JOURNEYS:
Expansion of the Strategic-Systemic Therapies

JOURNEYS:

Expansion of the Strategic-Systemic Therapies

Edited by

Donald E. Efron, M.S.W.

Brunner/Mazel, Publishers • New York

Library of Congress Cataloging-in-Publication Data

Journeys: expansion of the strategic-systemic
  therapies.

  Includes bibliographies and index.
  1. Psychotherapy. I. Efron, Donald E., 1944–
[DNLM: 1. Psychotherapy. WM 420 J86]
RC480.J68 1986   616.89'14   86–2640
ISBN 0–87630–419–6

Published by
BRUNNER/MAZEL, INC.
19 Union Square West
New York, New York 10003

This book is dedicated to my two daughters,
Laura and Sarah

Contents

Contributors

Harlene Anderson, Ph.D.
Galveston Family Institute, Galveston, Texas; and Private Practice, Boston, Massachusetts.

Brenda Atkison, M.S.W.
Madame Vanier's Children's Services, London, Ontario.

Insoo Berg
Director of Training, Brief Family Therapy Center, Milwaukee, Wisconsin.

Steve de Shazer
Director, Brief Family Therapy Center, Milwaukee, Wisconsin.

Donald E. Efron, M.S.W.
Madame Vanier's Children's Services, London, Ontario.

Mary-Jane Ferrier, Ph.D.   *96 School St. #2 S. Portland 04106*
Family Institute of Cambridge, Cambridge, Massachusetts.   *207-782-5188*

J. Scott Fraser, Ph.D.   *799-4844 home*
Crisis/Brief Therapy Center, Good Samaritan Hospital; and School of Professional Psychology, Wright State University, Dayton, Ohio.

Harold Goolishian, Ph.D.
Galveston Family Institute, Galveston, Texas.

Barbara S. Held, Ph.D.
Associate Professor of Psychology, Bowdoin College, Brunswick, Maine.

Evan Imber-Black (Coppersmith), Ph.D.
Faculty of Medicine, Family Therapy Program, University of Calgary, Calgary, Alberta.

Eve Lipchik
Associate Director, Brief Family Therapy Center, Milwaukee, Wisconsin.

John McFarland, M.D.
Family Physician, Auburn, Alabama.

Elam Nunnally
Associate Professor, School of Social Welfare, University of Wisconsin–Milwaukee; and Family Therapist, Brief Family Therapy Center, Milwaukee, Wisconsin.

Bill O'Hanlon, M.S.
Private Practitioner at the Hudson Center, Omaha, Nebraska.

Howard Protinsky, Ph.D.
Center for Family Therapy, Virginia Polytechnic Institute and State University, Blacksburg, Virginia.

George Pulliam, M.S.W.
Galveston Family Institute; and University of Texas Medical Branch, Galveston, Texas.

Michaelin Reamy-Stephenson, M.S.W., A.C.S.W.
Director of Extramural Training, Atlanta Institute for Family Studies, Atlanta, Georgia.

Janine Roberts, Ed.D.
School of Education, School Consulting and Counseling Psychology Program, University of Massachusetts, Amherst, Massachusetts.

Bill Rowe, D.S.W.
School of Social Work, King's College, London, Ontario.

Cheryl L. Storm, Ph.D.
Department of Marriage and Family Therapy and Social Work, Pacific Lutheran University, Tacoma, Washington.

Lee Winderman, Ph.D.
Galveston Family Institute, Galveston, Texas; and Private Practice, Houston, Texas.

Introduction

The Strategic-Systemic models of therapy are no longer revolutionary. We have moved beyond the heady early days of struggle. Harsh conflicts with practitioners of other models still occur, but it no longer is necessary to prologue each case with statements to the effect that the family or individual assisted so ably by ourselves was seen for *years* by misguided and bumbling followers of linear thinking. Indeed, our very success has ensured that we now have our full and equitable share of failures ourselves. We haven't lost our heroes — those pioneers whose efforts established systemic and strategic therapy within the mental health field — but we now know that the rest of us cannot treat our cases as if we were those heroes. We must develop our own ways of thinking about cases, of interviewing and intervening, of succeeding or failing.

The current challenge in the Strategic-Systemic therapies is to assist practitioners as they become more than beginners yet less than heroes. The entire field is maturing. Our literature needs to reflect this maturation. Revolutionary zeal must be replaced by positive and personalized efforts. This book has utilized two quite different methods in order to tap the energy of the field as it exists today — after the revolution.

The first method is taken in the *Journeys* section. It consists of autobiographical statements by three individuals and two groups. The individuals (Evan Imber-Black, Michaelin Reamy-Stephenson, and Bill O'Hanlon) and the groups (the Brief Family Therapy Center of Milwaukee, Wisconsin and the Galveston Family Institute of Galveston, Texas) have distinguished reputations in our field. They have greatly influenced countless practicing therapists through their therapy, teaching, writings, consultations, and workshops. Each brings a unique tale to this book. They were asked to describe their own "journey" through the strategic-systemic field—their personal histories of entry into this area, early careers, important influences and contacts, etc. They were given no special format for presentation of this material, only general guidelines. They were encouraged to find some organizing framework which worked for them. They were requested to be as open as they wished, short of embarrassing themselves or the readers. All of the writers reported that the task was difficult. It necessitated abandoning comfortable academic forms of presenting their ideas in favor of more personal statements of who they are, where they have come from and where they are going. Their ideas needed to be integrated with their histories.

The five writers succeeded in their task. Their stories are inspiring. They reflect the best of our own hopes and dreams. Each person and group come alive with a sparkle and glow that identifies them as models for all of us struggling along our own journeys. After reading the stories, I regretted not being able to personally work intensively with each of them. What a joy it would be to study in Texas and Milwaukee, to share coffee and cases with Evan, Michaelin, and Bill!

The second method, that of the section called *Expanding the Models*, is more traditionally academic. The idea was that the ever-expanding Strategic-Systemic models needed to be examined from the viewpoint of the maturing base for practice and theory. By so doing, therapists could come away with a sense of how these models are "deepening" (adding new theoretical insights), "merging" (joining concepts within the field itself or between the field and outside sources), and "widening" (applied in new areas previously unused to Strategic-Systemic thinking and practice).

The seven articles in this section speak to these themes. J. Scott Fraser thoughtfully describes the problems and possibilities inherent in attempting to integrate our conceptual models. Janine Roberts suggests ways in which concepts and practices from Haley's Strategic Therapy model and the Brief Therapy model of Watzlawick, Fisch, Weakland, et al. can be coherently added to Milan style interviewing and intervening. Howard Protinsky shows how Ericksonian therapy can be used within the context of Family Therapy. Mary-Jane Ferrier complements this suggestion with her own—that Milan concepts and techniques can be used with individuals, not only with full families. Barbara Held explores the theoretical and pragmatic aspects of using concepts developed in the individual psychologies within the strategic-systemic context. Cheryl Storm and John McFarland develop their ideas of how Systemic and Strategic models can be applied in Family Medicine; Don Efron, Bill Rowe and Brenda Atkison complete the book by presenting their model of Strategic Parenting, thereby moving the models beyond the therapy world and into new territory.

For an Editor, of course, it is next to impossible to know if this book accomplishes what it was intended to do. Has it actually brought to readers the sense of the growth of the Strategic-Systemic therapies? Has it allowed them to get their own bearings and set their own course? Have the people and ideas presented here influenced them in a positive and productive manner? I do know that I have been touched by the writers of the first section and made to think by the second section authors. For this, I wish to thank them. I would also like to thank Vin Moley and Karl Tomm, Vin for encouraging me to consider doing this book in the first place and Karl for helping me formulate the conceptual base of the total book and especially the first section. In addition, I would like to thank my colleagues at Madame Vanier Children's Services in London, Ontario, for their encouragement and patience. Similarly, my colleagues of the London Strategic-Systemic Therapies Study Group deserve recognition for allowing valuable time to be spent on the trials, tribulations, and triumphs of a first-time Editor. Finally, to all those who have helped me wrestle with the naming of this book, thanks, you can relax now!

Section I

Journeys

Chapter 1

Odysseys of a Learner

Evan Imber-Black (Coppersmith)

It has been my experience that, from time to time, I encounter a family, or an individual, or a larger system that both calls upon my collective knowledge to date and challenges me, stretches me, enables me to see more than I could see before. I have chosen to discuss my own development by reflecting on my recent work with one such family.

A TOUCHING CASE: REWORKING FAMILY MEMBERS' RELATIONSHIPS TO EACH OTHER AND WITH LARGER SYSTEMS

A family was referred to me for consultation by a psychiatric resident. The family consisted of two aging parents, Mr. George Simpson, 74, and Mrs. Carrie Simpson, 73, and their two grown daughters, Catherine, 48, and Ellen, 47. Catherine, a nursery school teacher, was married to Alan, a mechanic who owned his own business, and had a daughter, 20, and a son, 18. Ellen, presently unemployed, was divorced and had one son, 21. (See genogram.)*

The family was referred for consultation because Carrie was hospitalized due to a "phobia," reported to be of five years duration and allegedly commencing at the mutual retirement of her and her husband. They had led active lives until George retired because of emphysema and Carrie retired soon after. She talked about a great fear of germs and refused to touch anyone or be touched. She would not try on clothes, open doors, handle money, play cards, etc. because she feared germs were on the surfaces of all of these. Her

---

*Names and specific identifying information have been changed to protect confidentiality.

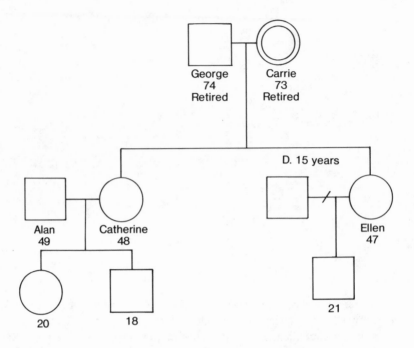

fears handicapped her in a number of ways: She would not shop or travel, she cried daily because she was so unhappy because of her situation, and her "phobia" was the main topic of family interactions and conversation.

This was her second hospitalization for this problem. During the first, a behavioral desensitization program was tried and failed. Following this, for three years she saw a psychiatrist monthly for antidepressant medication but with no change in her symptoms or her mood. A short course of marital therapy had been attempted and abandoned by the therapist because the couple insisted they had no problems as a couple and that only Carrie's symptoms were the problem. Professionals who discussed the case described Carrie as "resistant," the family as "uncooperative," and the overall prognosis as "hopeless." At the time of the consultation, Carrie was considered a "treatment failure" in the hospital and a source of enormous frustration to both professionals and family members. Serious consideration was being given to 1) psychosurgery; 2) shock treatment; 3) nursing home placement.

Reflections and Influences — The Family and Larger Systems

Before examination of any hypotheses internal to the family, the most salient feature seemed to be the relationship between the family and larger helping systems. The family was keenly aware of failed treatment efforts. Both family and larger systems (medical, psychiatric, and other therapeutic) were united in their view that Carrie was *the patient*, that she was, in fact, a "crazy lady." They were all frustrated and burned out. The case was presented to me with a tone of exhaustion and despair that seemed to mirror the family's attitude. Not much hope remained; yet "one more try" was being initiated. I knew I was entering a mine field, that I would need to carefully balance the family's requirement for a different experience with a larger helping system than any in their familiar repertoire with respect for prior actions promulgated by the other larger systems.

Entering the terrain of families and larger systems has been and remains the most challenging, risky, and exciting frontier of my work. In fact, the family and larger systems have been with me since childhood. I grew up in a family that interacted easily with many larger systems and carefully avoided others. My family is Jewish and my childhood was played out within the context of the American Conservative Jewish community in the post World War II period and the "Cold War" (e.g., McCarthyism, the Rosenberg case). I grew up hearing stories of my parents' and grandparents' experiences with anti-Semitism, and was keenly aware of discrimination practiced by many larger systems (e.g., educational, housing). My parents occupied leadership positions in international Jewish service organizations. Home and synagogue formed a synthesis of family and larger system.

As a young child, I proudly witnessed my father battling discriminatory practices in our local public school and eagerly listened to stories relating to his fights against quotas in his professional school, unfair labor practices, and restricted housing. I inhaled the idea that there were friendly larger systems and dangerous larger systems without any explicit discussion of this. My own entry into unfamiliar larger systems, foreign to my own family, began at the early age of three when I wandered off from a B'nai B'rith picnic into the midst of a gathering from a Polish Catholic Church and proceeded to dance to everyone's welcome. I grew up hearing this story with repeated delight and seeing a photograph which captured this event of 1947. Seldom does one explore new territory or break old boundaries without at least subtle permission.

Educational systems were respected and valued up to the point where I began to come home with ideas that challenged or in fact, ran counter to family rules. My adolescence developed within a context of tension, albeit ultimately manageable, between family and larger systems. Thus, the politics and processes of organizations were part of our daily lives and I watched and participated in and rebelled against and synthesized the world views from larger systems that entered our family sphere. A combination of comfort, fascination, dismay, and magnetic pull permeated my relationships with larger systems as I moved into teaching and community organizing as a young adult.

This period of my life was set in the larger context of the Civil Rights Movement. I taught in a ghetto high school in Chicago and worked as a volunteer for the Southern Christian Leadership Conference and the American Friends Service Committee. The suffering supported by larger systems (e.g., educational, welfare, political) became starkly apparent, as did the possibilities for hopeful change. The changes, however, were slow and an uneasy sense of "one step forward, two steps back," coupled with the first realization that I was, indeed, part of whatever system I felt compelled to try to alter, led me to want to learn more about the nature of human systems, particularly larger systems that impinge on the daily lives of people.

Thus, it was no accident that I ultimately chose a doctoral program with an available focus on change agents and larger systems and found there a mentor, Dr. Canice Connors. Fr. Connors, a Franciscan priest, a brilliant man and a dedicated teacher, taught me to *see* larger systems, to appreciate systematic analyses of their mandates, actions and goals, to understand the intricacies of human interaction in larger systems and to nurture qualities of mercy and justice within institutions. He provided me with opportunities to try my ideas within a supervisory context that offered an optimal combination of rigor and support. I learned how to enter larger systems, at diverse hierarchical levels, with a delicate combination of respect and challenge, tempering earlier stridency and taming earlier fear. Much of my work with Canice Connors involved hospitals and larger geriatric care facilities, thus bringing together many of the elements of the present case.

As I entered family therapy as the specific arena for clinical work with systems, my background in larger systems continued to influence my work. Here, my trainees and consultees led the way as case after case in Pittsburgh, Western Massachusetts, and Calgary, cities where I have lived and worked the last 12 years, involved problematic interaction both between families and larger systems, and among the larger systems, per se. I have been fortunate to have been received as a consultant and educator in a wide variety of settings (e.g., university, medical, mental health clinics, welfare, probation, public schools) and to have met a range of people who have been willing to experiment with me in assessing and intervening in families and larger systems (Note 1).

My work with families and larger systems has moved from an initial Don Quixote-like stance to a period of thinking it was my "mission" to "protect" families from larger systems, thereby discovering the symmetrical escalation I was helping to engender. Then I moved on to a purist systemic perspective, followed by what I now consider to be work that utilizes many systemic principles and practices, with, however, an eye on the ways that larger systems are bearers of sociocultural rules and assumptions that are often stronger and more powerful than family processes. Thus, they do not simply "interact as parts of the system," but rather shape implicit and often unexamined norms and values.

Primary in my thought and action as I entered the Simpson family was the need to understand the family's prior relationships to larger systems, to assess in what ways this relationship might be similar to internal family relationships, and to explore the possibilities of creating an unexpected relationship with a helper capable of facilitating change in a multisystem presently permeated by frustration, covert anger, and despair.

SYNOPSES OF SESSIONS 1-5

The family consultation led to a recommendation for family therapy to which both the family and hospital agreed. The hospital discharged Carrie, feeling there was nothing they could do for her, and hospital personnel backed out of the case. Unknown to me at the time, however, was the continued periodic involvement of Carrie's psychiatrist who, every two months, renewed her antidepressant prescriptions. The medication seemed to have no effect other than to support labelling Carrie as a "psychiatric patient" within both her family and larger systems.

Several salient issues became apparent early on:

1) George and Carrie struggled daily about her "phobia." The nature of this struggle consisted of George trying to convince Carrie that her fears were foolish and, in Carrie's words, "scolding her," and Carrie insisting that she could not do otherwise. Frequently, this escalated until Carrie cried and George walked out. Both denied any other problems, and objected strenuously to the designation "fight" or "argument."
2) Both George and Carrie had given up active lives five years earlier. Many of their friends had died or moved away and they were quite isolated. They had met originally as musicians and maintained this as part of their employment for over 40 years. When George's emphysema forced him to abandon his horn playing, Carrie protectively insisted that she was bored with the piano and gave up playing and teaching. When George's illness led to his complete retirement, Carrie maintained that she was now too afraid to continue her community work. A likely hypothesis is that their relationship had been structured along traditional male-female complementary lines, with George ostensibly "leading" and Carrie "following." As George became ill, the couple was unable to shift this complementary process and Carrie, in turn, became "sick," thereby maintaining earlier patterns.
3) Catherine and Ellen competed for the job of "saving" mother and father. They alternated supplying new ideas and discounted each other's ideas. Ellen generally appeared solicitous to the parents and angry with the ther-

apist while Catherine generally appeared angry with the parents and solicitous to the therapist.

4) The parents' problems had a powerful effect on the daughters' day-to-day
lives. Catherine and her husband fought frequently over her relationship
to her parents, and Catherine felt powerless and ineffective with her own
children. Ellen, who took a new job during the early phase of therapy,
stated frequently that she would give up her job and go live with her parents
if this would help. Both daughters appeared mired in unexplainable guilt
and spent most of their free energy struggling with a sense of knottedness
with their parents.

5) There was a strong injunction against the acknowledgment of conflict in
any of the relationships. Both daughters stated they could recall no open
conflicts between their parents when they were children, to which George
added, "I don't remember having any!" In a session with only the daughters, each said they believed the parents were now hiding conflicts and
pretending all was well, as each parent would complain ferociously about
the other in private and then deny this when the other spouse was present.
Thus, a pattern of secrets that everyone knew but disavowed permeated
the system.

6) There was a strong injunction against "outsiders." For Carrie, in particular,
"outsiders" included professional helpers *and* her husband and her in-laws
and children's spouses — in short, anyone but her daughters. For George,
"outsiders" included anyone outside the immediate family. Thus, attempts
by professional helpers appeared doomed.

A variety of interventions were attempted during the first five sessions.
These included: 1) a ritualized task designed to reframe the problem as belonging to both Carrie and George, and to interdict their daily struggles which
seemed to support the symptoms; 2) a sibling session, including Catherine's
spouse and Ellen's boyfriend, whose presence in the system became known
to me only when this meeting was convened; 3) a Milan-style letter sent to
each member positively connoting Carrie's symptoms and prescribing no
change. While these interventions had no apparent impact on Carrie's symptoms, they did have the effect of revealing more and more information about
the nature of family relationships, the powerful injunction against acknowledging open conflict that supported pseudomutuality both in the family and
between the family and larger systems, and the pervading sense that secrets
had the family tied in knots. At this juncture, therapeutic neutrality and the
somewhat unusual and cryptic nature of interventions appeared to be "news
of a difference" to the family sufficient to bring them back each time. Indeed, Catherine briefly dropped out and the letter served to encourage her
return with great curiosity. However, the team working with me and I felt

that bolder measures were needed if we were not to soon join the long list of treatment failures (Note 2).

Reflections and Influences — Early Work with the Family

Opening work with the family centered primarily in the patterns of practice of Milan systemic therapy, as understood and translated by the Family Therapy Program at the University of Calgary under the leadership of Dr. Karl Tomm. Before I studied family therapy, my graduate training had been theoretically broad, including intrapsychic, interpersonal, and organizational models of human behavior and change. Like many practitioners in the field of family therapy, my own work has been deeply influenced by the major leaders (e.g., Erickson, Bateson, Jackson, Minuchin, Haley, Watzlawick, Bowen, Boszormenyi-Nagy) of the last three decades and their concepts and practices remain visible as I hypothesize about and interact with families. The creativity and originality of the early Milan Team (e.g., the team of four) impressed me deeply when their work became available in North America, and I sought opportunities to learn from them and experiment with their ideas.

With the Simpson family, I began by utilizing circular questioning and neutrality, attempting to hypothesize regarding possible functions of Carrie's symptoms. I was aware of the importance of entering the system in a way that differed from their prior involvement with professionals. Since the family had already experienced a few years of negative judgment and advice which they chose not to follow, neutrality and circular questioning proved to be engaging and unusual enough to provoke their interest. Use of language was immediately salient as the family let me know in no uncertain terms that they did not have "fights" or "arguments," only innocuous "quarrels" and "scoldings."

Central to my hypothesizing process was the use of family developmental life cycle theory, a crucial body of ideas about human interaction that exists as background to all of my work. Here I see the early influence of Haley's translation of Erickson (1973), the idea that symptoms are often an expression of a life cycle transition difficulty, enriched by a much more complex and comprehensive view of life cycle issues as promoted by Carter & McGoldrick (1980).

Life cycle and human development issues have formed an important part of my education and training. While well-published family therapists certainly influenced my thinking in this area, I am keenly aware of the closer contacts with teachers who focused this domain, especially Dr. Nancy Elman, Sister Mary Louise Nash, and Lois Jaffee. I encountered these three women during my doctoral work at the University of Pittsburgh. Each gave me something unique that I now associate with my understanding of and ability to effectively use life cycle theory. Nancy Elman taught me theory within an abiding context of friendship and support. At the time we were both single parents, struggling with special life cycle issues of our own, and finding, I think, that good theories offer sensible framings both personally and professionally. Sister Nash helped me to learn more about the aging phase of the life cycle. She challenged commonly held notions about confusion and depression in the elderly with the idea that an accumulation of unresolved and unrecompensed losses within a context that ignores human dignity easily leads to symptomatic behavior. She modeled relationships marked by dignity and respect, and showed me ways to challenge institutional premises about people without engendering useless conflict. Lois Jaffee taught me directly and humanly about dying and death. A family therapist suffering from the final stages of leukemia, Lois chose to open her own life and the impact of her illness on her family to graduate students. Her teaching about life and life cycle issues was decidedly not theoretical. To be with Lois Jaffee and to learn from her meant to enter existential places in oneself, places that transcended theory and technique.

Thus, in regard to the family life cycle, all three women gave me the best that a teacher can give—keen knowledge and expertise, rich personal experience, and an invitation to learn clearly coupled with the expectation that I would act upon my learning in ways that would potentiate their efforts as teachers.

The present case seemed to exemplify a host of intertwining life cycle issues, centering on the aging and retirement of George and Carrie, the relationship of grown children to aging parents, and the leaving home stage of the youngest generation. Since the family insisted that Carrie's symptoms began when George became ill and the older couple retired, hypotheses and action related to this phase of the life cycle seemed salient. And yet, our work was failing and we were somehow off the mark.

At this point, the team became crucial to my work with the family. Working in teams is one of the most exciting contributions to my work from the original Milan team. The idea of collaboration in a team, as I have understood it and attempted to translate it in a training format (Note 3) seems profoundly compatible with philosophical underpinnings of a family therapy that seeks to facilitate and enhance a sense of justice and collaboration in families and larger systems, a lived experience of mutual influence, and a sense of valuing each member's contributions to a synergistic whole. I owe much to my trainees for my ideas about teams. At the University of Massachusetts, we took the professional peer team concept of the Milan group, and experimented with it in a training format that encouraged trainees to look as much to each other for learning as to me, their supervisor. The results were, frankly, startling. In an atmosphere of mutual support and encouragement that maximized collaboration and minimized competition, even rank beginners demonstrated capacities for effective work with very difficult families. We were inventive, exploratory, took risks, had fun, and helped families. (Notes 4, 5)

The team in the present case worked with me in several key ways. We shared responsibility for the conduct of the sessions and the interventions. Following the tiniest bit of progress, the Simpson's daughter, Ellen, would snap at me and treat me with derision, but the team kept me steady and facilitated my ability to remain open and curious about what was happening. At that awful point when I began to secretly wish the family would not show up, the team's enthusiasm saw me through. Finally, the team helped me to execute what became, in fact, the first major turning point in the therapy.

THE GROWN CHILDREN AS CONSULTANTS TO THE THERAPIST: AN IN-SESSION RITUAL

We met as a team at the end of the fifth session, which had been a session of the children and their mates. During the session, a strong bid was made to me by Ellen for me to see each parent individually so that I could hear their complaints about one another and thus become as immobilized by secrets as everyone else. I stated that we wanted to try something else first and would need their help. As a team, we had several building blocks for intervention — secrecy, outsiders versus insiders, rules regarding the open expression of conflict and who can say what in front of whom. We struggled to translate all of this into meaningful action and devised the following end-of-session intervention:

"I need your help at this juncture because, as we all know, I am an 'outsider,' and so your parents are very polite and diplomatic with me. I would like you to invite your parents to the next session. At that session, I want to ask you to serve as consultants to me, to be my team, to sit behind the one-way mirror and call me when I need to raise issues that your parents would not otherwise deal with because I'm an outsider. I want to ask you to keep this plan a secret between us. Are you willing to do that?"

The children appeared curious and a bit uncomfortable at the idea of keeping a secret with me, but agreed. I did not know if they would keep the secret, which was intended as both a metaphor for family relationships and a crucial rule-breaker regarding "outsiders." The session was set for three weeks away.

All came to the session. I asked the parents to wait and ushered the two daughters and their partners behind the mirror, where one team member was waiting to assist (Dr. Dusty Miller). They had, in fact, kept the secret. I explained the set-up, showed them the phone, and said I wanted them to call in two circumstances: 1) if they saw their parents being very polite or diplomatic with me as an "outsider," or 2) when they felt there were topics I needed to address. They practiced using the phone, and then I brought Carrie and George into the interview room. Both were surprised not to see their children.

I began by explaining our plan for the session, addressing why and when the children would call, framing myself as an "outsider," highlighting concerns of the children, and asking their permission to proceed. Both immediately feigned great comfort with the arrangement, at which point the phone began to ring with challenges from the children to the parents. I became a conduit for the expression of the children's distress with the family's rules. I could say and ask *anything* and attribute all to my callers, who rang me up about every five minutes!

In tiny steps, the parents began to acknowledge painful conflicts, insisting, however, that these related only to the last five years and that the children were mistaken if they thought otherwise. Both parents expressed frequent surprise at jointly hearing their daughters' views for the first time. I began to feel like a villain, pushing these old people. I struggled with feeling disrespectful. In short, I felt like one of the children. Just at this juncture, Dusty Miller called me out for a break. I went behind the mirror and discovered the emergence of a great split between the daughters. Catherine felt we were finally getting somewhere, that her parents were starting to deal candidly with each other and me, and that we needed to go on. Ellen felt we were potentially causing harm, that her parents needed to be protected, and that we must stop. This was the most natural team split I had ever witnessed; after conferring with my clinical team, I reported the split to the parents:

"Half of your children think that at this age and stage in your lives that you need to be pushed a bit to resolve some long-standing issues. Half of your children think that at this age and stage in your lives you need to be protected. As your therapist, I just don't know and I think only you can decide. If you decide at this age and stage in your lives that you need to be protected, then therapy is not indicated and I would certainly respect that decision. If, however, you decide that, no, at this age and stage in your lives you need to be pushed a bit and given a hand to resolve these painful issues, then therapy is indicated and I'd be glad to work with you." George rose up in his seat and said "Just what's this protection bit? Where do you get that idea?" I told him I was only reporting the ideas of his children and I asked them to discuss it and call me in two to three weeks.

I then met with my "consultants" and suggested that they, too, were faced with a choice, which was whether or not to continue in their roles as "protectors," and that I would be available to any or all of them in this regard.

Reflections and Influences

This session was simultaneously very scary and very exhilarating. Family rules about secrets, acknowledgment of conflict, and "outsiders" were challenged and frequently broken. I moved from the position of "useless expert" to one in need of consultation from the "insiders." A generational boundary was graphically drawn and this facilitated both the open expression of conflict between the sisters who previously feigned polite agreement about their parents, and the open expression of conflict between the parents. Crossgenerational coalitions were torn. Still, I was left with a deep sense of uncertainty that only time would answer.

As I think back now on my own personal and professional development, the ability to entertain and live with uncertainty, to take risks that are not careless, to be willing to journey to unknown lands with clients and trainees, and to respect the inherent strengths in people emerges as my most crucial learning, regardless of model, technique or context. While it is difficult to pin down the ongoing support for these capacities, or even to track their earliest origins, I am keenly aware of growing up in a context in which stories about courage and pioneering were frequent. Among these were my maternal grandfather who left Rumania alone at age 11 and traveled to England, and South America, ultimately arriving in the U.S. at age 13; my paternal grandfather who resigned from a Jewish service organization because it refused to admit his friend, a peddler; my mother who spent her childhood as the only Jewish child in a neighborhood marked by frequent anti-Semitic incidents; my father as the only member of his family to leave trade and seek university and professional school education. Named for my paternal grandmother, Esther, I grew up hearing simply that "she was a strong woman."

I am also clearly appreciative to two mentors in this regard, Dr. Fred Heslet and Dr. Mimi Silbert. Both imparted knowledge to me in the broad area of human interaction and communication, with Fred's work centering on groups, and Mimi's on psychodrama. While the skills in these areas have been clearly important to me, I am more certain that the entry into my life of these two people and what they offered me in a learning relationship of the dimensions described above was far more profound. I met Fred Heslet and Mimi Silbert in different contexts, at approximately the same time. Fred was my advisor in my master's program; Mimi was the director of a program training paraprofessional group leaders, with an emphasis in video analysis of communication and psychodrama.

At that time, I was newly divorced, the single parent of a two-year-old and an infant, living far from family and old friends. My immediate context was filled with criticism and doubt. We were fairly poor and I worked at an odd variety of part-time jobs while going to school. (A brief aside: Perhaps the most important of these jobs was selling Christmas trees, for here I turned from a major interest in stranger group interaction to family interaction as I watched such scenarios as: 1) "We have to get a scotch pine — *my* family always had a scotch pine." "Well, that's too bad, *my* family always had a fir tree!" and 2) to a six-year-old: "You can pick the tree dear — oh no, *you don't like that one — you like this one."* and 3) "I don't know if I really want a tree this year — my wife always picked them, you know, and she just died about a month ago.")

I was filled with a great deal of uncertainty at this time in my life. My confidence in myself was fairly low, and while I was endlessly fascinated by human interaction I certainly doubted my capacity to be very useful or effective. I think Fred Heslet and Mimi Silbert had a dramatic impact on my sense of myself, my talents, and my willingness to muster the "chutzpah" to become a therapist. They shared key qualities: the willingness to journey into *my* world, rather than insist that I fit into some stereotyped notion of "student," so as to facilitate my taking risks at a time when my inclinations were for safety and mediocre comfort; the amazing capacity to give "loving kicks"; and an interest in my development that required, indeed demanded, a thoughtful response indicating that I took seriously their well-seasoned judgment. Their availability, their refusals to accept self-deprecation from me, and their deep empathy combined to set me on a new course. Both valued strength, ambition, and courage in a woman at a time when messages from the culture were encouraging weakness and dependency. They shattered my old mirrors and held up new ones.

RESPONSES TO THE IN-SESSION RITUAL

I. Catherine called me in three weeks requesting an appointment for herself. When she came in, she reported the following:
1) A fight, the first of its kind in the history of the family, ensued following the session. The exact nature of the fight seemed less important to her than the fact that people were voicing their differences face to face.
2) Ellen announced to the family that she and her boyfriend were living together. It turned out they had been living together for quite a long time, but had kept this a secret and pretended to be living separately.
3) Ellen also acknowledged to Catherine that she was struggling with a drinking problem. Catherine had suspected this, but previously the two sisters were unable to discuss any important issues.
Catherine was unsure of what was happening and said she wanted therapy for herself to deal with a pervading and unexplainable sense of debt and guilt which she felt towards her parents. She was very tense, her blood pressure was abnormally high, and she felt trapped in relationships that were murky. She stated that she had felt such tension and anxiety in regard to her parents for as long as she could remember, and she feared a future like her mother's. She was aware, too, of a backlog of anger and resent-

ment towards her own children who treated her disrespectfully, but she feared expressing this to them. We agreed to meet in a one-to-one format that will be discussed below.

II. Carrie and George did not call as requested. Since I had purposefully left the question of therapy entirely up to them, I chose not to call. Three months later, Carrie called to request an appointment. It should be noted that this was the first time Carrie had ever called as all previous calls were handled by George or Ellen on Carrie's behalf. When they came for the appointment, a profoundly different mood prevailed as George and Carrie willingly entered into a discussion of their lives together, revealing a host of previously denied problems and unresolved conflicts (Note 6). Many problems centered in the sexual area and the couple had chosen to handle these by totally withdrawing from each other sexually. They had separate bedrooms and, over the recent past, used Carrie's "fear of germs" as an excuse to not even touch each other. This pattern was rationalized through reference to George's health problems, but our discussion together, in fact, indicated struggles relating to sexual communication that originated at the start of their relationship.

During this session, I was able to use humor for the first time with them, replacing the grim tone of previous sessions. We laughed together about Carrie washing George's face in bed many years before the start of her "phobia." Then, as George, despite his emphysema, sat smoking while Carrie claimed their physical distancing was for his health, I asked, "Suppose a doctor told you sexual intercourse would be better for George than smoking cigarettes?" Both laughed and Carrie affirmed that this might alter her views.

As this lighter and more open mood prevailed, Carrie related a secret, the interactional effects of which had established a family whose relationships with each other were marked by fear, defensiveness, criticism, and dissatisfying distance, and whose relationships with the outside world, in fact, mirrored the internal relationships. Carrie and George met and became pregnant with Catherine prior to marriage. Carrie's family sent them away so no one would know. George was afraid that his own family would find out and so tried to keep the matter a secret, but they discovered the information and behaved quite punitively and critically, especially towards Carrie.

Carrie and George lived together, but extreme poverty postponed a legal wedding. After Catherine's birth, Carrie asked her doctor for birth control information. His response was that she was young and should go home and have more children, thus initiating difficult relationships with helping professionals. Soon Carrie became pregnant again and only after the birth of Ellen did the couple wed. They chose to keep this past history secret from both daughters. They lived in constant fear of the girls discovering this information. Carrie hid their wedding certificate and they purposely ignored their anniversary.

Their relationship had been cursed by their families-of-origin and they began their family life in a context of fear and approbation. Their union was neither "blessed" nor celebrated. The birth of their children had been made a cause for shame by wider cultural norms and family beliefs reflecting these norms. Central life-cycle tasks were derailed. Subjects that might remotely relate to these circumstances were scrupulously avoided and gradually replaced by a focus on Carrie's "peculiarities," the tendency towards which had, in fact, begun many, many years before the couple's retirement. Both affirmed that they thought their daughters knew this past history, citing the daughters' scrupulous avoidance of the topic of the parents' marriage and that all had simply agreed to not acknowledge this. Thus, they mirrored the pervasive pattern in the system (prior to the in-session ritual) of "secrets" that everyone knows but cannot discuss together.

At the next session, I connected Carrie's symptoms to all they had told me and asked Carrie and George if they would like to make a videotape recounting their history for their daughters to see. George, the prior master of obtuse communication, responded immediately, "No, that's too indirect — let's just bring them in and talk to them!" Carrie agreed and then asked if it would be possible for her to speak to an expert about germs!

Reflections and Influences

Clearly, the in-session ritual of the grown children and their partners serving as "consultants" to me had a profound effect on the family at a number of levels. The pattern of secrecy that surrounded relationships at many levels was crumbling and being replaced by more directness, both within the family and between the family and professionals. The harsh symmetry between the family and outsiders seemed to have melted following the experience of the children directing the therapist's efforts in a complementary arrangement, which was a totally new experience for this family. Carrie's symptoms made sense from a new perspective, as did all of the prior treatment failures, including our own lack of success.

I began now to envision Carrie's symptoms as embedded in a complex three-generational web of metaphor standing for what could not be stated directly and of well-intended secrets that escalated to unfortunate proportions. The exact content of the original "secret" was clearly less important than the context in which it grew, the meanings people ascribed to it, and the escalating pattern of secret-keeping that pervaded and shaped all relationships until the only topic that could be discussed jointly was Carrie's "symptoms."

Secrets can be benign and useful boundary markers (e.g., the "secrets" adolescents keep from parents that ultimately aid in their differentiation) or secrets can be malignant, constricting, fear-inducing. As seen in the present case, many secrets take shape within conformist social norms. Unable to question such norms, cut off from varied points of view, or otherwise embedded in contexts that disallow difference, the "rule-breakers" feel compelled to become "secret-keepers," defined by others as "violators" of social values. In such circumstances, capacity for self-acceptance is eroded. Relationships with others become increasingly skewed by fear of discovery and elaborate metaphorical methods of communication are created.

My own response of suggesting a videotape is, I think, indicative of my being drawn into the pattern of protection and less than direct interaction. George and Carrie not only were ahead of me but were not willing to set me straight rather than treat me with polite dissembling! I was, at first, confused by Carrie's request to talk to a "germ expert" and wanted to ignore it. Fortunately, a trainee was behind the mirror and helped me to see that Carrie was asking for a way out of the corner into which she was painted (Note 7).

Unlike earlier segments of this case that I have related to direct influences in my training and development, here I would like to discuss influences in broader strokes. I see my work with the family at this juncture as influenced by a blending of intellectual forces in the fields of family interaction and family therapy, by an abiding interest in using the session, per se, in unusual ways, and by an intuitive belief that *most* people are doing the best they can *most* of the time, given contextual constraints. My ideas about this family reflect multigenerational models, including Bowen, Boszormenyi-Nagy, and the Milan systemic model; communication theories as put forth by the original Bateson project, especially the concepts of symmetry and complementarity; and the ways that systems can escalate through feedback processes and ideas regarding symptoms as metaphors, as described by Haley and Madanes.

As I look at this case, it is clear to me that it is now impossible to identify my work as belonging only to one school of thought. I dislike the word "eclectic" as I often think of it connoting wishy-washiness. Rather, I am suggesting that I find it impossible to attribute my work to only one model, and that to do so is to deny a rich heritage of ideas and to support a fiction that in systems therapy a variety of sources and resources have not profoundly influenced one.

The in-session ritual used in this case is an example of the synergistic effects on my practice of a variety of models and techniques. Years ago, Minuchin put family members behind the one-way mirror, not to comment or guide the therapist, but to observe and learn (Minuchin et al., 1967). The original Milan Team described inventive and effective rituals in which direct action between sessions profoundly affected symptoms. These rituals included elements of the unexpected and frequently addressed life-cycle issues (Selvini-Palazzoli et al., 1974, 1977, 1978). In more recent work, Selvini-Palazzoli & Prata have described prescribing a secret to the parents of a symptomatic child (unpublished).

Both structural and strategic therapists use the session, per se, to generate new action. Madanes, in particular, has described "pretend" interventions that are practiced in the session, as well as role-play directives in the session that lead to changes in relationships (Madanes, 1981). Psychodramatic practice, which formed much of my early clinical training, highlights the effective uses of pretending. Also coming together in this in-session intervention were: specific applications of working with symmetry and complementarity, as applied in my own work on families and larger systems; the notion of "teams," both the usual clinical teams discussed above and the pretend team composed of the grown children; and an elaboration of my earlier work suggesting creative uses for the telephone in therapy sessions (Imber Coppersmith, 1982). Thus, this one intervention, which I am suggesting was the turning point in this therapy, represents the amalgamation of the thought and practice of many who have influenced my work over many years.

The family poignantly reminded me of a fundamental belief that underpins my work. Hearing their story supported a notion of human beings struggling to make sense of their existence within broader contextual constraints that affect their capacities and their vision. Here is the not so unusual example of people obeying the dictates of both their families of origin and their wider culture, and doing what they, in fact, believed was best for their children. Within an atmosphere of fear and criticism, unable to accomplish normative family life-cycle tasks, George and Carrie tried to protect their children. Ironically, this very attempt to protect became the foundation for decades of escalating painful interaction within the family and between the family and the outside world.

Individual existence and family interaction are not explainable by stopping at the boundaries of the family, nuclear or extended. Rather, families exist within broad religious, ethnic, cultural, and societal rules that affect them profoundly. Just as family "rules" are often unspoken and implicit and sometimes mystifying and double-binding, so are the societal rules within which families are embedded, thus making them difficult or impossible to question and challenge on a personal basis. George and Carrie grew up in a time when evidence of premarital sex led to being shamed and made an outcast. These beliefs permeated their existence as a couple. Carrie's attempts in the 1940s to get birth control information from a male doctor were met with the kind of negativity and scorn that supported "keeping a woman in her place." To see George and Carrie's predicament as springing only from their family is to enter a victim-blaming mentality and to ignore complex social and political factors that affect and shape family organization. Here, our current models are strained to their limits. Developing assessment and intervention models that account for the family's embeddedness in complex sociopolitical rules, that appreciate symptoms from this perspective, and that appropriately challenge adjustment to a status quo that has brought human existence to the edge of destruction is unquestionably the next step for the field as a whole.

FOLLOW-UP

I. The Parents Talk to Their Daughters

George and Carrie invited Catherine and Ellen to the next session. The session was postponed once because George went on a fishing trip and Carrie went to her sister's. This was the first time George had been able to go away from home for many years, as previously Carrie would complain of her fears and George would give in and stay home, full of resentment. Carrie reported playing the organ at her sister's, which she had not done for several years due to her fear of touching the keys.

They kept the purpose of the session a secret, thus turning the tables on their daughters. (I had not instructed them or suggested this. It seems the family was discovering complex forms of "secrets.") My role in this session shifted to that of witness, as George and Carrie alternately told their daughters the origins of the family, the nature of the secret, their reasons for keeping it secret, and the effects it had on them to do so. At my bidding, they had brought their marriage certificate and showed this to Catherine and Ellen. Both daughters told the parents tearfully that they knew all of this already and had always wanted to talk about it, but felt they could not. Upon further exploration, however, what came out was that they, in fact, believed only Catherine had been born prior to a legal wedding and did not know for sure about Ellen. The escalating differences between Catherine and Ellen throughout their lives, their lack of cooperation with each other, and Ellen's beliefs that she could provide more for her parents than Catherine became clearer when set in this context.

Other secrets that the daughters had kept from the parents emerged. Old angers and misunderstandings began to be renegotiated. The daughters demanded that the parents stop triangulating them into their relationship, and that they include the daughters' partners in open discussions of issues rather than treating them as "outsiders." I occasionally translated intentions, but primarily remained as an empathic, outside witness during the session.

At the end of the session, I met briefly with the daughters alone and suggested that they plan a surprise "anniversary" party for their parents. Here, making a "surprise" replaced "keeping secrets." I then met briefly with the parents to set a time for meeting with a physician who would answer Carrie's questions about germs. As they rose to leave, George thanked me and shook my hand. Carrie, who had not touched anyone for many years, hesitated and then came forward and put both of her hands around mine and thanked me.

II. Therapy with Catherine

I met six times over eight months with Catherine, including four individual sessions, one meeting with Ellen, and one including Catherine's husband. The essence of our work together consisted of coaching Catherine in differentiating steps. I taught her about family process and gave her *Family Ties That Bind*, a Bowenian self-help book, to read (Richardson, 1984). She identified areas for work and diligently carried out strategies and experiments.

Following some successful work, she came to see me one evening very concerned and upset. The previous week, her son had treated her very rudely, pushing her out of the way in the kitchen. Without pausing to think or censor herself, Catherine poured apple juice on his head! She felt very guilty and wanted to know what I thought. To her surprise, I congratulated her, we had a good laugh, and her guilt evaporated.

As our work together progressed, she reported radical changes in her son, who now treated her with respect. She became more and more her own person, less subject to rules and roles not of her own making. At one point, I became concerned that all of her changes might precipitate trouble in her marriage, since her marriage had existed for many years with Catherine extremely involved in her family of origin. I invited her husband, Alan, to a session and found that my fears were unfounded as he let me know that he was delighted with Catherine's changes and that she was more relaxed than at any time in 22 years. Some symptoms are simply unfortunate, rather than functional! Though he was very close to his son, he applauded the apple juice shower and reported positive changes in Catherine's relationship to him and their children.

In the middle of my work with Catherine and following the session with the parents and daughters, Ellen asked to come in with Catherine. It was an odd session, during which Ellen insisted she did not want therapy. Her exact purpose for coming in was never clear to me. However, she did report that her drinking was no longer a problem and that she had felt "much freer" in the last five months (since the "children as consultants" session), though she had no idea why.

Catherine worked with me during a time when her children were leaving home, her parents were aging, and her husband was losing his business due to the recession and needed retraining. In addition, she and her husband sold their house and moved, and information regarding a 48-year-old secret was revealed to her. Through all these stresses, she became more confident, more autonomous, less anxious, no longer guilty. She decided to stop therapy, affirming that she knew she had further work that she wanted to do on her own. In our last session, she said that a stone had been lifted from her back and that her blood pressure was now normal!

III. Carrie and George Meet a New Professional

Carrie and George came for their session with the physician. I had arranged for an especially knowledgeable, kind and patient doctor to talk to them. He treated Carrie's questions with respect rather than as the paranoid delusions of a "crazy" woman. He took notes and carefully answered all of her questions about disease, germs, the lives of germs, where germs could live, how germs could be transmitted, etc. Carrie laughed and cried and talked of how relieved she was. George was a bit annoyed that she had not believed him when he told her not to be afraid of germs, but he, too, cried when Carrie announced that she was now ready to go buy new shoes, something she had been afraid to do for years. She turned to George and said it would be nice if he would hold her when she got upset!

Here it is important to note that during Carrie's hospitalization she had been sent *against her wishes* to talk to a microbiologist, who certainly knew a lot about germs! She had dismissed all he told her.

Several changes occurred following this session. Carrie decided she no longer wished to see her psychiatrist, citing her dissatisfaction with his constant recommendation of nursing home placement and his refusal to answer her questions about medication side-effects.

Carrie invented her *own* "behavioral" plan for eliminating her symptom by each week adding a new item that she could touch, metaphorically opening herself to the world, with a sense of her own empowerment to do so. The final item on her list was to invite people who had never been to their home over for a party!

REFLECTIONS AND INFLUENCES

Both the final stages and my overall work with the Simpson family involved four areas that I see as central to my broader work with families, including therapist/trainer positioning, rituals, empowerment and coming full circle, families and larger systems.

I. Therapist Positioning

My position as therapist shifted several times in this case. I began in a position of neutrality, as this term is defined by the original Milan Team (Selvini-Palazzoli et al., 1980). I adopted this position towards family members and towards the larger helping systems that were then involved. In retrospect, I believe this kind of neutrality allowed my entrance into the system and began to affect people's views towards Carrie as the symptom-bearer blamed for her own problems and facilitated a more complex view of the interactional network that underpinned Carrie's symptoms. By maintaining neutrality towards the hospital and other outside systems, I was able to avoid escalation about "whose treatment was best" and to avoid triangulation in which the family would take sides, replicate internal family patterns and thereby become more rigid and inaccessible.

During the staging and implementation of the in-session ritual, my position shifted. Rather than maintaining strict neutrality, I, in fact, first joined with the grown children in an alliance of keeping a secret, and then, in a series of complex moves, altered my position from 1) "one-up" in a complementary arrangement as the one who directed and gave instructions, to 2) "one-down" in a complementary arrangement as the one who took directions and received consultation, to 3) a simultaneous "one-down" vis à vis the children who guided me and "one-up" vis à vis the parents, whom I challenged with their children's direct questions, to 4) a neutral position once again as the "reporter" of the "team split" to the parents and "reporter" of the choice faced by the children.

Later, when Catherine requested therapy for herself, my position shifted again. I did not theorize her request as "a move in the family's game." Rather, I chose to work with her from a position that delicately combined systemic work (Note 8) with advocacy.

When the parents returned to therapy and related their story to me, I became the first "outsider" to be admitted to what had been a fortress. Here, I temporarily joined on their side, framing them as well-intended people victimized by pervasive cultural beliefs regarding pregnancy outside of legal marriage. I stepped out of a neutral stance to a deliberately accepting and empathic one — likely the first they had ever received in this regard and so providing the "news of a difference" that led to their choice to tell their daughters. I suspect that strict neutrality would not have been potent enough to overcome their expectation of judgment and criticism.

During the session in which the parents talked to their daughters, I was primarily an outside witness. I spoke very little, asked very few questions, and only occasionally clarified or reframed intentions.

During the session with the physician, I was a broker, bringing the parents together with a useful resource. I suspect a more purely systemic approach would have suggested they find such a person on their own. I conceptualized their request as an opportunity to facilitate a new experience with an outside helper and chose, rather, to serve as the broker.

Finally, as Carrie developed her own "treatment plan," I became her cotherapist, or she became mine. In sum, this therapy reflects a variety of relationship options, culminating in greater equity in both the family system and the therapist-family system.

When I reflect on my various positions as therapist in this and other cases, I am aware of a variety of intellectual influences on my work, including Minuchin & Fishman's (1981) discussions of therapist's use of self, the work of the Mental Research Institute (Fisch, Weakland & Segal, 1982), the Milan Team (Selvini-Palazzoli et al., 1980), and de Shazer's ideas about discovering the family's way of "cooperating" (1982).

On a more personal level, my ongoing work with Richard Whiting has often focussed on creative uses of the therapist that are not model-bound, but which tap imagination, humor, playfulness, and a sense of awe at being in the position of therapist.

More recently, I see my work influenced by the writings of many feminist family therapists (Goldner, 1985; Hare-Mustin, R., 1978; James & McIntyre, 1983; Libow, Rasking & Caust, 1982) who are pointing the way to a family therapy capable of addressing complex sociocultural and political variables that shape family life. Here, examining the position of the therapist becomes crucial. Our stance with families, the kinds of questions we ask, the assumptions we make, the boundaries we draw around problems, and the interventions we choose can either perpetuate a kind of family life in which a Carrie Simpson is blamed for her problems, cut off from the means of controlling her own body (Note 9), substituting an exaggerated caricature of such control, and generally treated as a "crazy old lady, " or else challenge this in ways that conceptualize and intervene in individual and family problems in a wider context of social rules and organizations (Note 10). This includes recognizing and acting upon the idea that the position of the therapist is both a personal and a political position.

II. Rituals

Ideas about the central place of rituals in human existence also inform my work (van der Hart, 1983; Wolin & Bennett, 1984). The presence or absence of cultural, religious, life-cycle, and daily rituals has, I believe, a profound impact on individuals, families and larger systems.

Rituals identify membership, define social roles and rules, provide opportunities for development and change without paralyzing fear, and facilitate the expression of feelings that can communicate connectedness.

The Simpsons were impoverished as regards rituals. They had no ritual to bless their union; their actual wedding was simply a legal device, divorced from families or any social network, prompting Carrie to say, "We didn't really have a wedding." They had no celebrations to mark the births of their children and, in fact, tried to hide the first birth from George's family. They avoided their anniversaries, thereby turning the day into a cause for pain rather than joy. One of the areas intensely discussed at the session when the parents talked to their daughters centered on the daughters' weddings. The parents, deprived of rituals themselves, found it impossible to embrace rituals for their daughters. Thus, prior to Catherine's wedding, there were many fights, threatened refusals to pay for the wedding, and threatened refusals to attend the wedding, all culminating in a less than joyous event. Ellen simply ran off to marry, thus perpetuating a lack of rituals. Perhaps one way to understand Carrie's symptoms and the interaction around them is that they provided unfortunate daily rituals for this under-ritualized family.

I am not suggesting here that families must necessarily follow traditional rituals. Indeed, many of these have become empty events rather than rich processes capable of altering meanings and one's felt sense of existence. The field of anthropology, however, certainly indicates that human beings are ritualizing creatures. I am, therefore, suggesting a therapy that examines the place of ritual in a person's or family's or larger system's existence, conceptualizes the problem in a way that includes ritual or its lack as part of the equation, and utilizes therapeutic rituals as interventions.

Therapy with the Simpsons attended to this dimension. It is interesting to note that early ritual interventions failed, probably because I had no knowledge of the lack of key life-cycle rituals in this family, and so was off the mark. Later, therapy sessions, per se, were ritualized processes and events, including 1) the children as "consultants," 2) the parents talking to their daughters, and 3) the carefully planned meeting with the physician. Each included procedural steps prior to the event itself during which relationships were undergoing marked changes. Each included metaphor and symbols capable of multiple meanings. Each was time-bound, providing safety for exploration of feelings and new options. Each contained pre-planned direction and opportunity for spontaneous interplay. Each marked the passage of the family to a new place, with hitherto unavailable relationship possibilities.

My work with rituals has had many influences, including my background in psychodrama, Milan Team rituals, and structural family therapy meal sessions. More personal influences have included the delightful period of experimentation with rituals with the University of Massachusetts teams discussed above (we became known as the team that "buried things" and were presented with a ribboned shovel!); working as the supervisor of students' comprehensives and dissertations on rituals (Note 11); work with Richard Whiting in which we experimented with life-cycle rituals, such as "weddings" and "adoptions," and added freezing and burning to the burial option; and more recent work with Karl Tomm, centering especially on variations of the original "Odd-Days-Even-Days" ritual (Selvini-Palazzoli, 1978). I have been fortunate to work in two contexts (University of Massachusetts Psychological Services Center, directed by Dr. Hal Jarmon, and The Family Therapy Program, University of Calgary, directed by Dr. Karl Tomm) that have supported imaginative exploration of rituals as potent therapeutic tools.

III. Empowerment and Change

I view my work with individuals, families and larger systems as in the service of empowerment. Such empowerment facilitates nonexploitative relationships capable of complex interactional options and personal choices. I believe people are empowered when they experience a sense of self, connected to a variety of contexts that enhance, rather than oppress their unfolding as human beings. At the end of therapy, Carrie took charge of her "symptom" and developed her own plan for its dissolution. Her earlier sense of helplessness and entrapment was replaced by a sense of mastery and liberation. Unlike many descriptions of family therapy in which an intervention seems to lead to a magical disappearance of a symptom, Carrie chose her own way, which symbolized a gradual resolution, which fit not only her own needs but those of the people she loved as well. Change sometimes comes in leaps, but often it is incremental, sensitively calibrated, manageable in ways that feed the next step.

Very few seeds become flowers overnight. Ordering flowers to grow generally results in frustrated gardeners and secretly angry plants. Taking credit for beautiful, healthy flowers is the height of hubris and the outer reaches of simplistic thinking. Appreciating the inordinate possibilities of growth and development marks a garden of empowerment.

IV. The Family and Larger Systems

Work with the Simpsons began with a focus on the family's relationship to larger systems. It ended with a similar focus. From beginning to end, the family's relationship to outside systems shifted from one that was frightened, guarded, and consistently one-down to one that was open, receptive, inviting of information, and capable of both complementarity and symmetrical partnerships in problem-solving.

An individual or family's relationship with larger systems, as represented by particular helping professionals, is a key variable in therapeutic success, regardless of model. Time spent assessing the family's beliefs and experiences with larger systems is often time saved from later struggles that replicate both internal and external family relationships.

A second implication of a focus on larger systems regards the possibilities of affecting the policies, structures and day-to-day operations of larger helping systems and the human services network. Many of the problems faced by families are either iatrogenic or exacerbated by their interactions with larger systems (Imber Coppersmith, 1985).

Critical analyses of the effects of larger helping systems on human functioning are needed. Models of larger systems that facilitate human development require our attention. An important recent influence on my work in this regard has been the L'Arche Community, a larger system living and working with mentally handicapped adults (Imber Coppersmith, 1984). At L'Arche, the helper-helped complementarity is frequently called into question and other relationship possibilities abound. I have been especially impressed with their careful attention to building structures and processes that focus on the value of relationships, struggle to overcome artificial distances, challenge stereotypes, and recognize the inherent worth of each individual. I am currently grappling with ways to translate or approximate their work with other larger systems (Note 12). For systems thinkers and practitioners who are immersed in the complex processes of human development and change, our field, I think, has a great deal to offer in examination of, consultation to, and creation of larger systems.

CONCLUSIONS

Writing this paper has helped me to see my work as an unfinished tapestry, composed of many threads, varied colors, and intricate patterns. I have been extremely fortunate in the composition of this tapestry to have students, teachers, colleagues, families, and personal relationships with special people who have worked along with me, collaborated on new designs, given me thread when I was sure the spool was empty, and generously valued the emergent pictures (Note 13). This tapestry speaks to me of a fundamental sense of human resourcefulness and the need to build contexts that make such resources manifest. All along the way, I have had teachers who believed in my resources and, regardless of their area of expertise, took the time to discover how I would learn best and what I needed to struggle to new places.

I have tried to be such a teacher to others, to be a therapist to families, and a consultant to larger systems who focuses on strengths rather than deficits. I have been rewarded in this effort by seeing the careers of talented students blossom, by witnessing the emergence of resources within the healing matrix of relationships in families and larger systems, and by the appreciation of colleagues for my endeavors. The Simpson family is only one example of what I consider to be my extraordinary good fortune in being able to develop myself in a field that has allowed me to enter people's lives, appreciate the human wish to make sense of relationships, and contribute, in whatever ways I have been able, to that sense-making.

Along the way I have learned that models of training, therapy, family life, and institutions can be prisons of conformity, unquestioned reflections of oppressive social structures, and ferocious traps of escalating competition. Models, in this sense, mystify what I see as our larger purpose as facilitators of systems where no one person's needs are met at the expense of others — systems, in short, of cooperation and justice. Our models can free us to do the best work of which we are capable. Here, I understand our models as lenses that allow us to see certain phenomena and prevent us from seeing other phenomena. If we are to remain open to the discovery of new perspectives, then, like good photographers, we require a variety of lenses for different circumstances, the flexibility to try new angles, and a spirit of experimentation. Finally, if we are to be human artists rather than technocrats, then even we have all of the latest equipment, we will appreciate our work as ultimately embedded in relationships and measured by the nature of those relationships.

NOTES

1. It is beyond the scope of this paper to detail all of this work with families and larger systems. The interested reader is referred to:

Bell, N., & Zucker, R. (1968-69). Family-hospital relationships in a state hospital setting: A structural-functional analysis of the hospitalization process. *The International Journal of Social Psychiatry, VX*, 73-80.

Harkaway, J. (1983). Obesity: Reducing the larger system. *Journal of Strategic and Systemic Therapies, 2*, 2-14.

Harrell, F. (1980). Family dependency as a transgenerational process: An ecological analysis of families in crisis. Unpublished dissertation. University of Massachusetts, Amherst.

Hoffmann, L., & Long, L. (1969). A systems dilemma. *Family Process, 8*, 211-234.

Imber Coppersmith, E. (1980). Expanding uses of the telephone in family therapy. *Family Process, 19*, 411-417.

Imber Coppersmith, E. (1983). The family and public service systems: An assessment method. In B. Keeney (Ed.), *Diagnosis and Assessment in Family Therapy*. Rockville, MD: Aspen Publications.

Imber Coppersmith, E. (1983). The family and public sector systems: Interviewing and interventions. *Journal of Strategic and System Therapies, 2*, 38-47.

Imber Coppersmith, E. (1985). Families and multiple helpers. In R. Draper & D. Campbell (Eds.), *The Milan Method*. New York: Academic Press.

Imber Coppersmith, E. (1986). The systemic consultant to human service provider systems. In L. Wynne (Ed.), *The Family Therapist as Consultant*. New York: Guilford Press.

Lee, J. (1980). The helping professional's use of language in describing the poor. *American Journal of Orthopsychiatry, 50*, 580-584.

Miller, D. (1983). Outlaws and invaders: The adaptive function of alcohol abuse in the family-helper supra-system. *Journal of Strategic and Systemic Therapies, 2*, 15-27.

Selvini-Palazzoli, M., Boscolo, L., Cecchin, G., & Prata, G. (1980). The problem of the referring person. *Journal of Marital and Family Therapy, 6*, 3-9.

Selig, A. (1976). The myth of the multi-problem family. *American Journal of Orthopsychiatry, 46*, 526-531.

Webb-Woodard, L., & Woodard, B. The larger system in the treatment of incest. *Journal of Strategic and Systemic Therapies, 2,* 28–37.
2. The team in this case consisted variably of Dr. Dusty Miller, Dr. M. J. Ferrier, Mr. Jerome Adams, and Ms. Marija Bakaitis. They have my deep appreciation for their creativity and their support.
3. The interested reader is referred to the following works of Dr. Janine Roberts who has graciously chronicled and analyzed my work with teams in a training format:

Roberts, J. (1983, March). Collaborative training teams in live supervision. *Family Therapy Networker.*

Roberts, J. (1983). Two models of live supervision: Collaborative team and supervisor guided. *Journal of Strategic and Systemic Therapies, 2,* 68–89.
4. This period (1978–1982) resulted in ongoing relationships for me with trainees who became valued colleagues and who are now doing innovative work in a variety of areas. While many, many students have contributed to my development, I am especially appreciative of Dr. Richard Whiting, Dr. Janine Roberts, Dr. Linda Webb-Woodard, and Dr. Dusty Miller.
5. This period also led to a number of papers which I could not have authored without these teams, including "Expanding Uses of the Telephone in Family Therapy" (1980), "Developmental Reframing: She's Not Mad, She's Not Bad, She's Just Young" (1981), "From Hyperactive to Normal But Naughty: A Multi-system Partnership in Delabelling" (1982), and "We've Got A Secret: A Non-Marital Marital Therapy" (1985).
6. My appreciation is extended to Dr. Karl Tomm who entered the case behind the mirror for this one session and helped me to significantly explore the connections between the couple's marital development and Carrie's symptoms in the present.
7. My appreciation is extended to Carol Liske, the trainee at this session.
8. I primarily utilized the ideas of Dr. M. J. Ferrier regarding systemic work with individuals, as well as Bowenian coaching ideas.
9. Carrie Simpson was denied access to birth control in the 1940s. Recently a 39-year-old client in a troubled marriage described appearing before a hospital abortion committee to be told by the psychiatrist that she was "being selfish" and denying her husband his rights.
10. The as yet unpublished work of Dr. Dusty Miller and Laurie MacKinnon which questions when neutrality at the family level may, in fact, align one with oppressive forces at the societal level has certainly informed my thinking in this regard.
11. My learning in this area was greatly enhanced by the research of Beth Culler and Judy Davis. Both studied and wrote about rituals. Beth Culler produced many creative therapeutic rituals; Judy Davis examined her own son's Bar Mitzvah as a ritual that facilitated profound relationship changes in the family. I thank them both.
12. My deep appreciation is given to Mr. Pat Lenon, Regional Coordinator of L'Arche in the Western Prairie Region, who facilitated my study of this unique larger system.
13. My special appreciation to my children, Jason and Jennifer Coppersmith, who have been proud of me and adapted to the sometimes unusual demands of my work, and to my husband, Lascelles Black, for his abiding support.

REFERENCES

Carter, B., & McGoldrick, M. (Eds.). (1980). *The Family Life Cycle.* New York: Gardner Press.
de Shazer, S. (1982). *Patterns of Brief Family Therapy: An Ecosystemic Approach.* New York: Guilford Press.
Fisch, R., Weakland, J., & Segal, L. (1982). *The Tactics of Change: Doing Therapy Briefly.* San Francisco: Jossey-Bass.
Goldner, V. (1985). Feminism and family therapy. *Family Process, 24*(1).
Haley, J. (1973). *Uncommon Therapy: The Psychiatric Techniques of Milton H. Erickson.* New York: Norton.
Hare-Mustin, R. (1978). A feminist approach to family therapy. *Family Process, 17,* 181–193.

Imber Coppersmith, E. (1981). Developmental reframing: She's not bad, she's not mad, she's just young. *Jnl. Strat. & Syst. Ther., 1*, (1).

Imber Coppersmith, E. (1982). From hyperactive to normal but naughty: A multisystem partnership in delabelling. *Intl. Jnl. Fam. Psychiatry, 3*(2), 131-144.

Imber Coppersmith, E. (1984). A Special Family with Handicapped Members: One Family Therapist's Learnings from the L'Arche Community. In E. Imber Coppersmith (Ed.), *Families With Handicapped Members*. Rockville, MD: Aspen Systems Corporation.

Imber Coppersmith, E. (1985). We've got a secret: A non-marital marital therapy. In A. Gurman (Ed.), *A Marital Therapy Casebook*. New York: Guilford Press.

Imber Coppersmith, E. (in press, 1986). Families and multiple helpers: A systemic perspective. In R. Draper & D. Campbell (Eds.), *Applications of Systemic Family Therapy — The Milan Method*. London: Academic Press.

James, J., & McIntyre, D. (1983). The reproduction of families: The social role of family therapy. *Journal of Marital and Family Therapy, 9*, 119-129.

Libow, J., Rasking, P., & Caust, B. (1982). Feminism and family systems therapy: Are they irreconcilable? *American Journal of Family Therapy, 10*, 3-12.

Madanes, C. (1981). *Strategic Family Therapy*. San Francisco: Jossey-Bass.

Minuchin, S., & Fishman, H. C. (1981). *Family Therapy Techniques*. Cambridge, MA: Harvard University Press.

Minuchin, S., Montalvo, B., Guerney, G., Rosman, B., & Schumer, F. (1967). *Families of the Slums*. New York: Basic Books.

Richardson, R. (1984). *Family Ties That Bind*. North Vancouver: International Self-Counsel Press.

Selvini-Palazzoli, M., Boscolo, L., Cecchin, G., & Prata, G. (1974). The treatment of children through the brief therapy of their parents. *Family Process, 13*, 429-442.

Selvini-Palazzoli, M., Boscolo, L., Cecchin, G., & Prata, G.(1977). Family rituals: A powerful tool in family therapy. *Family Process, 16*, 445-453.

Selvini-Palazzoli, M., Boscolo, L., Cecchin, G., & Prata, G. (1978). A ritualized prescription in family therapy: Odd days and even days. *Journal of Marriage and Family Counseling, 4*, 3-9.

Selvini-Palazzoli, M., Boscolo, L., Cecchin, G., & Prata, G. (1980). Hypothesizing, circularity, neutrality: Three guidelines for the conductor of the session. *Family Process, 19*, 3-12.

van der Hart, O. (1983). *Rituals in Psychotherapy: Transition and Continuity*. New York: Irvington Press.

Wolin, S., & Bennett, L. (1984). Family rituals. *Family Process, 23*(3), 401-420.

Chapter 2

Fragments for a Therapeutic Autobiography

Bill O'Hanlon

When I first considered writing this piece, I thought of the many ways to approach it. Each way I considered seemed to have its merits and each way seemed to be incomplete, only part of the story. What we leave out and what we include influence the story so much. Any version of our past is necessarily distorted, warped in a certain direction. As some pundit has said, "It's never too late to have a happy childhood." The best we can do, I believe, is make up a story about the past, based on our faulty reminiscences. As I wrote my story, various memories occurred to me and I thought as I wrote that eventually they would come together as a unified whole. Instead, I find myself with fragments, short vignettes. I decided in the end to leave them as that and let the reader make his own story from them. What follows, then, is the rather fragmented story (stories?) of my path to becoming a "strategic/ systemic" therapist and trainer.

LIVING IN THE MATERIAL WORLD

I decided to kill myself in 1970. I was a very shy, sensitive young man who was having trouble making it in the material world. I was in my first year of college going through those existential and value crises that young people often go through. A friend talked me out of killing myself and I was left with a dilemma which has guided my personal and therapeutic life since that time. I determined that since I had decided to live here on this planet, in this body, I wanted to have a life that worked and I wanted to be happy. Therefore, the question was, for me, "What makes a life work?"

Psychotherapy seemed a good place for the inquiry. It was concerned with that question and related ones. How do people get in difficulties and how do they get out of them? How do people get their lives to work and how do they attain happiness? What can people do that can make a difference in the quality of their lives and in their circumstances? Various therapeutic schools claimed to have at least some of the answers to these questions and most were actively engaged in the inquiry.

I mainly read at first. I read voraciously, mostly self-help and psychotherapy books. I actually found some useful stuff that way. Two things stuck in my mind that were very helpful. One was Albert Ellis' stuff, you can influence your happiness by your beliefs and by challenging irrational beliefs. That was something I could do on my own and did. I challenged my dramatizing of my misery and my situation. I challenged my powerlessness. The other was Gestalt and Ram Dass spiritual stuff. The idea that all it took to be happy was to give up the struggle to be happy and to let yourself BE where you are had a powerful impact on me that has never gone away. I remember being struck with the rather obvious insight that the way to be "self-actualized" was to continue to be the way I was. I had often longed for the oasis of self-actualization and it always seemed like a mirage, because I never could actually reach it even though I could see it in the distance. When I gave up trying to reach it, it was right under my feet.

O.K., so I had left misery-land behind and was now O.K. the way I was. I was content with who I was, but my life still didn't work. I was disorganized, chronically in financial straits, always late for things, painfully shy, and didn't seem to have the discipline to achieve my goals. I "had potential." But it wasn't clear whether I was a dreamer doomed to constantly have unrealized potential or whether I would turn out to "be somebody."

The ultimate test for whether I had mastered this life would be, I thought, when the results in the "real world" reflected that mastery. When, instead of dreaming about and longing for the things I didn't have and hadn't accomplished, I would have accomplished those things and have those things in my life. I decided I wanted a few things. I wanted to love and experience and know that I was loved. I wanted to make a contribution to other people, to the world. I wanted fame and fortune, not necessarily for themselves but because they would give me the clout and credibility to have an impact on people and on the world. And because that would be a good testing ground for the inquiry and experiment that I was conducting. If I, as messed up as I was, could make good, anybody could!

CLARITY BEGINS AT HOME

I have a confession to make. I have never been in therapy. Worse than that, I'm proud of it. I know that may sound like heresy, but I'm of the persuasion (with Haley and others) that therapy is the problem to be solved and it is best to avoid it if at all possible. I certainly don't view therapy as something that everyone (or even every therapist) should have. I think of therapy as analogous, in some ways, to getting my car repaired. At times it may become necessary, of course, but one hopes it doesn't. If it does become necessary, one wants it to be over soon and as inexpensively as possible. Human beings aren't cars, of course. I think that humans have self-repair mechanisms that require even less service and repair than autos.

I used to be a seeker of sorts. I searched religions, therapies, self-help groups, philosophies, etc. for THE ANSWER. Some years ago I went through the infamous est training. Much has been said in praise and damnation of est. I enjoyed it quite a bit and managed to avoid being an "esthole." One wonderful result for me in attending the est training was that I stopped searching for THE ANSWER. Not that I stopped being intellectually curious or trying out new philosophies or anything like that. I just finished the search for something that would finally make me whole and complete and at peace. I don't seek therapy to get fixed, because I'm not broken!

I much prefer to sort out my difficulties within my natural contexts, my family and friends. I'm wary of therapy for all the iatrogenic problems that it can give rise to. One can seek therapy for some very simple difficulty and leave with all sorts of esoteric psychological problems one never knew one had.

LIVING WITH THE ROBOTS

For many years I had really long hair (down to the middle of my back) and I remember very clearly when I decided to cut it short. I was on my way from Phoenix to New Orleans, riding with two close friends to attend a psychotherapy conference. My two friends drove and talked all night while I dozed fitfully in the cramped back seat. As the sun was coming up, I began to awaken and heard one of the friends say to the other, "You know, people are robots. They see Bill with his long hair and 'hippie' clothes and they make all sorts of assumptions about him that aren't true—that he does drugs, that he's irresponsible, has no money, etc. Then they see me (my friend looked as if he had just stepped out of a college fraternity, very clean-cut, but he lived much more of a "hippie" life than did I) and make all sorts of conclusions that aren't accurate. I have instant credibility with most people, whereas Bill has a strike against him at the start." As I lay there in my hypnogogic (or hypnopompic, I can never keep them straight) state, I thought, "He's absolutely right, people are robots, and what am I doing pushing the wrong buttons?!" When we arrived in New Orleans, I shaved off my beard and when I arrived back home, I got my hair cut short.

Two things I noticed right away: 1) Store employees stopped following me while I was grocery shopping (and I had always thought I was just being paranoid) and 2) I was much looser with my language and behavior in therapy. I no longer felt the need to act so "straight" to gain rapport in therapy. People did respond differently to me.

OUT OF THE SEA OF PSYCHOLOGY

One of the things that has emerged for me in the past several years is the utter uselessness of explanations and analysis of motives and meanings in being able to get happy and make a life work. This seems especially true in psychotherapy. We have already gone down the road of psychology and down that road lies no results. Psychotherapy has notoriously been shown to make no difference with people's problems overall. I grew more and more sceptical of explanations as I went along in psychotherapy. Each theorist and school have their own pet explanations for why people change and why they stay the same. But what ultimately makes an impact in therapy is what the therapist does and says.

I liked Bandler and Grinder's early (pre-NLP) work (1975a, 1975b) because it was long on action, flexibility, and observation and short on explanations and hypotheses. The Milan folks are fond of saying that one shouldn't "marry" one's hypothesis, but I'm more inclined to say one shouldn't even go out on a date with one. I think hypotheses are mere distractions at best and at worst become self- (or other-) fulfilling prophesies. Jim Wilk and I have a joke that we tell in our trainings. We say that we think all brief therapists ought to have a couch in their offices. Lest you think we have regressed to analytic or psychodynamic approaches, however, we assure you that the couch is not for the client, it is for the therapist to use whenever he gets a hypothesis—he should lie down until it goes away!

The radical shift I have gone through after working in a strategic, systemic, Ericksonian, contextual way for some time is that I am not concerned with how problems arise (not much new here, most modern therapists avoid the search for etiology), nor with how they are maintained in the present (this is somewhat radical, as most therapies and therapists these days are concerned with discerning and altering what currently maintains problems). I am even unconcerned with what functions the problem might serve for the person or the system (and this is perhaps the most radical stance of all, as most therapists are convinced that there is a function for the symptom and that it must be taken into account if the symptom is to be resolved and no other problems are to arise). I am only concerned with what will create the conditions for change, what will resolve the symptom, dissolve the problem.

Therapy has been stuck in a sea of explanations, mostly derived from psychology and medicine, the main disciplines from which psychotherapy emerged. No matter which direction we move in this sea or what the evolution of psychotherapy involves, it will always be in the realm of possibilities allowed to sea creatures. I propose that it is time to emerge from the sea of psychology, from the realm of explanation, into the realm of action. New possibilities, as undreamed of as eagles and elephants to the creatures of the sea, are possible when we emerge from the sea of psychology onto the dry land of action.

ENTERING THE REALM OF ACTION

Therapy has, I think, been pretty good at helping people accept themselves the way they are, with the feelings, thoughts and experiences they have or have had. This, however, is not enough much of the time to solve the problems that are brought into therapy, although people usually feel better when they come to accept themselves the "way they are." Where therapy has fallen short of the mark has been in the area of getting people to take action to solve their problems, to make changes by DOING something.

This is not to imply that internal experience (thoughts, feelings, and the like) do not exist or have an impact on people's lives. Of course they do. But what ultimately makes a difference in people's lives are the actions which they perform. Analysis and explanation rarely further the action in people's lives and is often what they do instead of action.

Of course, this view about therapy is very much influenced by what I have been experiencing in my personal life. I decided at a certain point that I wanted to be an international trainer and publish several books. I had my doubts about whether I could do that and so did other people. Look at all the things that were stacked against me: I had a masters degree in a field that accords status mainly to doctoral level practitioners and physicians; I was from NE-BRASKA, not exactly the hub of therapeutic innovation ("Do you practice your therapy on cows or something?"); No one had ever heard of me, etc. At a certain point in my development, I decided to stop just dreaming and wondering whether I could accomplish my goals; I started to take actions towards them AS IF they were going to be accomplished and then let the world teach me where the limitations were.

One time I was on a teaching trip to England, where I stayed with Jim Wilk, who was coauthoring a book with me. I told Jim that I would like to complete the whole first draft of the text while I was in England, since we write much better when we're face to face. Jim was quick to point out that there was no way for us to complete the draft in the time available. I got very upset and we had quite a row, until I said, "Look, Jim, what I want is for you to do action and then tell me what's possible. Don't decide beforehand what's possible and what's not!" He agreed and we set to work. I think that clients and therapists alike often decide beforehand what's possible and what's impossible, closing an issue that I would rather have left open. I like to work from the assumption that what I am trying to do is possible and then let the world inform me (by the success or failure of the actions to bring about the goal) what to do next or whether it is possible.

THE ONE-SESSION CONSPIRACY

I remember hearing about the beginnings of family therapy, where several individuals and groups had independently started seeing whole families together in their offices, but didn't know that anyone else was doing so. This was such a radical idea at the time that therapists didn't talk about it with their colleagues, fearing censure and derision. At national meetings, over late night drinks or in conversations in the halls, people started to mention, tentatively, that they had been seeing the whole family together. As they discovered kindred colleagues, who were also doing family therapy, they grew emboldened and started writing and teaching others about family therapy. From that emerged a growing national movement leading to the widespread acceptance of the approach around the world.

I feel somewhat the same way about writing and talking about my "one-session cures." At first, I thought them to be lucky flukes and dismissed them. But as they happened more frequently, I started to think I might have something and wanted to talk to others about the phenomena. I was concerned that I might lose my credibility with people and be seen as a braggart or merely fooling myself. I mentioned it to my colleague Jim Wilk on my first visit to England in 1982 and he confessed that the same thing had been happening to him on occasion. I have since found that it happens occasionally or often for others in the field, but no one has been able to offer a good formula or approach for making it happen more often or more predictably. Jim and I decided we would give it a try, which led to our collaboration on a new book (O'Hanlon & Wilk, in press). We figured that the key must be in the assessment process, because in these cases we rarely got a chance to do any formal "interventions," as the client knew that the problem was gone before we got the chance to do any "tricks." My assessment process has changed over the years and now seems to reflect an entirely different set of assumptions than I previously held (when I never got one-session results). We decided to articulate those basic assumptions and to recapitulate the process of challenging our previous assumptions and those presuppositions deeply embedded in all of psychotherapy.

GROWING WITH ERICKSON

I met Milton Erickson in 1973. I worked in the Arizona State University art gallery and he came with his wife and daughter to buy a Seri Indian ironwood carving. After I had carried the art piece down to their car, someone

at the art gallery told me about Erickson and showed me an article that was
in Time magazine that week about him. I read that article and went out immediately to buy *Uncommon Therapy* (Haley, 1973). I was intrigued and read
all that I could find on his work. It took me until 1977, as shy and as much
of a procrastinator as I was, to finally contact Erickson to study with him. I
wrote him a letter in early 1977 telling him that I'd come up with several
schemes to visit him (I'd write an article or a biography to expose him and
his work to a wider audience, I'd trade him gardening for teaching, etc.), but
that in the end I really just wanted to visit and learn and I didn't have much
money. I went away for the weekend and when I returned my roommate said,
"The strangest guy has been calling early in the morning, asking for the
O'Hanlon Gardening Service. He won't leave his name or number, just says
he'll call back."

The next morning, right on cue, came the call for the O'Hanlon Gardening Service. I took the phone and said that this was Bill O'Hanlon. He asked,
"Don't you think you ought to survey the territory before you decide to take
the job?" I answered yes, and asked if this was Dr. Erickson. He answered
that it was and we arranged a time for me to come visit. He showed me his
garden and set me to work in it. I had thought we were speaking only in
metaphor, but noooooo! I actually worked in the garden. Working with him
was very disconcerting and I left after several months more confused than
when I had started. From that experience, I vowed that I would figure Erickson out. I knew that I was on my own with that. He didn't clarify what he
did at all when I studied with him, but I became convinced that what he was
doing was very powerful.

In 1980, I started a private practice. As those of you who have done the
same know, one has a lot of time on one's hands when one starts a practice.
I went back and reread everything that Erickson had written, what others had
written about him, and listened to tapes. What emerged after a time was a
clarity about Erickson's approach that has been the basis of the things I teach
in workshops and has made a profound impact on my therapeutic results.

WORKING THE PSYCHO-JET SET: BECOMING A THERAPY TRAINER

The workshop leader was a well-known practitioner and teacher of Gestalt
therapy and he was attempting to teach the (then-new) techniques developed
by Bandler and Grinder (later to be called NLP). As I sat there in the workshop, I grew more and more frustrated. Although a novice therapist, I could
tell the presenter didn't know his subject. I had read several books on the subject and been to a workshop with Bandler and Grinder earlier in the year.
This man was pitiful! I was appalled.

Something inside me snapped. I had for the past several years been a "workshop junkie" and was disgusted with attending disappointing training after training. While driving home from that workshop with a colleague, bitter about wasting my time and money, I rashly declared, "I could have taught that workshop better and charged less money!"

Later, I thought to myself, "Okay, big shot, if you think you're so terrific, go out and teach a workshop!"

Currently, I teach workshops all over the country and occasionally in Europe.

Blissful Ignorance: Getting Started

Okay, so I was going to do a workshop. The only problem was that I didn't have a clue as to how to do that. A friend suggested that I talk to friends of his who had just started a graphic design business, as one of the first things I would need was a brochure. They kindly guided me through my first brochure, pointing out that before I could do the brochure, I would need to secure a place to teach the workshop (generally a church hall, college classroom, auditorium or hotel meeting room). I called hotels, expecting to be quoted outrageous prices, but was pleasantly surprised to discover that a smallish room (holding 30–50 people) generally ran $40–$70. I chose a date and reserved a room. Next came the brochure preparation. I used brochures I had received in the mail as guides for writing mine. The graphics people designed and printed the finished product (for about $75). I put together a mailing list from the yellow pages in the phone book and from a social services directory. I hand addressed, hand stamped, and mailed out several hundred brochures (about $40), as well as handing out many to friends and colleagues.

Lo and behold, about 20 people showed up at that first workshop (at $20 apiece) and I made a small profit. More than that, however, I discovered that I *loved* to teach and that I could put together a workshop. I was hooked. During the next year or so, I taught several more workshops, each one showed a modest profit, and I became more proficient in both the teaching and coordination of workshops.

I have had my ups and downs along the road. I have had workshops where only two people showed up, as well as some where several hundred showed up. I have met some wonderful people, some of whom have become good friends.

When I was teaching at a family therapy conference in Germany several years ago, I had dinner with Boscolo and Cecchin, from the Milan group. After I was introduced to them and told them that I taught workshops around the U.S. and lately in Europe, they said, "Welcome to the Psycho-Jet Set!"

I currently teach about every weekend and see about 10 clients per week during the week. With my writing and editing work, as well as my family and social life, I keep quite busy.

RIGHTEOUS INDIGNATION

Some people ask me how can I keep such a hectic teaching and traveling pace going. If I did it just for the money, I don't think I could. I have this burning sense of righteous indignation when I hear of some of the things being done in the name of healing. People drugged out, people told that they will never change or that it will take a minimum of a year to solve their problems, people sexually abused in the name of therapy, etc., etc. I have made a resolve to alter the course of modern therapy and the energy of that keeps me going. My quest is paralleled by that of many former "hippie radicals" who have now gone on to become professionals but have not lost their revolutionary fervor or desire to make a contribution.

Buckminster Fuller (one of my heroes) had a metaphor that he used to explain how one person could make a difference. There is a little rudder on the big rudder of modern ships that is called the "trimtab." Turning the trimtab, which takes relatively little effort, makes a larger difference in the rudder, which would have taken a lot more effort to turn. In this way the ship is turned with relatively little effort by a small difference that makes a big difference. Fuller said, "Just call me trimtab!" Me too. I want to make a difference in the larger field of therapy and I have my plans about how to get to that trimtab. One of them is through writing. This article is part of that process.

I had some friends who had a musical group when I was in college. They had one song that had a line in it that has stayed with me: "We are all flutes through which the breath of God should pass." While I'm not a religious person, I am very spiritual. I feel as if the Universe (or God or whatever) is using me as an instrument. My job is to get my self and my life as clear as possible so that the notes will sound pure. My job is to get my life to work and make a contribution to other people.

I had a psychiatrist friend who had a theory of the world that he called "benevolent paranoia." He thought the world was set up to work absolutely and our job was to discover what the world wanted us to do. When we did, it would reward us (with little pieces of paper which we could trade in for things we want, with love, with status, etc.). I hold a similar view. The analogy I use is that this planet and our species are like an ant colony in some ways. Each ant has its own life experience and individual urges, yet somehow they are all working in harmony and get the job done at a social level by following their individual paths. I think each of us has a part to play in making our planet work and our species a success. To discover that requires only a sensitivity to what works and what doesn't for you (no one else can decide for you, intuition is your rudder), a commitment to integrity, and a willingness to try many things to discover what the universe needs at this moment. The Mel Brooks movie "Blazing Saddles" has a line which I remember from time to time and use as a criteria for deciding whether this path is right for me or not. The villains ask the preacher to say a prayer before they go into battle and the preacher says, "Dear Lord, is what we're doing really important or are we just jerking off?"

I think that the contextual/strategic/systemic/Ericksonian approaches can make a difference for individuals, groups and societies. What we're doing *is* important. We're not just jerking off.

REFERENCES

Bandler, R., & Grinder, J. (1975a). *The Structure of Magic, Volume 1*. Palo Alto, CA: Science and Behavior Books.
Bandler, R., & Grinder, J. (1975b). *The Patterns of the Hypnotic Techniques of Milton H. Erickson, M.D., Volume 1*. Cupertino, CA: Meta.
Haley, J. (1973). *Uncommon Therapy: The Psychiatric Techniques of Milton H. Erickson, M.D.* New York: Norton.
O'Hanlon, B., & Wilk, J. (in press). *Shifting Contexts: The Generation of Effective Therapy*. New York: Guilford.

Chapter 3

No Bolts from the Blue

Michaelin Reamy-Stephenson

> The pulse of life beats with the pulse of the flood, maps are constantly out of date. . . . The river and the forest reflect each other's needs precisely.
> — *The Amazon* (A documentary), Jacques-Yves Cousteau.

My introduction to strategic and systemic therapy came at a critical juncture of my life — a painful ending and new beginning. I had, within the last two years, left a once-settled, meaningful life in Beirut, "the jewel of Phoenicia," the crossroads of Europe, Asia and Africa. One Saturday in October, I had been standing with a group of parents at the American Community School watching a little league game. I could hear the guns — street fighting, the Lebanese Civil War contained — three blocks away. Something clicked. I had been kidding myself. The situation was not getting better. It was not safe. I could not protect my children or my Lebanese friends. Two days later I left with my husband and children — a home and life of five years. Sheets were left on the beds, food in the refrigerator. There was no time for good-byes.

The grief was immense — a brutal uprooting, a loss of identity, a shattered world view. A divorce from my husband of 17 years followed in the wake. With a near frantic desperation, I pursued a course of graduate study at Georgia State University in developmental psychology. (I had long nurtured an interest, vaguely defined as "preventing emotional disturbances in children.") Here, while developing an animal model for fetal alcohol syndrome, a study that was to lead to a masters thesis, I developed a severe lung allergy. I had been spending hundreds of hours in a small room observing rats —

specifically, nesting behavior and mother-infant interaction. Apparently, I was allergic to dried rat urine.

A second academic launching was initiated at the University of Georgia M.S.W. Program. Before classes began, I took a breather. My boyfriend (and now husband), Rick, and I traveled to Mexico. We made our way leisurely across the Yucatan Peninsula, stopping to visit Uxmal and Chichreën-Itzä, beautifully preserved ruins of Mayan civilization. I found the ruins strangely reminiscent of the Egyptian pyramids—the "other worldliness," the lowered center of gravity. I felt a connectedness, a link to a facet of myself that had been reawakened. We settled in for the remainder of our holiday on Isla Mujeres, an island off the coast of the Yucatan Peninsula. Here we immersed ourselves in skin diving, exploring the coral reefs, swimming through giant schools of brightly colored fish.

Wandering into a small cafe for lunch one day, we were greeted from the corner by the sole customer. Striking up a conversation, he joined us for lunch. He told us he had been attending a conference on the mainland for editors of *Family Process*. He mentioned a book called *Change* (1974) that he had recently coauthored with Watzlawick and Fisch. He was John Weakland. To us he was a charming fellow-adventurer who eagerly joined us for skin diving before we bid him farewell that evening as he boarded the ferry for Cancun. His parting words to us were, "If you're ever in Palo Alto, give me a call—I'd like to return the hospitality."

Several months later I spent a delightful afternoon with John at his home looking out over the Palo Alto hills. He generously responded to my well-kindled interest, giving me suggested readings in strategic and systemic therapies. As I pursued the readings, my interest grew to excitement, my excitement to near passion. It was thrilling and it was exhausting. At times it was difficult to "turn off the wheels." I was reminded of a well known Atlanta therapist who, finding himself in a similar dilemma, awoke one morning with the plea, "Lord, please don't grow me today." During my social work internship, flying about the country, I attended workshops of some of the masters— Haley, Lynn Hoffman, Minuchin. I sold my silver flatware to finance one trip.

GATHERING ASSUMPTIONS

The way I gathered theoretical assumptions reminded me of the way I learned to gather blackberries as a child. My father made his living as a commercial artist in New York City. Born a Virginia farm boy, he planted every square inch of our quarter acre plot in Westchester County—mostly in berries. There was every kind you could imagine—blueberries, currants, gooseberries, raspberries, blackberries. It was the job of my brother Ken and I to pick the berries. I remember working frantically to pick every last blackberry before Pop returned on the 6:15 PM bus. We lined the overflowing boxes in neat rows on a grass strip reserved for walking. As his footsteps approached, my heart would skip a beat. I knew I had missed some berries behind the web of a huge orange and black garden spider. And then the dreaded and familiar question, "Have you gotten them *all*?" A tentative "Yes." Without fail, Pop would lift up a lower branch in some out-of-the-way spot. The branch would be loaded with plump ripe berries, the best of the lot. His lesson was well learned.

An assumption that I gathered and have clung to fiercely is one of Haley's. This is the assumption that the value of a theory for clinical practice is whether "it works," i.e., whether it helps people get over their symptoms or presenting problems, not whether it is "the truth" (Haley, 1979). Another relevant assumption I gathered was from the work led by Bateson in the early 1950s with schizophrenic children and their mothers (Bateson et al., 1956). This is the assumption that "how you communicate determines how you think." Hence, I assume that if one talks like one's theory is the objective truth, before long one will be believing just that.

Making Links

As I sorted through and gathered assumptions, *I focused on finding links, finding commonalities* among schools of strategic and systemic therapies. Again, a pattern that had worked for me as a child emerged. My parents had left their south Georgia small-town roots in young adulthood. My father's father was a former Baptist preacher, my mother's father the town doctor. However, my parents had attempted to throw out the religion and racism so central to their upbringing. They had settled in Greenwich Village—my father a struggling artist, my mother a social worker. As children, we grew up with stories of those days. Spaghetti for Sunday supper is a tradition in our family to this day—a testament to those depression days when they would gather with their friends from various ethnic groups and all throw in a quarter for supper.

After my brother and I were born, my parents sought fresher air and more room in the suburbs. That's where the quarter-acre farm complete with barn and berries came in. Our house was one of several old houses on a narrow strip, a remnant of the past. The strip was buffered from the outside world by woods and a grassy field. My school mates seemed to live in another world beyond, in the brick apartment building or the new housing development. Their parents were politically conservative and churchgoers. Mine were voting for Henry Wallace, supporting Paul Robeson, and vehemently anti-formal religion. I believe my parents had thrown out the wheat with the chaff. They had thrown out religious dogma and racism but had kept the assumption of objective reality, the Aristotilian duality that in their world view made liberals good, conservatives bad; non-religious people worldly, religious people ignorant. They were intolerant of intolerance.

As a child, I found ways to connect these two worlds, to integrate them. Wandering through the gate and down what became a well-worn path across the field, my brother and I peddled fragrant lilacs from our yard and my hand-wrought shell jewelry in the surrounding neighborhood. In retrospect, I think this was less for money, more for connectedness — a kind of peace offering. I ached to have my parents make some connections, for them to see that there were also some nice people over there with whom they had something in common. There were a few connections, but very few. I do remember my father renting a Victory Garden in the apartment complex and sharing enthusiasm over some "Big Boy" tomatoes with a nice man who tilled the adjoining plot. It was a warm feeling. Recently my father died of cancer. Two weeks before his death he shared with me his feelings of isolation. He acknowledged that he had never liked "not being in the mainstream." I believe he wanted to have the mainstream think like he did. The assumption of objective truth, of an objective reality, didn't work for him.

I was seeking a theoretical framework and as I studied the work of the MRI Group, Haley, and Minuchin, I found commonalities in what appeared to me the essential "working" theoretical underpinnings. Differences were surely there. These differences, however, seemed to me more in emphasis, tactics, and personal style. They all appeared to be directive, clearly goal-oriented. MRI's concept of "the more-of-the-same" attempted solution (Watzlawick et al., 1974; Weakland et al., 1974) could be seen as part of Haley's sequence supporting "the type of behavior," e.g., temper tantrums, that was defined as the problem (Haley, 1976). Haley's fine-hewn concepts of hierarchy and sequence helped me understand the relationship between Minuchin's family structure and behavior patterns (Minuchin, 1978). In a nutshell, the behavior patterns could be seen as maintaining the family hierarchy, i.e., status or power ladder. With child-focused problems it seemed they were all advocating for the therapist to get the parents to work together in applying fresh solutions in dealing with the identified patient's behavior. This made good sense. I remembered vividly an experience on one of my travels to Kenya. A maitre d' had stood by helplessly while a mother attempted to develop a consensus with her children *while* they skated amongst the tables as to whether it was appropriate for them to roller skate in the hotel dining room. The father had made an attempt to structure the children; rebuffed by his wife, he had retired to the garden.

A BEGINNING WORKING FRAMEWORK

In time, I began to weave theoretical assumptions that I had gathered into a working framework that looked something like this (being visual, it was helpful for me to try to diagram the process):

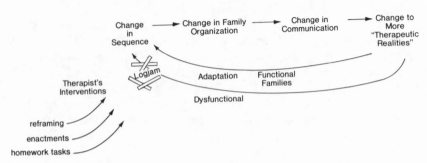

Haley had introduced me to the top half, i.e., the relationship among sequence→organization→communication→realities (Haley, 1979). I had added the feedback loop which underlined for me the constant renewing adaptive process often involving second-order change followed by well functioning families. Haley had pointed out that most "psychiatric symptoms" seem to arise at times when someone enters or begins to leave the family system, i.e., at important life stage transitions such as birth of a child, entry into adolescence, leaving home, death of a family member. It was really quite amazing that the great majority of families seemed to go through this process quite naturally in spite of the lack of rituals (e.g., puberty rites that exist in primitive cultures) to clearly delineate expected changes in behavior at critical points in the individual and family life cycle.

I began to see families presenting for treatment with an identified patient as frozen in time, stuck in a logjam preventing movement through the life stage transition. These dysfunctional families could be perceived as responding to demands for change (from inside and outside the family system) and the resultant raised levels of stress by rigidly maintaining the accustomed behavior patterns (repeating the same attempted solutions) and reifying the existing family structure, thus blocking the possibility of alternatives (Minuchin, 1978).

I began to see the job of the therapist as breaking the logjam, allowing the family to move forward in the life cycle. I had formulated a beginning working theoretical framework. In deciding how to go about breaking the logjam, I was confronted with differences among the master strategic and systemic therapists. It seemed that Minuchin's structural therapy emphasized enactments in the therapy sessions, whereas the strategic therapists put even more emphasis on homework tasks. The essential commonality seemed to be creating a new experience for the family, i.e., breaking the rigid behavior pattern supporting the symptom. Another theoretical assumption was essential here — that it is impossible to change without experiencing something new (Haley, 1979), that an emotional system responds to action, not interpretation (Papp, 1976).

I found that the hours spent watching sequences of behavior among mother and infant rats had not gone for naught. The experience helped train my eye. Inquiring into attempted solutions of various family members proved to be an efficient way to map out the rigid sequence.

I experimented with enactments and homework tasks. It didn't take me long to realize that what Minuchin (being a man, an M.D. and having a foreign accent) could pull off in a family session would not work for me as a woman social worker. As I had noted commonalities in theoretical underpinnings early on, I began to note that tactics associated with a particular school of structural or strategic therapy appeared to in large part grow out of the personal style of the founder of the school. Minuchin appeared to be more of a pursuer, hence his emphasis on enactments. This fit with his background in child psychiatry. In contrast, strategic therapists such as Weakland and Haley seemed to be more distancing; therefore, there was the emphasis on change outside the session. In a corresponding way, this fit with their backgrounds in anthropology and communications. I worked to find my own balance.

At this point in my clinical work, I had made little attempt at dramatic reframes, which still felt risky. I combined positive connotation, normalization, and gentle nudging reframes to enlist compliance with homework tasks. In time, as I began working with more difficult families, I learned that this was not enough.

Early Application of Theory

I used the opportunity of my internship to gather considerable clinical experience in working with school avoidance, the subject of my masters research project (Reamy-Stephenson, 1979). Several cases were sent my way. In working with this project, I found Haley's emphasis on clarifying the hierarchy and avoiding crossgenerational coalitions to be a particularly efficient way of breaking dysfunctional sequences. In addition I found that these concepts could be used beyond the boundaries of the family and school. The core issue was taking the decision about whether or not to go to school out of the hands of the child. Instead, parents and school officials were enlisted to give the child one clear, consistent message. "It is the law that you go to school. You don't have to like it; however, school attendance is not negotiable."

I remember one case particularly well. Billy was 13 and had been staying out of school for the better part of a quarter. From an intrapsychic point of view he appeared profoundly depressed. His anxiety level was so high that his speech would indicate a "thought disorder." Fortunately, I had heard Haley offer therapists an illusion of choice: You can say the kid is depressed so he is missing school and other peer activities or you can say the kid is missing school and other peer activities and so he's depressed. When I chose the latter frame, defining the problem as an "interproblem," i.e., a problem among people, I was able to stay grounded enough to focus on clarifying the hierarchy by backing his single-parent mother and organizing the necessary networking to get Billy back to school immediately. The change in Billy's behavior to a relatively cheerful, active adolescent within a matter of days was enough to convince me of the power of this therapeutic tool.

I had seen this concept of hierarchy in operation on a photographic safari in East Africa. A favorite pastime of mine was watching the animals come to water each night. As the late afternoon drew near, hundreds of water buffalo had appeared as mere specks on the horizon, forming what seemed an endless trail, zigzagging across the African plain, and in the span of an hour culminating in a thundering blackened mass in the water hole at the base of a cliff beneath our lodge. After taking their fill, the buffalos reversed their path, their trail disappearing as it had earlier appeared on the horizon. Shortly after nightfall, a rustling would be heard. Rhinoceros would move out of the shadows into the reach of the floodlights that surrounded the water hole. Their drinking would be disrupted when the lions arrived. The rhinoceros, after an almost imperceptible flurry, politely retired to the shadows until the lions were satisfied. In a similar manner the lions deferred to the elephants. The hierarchy was clear; the watering of many hundreds of animals proceeded with barely a hitch.

About this time I wrote to John Weakland, expressing my appreciation for his well-chosen reading list — highlighted by his book, *Change,* which he had advised me not to take too seriously — and my excitement over my early application of systemic therapy. I asked if I could consult with him further. He wrote back:

> I see that in spite of my warnings about *Change* and strategic therapy you have become involved nevertheless. I will be happy to talk with you further, if you insist on taking such risks.

Throughout my life, my experiences as student and teacher have been closely intertwined. This certainly fit with being the eldest sister in a large family where, predictably, the role of student of parents was quickly followed by the role of teacher of siblings. This pattern persisted in the arenas of swimming and tennis as it did in family therapy.

As I persisted in my own training and beginning teaching, I did a lot of observing. I was struck by how many students (and beginning therapists) demonstrated a cognitive understanding of systems. They had studied Haley and Minuchin. They were able to map family structure and point out triangles, yet had extreme difficulty in the practice of systemic therapy.

I was puzzled. These were not incompetent individuals. I looked closer. A pattern emerged. These therapists consistently complained about hostile parents, about fathers who wouldn't come to sessions, about "resistant" clients who dropped out of therapy. It was not that I hadn't struggled with these same problems; I had. But I still kept my enthusiasm for this way of working. The difference was subtle. I began to see that their systemic thinking did not expand beyond the family unit. The therapist's part in the parents' hostility, in the clients' resistance, had been overlooked. They were not seeing themselves as part of the family system (Keeney, 1979; Hoffman, 1983). I was still taking the rap, beating myself over the head for every hostile parent or missed appointment. I took a moment to reprimand myself for being an overly responsible big sister and went off to Galveston to learn more about dealing with resistance from Harry Goolishian and Paul Dell. I had just begun seeing a family with a nine-year-old male encopretic. My usual approach didn't seem to be working.

A Significant Workshop

The Galveston workshop was an important one for me (Dell & Goolishian, 1979). Goolishian and Dell presented their own integration of theory at that point in time, highlighting the work of the MRI Group. They added their own emphasis and twist and I liked it. They presented a bibliography which included readings from out-of-the-way spots, from the lower branches. One assumption that I gathered at that workshop was the assumption that you can be a good strategic therapist if you avoid drifting (stay goal-oriented) and avoid fighting resistance. This *emphasis* was helpful, doubly helpful as I hulled out assumptions to underline with students. In more recent years I have found the tendency to drift, to spend the better part of a session seduced into focusing on tangential issues, to be common with students. This tendency fits often with their past training where an emphasis was on empathic listening.

Goolishian and Dell presented their assumption that resistance lies not in a person but between people. In retrospect, this assumption was implicit in much of the strategic literature but it was helpful to have the assumption stated so clearly. I felt a kindred spirit, a validation of what I was believing at a gut level. It was okay to beat myself over the head when I came up against hostile parents — and then learn to avoid (or use) that resistance. Dell showed a tape of himself as therapist interviewing a young diabetic woman who was literally killing herself by eating improperly and refusing her insulin injections. He did a masterful job of reframing stubbornness into strength of character.

Another assumption was introduced—the assumption of non-objective reality, the idea that reality like beauty is in the eyes of the beholder. That what you look for determines what you find. At first I felt a bit like I had felt when I was first exposed to the concept of null hypothesis in a statistics class. At the time I could not realize how central this assumption of non-objective reality would become in my clinical work and, indeed, my teaching.

Midway through the first day of the conference, I found myself sitting in my hotel room faced with a homework task that had been given over the lunch break. Actually we had been given a choice of tasks. However, I had failed at my first try. (I had been unable to convince a drugstore clerk that he should reduce the fixed price of a toothbrush by two cents.) Ten minutes remained before the workshop resumed. Only one alternative remained: to call a long distance operator and find out 1) the weather in that city, 2) the name of a good restaurant, and 3) the price of Levis. We had been reminded of the objective truth about telephone operators, i.e., they could only give out telephone numbers. This was supposed to be related to being a strategic therapist. I wasn't sure I wanted any part of it. I found myself in a double bind. (My value system required that I respect and obey the objective institutional rules *and also* that I do my homework.) Fortunately the homework injunction won out. Taking a deep breath, I dialed the operator in Atlanta.

Going back in time, I "pretended" I was just returning from overseas. I responded to the operator's "Can I help you?" with "Oh, how wonderful it is to hear an American voice." She responded warmly with, "Oh, how is that?" I told her that I had just embarked in the United States after living overseas for two years, that I was looking for a friend, and I would be so grateful if she could help me. She answered "surely" and began searching the Atlanta listing for my friend, Beth Shumaker. At this point I interrupted to ask, "By the way, what's the weather like in Atlanta?" She responded "Someone just came in and said it was beautiful." I responded, "Great, I was looking forward to some Atlanta sunshine." She then told me that there were several B. Shumakers listed, but no Beth. With dismay I explained that I was just about out of money, then added, "Perhaps I could try them all when I get to Atlanta. And could you tell me the name of a good restaurant where I could have a bite to eat and use the telephone?" She directed me to an airport restaurant where she thought that would be possible. (Two down, one to go.) Taking another deep breath, I told her that she had been so helpful and that I had one more problem with which I wondered if she could help me. She answered, "I'll try." I then told her that I was down to my last pair of jeans, that they were ripped, and in fact I had a sweater tied around my waist to conceal the rip. I asked if she knew how much Levis were running these days. She responded, "I think you could find a pair for about twenty dollars." After I turned in my homework, one of the other workshop participants commented enthusiastically, "You must be a good strategic therapist." I thought—little does he know.

I remember that plane flight back to Atlanta, looking out over the Texas flatlands. I was still spinning from my experiences at the workshop followed by a reunion with Betty, my best childhood friend. We hadn't seen each other for 30 years. We used to make hollyhock dolls behind my barn, then ride our bikes out the gate and across the field to her home in the brick apartment building. As I began to settle in, I experienced a rush of thoughts and images, interconnecting patterns. Most of the trip was spent back in Africa and Lebanon. I thought of the Somali greeting, "Ma naabid ba" (Is it peace?) and the traditional response, "Ma naabid" (It is peace). How strange those words had seemed when they had first been translated for me—and how they came to seem very natural as I experienced the culture of nomadic herdsmen competing for sparse grazing lands. And then I was in Lebanon restoring a home perched on a mountain overlooking the Mediterranean and hiding my surprise as a Lebanese house painter munched on a whole cucumber for his coffee break. How I had smiled inwardly, imagining the response of other painters restoring our house years before in Connecticut. It would be strange behavior out of context. And then how this behavior came to fit in a culture that valued fruits and vegetables as Americans value sweets and junk food. I remembered the reference in *Change* (Watzlawick et al., 1974) to the experience of members of the Peace Corps. In a parallel way, having through my experience once become a member of a new culture, "foreigners abroad," I could no longer look upon the United States only as an "insider." It was like being behind a one-way mirror.

Two days later, back in Atlanta, I sat with the family with whom I had felt stuck: Mr. Jones, who worked as a janitor, the identified patient, nine-year-old encopretic Leroy, and four-year-old Susie. This was the second session. The mother, Mrs. Jones, had come to the first family session without her husband. She had presented her perception of Leroy as retarded and shameful, Susie as bright and beautiful. I had taken some individual time with Leroy during that first meeting. His speech was hesitant and hard to decipher, but I didn't think he was retarded. A phone call to his teacher had confirmed my hunch.

As I noted above, before Galveston I had felt relatively secure concentrating on breaking rigid sequences of behavior without the use of major reframes. I had sensed in this case, however, that amplifying Leroy's strengths and encouraging his parents to provide him with more learning experiences would backfire. I had been pleased that Mr. Jones had responded to my invitation to come to the next session. I had counted on having both parents there, hoping to grasp the opportunity for an enactment and to interrupt the sequence around the encopresis through homework tasks. But now Mrs. Jones hadn't shown up. Mr. Jones explained that she couldn't leave the computer.

I was feeling responsible for her absence since I had just gathered the assumption that resistance lies not in the client but between the client and the therapist. To top it off, here I was drifting. Attempting to hide my awkwardness and fear from Mr. Jones, I turned my attention to Leroy and Susie who were playing with the pieces of a board game on the floor beside us. I could understand Leroy's mumbles enough to see that he was setting his sister straight concerning the colors of the plastic pieces and showing her how to count the boxes. I commented to Mr. Jones on what a fine teacher Leroy was for Susie, asking his permission to call his wife at the office and share my observations. Reaching Mrs. Jones, I shared these observations, adding a casual reference to the literature that showed how children learn most from their older siblings (who themselves have primarily learned from their parents).

The next week Mrs. Jones burst into my office sharing excitedly a recent happening. It seemed she had given Leroy a 32-piece puzzle, left the room, and returned a few minutes later to find it completed. She then added, "I think I probably just haven't given Leroy enough opportunities to learn." By the next week, a child who had been kept in shame behind closed doors was jogging around the block with his mother. Two weeks later he was playing backgammon with his father. It seemed upwardly mobile Mrs. Jones could not tolerate having a retarded, shameful teacher for her bright, beautiful daughter — or the implications of having been the teacher for such a son.

I also worked to break the rigid sequence around the encopresis through symptom prescription. This case allowed me to solidify what I had learned in Galveston. Although I believe that prescribing the symptom was important in breaking the sequence, I don't think it would have been enough. The critical piece in leading to second-order change, as I see it, was reframing a perceived-as-retarded, shameful boy as a teacher to his bright, beautiful sister.

I was beginning to see reframing not as a technique but simply as another way of perceiving a situation, another way of sorting and arranging data. My enthusiasm took another upswing. As I began sharing my enthusiasm with more traditional therapists, I began to feel more and more isolated. I called John Weakland, who suggested that I refrain from public expressions of enthusiasm and find (in addition to my husband) one person with whom it appeared safe to share my interest in strategic therapy. Harry Goolishian had suggested that I look up Carrell Dammann, Director of the Atlanta Institute for Family Studies (AIFS) right at my doorstep in Atlanta. After meeting her and hearing her ideas, I learned another important lesson. All of the best berries were not in out-of-the-way spots. Some of the choicest berries were in front of my nose.

A Significant Training Experience

As I completed my master's degree in social work, I began my association with Carrell and AIFS as a member of an advanced live-supervision group which she taught with Michael Berger. I am still grateful for the boost Carrell gave to my feelings of competence at a critical time. I felt validated both for my enthusiasm and for my beginning efforts as a strategic therapist. She seemed to recognize a glimmer that could be amplified. She exempted me from the preliminary two years of training, valuing my primarily self-directed learning experience. Of course, this added to my performance pressure of which I already had a healthy self-inflicted dose. The first few times I was to be supervised live, I stayed up half the night with a legal pad planning the session. Goal-oriented, yes. But I was up the creek when the family showed up with a basket full of new data.

The experience of live group supervision in itself was invaluable. I had observed therapy sessions through a mirror before. However, I had never flowed back and forth between participant therapist and group observer as we each took our turns over a four-hour block of time on Friday mornings. As Carrell Dammann and Michael Berger have pointed out, the context of live supervision gave me the opportunity to experience both the affective field of family and therapist in the room and experience the perspective that comes with viewing family and therapist from behind a mirror (Berger & Dammann, 1982). And as a member of the group, defined as trainees, I could in turn both experience and observe the telephoning supervisor as part of the supervisor/therapist/family system. The experience in live supervision came on the heels of my excitement over the assumption that resistance lies not in the client, but between the client/family/therapist. I expanded the assumption to include the supervisor as part in and part of the client/family/therapist system.

Carrell and Michael were a fine combination as trainers. Carrell brought her strategic bent à la Haley and Erickson, Michael a blend of structural and Bowenian. Dramatic, carefully embroidered reframes, often interlaced with humor, were an everyday occurrence. I appreciated Carrell's elegant way of getting to the point and staying symptom-focused. This was a timely compliment to my fascination with detail. Michael's gift for spontaneous generation of double-binding family-of-origin frames was a delight to experience. What he calls "the strategic use of genograms" (Berger & Daniels-Mohring, 1982), framing a person's symptomatic behavior as loyalty to a despised relative, worked like a charm.

The point, consistent with the working framework I had developed for myself (see p. 44), was still to break rigid patterns of behavior around the symptom. However, as I began to work with more and more difficult families, i.e., where logjams had existed for a long time, I realized that there were usually a number of rigid sequences that could be seen as supporting the symptom, a number of triangles involving crossgenerational coalitions in which the identified patient was a participant. The training experience at AIFS underlined and clarified for me what I had experienced earlier with the encopretic family. I now felt grounded in the assumption that developing a systemic frame can in itself elicit (and sometimes challenge) the emergence of new behavior patterns. I learned to use genograms strategically. And Carrell and Michael let me tell stories in family sessions. Even the one about crossing the Jordanian desert on a camel.

AMPLIFYING AND EXPANDING THEORY WITHIN A PSYCHIATRIC CONTEXT

Following the completion of my M.S.W., I took a job as a social worker on an adult unit in a private psychiatric hospital (Reamy-Stephenson, 1984). My job was to conduct group and family therapy. This was an intense period. I moved slowly in the beginning. Perhaps it was John Weakland's earlier sage advice. I kept a damper on my enthusiasm for strategic therapy and did a lot of observing. Possibly what best describes my thinking during this period is to say that certain theoretical assumptions came to the fore, were amplified and expanded.

I discovered that the same assumptions that worked with clients worked with coworkers, psychiatrists, and other members of the therapeutic team, e.g., resistance didn't lie in a psychiatrist with whom I was working any more than it lay in a client. I found that just as family members were applying well-meaning "attempted solutions" that were maintaining the symptom, so were staff members. Also, patients appeared to be placed in a classic double bind. They were encouraged to work on their problems in individual and group therapy, at the same time that they were given a more indirect message that their mental illness, e.g., schizophrenia, was incurable. Haley (1979) had raised the possibility that the more crossgenerational coalitions in which the identified patient was participating, the crazier the behavior. This assumption seemed to work. I remember one case where a young woman in her early twenties became particularly mad around the time of discharge. I quickly counted seven crossgenerational coalitions that were readily apparent among Linda, mother, father, psychiatrist, mental health assistant, director of nursing, night shift, night nurse, and day shift in various combinations.

I clung fiercely and silently to the assumption of nonobjective reality, at times by my fingernails. I was surrounded by a pathology-seeking reality.

What you looked for determined what you found. I remembered how a friend of mine was able to survey any clover patch and come up with at least one four-leaf clover. When Americans look at a full moon they see the "man in the moon." The Japanese see an aging rabbit. Here just about everybody seemed to be looking for pathology, for proof of schizophrenia — disordered thinking, hallucinations, delusions — and they found it. Any remnant of uneasiness I had about reframing being a tricky, manipulative "technique" soon vanished. I began to see the diagnostic framework (DSM-II) as negative reframing. If a strategic family therapist could get a person out of the identified patient role, a person whose family had already paid some $300,000 for traditional psychiatric care, how could this process be called tricky and manipulative and the traditional alternatives good, caring psychiatric care?

In time, I began to receive referrals for family therapy from the attending physicians. I was challenged to arrange the concrete facts around the symptom into different patterns, to change the meaning attributed to the situation, and thus its consequences (Watzlawick et al., 1974). Tommy's case was a good example. A strapping young man of 26, Tommy had been diagnosed on admission as having a severe germ phobia, speech impairment, and moderate retardation. Tommy had been adopted at 10 months and reportedly weighed only 10 pounds. Since he was especially vulnerable to germs as an infant, doctors advised Tommy's parents to keep him away from crowds. His father, who had a serious heart ailment, had recently retired from his work as a druggist. Tommy had been staying home, talking in a bizarre sing-song, up-and-down manner, and washing constantly — using some 30 towels and washcloths a day. He drained the hot water tank daily while his parents stood by helplessly, patiently.

The situation could be perceived as a leaving home logjam. Certainly, Tommy's behavior helped keep his parents' mind off father's heart ailment and what could be an empty retirement. Fortunately, the universe again provided me with a helpful experience to bring to therapy. I happened to have a 14-year-old son who had just discovered girls as well as shampoos and was driving me crazy leaving piles of towels around the house. Aha! Tommy could be framed as a moderately retarded 26-year-old man with a severe germ phobia and speech impediment, requiring long-term, expensive psychotherapy and speech therapy. *And* Tommy could also be framed as a 14-year-old boy in the body of a 26-year-old man who desperately needed his parents' help in catching up with his body. Fourteen-year-olds typically need their parents' help in providing 14-year-old experiences, e.g., experiencing limits on their use of towels and hot water.

Tommy's parents chose the developmental frame. They proceeded to set limits on the use of towels and hot water and Tommy began his step-by-step change to more age-appropriate behavior. The germ phobia quickly disappeared.

Another assumption was amplified during this period, a corollary of non-objective reality, the assumption that what you believe determines what is possible. Rabkin (1977) pointed out that clients come into treatment not because they have symptoms but because they are feeling hopeless about their symptoms. I needed this assumption, both for my clients and for myself as a strategic therapist working in this context. This was Tommy's first hospitalization. However, there were many patients who had joined the ranks of the lifers and were beating a path between their homes and the hospital. I needed to work on the hope first. I began to look for colleagues who believed patients could change. I found a few—most importantly, Steve Howard, the psychiatrist who directed the unit, and Harry Kramer, a charismatic young mental health assistant who was powerful within the informal hierarchy. I found another attending psychiatrist, Jesse Peel, who tended to nurture strength in his clients rather than weakness. He had an embroidered saying framed on the wall in his office: "Ships are safe in a harbor, but that's not what ships are for."

As I began work with clients and their families, I assumed they were feeling hopeless. Concentrating on seeding hope, I used forward-sounding words, e.g., labeling an identified patient's level change earned on the unit as the first step forward.

The assumption that how one talks determines how one thinks became amplified in my thinking and my clinical work. I liked a quote from Socrates that had appeared on a Lankton brochure: "The cure of soul is accomplished by certain charms and these charms are fair words." I often gave clients a secret note as they left the first session. On it was written, "When you look at your wife (husband), can you tolerate the possibility that things could get better in your life?"

The discovery of the assumption that one can amplify an assumption by focusing on it continues to fascinate me. I delight in the observation that introducing a large, peach-colored seashell into a room will amplify the peach color in the wall covering, in a painting, a throw pillow, even in my daughter's cheeks. Certainly this principle is inherent in strategic clinical work, in what Lynn Hoffman (1981) calls amplifying small deviations. As I focused on the assumption that "what you believe determines what is possible," some memories emerged from the past. Through the years my parents had taken pride in finding rundown old houses (which most people perceived as "haunted") and transforming them into showplaces. My parents were able to see the sound structure beneath the falling plaster, to see a speck of pine patina under layers of paint, and create a beautiful mantel. I was struck with how one could look at dysfunctional families in a similar manner. Jeff Zeig (1980) had once pointed out to me that there are many things we know and do intuitively as therapists. Yet if we recognize this process and purposefully focus on it, we add more power to our interventions. I believe the same thing works with assumptions.

There was a case that helped me find hope. Joe, a man in his late fifties, had been in the hospital several weeks with a diagnosis of paranoid schizophrenia. He worked in a huge plant as an electronics technician. Joe had been a loyal, competent worker for 28 years. His wife worked in the same plant. Joe had been hospitalized after a period of bizarre paranoid behavior. He had been acting increasingly terrified at home. While driving home from work he would look over his shoulder, pleading with his wife that his life was at stake. One evening he ran to a neighbor's house, claiming someone was out to get him. His wife called his brothers and they brought him to the hospital. On admission, since there were few male staff members that evening, Joe's brothers were asked to take (drag) him to the behavioral control room.

In the hospital, Joe continued to act frightened and tried to escape. All Joe would say in group therapy was, "There is nothing wrong with me except my hearing" and "I want out." This was perceived on the unit as Joe's resistance to therapy. More recently he had become withdrawn and refused to talk. The attending psychiatrist understood that Joe had a nerve deafness of 10 years but read lips effectively. Yet, when he met with Joe and his wife, Mary, Joe didn't seem to understand him. The psychiatrist assumed that his beard got in the way of Joe's lip reading and referred them to me. I didn't have a beard but I encountered the same problem. Introducing a large blackboard into the session, I wrote a few words on the board and verbally asked him to read. He jumped up quickly and grabbed the eraser. His bizarre behavior took on a different meaning; I realized that he had confused the word "read" with the word "erase." I began writing on the board, encouraging him to ask questions. There was a visible lessening of his anxiety. His wife explained that he had always been the strong silent type and had never been in the habit of asking questions.

We discovered all kinds of misunderstandings. The Employee Assistance head from his plant was willing to participate. His brothers came back also. Joe's fears began to make perfect sense. It seems there had been a strike at the plant in which Joe had participated as a loyal union member. After the strike, he had been assigned to work next to a "scab," a worker who had crossed the picket line (unbeknownst to Joe). Workers came by and glared in Joe's (and the "scab's") direction. He assumed they were glaring at him. He picked up bits and pieces of threats. About this time, he received a rejection for a promotion. He had failed to ask questions, failed to find out that the position with its proximity to dangerous machinery required a normal range of hearing. His fears increased and the scenario reached a crescendo when his trusted brothers appeared out of the night and, without his understanding why, packed him off to the hospital.

In addition to clearing up the misunderstanding with Joe, his family, his employer, and the hospital staff, I gave Joe a pad of paper and the assignment to ask questions. We met with his floor supervisor and worked out a daily briefing period to be implemented when Joe returned to work. Joe's paranoia and anxiety diminished dramatically, almost overnight. Joe was right. The problem was his hearing, *plus* his and our attempted solutions. I'll always remember one of Joe's last group therapy sessions when he poignantly described his life in a soundless world. He was soon able to leave the hospital, return to productive work, and enroll in a course in lip reading. Along with hope, this case gave me a profound sense of unrest. I wondered about the other 19 "mental patients" on the unit.

SOME NOTES ON TRAINING

"Argue for your limitations and sure enough, they're yours" (Bach, 1977, p. 100).

Early in 1982, I left my position at the private psychiatric hospital to join the staff of the Atlanta Institute for Family Studies. By 1983, my interest in teaching had expanded to include a considerable amount of training of other therapists and my designation as Director of Extramural Training for the Institute.

Not surprisingly, the same illusive assumptions that I have found most central and workable in my personal life and clinical work I find central to my teaching. In a nutshell and in summary:

1) The assumption of non-objective reality (i.e., reality like beauty is in the eyes of the beholder) and its corollaries:
   (A) What you believe determines what is possible;
   (B) What you look for determines what you find.
2) You can't change until you experience something new.
3) Resistance lies between people, not in people.

These assumptions appear to me to be central to thinking ecosystemically, yet they seem to be brushed over or rushed past in the training process. My guess is that they are so much a part of the world view of the master systemic therapists, so taken for granted (like the assumption that the sun will rise and set tomorrow) that they are brushed over (Reamy-Stephenson, 1983). It is not surprising to me that the majority of the master thinkers and/or clinicians such as Bateson, Weakland, Haley, Minuchin, Watzlawick, Hoffman, Papp, have come from fields other than psychiatry and psychology (e.g., anthropology, communications, art, theatre). Or they have experienced different cultures firsthand, or are multilingual, thus having different ways of looking at things and repeating patterns. *Nonobjective reality has been a central experiential theme.*

I see one of the biggest logjams in the training process at the point where objective-thinking trainees – already experienced after two to four years of graduate training in how to label and put people into boxes – meet the enthusiastic systemic trainer. In our enthusiasm as trainers, and having ourselves grown up surrounded by Aristotelian duality, I think we often come across as having the truth rather than a theory. Typically, family systems theory is presented as a drastically different way of thinking and working, foreign to the trainee. Students often get the idea that they have to throw out everything they've learned and start from scratch, as if being a systemic therapist requires a leap across the Grand Canyon. And they get immobilized. Or push for learning clever interventions which they plug in indiscriminately with no respect for the ecological niche of the client or family.

I find it helpful, in the Ericksonian tradition, to attempt to "start where the trainee is at," to meet the trainee at his model of the world. I've found it helpful to begin the training experience with these elusive underlying assumptions, to make links from the beginning to the students' past experiences (fleeting and deviant as they may be) that confirm these assumptions, and then to amplify them. Part of the focus is on validating the relevance of their experience in music, biology, art, organic gardening – in pattern viewing and pattern creating – and then making a link to ways of looking at presenting symptoms. I give them practice in arranging data around a case, using a traditional pathology-focused frame as well as several other frames, e.g., a developmental frame and a protective frame. The point is to link past experiences with current practice in pattern viewing and creating. The challenge is in finding a pattern and corresponding view that challenges the client/family and fits with a forward-looking, change-oriented view and appropriate behavior.

Through this process I find that students flow naturally into reframing, which is no longer seen as a technique but as simply another way of viewing a situation. In the Ericksonian tradition, an emphasis is put on amplifying relevant past experiences as resources rather than focusing on past experiences as irrelevant liabilities.

In a corresponding way, the *power of the belief system* is explored. I talk about my experience as a swimming teacher in Somalia. My classes had children from 14 nationalities. Many of the students had had no previous swimming experience. There were young girls from India who were shedding the flowing saris of their mothers for bathing suits. When I returned to the United States, I was struck by the surprise of other swimming teachers as they learned that these children had all learned to swim in deep water. I realized that it had never occurred to me that any of the children would not learn to swim. If you had swimming lessons, you learned to swim. I don't think it was my technique that fit with the children's success as much as my belief system. Trainees, in turn, share experiences from their own lives, e.g., a friend who had a massive stroke who learned to speak fluently again, defying all medical prognoses. These experiences are then linked to beliefs about mental illness, about our clients, and about the possibility for change. Not surprisingly, I tend to err on the side of revealing my "belief in people" (clients, trainees) too much. I've learned to compensate by frequently introducing caution with change, prescribing small steps, and sometimes acknowledging that I fear I am believing in my clients or trainees more than they are believing in themselves.

Focusing on the assumption that *resistance lies between the therapist and the client (or colleague) rather than in the client (or colleague)* seems to be a natural way to have trainees begin to see their part in the client/family system or work system—to see that their behavior matches the behavior of clients and colleagues. Time is spent discovering and exploring each trainee's body of habitual assumptions out of which he or she responds. Early on, as an evaluation tool, I like to have the individual trainee explore his or her own personal resources as a therapist, to note that every resource can be seen as a liability, every liability as a resource. For example, empathy (widely perceived as a desirable quality for therapists), when overabundant, can fit with minimal gatekeeping (ordinarily perceived as essential in a directive therapy) and with clients who complain about "not getting anywhere." At the same time, gatekeeping, if overly rigid, can fit with difficulty in joining and with clients who feel unheard and discounted.

I share my metaphor about picking blackberries. I point out how thoroughness and attention to detail can lead to exciting discoveries in out-of-the-way spots, but also can lead to missing the forest for the trees. Through the course of training, students are encouraged to find their own balance that works best for them—to use their own person effectively within an ecosystemic theory—not to try to be a facsimile of Minuchin or Haley. This, of course, means taking risks, often breaking lifelong patterns of behavior. The trainee who appears cautious is challenged to begin taking small risks, first in his personal life and then in therapy sessions—perhaps by using a well-planned but dramatic reframe supported by supervision.

I find that giving trainees homework tasks—beyond reading assignments—is central to amplifying the assumption that *you cannot change until you experience something new.* Such tasks might include climbing a mountain or modifying an internal map around risking or thoroughness. In retrospect, I am in awe of the impact of homework tasks on my own development as a therapist. Two stand out. I've described the task around calling the long distance operator. The other experience was more recent at a workshop with

Carter and Gilligan in New Orleans (1983). At the lunch break they suggested we do something different, break some rigid old pattern. They suggested, for example, that one might take one's steak off the plate and cut it on the table cloth.

My husband and I proceeded to our lunch. We had an intimate lunch at a charming little cafe and then took a walk along the river. When we returned refreshed for the afternoon session, Carter and Gilligan began to inquire about the homework assignment. I was horrified. I had totally forgotten to do my homework! And then a feeling of delight overcame me. I had indeed done the homework. Enjoying a free-spirited lunch break without doing my homework was breaking a rigid pattern for me. And nothing awful happened. Since that experience, I've found I have much more fun at conferences. I take more breaks and am more selective with scheduled learning experiences.

A Comprehensive Training Program

In October of 1984, at the Atlanta Institute for Family Studies, we as a staff began a major team effort to develop a comprehensive two-year training program for externs, i.e., therapists who are practicing in other settings. The emphasis is threefold but not compartmentalized. The beginning emphasis, as I have described, is on the individual systems of the therapist and client. In addition to exploring habitual assumptions of the trainee, we include studies in child and human development. We have realized that it is hard (and dangerous) to expect trainees to learn to "normalize" behavior — especially young therapists who have had limited life experiences, e.g., no experience in parenting — when they have not been exposed to a framework of "normal" human development. We no longer move directly into what is now our second area of emphasis, the therapist/family system.

When we do move into focusing on initial sessions, setting goals, and developing frames, we put considerable priority on the use of tapes, preferably video. This is sometimes a problem as not every agency will allow taping. Arranging for trainees to see families in our low-cost clinic (The Metropolitan Family Study Center) helps. Live supervision is arranged whenever possible. In any case, a hands-on approach seems to work much better in the early stages of training. I believe supervision based on case presentation without tapes is helpful for conceptualization and efficient for advanced students who are already thinking and practicing ecosystemically. For the beginning student, however, a lot of important data seem to slip through the cracks. It is difficult to evaluate whether the frame didn't fit or whether the therapist got stuck in presenting the frame to the family. Using tapes is very time consuming and there is never enough time, but I find them invaluable.

Live supervision still emerges for me as a highly effective means of teaching therapists to think and act systematically. As noted earlier, group live supervision offers the therapist the rich opportunity provided by the bicameral nature of the context. Of course, this assumes a group situation where at least one other trainee is participating. Having participated in live supervision, students seem to be more readily able to get outside of themselves even for a brief moment and see themselves as "part in" the family system.

The hands-on opportunity has other helpful trade-offs. Recently, I was working with a rather sophisticated therapist who seemed to have developed considerable resources as a strategic therapist. She believed people could change and was a natural for positive connotation. She did not have the flexibility to tape her sessions and I agreed to work with her around her presentation of case material. However, she seemed to be spinning her wheels with Gary, a 24-year-old young man who had been on the chronic path. I suggested she bring her client in for live supervision.

When she had spoken of him in previous sessions, it had been clear that she was trying to amplify his potential. But he continued to define himself as a mental patient and drag his feet on homework assignments. Not succeeding in enlisting in therapy his widowed mother with whom he lived was a major part of the problem. However, there was another piece. When I met the therapist in the waiting room, I suggested we consult before her session with Gary. As we left the waiting room, she leaned over and spoke reassuringly to Gary. I believe she patted him on the shoulder. If I had not seen Gary, I would have guessed she was speaking to a five-year-old. A confusing message. This brief observation gave us a rich opportunity to focus on subtleties of voice tone and body language which are such powerful tools for change — and such powerful components of "walking on eggs," a primary crazy-maker.

The third emphasis of our two-year training program is on the therapist/family/agency system. From the beginning we develop the idea that how one practices family therapy will be greatly determined by the context in which one works (Berger & Jurkovic, 1984). For example, how a problem is framed, the language that is used (with colleagues and families), and the interventions carried out will all depend on the context. Typically, our trainees come from a variety of settings — nursing homes, psychiatric hospitals, group homes, general hospitals, psychoeducational centers, and private practice. We are recognizing that there are definite advantages to carrying out training on the spot, at the agency (although there is certainly a benefit for students to be exposed to their colleagues' work in contrasting settings when they are developing the concept of individualizing therapy to the context). Gregory Jurkovic of AIFS has been developing and carrying out two such innovative agency training programs — one with psychoeducational centers, the other with the juvenile court system.

One last comment about training. I agree with Bergman's (1984) tongue-in-cheek suggestion that every beginning family therapist should have a one-year grant to support practice in losing families. The pressure of maintaining families for supervision and/or supporting a beginning private practice work counter to good therapy. It is difficult to take risks, set limits, and avoid walking on eggs when you need families as much as or more than they need you.

AN ECOLOGICAL SHIFT

In the summer of 1983 while attending an international family therapy conference in Brussels, I participated in a workshop with Bunny Duhl (1983). An exercise she conducted helped me capture the state of my theoretical framework. She asked us to choose an animal and develop a metaphor that fit with one's style of learning. I chose a large bird who was struggling to move her nest from tree to tree, from mountain peak to mountain peak. Each move took more effort as her wings tired. Yet each move was rewarded with a more expansive view, a broader perspective. At times she yearned for the comfortable nest below amidst the forest, protected and secure. The bird had been building her nest out of a multitude of what would appear to be disparate bits and pieces of varied colors, textures, and sizes — from the seashore, the woodlands, the precarious mountain slopes. She delighted in her discoveries — each piece was carefully examined by itself and then in relation to the nest. Well-used and fresh pieces alike were discarded. Others were woven in new combinations into the nest. As time passed, the nest began to take form and pattern.

In the past few years, as I have been immersed in an abundance of clinical work and training activities, I have found myself struggling for perspective, resisting fusion with other family therapists. At times, I have felt much like I have felt after a long day of back-to-back family sessions — fused for a moment, not sure where my boundaries end and others' begin. My response has been — like the bird in the metaphor — to pull away, and in that pulling away to at times draw away from theoretical discussions, to be more selective with readings and workshop attendance. It seemed necessary for survival as a therapist and teacher.

As I have allowed myself more distance, I have become increasingly aware of what appears to be a developing rift in the field — a rift between theoreticians such as Paul Dell, and Brad Keeney, and those who I once heard define themselves as the "foot soldiers," or front-line clinicians. The former emphasize the importance of epistemology, the latter question its relevance to their work as clinicians. Again I find myself drawn to working on bridging the gap, e.g., finding the clinical relevance of (what might appear to some) nit-picking differences in use of language. Clinical relevance is of particular interest to me. The assumption that the value of a clinical theory is determined by whether or not it works remains of central importance. And certainly I experience my thinking as growing out of my clinical work as my clinical work grows out of my thinking — just as there is a constant exchange between myself as a perceiver and constructor of reality and the world (what's out there and what's happening).

To attempt to bridge this gap in some small way is, of course, no small challenge. To articulate my beginning thoughts through a left brain digital form, i.e., the written word, makes the task even more formidable. The essence of the dilemma for me is captured in a recent remark of the comedian, Steve Martin: "Talking about music is like dancing about architecture" (or is like writing about thinking about thinking about therapy).

Early Attempts at Bridges on the Conceptual Level

Causality or fit, a nitpicking difference? From my first exposure to Dell's (1981) work in epistemology, most specifically his *focus on fit in contrast to causality*, I have been intrigued. He seemed to be describing on a theoretical level what I had been intuiting.

For some time I had found my beginning theoretical framework inadequate (p. 44): The arrows suggested a causality, however circular, that did not adequately capture the thinking that had been evolving along with my work as a clinician and trainer. In my attempt to modify my theoretical framework to fit my experience, I had found myself drawn back to the work of Bateson and, more recently, the work of Maturana. The MRI Conference "Maps of the Mind, Maps of the World" in 1983 amplified this interest and introduced me first hand to the work of Von Foerster and Von Glasersfeld, validating my interest and near preoccupation with the process of reality construction and more specifically the assumption of nonobjective reality (Reamy-Stephenson, 1983). Paul Dell's (1985) recent clarification and integration of Bateson and Maturana has been immensely helpful. I find particularly relevant Bateson's perception of character structure as a "body of habitual assumptions" (Bateson, 1972, p. 314). It seems a link can readily be made here to Maturana's concept of structure: a constantly evolving structure that specifies which events in its medium a living system can interact with, and how that living system will behave under any and all interactions (Dell, 1985).

It is a common experience in life (certainly in therapy sessions) to hear people say, "He made me feel angry," "She hurt my feelings." It particularly bothers me to hear a therapist ask, "How does that make you feel?" I think these statements imply causality — linear (or linear as a segment of a circular loop). In either case, I think they ignore the individual structure of the person feeling and reacting to that feeling. For example, there's no predictability about how the sight of a moving van will "make someone feel" unless we know more about his or her individual structure. The sight of a moving van elicits feelings of excitement and adventure for me, feelings of anxiety and disruption for my husband. I had lived in the same house all during my school years. A move after high school graduation had been a positive one for me and my family. In contrast, my husband had moved constantly as a child, which demanded a new school adjustment every one or two years.

I've already stressed an assumption central to my work: How one talks determines how one thinks. I'd like to update my assumption: How one talks fits with how one thinks. As a therapist one can get at the thinking through reframing and thus influence the talking. And one can also nudge and challenge people into talking differently and thus influence their thinking. I do both. I nudge people toward saying, "When you forget my birthday, I feel angry and sad" rather than saying, "You made me angry and sad on my birthday." It may appear to be a nitpicking difference. I believe subtle changes can make a profound difference over time in people acknowledging and normalizing differences in experiences and assumptions, while diminishing blame which gets in the way of functional relationships.

In my fascination with the process of reality construction over the last few years, I have concentrated more and more on discovering the internal maps which I as a clinician or trainer, as well as my clients and students, bring to our work together. Some maps work for us; other maps are outdated and lead us into predictable logjams. It seems Bateson was describing the process of formulation of internal maps which relate to the particular set of habitual assumptions that we have when he wrote:

> The patterns and sequences of childhood experiences are built into me: Father did so and so; my aunt did such and such; and what they did was outside my skin. But whatever it was I learned, my learning happened within my experiential sequence of what those important others—my aunt, my father—did. (Bateson, 1979, p. 15)

Having been raised in a family pervaded with an objective Aristotelian duality, getting lost in my own reality is predictably my Achilles heel. I am both dismayed and delighted at my routine discovery of how readily I get locked into a mind set, an internal map of assumptions, at that point in time.

Last year I was with my husband on our way to the state legislature during a lunch break. We were part of a grass-roots effort directed at licensure for marriage and family therapists. Being in a rush we picked up a hamburger at a fast foods "drive-thru." As we approached the state Capitol, I was feeling increasingly uncomfortable with the onion on my breath and hands. (In my family of origin, I had been taught never to eat onion before social occasions.) As I leaned forward to sign in at the security desk, the guard exclaimed,

"Pardon me, Ma'am, but you smell great!" I was horrified—see, I did smell like a greasy hamburger. Then, in a flash I realized my error—he was referring to L'Air du Temps, my French perfume. I have a vast collection of such experiences. Some are in relation to clients.

Several years ago a client, 22-year-old Tom, used to call in despair and tell me that life wasn't worth living. I had caught myself spinning my wheels, repeating the attempted solution of trying to suggest some new experiences to elicit more positive feelings. He would respond with one "Yes, but" after another and usually end up hanging up on me. The sequence continued with Tom calling back promptly to apologize and the game would continue. I had recognized that my attempted solution was the problem. I resolved to break the sequence and told Tom that our conversation would be limited to five minutes and that if he hung up on me he would have to wait to talk until the next session. Then I waited for him to test my resolve. Predictably, Tom telephoned. After three minutes, as I was struggling against being seduced into being positive, the phone on the other end was hung up. And sure enough there followed a rash of telephone messages from Tom. I didn't respond. Finally, on the second day there was a more detailed message: "I didn't hang up the phone the other day. Someone on your end picked up the extension phone and then hung up." Hmmm. . . .

In each of these interactions—one from my personal life, the other from my work as a therapist—I perceive myself as behaving in relation to the context of which I was a part. However, it is not enough to consider the context. *Another person under the same circumstances very likely would have responded differently. What defined the precise interaction was the coupling or fit between myself with my internal maps at that point in time (or perhaps my Batesonian body of habitual assumptions, or Maturanian structure) and the context, which includes others with their own set of maps.* In my view, an assumption of causality (linear or circular) cannot adequately explain or predict the *individual nature* of these interactions.

Communicating and Thinking in Terms of Fit:
An Aid in Avoiding Resistance

It is perhaps in the area of resistance that I find the concept of fit most helpful. It seems to work better, to be more consistent with the assumption that resistance lies between people, not in a hostile defensive client (or colleague). I find it important for myself as therapist not only to discover the relevant internal maps out of which clients behave which are maintaining the symptom but also to anticipate some of their habitual assumptions as we begin our first contact.

For example, I assume that clients emerging from western civilizations will assume objective reality and, consistently with this view, will further assume that the therapist will be determining which client (e.g., husband or wife) is right and which is wrong—that I will be validating one person's view as the truth and blaming the other(s). I attempt to head off resistance from the beginning by stating: "You may not feel this way but I find a number of my new clients come in expecting me to be a judge and to be determining who is right and who is wrong." I go on to say, "I find that pointing fingers is not particularly helpful for families and I also don't think things are that simple." I routinely detect a lessening of tension, a sense of relief, sometimes a rather dramatic shift.

I proceed to seed and amplify the assumption of nonobjective reality. Rather than moving quickly to a common definition of the problem, I place my emphasis on developing and normalizing the idea that both of them will have their own view of the problem (based on their body of habitual assumptions) and that based on their assumptions, their behavior, i.e., their attempted solution, makes perfect sense. There are no bolts from the blue. I state further that it is actually very helpful for me if they do have different views because then I can better determine where they are getting stuck. As I seek each person's down-to-earth, human perception of the problem, I predict that "naturally" as this view is presented someone else in the room may feel uncomfortable.

In welcoming and acknowledging each significant person's perception of the problem, I find a natural bridge to the concept of internal maps. I find consistently that family members become stuck at very predictable places considering their past experiences and assumptions growing out of those experiences. The case of Sandra and her family is an example.

Sandra had been diagnosed schizophrenic about the time she enrolled in college. Predictably, I found her parents had long perceived her as especially vulnerable and needy of protection and had treated her as such. I found that the family had been out to visit the Grand Canyon when Sandra was 18 months old. It seems Sandra had managed to squeeze under a guard rail and had been rescued just before plunging into the Canyon.

Gems like this frequently pop up in the process of doing genograms, where I tend to focus on themes and metaphors that seem relevant to the symptom, e.g., related to the redundant attempted solutions of family members. I find it helpful to talk about maps: how we all have them and how they helped us survive in an earlier environment—perhaps a substitute for instinct in a species with a highly developed brain—and how they sometimes get outdated and need to be modified, e.g., the map that Sandra is especially vulnerable and in need of round-the-clock protection. As in the case of Sandra's family, I find that an *emphasis by the therapist on communicating and thinking in terms of fit rather than causality dramatically reduces resistance.* I think one explanation is that people (who are already blaming themselves and who typically have felt blamed by others, e.g., extended family, school officials, mental health and other professionals) feel a significant reduction in blame. Paradoxically, I find that when an emphasis is placed on giving credit and avoiding blame, clients more readily own responsibility for their behavior.

In retrospect, I believe my part in the relative success of breaking the cycle of chronicity of a number of inpatients within the context of a private psychiatric hospital fits with the assumptions central to my world view at that point in time—the assumption of nonobjective reality and the assumption that resistance lies not in the client (colleague) but between the therapist and client (colleague). I believe I headed off considerable resistance that would have prevented change by anticipating that clients would already feel blamed by themselves and others. Also, it was helpful to assume that clients would be feeling helpless, hopeless, fed up, financially stressed. These feelings fit perfectly with their experience over the past years. Again, no bolts from the blue. Furthermore, it made perfect sense that family members (especially spouses and parents of the chronic identified patient) would present at the first session as "hostile," expecting me to blame, demand that they miss work to attend sessions, and add more financial burden to their mountain of bills.

I have given up the idea that carnivorous families are out to get me as a therapist, even though it sometimes feels that way (and certainly we all seem to profit from a little "linear moralizing" among colleagues) (Bergman, 1984). I don't believe people like being miserable or having an identified patient, nor are they singularly and purposely out to keep the status quo. Consistently when I am sensitive to their need for credit and their assumptions based on past experience of being blamed by others, the "hostility" disappears and people appear eager to work on changing. Consistent with this view, I am now receiving self-referred families who have heard of my interest in breaking the cycle of rehospitalization and seem to work to do just that.

Ecological Niche

A theory that denies our existence as biological entities and more specifically as mammals with a highly developed nervous system and brain has never seemed relevant to my work as a family therapist.

There has been a tradition in my family of reverence for life and a corresponding assumption of connectedness of the human species to other life forms. In fact, my father's 1926 exodus from home at 17 had followed on the heels of a severe rift with his father. Pop had been caught by his Baptist preacher father poring over Darwin's *Origin of the Species*. In his later years, Pop lived and breathed his fruit orchards. It was sometimes difficult to see where Pop ended and his trees began.

My interest in connectedness to other life forms was amplified in my early years as a science teacher and more recently in my brief studies at Georgia State in comparative psychology. Here I was exposed to ethological strategy as developed by Niko Tinbergen and Konrad Lorenz: the combining of rigorous observations of animals, usually in their natural habitat, with evolutionary analyses of the observed behavior patterns.

My natural preference for a broader ecological perspective has been amplified in my work in the past few years in the context of the Atlanta Institute for Family Studies. A neighbor who was a retired plant manager once told me about some wise advice his boss had given him: "Take care when you hire new employees. They will determine the kind of person you are." This assumption appears to work for partnerships too. The six partners at AIFS, in choosing a close working association, have influenced and been influenced by one another in our thinking, in our clinical work and in our personal lives. Thinking in terms of linear or circular causality cannot explain the changes I observe.

Paul Carter's presentation (1982) on rapport at the 1980 International Conference on Ericksonian Approaches to Hypnosis and Psychotherapy comes to mind as more relevant. Paul focused on the Ericksonian concept that as individuals we are multifaceted, much more than we are conscious of, more than a singular point of view. He emphasized that as individuals we have more resources, more brain cells than we can possibly use in a lifetime. Integrity was perceived as the process of experiencing one's wholeness and aligning oneself with it.

It seems that in our interactions at AIFS as partners and in the coupling of our thinking and clinical work, our individual structures and our habitual body of assumptions have been altered; facets of ourselves have been accessed and amplified, others subdued. New maps have emerged.

A focus of our co-evolving work at AIFS has been an emphasis on individualizing family therapy to the context in which the therapy is practiced. Our work came together in *Practicing Family Therapy in Diverse Settings* (Berger & Jurkovic, 1984). This book represents an emphasis on the therapist/family system being inseparable from its ecosystem, e.g., the context of the psychiatric hospital where the identified patient was a patient and I was a staff member. I am no longer thinking in terms of doing "family therapy" but rather of practicing an "ecosystemic therapy." I quickly discovered that in working with those perceived as "chronic" mental patients, the assumption of circular causality wasn't enough. It helped. As described earlier, it was extremely productive to zero in on sequences, to change attempted solutions of immediate and extended family members and of other professionals, and to change their belief systems about the IP out of which they respond.

I still find this emphasis a central core of my work. However, if second-order change is to occur and the long perceived identified patient is to move toward a more functional life in more than a temporary way, it seems a more comprehensive look must be given to the ecological niche of the IP. For example, a 25-year-old who has been labeled schizophrenic and who has been vegetating at home for seven years has missed out on many developmental tasks, e.g., development of social skills. He is "out of sync" with his chronological age peers. Assuming that we are, to a significant extent, our experiences, he is more like an 18-year-old or perhaps a 14-year-old in the body of a 25-year-old. Considering his physical development, however, he is no more in sync with a 14- or 18-year-old. *Unfortunately, a comfortable fit with other young adult chronic patients is readily available.* A developmental frame is particularly helpful in these cases as a rationale for a concentration on the development of social skills missed during the period of absence from "normal developmental activities."

I have found young adult groups, with the focus on the leaving home transition (in contrast to a group for schizophrenics), to be an important adjunct to family therapy, of an ecosystemic approach for such an identified patient. In these groups, young people representing a variety of traditional diagnoses (e.g., eating disorders, schizophrenia, borderline personality) interact. Homework tasks are given, backed by peer support, directed toward pursuit of employment, educational goals, driver's license, peer contacts outside the group, etc. Group members move toward advocating at home for more responsibilities and corresponding privileges that fit with being a young adult in their ecology rather than a mental patient.

It makes sense to me, taking an ecological view, that as a therapist I will need to be more of a meddler in families with long-standing problems. More of the ecology fits with a chronic identified patient—the intrasystem of the client as well as the complexities of his or her environment. Not only does the belief system of a myriad of significant people in the identified patient's ecology need to be changed, but also the IP's belief about himself. My task as a therapist in such cases is changing the fit so that, one might say, the ecological niche no longer requires a crazy person and the person no longer requires a padded cell for a niche. The river and the forest reflect each other's needs precisely. A change in the river will fit with a change in the forest.

For a time, I had trouble integrating the concept of hierarchy with an ecological view. I didn't want to throw it out—it worked too well as a tool. The issue for me is the *clarity of assumptions* about who does what and how. I now think of a confused hierarchy as confusion about decision-making in a segment of the ecology. Haley's (1976) assumption that there is something pathological about crossing generations to form coalitions works beautifully. I'm able to fit this assumption into an ecological perspective around the issue of clarity. There is something inherently confusing about individuals from different generations participating in peer-like behavior. It feels like a double bind; you are my friend and I am your mother. It seems roles are inherently defined by a body of habitual assumptions. Once a child to a parent, I believe, always a child to a parent at some level, and vica versa. It seems the assumptions respective to parenthood and peership are inherently confusing when coupled. Conflict and confusion are inherent in the fit. This does not mean that children and parents cannot move toward a functional adult: adult relationship. I don't think this is the same as being a friend. As noted earlier in the chapter, Haley (1979) has pointed out that symptoms seem to emerge at times when someone enters or leaves the system. Again, we have the issue of confusion — adjustment to demands for change in regard to who does what and how.

In taking an ecological view, I assume that as a therapist my fit in what could be perceived as unrelated parts of the ecology impacts the course of treatment of my clients. Thus, failure to join effectively with colleagues appears to have the potential for drastically impacting the client (Reamy-Stephenson, 1984). In an inpatient setting, for example, if an attending physician is not involved in the change process nor credited for his contribution, a precipitous discharge or, in one case, an order for electroshock therapy can follow. Formerly, as director of social services of such a hospital, my detailed attention to administrative tasks, e.g., documentation for which the hospital administrator was ultimately responsible, fit with the administration's support for my work with families. Private psychiatric hospitals are money-making organizations. It would appear that the number of empty beds influences the director of admission's perception as to whether a person should be admitted or treated on an outpatient basis. Correspondingly, I believe the number of empty spaces in a private practitioner's appointment book influences his or her decision as to whether a client/family should be seen on a weekly or biweekly basis.

Several concerns have surfaced for me since I've acknowledged an ecological view. I now own my role as a meddler. The word *meddler* has a rather negative feel to it. *Helper* would sound nice but it might soft-pedal the issue of the therapist's subjectivity in intervening in other people's lives. I have always believed that therapists are in a powerful position. My belief has intensified since I began working with "chronic families" and began seeing the impact of professionals' belief systems on families in treatment. I attempt to control the degree of meddling — by staying focused on the symptoms or presenting problems of the client/family, whether it be a child-focused problem, marital conflict, or repeated hospitalizations. However, it is not my experience that presenting problems of a long-standing nature will disappear with minimal involvement of the therapist. As I have described in some detail, I believe more of the ecology needs to be impacted and that means more meddling.

An ecological view requires that the therapist be seen as part of the client/

family's ecology from the first contact. One way I reduce meddling is to avoid becoming central to families, amplifying and challenging the emergence of their own resources from the start. Although I seem to join intensely with families in sessions, they seem to rely on their own resources between sessions. I *expect* them to. Somehow this gets across without my ever saying it explicitly. With an occasional exception, I get very few cries for help. I don't want to be needed by my clients. I already feel needed in about as many arenas in my personal life as I can handle. I think this fits with my client families' behavior. If clients are in a severe crisis, I schedule more frequent sessions for a week or two, giving me more opportunities to rally their own strengths and resources.

Another issue emerges for me as I take a more ecological perspective. I realize that as I meddle in client families' lives, assuming all good intentions, I'm also meddling in the lives of others who haven't contracted for therapy. I have noticed in a number of families, particularly those with a long-standing IP, that there appears to be a pattern of focusing on a "problem person." I often observe this pattern in families where the assumption of objective reality prevails in the extreme (i.e., hot:cold . . . black:white . . . sin:grace . . .). It is as if there has to be a problem child or person—someone in the bad box— to allow the others' existence in the good box. In these families, I find that removal of one person from the IP slot can leave a void that seems to suck up another IP (symptom substitution?) to fit with the family's world view. The assumption may be that someone will be crazy in each generation, which would fit with the family's history. The new IP may appear somewhere beyond our awareness, e.g., a first cousin. When I allow myself, I get concerned that at times we may be merely passing the hot potato.

Over the last two years I've worked with two chronic families from the same church. In each case the wife had been in and out of hospitals for many years with a diagnosis of schizophrenia. Mary and her family were referred to me after Ruth had terminated and was well on her way to a functional life. They attended the same Sunday school class. I noted that they never seemed to be "crazy" at the same time. It was as if they were on alternating shifts. As Mary and her family move toward termination and Ruth remains functional, I have wondered if someone else has emerged as the problem person for the Sunday school class. I hope not. I'm almost afraid to ask. Can a town exist without a town fool? In spite of these concerns, I seem to keep meddling.

SOME COMMENTS ON THE FIELD

"There is no such thing as a problem without a gift for you in its hands" (Bach, 1977).

Certainly, practitioners of family systems therapy are no longer an isolated, radical fringe group. There has been a mushrooming of interest among mental health professionals. Yet Minuchin has pointed out that in spite of the upsurge of interest in family therapy, we have had little effect on the institutions that serve people (Minuchin, 1984). I have seen considerable evidence of this. An obvious example is the brand of family therapy often seen in psychiatric hospitals. Family therapy as adjunct to the "real" therapy being conducted by a pathology-seeking individual therapist is focused on helping the family adjust to having a schizophrenic member—or, essentially, to keeping the family off the psychiatrist's back so that he can get on with the important business. Unfortunately, I think part of the problem is that the family therapist often is not thinking ecosystemically; he is coming, unbeknownst to self, from a linear model. She considers herself systemic because she is working with the whole family. My fear is that rather tragically this only serves to further define an identified patient (his belief system about himself included), and underline the rigid pattern of status quo.

However, I do believe we are making inroads. In Atlanta, there are indications that some of the employee assistance heads of major corporations are pairing family therapy with keeping patients out of the expensive hospital circuit and pursuing locally prominent family therapists as preferred providers. I have been struck with how the push toward the remedicalization of psychiatry (and the comparatively recent biochemical/neurological emphasis in psychiatry) fits ecologically with the more generalized burgeoning interest and promise of family systems work. Psychologists seem to be defining their turf in a corresponding way. Anyone who has recently struggled through the reams of documentation materials required for the American Psychological Association's Continuing Education providers will have had a good taste of it. Recently, a bill was passed in Georgia licensing marriage and family therapists, clinical social workers and counselors. Family therapy is probably the most common modality used by all three groups. Interestingly, one of the primary sources of resistance, which had earlier delayed passage of the licensing bill, was with the established state-employed social workers involved in case work.

I recently perused the employee manual of a centralized insurance program for a major network of private psychiatric hospitals. As is most commonly the case, any reference to family work was found under "mental health benefit exclusions." Family work was not even given the validation of being labeled a therapy. Instead, marriage counseling and family counseling were listed under excluded services, along with vocational or religious counseling and consciousness raising. Failure to recognize the value of family therapy? Or recognition of the value of family therapy and its threat to the establishment? Perhaps some of each. I like to think that the tightening of the belt so pervasive in health care today will in time fit with a new valuing of family systems work. It would make sense.

As I began this chapter, I indicated that I have been struck with the commonalities among the leaders in the family systems field and that I tend to see their differences more as personal style (and working context) than conflicting theoretical bases. It was reassuring, recently, to see Minuchin clearly validate his early work with Haley, Montalvo and Whitaker. And to read his words: "The terms structural and strategic . . . were created to sell our products, just as Pierre Cardin brands the buttocks of all his jeans" (Simon, 1984, p. 29). Having moved into new experiences beyond his formal retirement from Philadelphia Child Guidance, Minuchin seems to have attained a perspective that is refreshing. Perhaps he can be meta to the field in a way that others more enmeshed in the field cannot.

I think Minuchin is referring to the human propensity for being territorial, for staking out one's turf. We see it in other mammals—I am reminded of it every time I take a walk with our dog and we are confronted with a barking beast, or several, on every block. Again, I'm reminded of the Somali nomads staking out their claim to sparse grazing lands and their greeting, "Ma Naabid Ba"—Is it peace? I once heard an expert defined as anyone who lives and works a hundred miles away. I think the second, third and fourth generations (if there are such) are still staking out their territory, and as mammalian creatures competing for grazing lands. I continue to be frustrated when I attend panels on theory and epistemology. The participants have so much to offer, but they usually appear to be talking past each other—not listening—focusing on differences and reifying theory. I always find myself wanting to make links, bridges. And then I feel as if I am back at the dining room table with my parents or walking along the path to the brick apartment building. Perhaps I'm just conflict avoidant.

It is predictable that as the territory becomes more and more populated, family therapists will describe more and more finely-defined plots and put up fences for privacy. One can see this happening in the broader field of psychotherapy. There are specialists in eating disorders, in borderline personality, in suicidology, in group therapy for young male schizopaths, and other areas. I see the same pattern in the family field, as one can see from the offerings of the major publishing houses. As products of Western civilization, we have a tendency toward Aristotelian duality that promotes the defining of boxes around people and turf.

Certainly, I think it is valuable to learn from our clinical experience and move toward quicker detection of redundant patterns among systems presenting an identified patient with specific symptoms. Haley (1979) has suggested the value of a clinical nosology for more efficient systems therapy. Having done a great deal of work with school avoidance, I have seen a repetition of the same pattern and have relied on the same interventions—with some individualization. Probably what distresses me most is the tendency to leave the theoretical base behind, the real essence of an ecosystemic therapy, and get caught up in techniques as therapists become specialized. As trainers we have enough trouble challenging students to focus on theory when they are chomping at the bit to learn techniques.

I would like to hold onto such gems as the MRI concept of small difficulties becoming problems through the application of "more of the same" attempted solutions. The attempted solution becomes the problem. I find this applicable at all levels of system, from my experience with poison ivy (where my body's attempted solution to an allergen, invisible to the naked eye, emerges in a miserable rash) to the arms race (where the escalating cycle of producing bigger and "better" weapons develops from a relatively small difficulty among nations). I especially appreciate the applicability of this principle to systems therapy.

From another perspective, I am concerned about what is happening in the general population as more areas of specialty are being defined in the general psychotherapy and family therapy arenas. For example, more and more cases of eating disorders appear to be emerging. One way to look at it is to say that earlier these cases went undetected. Another perspective is that small deviations in normal eating behavior—e.g., a temporary loss of appetite in an adolescent—are being amplified through the attempted solutions of concerned family members who have been exposed to the rash of articles and media presentations on eating disorders by eating disorder specialists. What you look for determines what you find. I fear that a similar pattern may be developing around teenage suicides. Certainly, this is not the whole picture. However, when I allow myself an ecological perspective, changes in the therapy field seem to go hand in hand with changes in the general population, and it is not a one-way street.

From the beginning, it seems strategic/structural therapy has been criticized as being manipulative and disrespectful to the client. I fear an emphasis on techniques and their consequent misapplication will bring further loss of credibility. This is indeed ironic when a well-trained ecosystemic therapist should be in perhaps a prime position for respecting the ecosystem of the client and client family.

Recently, Dell (1984) defined the family systems field as temporarily stagnant and predicted a breakthrough in 1986. He believes it will come in connecting the systemic and transgenerational. Goolishian (1984) reminded us that stagnant ponds are teeming with life. My concern is that if a breakthrough came, nobody would notice it. We might all be too busy defining our turf and building our fences. The most promise for me is in the coming together of family therapists with thinkers from what have once been considered diverse disciplines, e.g., Maturana, von Foerster, von Glasersfeld, Umpleby, as I experienced in 1983 at the conference, Maps of the Mind, Maps of the

World, sponsored by the Mental Research Institute. I have always believed the lines defining disciplines were arbitrary. When I look at the bookshelf in my study, I find Erickson's collected works and *Change* (Watzlawick, Weakland & Fisch, 1974) surrounded by *The Silent World* (Cousteau, 1953) and *Only One Earth* (Ward & Dubos, 1972).

My continued delight in attempting to define and practice an ecosystemic therapy fits with my love of challenges. I'll occasionally attempt a black slope in skiing but I'll go around the mogels, not over them. In owning my role as a meddler, I'm trying to be increasingly respectful of people's lives — of their ecosystems. I find one of my biggest challenges is to avoid burnout both clinically and professionally. I'm trying to leave the berry patch more and more frequently. A hideaway on a barrier island in the Gulf of Mexico seems to help.

One of the most exciting things about being a family therapist is that every life experience enriches one's practice. I had experienced considerable loss in my life which had helped me better join with clients who were suffering losses and help them past log jams. But until this year I didn't know what it was to lose a parent — a father. I recently heard an interview with a master clarinetist on public radio. The interviewer began focusing on deficits he perceived in the musician's childhood. After all, he had sacrificed his junior high school years in endless hours of practice. The musician acknowledged that he indeed had had some dark and sad experiences. He went on to say that these experiences had helped him communicate classical music to his audience — as so much of music is dark and sad.

One final comment. An ecological view would appear to challenge the concept of purpose. Maturana (1983) has stated clearly his assumption on evolution: survival of the fit, not the fittest. A profound shift. The intention lies in the perception of the observer. Perhaps it is the illusion of purpose and responsibility that keeps the human species going, keeps us alive as individuals and as a species . . . keeps family therapists in business. With a brain so highly developed that abstract questions can be considered, long-range planning can be discussed. At least it appears so. One thing seems apparent: The *why* appears to be beyond human understanding, beyond the computing of the human brain (Watzlawick, 1983). And indeed the human spirit keeps searching. . . .

      way up in the Henegar's
tree just now
picking the last apples, and the wind over the hill
coming on . . .

                  swaying
I reached and it blew them down; swaying again

reached, and it blew them toward me; again
reached, and it blew us together,
                                    me and the branch
the branch and the breeze
                            whispering together
bending, almost breaking:

and on the near ridge crest
on the slate-grey sky, I saw Jack's cows
standing on Gerald's new roof
and the workmen hammering at their feet
        and thought

bowed to the hammers for their bread
as they to the grass: hammering on
ruminating on: the wind blowing
on and on . . .

        I to the apples
apples to the branch, branch to the wind
I to the branch to the wind
and the beef, and the workmen:
        where my brothers
is the altar; and whose
is the sacrifice; and for whom
bow the apples,
blows the wind
        as I reached for the apples
was I reaching for the wind
in the top of the tree
the branches swayed

and I too swayed
and sang.

        Michael Martin (1977)

REFERENCES

Bach, R. (1977). *Illusion: The Adventures of a Reluctant Messiah*. New York: Dell.
Bateson, G., Jackson, D., Haley, J., & Weakland, J. (1956). Toward a theory of schizophrenia. *Behavioral Science, 1*, 251–264.
Bateson, G. (1972). *Steps to an Ecology of Mind*. New York: Ballantine Books.
Bateson, G. (1979). *Mind and Nature: A Necessary Unity*. New York: Dalton.
Berger, M., & Dammann, C. (1982). Live supervision as context, treatment and training. *Family Process, 21*, 337–344.
Berger, M., & Daniels-Mohring, D. (1982). The strategic use of Bowenian formulations. *Journal of Strategic and Systemic Therapies, 1*, 50–56.
Berger, M., & Jurkovic, G. (1984). *Practicing family therapy in diverse settings*. San Francisco: Jossey-Bass.

76   *Journeys*

Bergman, J. (1977). Personal communication.
Bergman, J. (1984). Personal communication.
Carter, P. (1982). Rapport and integrity for Ericksonian practitioners. In J. Zeig (Ed.), *Ericksonian Approaches to Hypnosis and Psychotherapy*. New York: Brunner/Mazel.
Carter, P., & Gilligan, S. (February 4-6, 1983). Personal communication.
Cousteau, J. Y. (1953). *The Silent World*. New York: Harper.
Dell, P. (April 23-25, 1981). Workshop on *Dialogues in Family Therapy*.
Dell, P. (October 18-21, 1984). An institute on theory, 42nd Annual Conference, American Association for Marriage and Family Therapy.
Dell, P. (January 1985). Understanding Bateson and Maturana: Toward a biological foundation for the social sciences. *Journal of Marital and Family Therapy, 2* (1).
Duhl, B. (September 22-24, 1983). Congrès internationale: *Approches Thérapeutiques et Modèles de Formation en Thérapie Familiale*. Brussels, Belgium.
Goolishian, H. (1984). An institute on theory, 42nd Annual Conference, American Association for Marriage and Family Therapy.
Goolishian, H., & Dell, P. (Mar. 17-18, 1979). Workshop on *Strategic Family Therapy*, Galveston, TX.
Haley, J. (1976). *Problem-solving Therapy*. San Francisco: Jossey-Bass.
Haley, J. (April 5-6, 1979). Workshop on *Strategic Therapy*, Washington, D.C.
Hoffman, L. (April 23-25, 1981). Personal communication.
Hoffman, L. (1983). State of the Art, *The Family Therapy Networker, 1* (7).
Keeney, B. (1979). Ecosystemic epistemology: An alternative paradigm for diagnosis. *Family Process, 17*, 195-205.
Martin, M. (1977). *Way Up in a Tree Just Now*. Emory, VA: Iron Mountain Press.
Maturana, H. R. (July 29-31, 1983). Conference on *Maps of the mind, maps of the world*, sponsored by the Mental Research Institute, San Francisco, CA.
Minuchin, S. (1978). *Families and Family Therapy*. Cambridge, MA: Harvard University Press.
Minuchin, S. (1984). An interview with Salvador Minuchin. *The Family Therapy Networker, 8* (6).
Papp, P. (1976). Brief therapy with couples groups. In P. Guerin (Ed.), *Family therapy*. New York: Gardner Press.
Rabkin, R. (1977). *Strategic Psychotherapy*. New York: Basic Books.
Reamy-Stephenson, M. (1979). *In search of a comprehensive theory/treatment paradigm for school phobia/school avoidance*. Unpublished manuscript, University of Georgia School of Social Work.
Reamy-Stephenson, M. (1983). The assumption of non-objective reality: A missing link in the training of strategic therapists. *The Journal of Strategic and Systemic Therapies, 2* (2), 51-68.
Reamy-Stephenson, M. (1984). Psychiatric inpatient units. In M. Berger & G. Jurkovic (Eds.), *Practicing Family Therapy in Diverse Settings*. San Francisco: Jossey-Bass.
Ward, B., & Dubos, R. (1972). *Only One Earth*. New York: W.W. Norton.
Watzlawick, P., Weakland, J., & Fisch, R. (1974). *Change: Principles of Problem Formuation and Problem Resolution*. New York: W. W. Norton.
Watzlawick, P. (July 29-30, 1983). A conference on *Maps of the Mind, Maps of the World*. San Francisco, CA.
Weakland, J., Fisch, R., Watzlawick, P., & Bodin, A., (1974). Brief therapy: Focused problem resolution. *Family Process, 13* (2), 141-169.
Zeig, J. (April 4-5, 1980). Personal communication.

Chapter 4

A Study of Change:
Therapeutic Theory in Process

Elam Nunnally, Steve de Shazer,
Eve Lipchik, and Insoo Berg

The study of change reported here takes place within the Brief Family Therapy Center (BFTC) in Milwaukee, Wisconsin. The Center is dedicated to research, theory building, and training in relation to clinical practice.

What are the true origins of a center like this one? With no outside private or public support and no foundation grants, what motivates a small group to sacrifice their salaries for videotapes and one-way mirrors? To answer these questions, we encouraged Steve de Shazer and Insoo Berg to reminisce:

> We had no five-year plan. We just wanted to be in the forefront of thinking in the family therapy field. We wanted to be the MRI of the midwest and provide the very best training possible for the next generation of family therapists. Our way of working together seemed to parallel our way of working with families. We developed a 'Z' model of openness and participation. Anyone could watch anyone at work and comment on their handling of cases. No one seems to be threatened by anyone else's competence. We seem to find each other's competence more reassuring than otherwise.
>
> The purpose of this joint is to provide a milieu for creativity, a collegium of scholars. Alex Molnar talks about the academic freedom which he finds more of here than in the University.
>
> Alex also has an interesting way of conceptualizing our practice model. He speaks of it as a virus, in the sense that it's always in process of change and development, and with every change it just seems to get more robust.
>
> That's a characteristic of our group as well as our model: We take the attitude that change is inevitable and we value the process of change and the experience of it, the excitement of watching ourselves grow and pushing ourselves on. Whenever we start to get bored with the model, we change it. Some of the changes seemed to have developed out of random events. We appreciate randomness, too. Looked at in one way, I guess you could say this all happened by accident.

   This is the history of an organization — Brief Family Therapy Center (BFTC) — and of an investigation into the nature of cybernetic change, which took place over nearly a decade and involves a sizeable dramatic personae. The organization provided the context in which creative thinking could occur: the interplay of practice, research, training, and theory building. The cast of characters includes:

- Insoo Berg, M.S.W. — A founder and now Director of Training.
- Marilyn Bonjean, Ed.D. — Specialist in gerontology; Director of Social Services at the Marian Catholic Home, Milwaukee.
- Calvin Chicks, M.D. — Medical Director, Psychiatric Consultant, and former trainee.
- Steve de Shazer — A founder and now Executive Director.
- Jim Derks, MSW — A founder, now on the staff of Family Health Plan, Milwaukee.
- Ron Kral, M.S. — Educational Psychologist and member of the staff of Brookfield Public School System.
- Marilyn La Court, M.A. — Former staff member, now on the staff of Family Health Plan, Milwaukee.
- Wallace Gingerich, Ph.D. — Research Associate, and an Associate Professor in the School of Social Welfare, University of Wisconsin-Milwaukee.
- Alex Molnar, Ph.D. — Research Associate, and an Associate Professor in the School of Education, University of Wisconsin-Milwaukee.
- Eve Lipchik, M.S.W. — Associate Director.
- Elam Nunnally, Ph.D. — A founder, and an Associate Professor in the School of Social Welfare, University of Wisconsin-Milwaukee.
- John Walters, M.S.W. — Training Associate.
- Michelle Wiener-Davis, M.S.W. — Research Associate.
- Marvin Wiener, M.D. — A founder; now with Family Health Plan.
- James Wilk — Therapist in Residence, 1984–85.

The investigators chronicled in this report, like all diligent Poirots and Holmeses, have sifted through numerous clues and red herrings in pursuit of their quarry — cybernetic change. They believe that they have narrowed the evidence down sufficiently to make a progress report which may be of assistance to like-minded investigators elsewhere, whose contributions in turn will help them carry their investigations forward.

   The four principal investigators came from different directions: Steve de Shazer had earlier developed an Eriksonian practice incorporating perspectives from sociology and from eastern, i.e., Taoist and Buddhist, philosophy. Insoo Berg was heavily involved in training therapists and intensely concerned with the question of how therapists learn to do what they do. Elam Nunnally was preoccupied with family communication and family development and with the question of how changes in communication can produce changes in family relationships. Eve Lipchik was invested in finding ways to hypothesize about problems so that solutions were possible and also with identifying interviewing skills congruent with effective problem-solving. A fifth investigator, Jim Wilk, in residence for a year, will report his observations of the other investigators at work from a new-to-the-scene perspective.

In the mid-1970s, Insoo, Steve, Jim Derks (and Elam on a volunteer basis) were working together in a community agency in Milwaukee, drawing on de Shazer's earlier work in Palo Alto and on the work of the Mental Research Institute. It was not easy, as a maverick group in a traditional setting, to practice the type of exciting and unorthodox therapy which evolved. Therefore, they decided to break out on their own and establish a setting in which they could practice and research as they pleased and, hopefully, make a living at it. It was a daring move which was made in several stages and proved to be both exciting and frightening.

In the first year of operation, Jim and Steve, the two pioneers, essentially donated their time and energy to start the Center. Fortunately, they had spouses with full-time jobs who were willing to support them. Since neither of them had experience or training in how to run a business, there was some "culture shock" involved in a shift which forced them to be administrators as well as staff members.

The first cases were seen in the living room of Insoo and Steve's house. The video camera was set up on the stairway to the second floor, which is where the team adjourned for consultation breaks. The camera operator sat on the stairs behind the camera while the therapist talked with the family. Sometimes a family member would direct a comment to the operator, perhaps to be friendly. In an effort to behave in a professional manner, the operator would remain silent. After all, he/she was "behind the mirror." Families had a hard time understanding all this when the therapist attempted to explain it.

As business picked up, the decision was made to professionalize the operation. An appropriate location was chosen and a small suite of offices rented. Signing the three-year lease was frightening for the corporation officers, who had to assume financial liability. Each loaned the corporation $600 to get under way. The space we had rented was big enough for only two therapy rooms with an observation room in the middle that would accommodate about six people (who were willing to be sardines). Trying to install a one-way mirror was no easy task. Continuous problems with defective mirrors meant that we usually had a huge hole in the wall where the mirror should have been. For over two weeks we asked families to pretend that there was a mirror on the wall and the team members behind it were invisible. To our surprise, the families did just that!

When there were two cases to be observed simultaneously, as frequently happened in the evening hours, two teams would jam into the observation room back to back. One team used earphones, which prevented them from talking to each other, while the other team used the overhead speaker system which had to be turned down so that the team with the headsets could hear through their earphones. Sometimes eight or ten people would be jammed into the observation room, and in the summer the heat in the room was unbearable. A trainee who was taking a week-long course in July nearly passed out. She still talks about the experience, but she also still sends us cases periodically.

Initially, the group was organized in an egalitarian mode, with everyone sharing both in work and income. Members of the group took turns doing everything, from vacuum cleaning and watering the plants to typing letters and answering the phone. The group took pride in this egalitarian division of labor and informally assigned tasks according to professional degrees and credentials. Thus, Marvin Wiener, M.D., who had the highest academic credentials, took on the lowest task, that of watering the plants.

We outgrew our office space almost as soon as we occupied it. Every desk and nook and cranny had to be shared. It was like a large family living in a small house. Every decision, business or clinical, however small, was made by group consensus. Each of us was familiar with everyone's cases and perceptive visitors commented on how we seemed to have developed a verbal shorthand for talking about cases or classes of interventions. This probably resulted from our habit of nicknaming cases rather than referring to them by family name—for example, the "piano case," the "fog case," and the "do a bat boy" intervention. Some of the case names were even more colorful, such as "When the Brewers are in town," "Barbie doll," and "4th of July." We didn't think this custom colored our perception of cases, but we did get into trouble with our "Wicked stepmother" label (Nunnally & Berg, 1983).

Even during this early phase of close-knit and egalitarian group life, some differences in styles and special interests developed among the group members. Steve was good at keeping track of the checkbooks as well as at articulating theories; Eve was not only good at making contacts with new referral sources but she also kept track of internal organizational issues; Insoo had been in the Milwaukee therapy community the longest and brought in cases; Elam, with his academic connections and established reputation, provided some necessary credibility for the group.

We grew and prospered gradually but not without growth pains. It was hard to balance our ideal of remaining a "think tank" and the pragmatics of surviving as a business organization. Our dreams of total egalitarianism gradually gave way to a more formalized hierarchy which adhered to the principle of "more pay for more work." We outgrew our space, which was a sign of growth; however, our new larger quarters, in which we each had our own office, were a mixed blessing. More space meant more distance from each other and a need to portion out the work even more specifically. Differences in personalities surfaced more. We found we had to schedule specific times for team work in order to retain the concept of team. Threats to the cohesion of the group made it necessary to reassess the aims of the Center and redefine our individual roles, leading to shifts in the membership of the group.

Although we agreed on a single model of systemic, brief, problem-solving therapy, and in our discussion of cases everyone understood what the other was describing, distinct differences in personal style began to emerge. Trainees and visitors have frequently commented on these differences. Steve, who uses the least number of words and makes the most use of silence, does the shortest sessions. Elam, who has a low-keyed and very nurturing and soothing way about him, always runs over the hour with his sessions. So do Eve and Insoo. Eve designs the most elaborate intervention messages, clearly related to formalized hypotheses, and composes marvelously impactful follow-up letters. Insoo is the group's most accomplished actor, with a range of performances from "oriental inscrutable" to calm reassurance to abject terror. Insoo's tendency to confuse grammar in her intervention messages, following the consultation break, often seems to have a hypnotic effect on clients.

In moving out of the traditional mold and setting up a new, untraditional organization, we discovered that we still had to relate to the forces of traditionalism within the mental health community. The delicate balance between adapting to the community and maintaining our unique orientation was difficult to achieve and is difficult to keep. We had to articulate to others what made us different and at the same time prove how we were valuable to the therapeutic community. This public relations problem forced us to be clear about our systemic thinking so that we could present it in concise, understandable terms.

Withal, we continued to experience some sense of isolation within the Milwaukee community, which led us to look for other ways of connecting with people who "work this way." Steve began to publish the *Underground Railroad* which was first distributed at conferences and sent to a few colleagues who shared our ideas. We now have a mailing list of 700. Publications of individual members also served to communicate with the family therapy world "outside" and to get feedback. Conducting workshops and seminars in the community, around the country, and in Europe has been another means for networking with like-minded practitioners and helps us to compare and contrast our work with other models.

Another important element in sharpening our thinking was the Brief Family Therapy Center Training Program. It became apparent very early that the Training Program provided an unexpected bonus in the evolutionary processes of concept development and theory construction. Trainees have a way of asking very basic and thought-provoking questions, forcing staff to become more clear about their thinking. At this time, training is considered an integral part of the Center's practice/research/theory building enterprise.

THE RESEARCH PROGRAM

As we see ourselves, BFTC is a "research program" whose job it is to figure out the puzzles within our paradigm. Studying and solving these are not easy tasks and over the years we have come to the conclusion that all we can ever hope to do is to approach useful solutions to the paradigmatic puzzles.

"Where did that intervention come from?" All brief therapists are plagued with this question whenever they show and/or describe their work; attempting to answer it in the most useful fashion constitutes much of our research program. An early research effort was the accidental result of not having the video camera and the VTR behind the mirror with the team (as it is now). Instead, it was in a separate room, meaning we used a three-room suite which consisted of: 1) therapy room, 2) observation room, and 3) video room. The video room was also a working office, with a typewriter. Usually the person assigned to video taping did the job with the sound turned off, while occupied with other tasks.

One day (in 1979) while in the video room, the research team (Alex Molnar and Steve de Shazer) turned on the sound and watched (rather than working on a grant proposal they should have been doing). Their discussion shifted from just talking about their observations and what the intervention might look like to speculating about what kind of intervention the rest of the team (who were in the observation room) might develop. As a lark, they developed an intervention which they planned to compare with the one the therapy team developed. When they later compared their intervention with that of the therapy team, they found it to include the same homework assignment and some of the same compliments. However, as they compared how they had arrived at their interventions, it became clear that their thinking had come from several widely different directions. For a period of time, this comparison activity continued, which greatly contributed to our understanding of where interventions come from.

This research also led to our current routine in situations where two training teams observe the same case. During the intermission, each team goes to its own room and designs an intervention. Later on, the two intervention messages are compared for similarities and differences. This comparison not only helps trainees understand how to construct interventions, but also demonstrates to them the useful notion that THERE IS NO ONE RIGHT INTERVENTION.

Similarly, the "formula first session task" research project developed from the team's approach to a particular case. The therapists involved on a case designed the original message ("Notice what you want to continue happening") to fit a vaguely defined situation. When de Shazer and Molnar talked about the results reported in the second session (a list of concrete and specific changes which led to the family's solution), they wondered what was going on. The pattern could be simply described in this way: The family described a lot of vague complaints with no specific ways of measuring success; the team gave a message about watching for GOOD THINGS happening in the interval between the first and second sessions (implicitly predicting change); and, in the second session, the family reported concrete changes that led in the direction of a satisfactory solution.

The research team wondered what was going on, and wondered if we had serendipitously stumbled onto something about the universality of the change process. After using the message with several cases and getting similar reports, they decided to organize a study. They reported on their observation to the rest of the team and asked the whole team to use this intervention message with as many new clients as possible and to report what happened in the second session. They were asked to use the message unless they had good reasons not to, and to report those specific reasons for not using it so that we could understand the range of conditions under which the message was a useful intervention. Therefore, at the end of the second session each therapist was asked to fill out a simple one-page report.

We were surprised to find that we used the formula task with two-thirds of our clients in the first session, most of whom reported that good things had happened and that some of these were "new" or "different." All of these clients reported what happened in concrete terms, and 82 percent reported that at least one of the worthwhile things that happened was new. Fifty-seven percent reported that things were "better," and only 10 percent reported things as somehow "worse." In some cases the clients even reported enough increased satisfaction that the second session also became the last. We began to see that the therapeutic task had shifted from *promoting* change to 1) eliciting news of difference, 2) amplifying the differences, and 3) helping the changes to continue.

These concrete responses to vague instructions, along with data about how the therapists in turn responded to these, led us in a new direction. Once again the entire group initiated a research effort, this time to look at what the therapist was doing in both the first and the second sessions. The new research team — Wallace Gingerich, Michelle Weiner-Davis, and Steve de Shazer — noticed that the therapists' questions about exceptions to the complaint (e.g., "When is it that he doesn't nag you?") were coming earlier and earlier in the first session, which was consonant with our philosophical belief that change is a continuous process. Weiner-Davis took this even further. She had therapists in her agency (which uses the BFTC approach) ask clients at the beginning of the first session about changes that had occurred between the initial phone call to make the appointment and the first session. Again, two out of three reported changes of the type they wished to continue (Weiner-Davis, 1985).

ONE-WAY MIRROR: EVOLVING THE CONCEPT OF TEAM

Early in the history of BFTC, prior to moving to the Center, Insoo, Steve, Jim Derks and Elam began experimenting with use of the one-way mirror. We tended to use our peers behind the mirror as on-the-spot consultants. Contact with the "conductor" of the session was usually over the phone. We would call in suggestions when the conductor of the session was having difficulties. Infrequently, a therapist from behind the mirror would go into the room to deliver assistance.

Initially, the one-way mirror was thought of as just a special part of a wall. The observing group and the therapist remained as separate as they would be if the wall contained no mirror. They would meet before and after each session to discuss the session and to plan the next one. Insoo recalls the day we invented the "consultation break": "It was while we were arguing over what to do with one particular obesity case. Therapist and observers were in disagreement over whether we should focus on the client's overweight which depressed her or first work on her depression which made her overweight. Following several emotionally charged phone calls which became heated as the session went on, we decided to take a time out. Once the disagreement was settled, a plan was jointly developed for the remainder of the session. From this beginning, a consulting break became routine with the staff." (We use the break "to sort things out and collect our thoughts" even when no one is behind the mirror.)

It was not until sometime later, however, that the clue of the one-way mirror and the use of the consulting break led us to evolve the concept of the "team." The group behind the mirror continued to view therapist and family as being on the other side of a wall and the therapist, too, would behave as if working alone except for a routine consultation break. One day a client helped to change that when she asked the therapist to tell her what the observers thought about her situation. Although unexpected, the request seemed reasonable enough, and the group phoned in a short, complimentary statement about the client's efforts to deal with the problem. The client beamed and the therapist went ahead as if nothing important had happened. But something terribly important had happened. The wall between therapist/client and observers had been breached. The interaction between observers and clients became a regular part of the therapy format, which eventually developed into a new model which demanded a new theory of change.

The observers began to work with the therapist behind the mirror during the consulting break to construct the major intervention as a statement from the team to the family. Unknown to us, a group in Milan (Selvini-Palazzoli, et al., 1978) and a group in New York (Papp, 1977) had begun to use the group behind the mirror in much the same fashion. As this approach became more and more refined, the roles of the therapist ("conductor") and of the observers ("team") became defined in ways that forced the team to become even more involved in the therapy session. Eventually, therapist and observers began to see themselves as a single unit, as a team, which led to seeing the family and therapy team as a larger suprasystem — an ecosystemic perspective.

The team behind the mirror assumed the roles of designing interventions and observing the results. In front of the mirror, the therapist's role was to establish rapport and collect data that the team needed in order to design interventions. After the consulting break, when the therapist returned to the clients, he spoke for the whole team.

These new definitions of roles for conductor and observers were not without certain costs. Eve Lipchik recalls: "My first memory of the Brief Family Therapy model as I saw it in practice in 1979 was of a heavy emphasis on the team. An appropriate slogan for the work at the time might have been 'the team is the method.' It seemed then as if the 'real' work was done behind the mirror where the polyocular views of the various therapists on the team, including the conductor, were blended to produce a way of giving 'news of a difference' to the family. Little energy was spent in thinking about the role of the conductor. My own impression was that it was considered an easy role, almost menial in contrast to the creative, intellectual process that went on behind the mirror. Personally, I found it more difficult than working behind the mirror because it felt simultaneously like a nonverbal interaction with the people behind the mirror and a verbal one with the family. The message that I had gotten was not to do any thinking on my own about the problem while interviewing, but just to obtain information necessary for an intervention for the people behind the mirror. Thus, my energy seemed to be diffused and I never felt truly engaged in either direction. On the other hand, the conductor was given the power to have the final say about the content and form of the intervention, even to veto it, because he or she had been the one in the room with the family. There seemed to be a decided lack of fit about all this for me."

As noted by Kuhn (1970), paradigm shifts are likely to occur at a point when one begins to be troubled by the ambiguities or the inadequacies in the old paradigm. The lack of fit noted above contributed to shifts at a pragmatic level of interviewing behaviors, accompanied by shifts in focus of intervention and in our perspective on the change process. From our interest in study-ing the team and how it does its work, a new definition of the role of the conductor evolved. This led to a shift from studying family systems and how to change them to studying the change process itself. The object of study, then, became the interaction process of the suprasystem composed of clients and team.

This shift to an ecosystemic view began to put the interview and the work of the therapist conductor into a new perspective. The interactional patterns between a conductor and a family became as significant as the patterns described and observed in the family system. The interactional patterns between the team members behind the mirror became as important as the pattern be-tween them and the family via the intervention. The conductor's interactional pattern with the family could be different from his interactional pattern with the rest of the team, when necessary. All patterns are recursive and had to be considered even if at any one time they weren't of equal importance. The interview between the conductor and the family came to be seen as signifi-cant in itself, not only because of the information obtained but because *how* it was obtained determined both the extent of information that would be forthcoming and whether or not the family would be motivated to change and to continue to change. That is why we had instinctively given the conduc-tor the final word about interventions.

The greater focus on the interviewing process resulted in greater attention given to behaviors for maintaining rapport and led to closer examination of the kinds of questions used in the interview. The role of the conductor was further influenced by a great epistemological or theoretical shift begun in 1982, from "isomorphism" to "fit," from an emphasis on resolving problems to an emphasis on designing solutions. This shift changed the interviewing process.

FOCUS, CIRCULARITY, AND THE INTERVIEWING PROCESS

Our epistemological shift in 1982 significantly influenced and changed the interviewing process at BFTC. The questions we had to ask in order to assess the results of our experiment with the "formula first session task" forced us to increase our push for information about minute differences between past and present behaviors indicative of favorable change. This took us more and more away from details about problems and how they are maintained and more and more towards a focus on solutions and how to help the family con-struct them. Solutions were seen as a reality different from the one in which complaints lead to unsolvable problems. Thus, the interviewing process was adapted to purposefully connect complaints with solutions.

The concept of circularity and the technique of circular questioning described by the Milan group (Selvini-Palazzoli et al., 1980) had already been incorporated into our model. However, there were no specific guidelines for using these tools within our model. The understanding was, loosely, that one used linear questions only when absolutely necessary and that circular questions were more desirable because they addressed differences and relationships. We realized the need for a more definitive set of concepts to guide the interviewing process. The framework we evolved (Lipchik & de Shazer, 1985) is summarized below.

In order to determine what intervention will fit family members, one needs an understanding of their view of why and how the presenting problem exists and their ideas about solutions and how these come about. Furthermore, the team needs an understanding of how each individual sees the part they play in the problem and solutions as well as the parts others play. We elaborated and modified the concept of linear and circular questions to Individual and Systemic Questions and Direct and Constructive Questions.

- *Direct Questions* are used to gather information about how the complaints are viewed presently and how they arose.
- *Constructive Questions* are future-oriented inquiries about possible solutions.
- *Individual Questions* seek such information as why a person thinks a problem exists, when he or she thinks it began, what the reasons for it are, and what will have to happen for it to change.
- *Systemic Questions* search for information about differences and relationships, such as who is most affected by this problem, what one member of the family does when another is upset, and how family members will interact differently when the problem no longer exists.

These question types constitute a matrix:

	DIRECT	CONSTRUCTIVE
INDIVIDUAL	individual/direct	individual/constructive
SYSTEMIC	systemic/direct	systemic/constructive

In the earlier version of our brief therapy model, the "intervention" was viewed as the specific set of messages which followed the consultation break. Behavior of the therapist/conductor preceding the break was seen as almost exclusively data gathering and rapport building. With the shift to a focus on solutions, and informed by the concept of "fit," it became clear to us that the therapist behaviors preceding the break now constitute a major part of our intervention. Through skillful use of the question-matrix, the therapist helps the family construct complaints into solvable problems and helps them to recognize changes and expand these toward their solutions. The question-matrix is proving to be an extremely valuable tool in our melding of exploration and intervention.

Arriving on the scene in the Fall of 1984, Jim Wilk observed: "At BFTC, the notion that clients already have the resources they need to solve their problem is an important assumption. The client, as a general rule, may have been unsuccessful in dealing with the difficulties, but there always seem to be *exceptions* to this rule. Both the BFTC model and clinical epistemology (the model Bill O'Hanlon and I have developed) emphasize the search for and utilization of these exceptions. Both approaches attempt to determine the limits of the 'symptom context' and to build upon those contexts in which the symptom does not arise. From my earliest contacts with BFTC, this was present in the form of the interest in finding *clues*—if you listen to the client he will eventually give you the clue or key to solution. The use of compliments, particularly as they seem to be used currently at BFTC, simply recognizes and draws attention to what clients are already doing right."

CLUES TO UNDERSTANDING THE PROCESS OF CHANGE

At BFTC research, theory, and practice are considered to be elements of the same "thing," each informing the other. Therefore, for a theory of change to fit, it must meet certain criteria:

1) It needs to fit within the constraints of our observation and experience;
2) It needs to guide practice in some way, i.e., it needs to inform clinical practice about the sorts of things to do and not to do;
3) It needs to guide clinical research activities;
4) Construction of theory must be informed by clinical practice and clinical research.

What sort of things are we talking about when we talk about "change"? For us as brief therapists, influenced by Milton Erickson, it is perhaps easiest to think about "change" as #1) *whatever happens that makes the client's life more satisfactory* and to let it go at that. But we are also interested in the more theoretical and epistemological issues involved in the whole concept of change.

In the field of family therapy, the concept of change has been, and continues to be, defined in a variety of ways. At first, we tried to fit our observations into the #2) *first-order change, second-order change* frame suggested by the brief therapists at the Mental Research Institute (Watzlawick, Weakland, and Fisch, 1974). There is a certain desirable simplicity to this view, but we found the distinction slippery and not too useful because either type of change could lead to a satisfactory solution. Thus, we continued on the alert for something that would fit better with our observations.

We next tried to fit our experiences into the #3) *continuous change/discontinuous change* frame suggested by Prigogine, Nicolis, & Babloyantz (1972) and by Dell & Goolishian (1979). Continuous change might be described in this way: A child wets the bed five out of seven nights before therapy starts, and this frequency decreases to four, then to three, etc. Discontinuous change could be described as a drop in frequency from five to zero in one step. Again, either type of change pattern could be satisfactory to the client, and so the distinction did not appear to be as useful as we had at first believed. Furthermore, neither of these concepts seems to deal with the patterns as we saw them.

Casting about for more useful clues, we next tried to fit our work into Maruyama's (1963) distinction between #4) *homeostasis* (deviation-counteracting processes) and *morphogenesis* (deviation-amplifying processes) or Wilden's (1980) more Batesonian framework for the same distinction. This seemed more hopeful because morphogenic processes (small differences which make a difference that is disproportionate in the long run) could be described as a clinical focal point which includes continuous and discontinuous processes. However, this led us full circle back to #1: changes are either satisfactory to the client or not.

None of the concepts of change above fit very well with our experience and our observation. In particular, none of these described the relationship between the client and therapist which we see as important to the clinical processes of change. It appeared to us that none of these theories could serve as a guide to what the therapist should do or should not do.

We next tried to fit our experiences into #5) Thom's *catastrophe theory*. This held a lot of promise for two reasons: a) depending on which version of the theory one used, anywhere from five to nine distinct change processes could be mapped, and b) all of the maps are drawn to include both the change process and the "forces" which prompted the change being described. Thus, one map could be used to describe the process of change which included both client and therapist. But the same difficulty remained as with other change concepts: Any of the nine processes of change could make life more satisfactory to the client.

Meanwhile, our clinical practice continued and we observed three more elements which needed to be included in any theory of change that could be *useful to therapists* regardless of the theory's sophistication and elegance:

1) We noted that clients would frequently report that concrete changes in the area of complaint were made between the first and second session which made things "better."

2) With increasing frequency we noted that clients reported changes outside the area of complaint which made things better for them in general.

3) With increasing frequency we noted that clients reported changes inside the area of complaint between the initial phone call and the first appointment which made things better.

We noted that we then worked to keep these changes going and that this approach led to increased client satisfaction and fewer sessions per client.

All along, some of us at BFTC had held a #6) *Buddhist view of change.* Philosophers, at least since Heraclitus and the ancient Buddhists, have believed that change is constant and that stability is an illusion. This definition fits the above observations: All sorts of changes are happening all the time. But often therapists seem to behave in ways and to have theories that indicate the opposite belief, i.e., concepts of homeostasis and resistance. The most notable exception has been Erickson's work and the work of the brief therapists (e.g., Haley, 1963; Weakland, Fisch, Watzlawick, & Bodin, 1974; de Shazer, 1975). At least implicitly, their work is rather congruent with the Buddhist belief. As Haley (1967) pointed out, Erickson behaved as if he believed that change was inevitable and that *not* changing would be a surprise to him. Bateson's work (1979) was also congruent with this idea when he drew the distinction between "differences that make a difference" and "differences that do not make a difference." The latter differences, since they do not make a difference, contribute to the illusion of stability.

Any behavior that is seen as new or different can be used as part of the therapeutic construction of a solution. It does not need to be a bit of behavior that is seen as part of the complaint pattern. Even if the new behavior first occurred before the first therapy session, it can be labeled as the start of the solution. Thus, any difference can be developed into a difference that makes a difference as long as the new behavior (or newly perceived behavior) is "sacramental," i.e., is perceived as an "outward and visible sign of change."

Clearly, any theory of clinical change needs to include the influence of the observer, i.e., the Heisenberg hook. Although the process of change can be seen as constant, the therapist/observer's influence is part of what makes for the distinction between a) differences that make a difference and b) those differences which make no difference.

Simply, satisfactory clinical change, or a difference that makes a difference, is *constructed* by the therapist and the client out of the various differences which are part of the constant process of change. Conversely, the "facts" of a situation can be different without the client noticing it; therefore, the difference makes no difference and things are not better. Whether a difference is part of making life more satisfactory is a matter of perception and interpretation, not a matter of fact.

From his perspective, Jim Wilk suggests that "perhaps one of the most important and powerful features of the BFTC approach, now clearer than ever before, I think, is the emphasis on what's right instead of what's wrong—an emphasis on solutions instead of problems. As the BFTC model stands now, problem talk is actually bypassed by focusing on solutions that would eliminate the complaint. This is done through questions getting the client to focus on what things will be like when therapy is successfully completed, e.g., 'What will your life be like after this problem is solved?' and 'How will we know when we can stop meeting like this?'"

RED HERRINGS

In our investigation into the nature of cybernetic change, some of the clues we have followed seem to have led us nowhere in particular. This is not to say that the examination of such clues is unproductive. Far from it. Our study of "clues" such as catastrophe theory, first and second order change, etc., has helped us to clarify our thinking, and sometimes retrace our steps and move off in another direction. We call them "red herrings" because they did not point to the direction in which we eventually moved. Among the various clues in this class, perhaps the most important ones for us were the concepts of "resistance" and "paradox."

Resistance

In our main observation room, displayed in a prominent location, is an "Obituary for Resistance." Insoo Berg (1984) writes that Resistance "died peacefully of natural causes one Friday afternoon in July, 1979 behind the one-way mirror at The Brief Family Therapy Center. Present at his deathbed were friends and close long-time associates who came to share the realization that resistance had been losing his strength for some time."

At BFTC the concept of resistance began to fade at the time the team "came through the mirror" and a paradigm shift occurred wherein we began to think in terms of a family and therapy team suprasystem instead of viewing the family as a system "out there." Earlier, we had tried to figure out ways to utilize the resistance in the service of change. The family's resistance was seen as a natural occurrence, given the homeostatic tendencies of systems. This view was "entity-oriented" rather than pattern-oriented and turned the therapist and the family into opponents. If we look at the therapy situation with homeostasis as the organizing concept, then the clinical equivalent—the concept of resistance—is reasonable and necessary because the therapist/observer is outside the boundary of the system. If the therapist is included in the description, however, then morphogenesis becomes the organizing concept, since the focus of therapy is on changing. The openness of the subsystems and their ability to change in order to survive suggest the concept of "co-operating" as a viable alternative to the concept of "resisting."

At about the time we were shifting our thinking to include the team as part of the treatment system, we were studying and attempting to classify the outcomes of task directives. We were accustomed to thinking of *any* client response to a directive as information to be used in constructing the next directive. For example, clients who were found to oppose directives were instructed to do "more of the same," and clients who complied with specific concrete directives were given additional specific concrete directives. A logical next step was our recognition that we were treating *each* response as the client's particular way of cooperating with us, while our response to the client's response was our way of cooperating back.

The logic of this step, however, became apparent to us only as we shifted away from homeostasis as an organizing concept. We recognized then that client behaviors we had formerly labeled as "resisting" could better be conceptualized as "cooperating." The death of resistance and the birth of cooperating proceeded from our need to reconceptualize our research concepts consistent with the paradigm shift. Pragmatically, we find that the "death of resistance" means that we do not view the therapy session as a battle nor our clients as opponents who must be outwitted or otherwise somehow defeated by us in order to help them.

In Jim Wilk's view, "the concept of cooperation remains central to the approach at BFTC. In the Ericksonian tradition, this is often discussed in terms of 'utilization'—utilizing whatever the client brings in order to arrive at a solution and this places the responsibility on the therapist and the therapy team to cooperate with the client's way of cooperating. This, in my view, is a very ordinary, commonsense, and respectful way of putting this matter, which is sometimes discussed elsewhere in somewhat more mystified terms—'gaining and maintaining rapport'—or more epistemologically suspect terms such as tiptoeing around the resistance. This notion of utilization-as-cooperation is now very much a part of the culture at BFTC."

Paradox

Until 1978 or 1979, the terms "paradox" and "paradoxical intervention" were part of our everyday working vocabulary at BFTC. But as we learned to cooperate with our clients instead of "dealing with resistance" and viewed the family/team as the system to change, we used the term less and less often. Although the interventions we devised continued to surprise our clients and us at times, we came to see them as surprising and interesting and nothing more, rarely as paradoxical. This was so despite the fact that a substantial portion of our interventions contained some variant of "symptom prescription." Increasingly, we saw ourselves as simply giving directives that mapped on to the clients' complaint pattern (isomorphism).

Sometimes we wondered uneasily if we were inadvertently discarding something we really ought to keep, but eventually we found some reassurance in the questioning of "paradox" by other clinicians and theorists that began to appear in the literature (e.g., Dell, 1981). As we shifted to a focus on solutions and substituted the concept of "fit" for "isomorphism," we seemed to find even less use of the term "paradox." This is not to imply that we thought the term was somehow "wrong" or totally useless, but rather that we had found tools that appeared more useful and more consistent with our way of thinking about systems. We are not ready to write an obituary for this concept, despite its marked decline. For some few interventions, the term seems to remain applicable.

CLUES TO INTERVENTION DESIGN: THE CONCEPTS OF BALANCE, ISOMORPHISM AND FIT

In our pre-1979 period we were influenced by the concept of homeostasis. To describe processes which maintain homeostasis (homeostatic mechanisms), de Shazer (1978, 1979) developed a model based on Heider's (1946) balance theory. The model, which Steve started to build in 1972, described the problem as one that is maintained by the balanced state of the relationships between and among family members. The model offered guidelines to help the therapist move the family from one form of organization (balanced state) to another. The balance theoretical model, unlike most models built on homeostatic concepts, included a concept of change. As a team, we worked with the model for more than a year. We found that with experience we were often able to use the model within the 10-minute consultation break to map a family and identify the type of intervention specified by the model. But we had to find a replacement for the model as our interest in homeostasis and resistance gave way to an emphasis on change and on "cooperating" and as the team "came through the mirror" and embraced a concept of family/team suprasystem.

In the balance theoretical model, the therapist views the clients as "out there." Basically this was a closed-system model that drew a boundary between components of an ecosystem. Furthermore, it seemed to us that the notion of balanced states of relationships is too easily equated with no-change or with resistance to change. The concept of "isomorphism" seemed to offer greater promise for our evolving model.

Our ecosystemic view of a family/team suprasystem suggested that there needed to be something about the pattern of interventions and the family's complaint pattern, along with something about the interaction between these two patterns, that can promote change. Briefly, if change is going to be involved, then the intervention pattern needs to be closely related to the family's pattern so that the intervention pattern can serve to reframe or redefine the family's pattern.

A metaphor about the "bonus" of depth perception that we receive from the two eyes seeing the same thing from different angles helped us to grasp the concept of isomorphism and its importance (Bateson, 1979). The right eye's view can be mapped onto the left eye's view isomorphically; the meaning of this is the phenomenon of depth perception. The brain can be described as receiving two messages: 1) each eye's view of the same thing and 2) "news of the difference" between the views of the two eyes.

The concept of isomorphism guided the therapy team to "describe the family's patterns (A) in such a way that their reframed description (A') can serve as a guide for designing an intervention that can be mapped onto the pattern the family has described and shown (A). The elements of the team's description need to correspond to the elements of the family's description and the patterns it has shown the team in the therapy session(s). Furthermore, the team's description (A') needs to be from a different angle so that the family (at least potentially) can receive the news of a difference, a perceptual shift, which promotes change in the family patterns. The resultant behavior change will create a different subjective experience (de Shazer, 1982, p. 9). For example, we provide one couple with another view of their loudly argumentative interactions: They are in a transformational period of their marriage, "struggling to leave juvenile romance behind and achieve mature intimacy."

Although the concept of isomorphism served us rather well, in time our recognition of certain ambiguities led us to look for a replacement. It was the results of our research with the formula "first session task," begun in mid-1982 (de Shazer & Molnar, 1984), which suggested that isomorphism might be too limiting a term. It is hard to imagine that the same homework task, worded in the same way, could have even a very limited degree of isomorphism with two-thirds of our clients' complaint maps! The response to this task necessitated a change in our thinking. If we retain the isomorphism metaphor, then what is it that the map of the intervention is isomorphic with? As we reflected on our experiment, we began to find the concept of isomorphism lacking in descriptive power and pragmatic usefulness.

Isomorphism dealt with the relationship between the complaint pattern and the intervention pattern, but our experiment pointed to solutions and how they work: Solutions seem to have more in common with each other than the problems they solved would have suggested. At first this seems counterintuitive, but case after case has illustrated the usefulness of this way of thinking.

By 1982 we had begun to use the term "fit" as a shorthand replacement for the term "isomorphism." The concept of fit describes the relationship between (a) the map of the constructed problem (client's complaint, as interpreted by the therapist, plus potential solutions) and (b) the map of the intervention. This is seen as being similar to the relationship between (a) a lock and (b) the keys that open that lock. Within this metaphor, "formula tasks" can be seen as particular kinds of keys that work or fit in many different locks, i.e., skeleton keys. Thus, rather than the two maps (A and A') being isomorphic, the concept of fit suggests only that the therapist's map of the intervention somehow fits within the constraints of the problem (complaint plus potential solutions) as constructed by the therapist and client.

This suggests that we had been doing our work backwards! We had been looking at "Problems: Complaints and how to solve them," while the concept of fit suggests rather that we need to look at "solutions and how they work." And we do not need to know how a particular lock (complaint) is constructed in order to find a skeleton key-like intervention that fits in such a way that it opens the door to a "better," more satisfactory future for the client. Therefore, things go wrong when the therapist has not developed a fit between the problem he and the client have constructed and the intervention that he, the therapist, has constructed. In practice, fit seems to be achieved when the therapist and the client have constructed ways to know when the problem has been solved and the intervention can be seen to lead in those directions.

CONTINUING

We decided to end our report at this point, or, more accurately, pause in our reporting, because we expect to continue issuing reports from time to time. This is an arbitrary punctuation in an ongoing scenario. (Anyway, there are only so many pages allotted.) We have found it useful to reflect back on the road traveled, surprising to find where we are now, and exciting and also scarey to think about what we may find, or may build, around the next bend in the road.

Over the year in which we wrote this report our thinking changed, necessitating rewrites. Since we expect our clients to change and our client/team suprasystems to change, we needn't be surprised that we changed too. However, a year from now you might not hear a statement like this from us, because our thinking about change will change.

REFERENCES

Bateson, G. (1979). *Mind and Nature: A Necessary Unity.* New York: Dutton.

Berg, I. (1984). Obituary for resistance. *Family Therapy News.*

Dell, P. (1981). Some irreverent thoughts on paradox. *Family Process, 20*(1), 37–42.

Dell, P., & Goolishian, H. (1979). Order through fluctuation. Presented at A.X. Rice Institute, Houston, Texas.

de Shazer, S. (1975). Brief therapy: Two's company. *Family Process, 14*(1), 78–93.

de Shazer, S. (1978). Brief therapy with couples. *International Journal of Family Counseling, 6,* 17–30.

de Shazer, S. (1979). Brief therapy with families. *American Journal of Family Therapy, 7,* 83–95.

de Shazer, S. (1982). *Patterns of Brief Family Therapy: An Ecosystemic Approach*. New York: Guilford.

de Shazer, S., & Molnar, A. (1984). Four useful interventions in brief family therapy. *Journal of Marital and Family Therapy, 10* (3), 297–304.

Haley, J. (1963). *Strategies of Psychotherapy*. New York: Grune & Stratton.

Haley, J. (1967). Commentary on the Writings of Milton H. Erickson, M.D. In J. Haley (Ed.), *Advanced Techniques of Hypnosis and Therapy: Selected Papers of Milton H. Erickson, M.D.* New York: Grune & Stratton.

Heider, F. (1946). Attitudes and cognitive organization. *Journal of Psychology, 21* 107–112.

Kuhn, T. S. (1970). *The Structure of Scientific Revolutions* (2nd ed.). Chicago: University of Chicago Press.

Lipchik, E., & de Shazer, S. (1985). The purposeful interview. Unpublished manuscript.

Maruyama, M. (1963). The second cybernetics: Deviation-amplifying mutual causal processes. *American Scientist, 5,* 164–179.

Nunnally, E., & Berg, I. (1983). We tried to push the river. *The Journal of Strategic and Systemic Therapies, 2*(1), 63–68.

Papp, P. (1977). The family that had all the answers. In P. Papp (Ed.), *Family Therapy: Full Length Case Studies*. New York: Gardner Press.

Prigogine, I., Nicolis, G., & Babloyantz, A. (1972). Thermodynamics of evolution. *Physics Today, 23,* 11–23.

Selvini-Palazzoli, M., Boscolo, L., Cecchin, G., & Prata, G. (1978). *Paradox and Counterparadox*. New York: Aronson.

Selvini-Palazzoli, M., Boscolo, L., Cecchin, G., & Prata, G. (1980). Hypothesizing-circularity-neutrality: Three guidelines for the conductor of the session. *Family Process, 19* (1), 3–12.

Thom, R. (1975). *Structural Stability and Morphogenesis*. Reading: Benjamin/Cummings.

Watzlawick, P., Weakland, J., & Fisch, R. (1974). *Change: Principles of Problem Formation and Problem Resolution*. New York: Norton.

Weakland, J., Fisch, R., Watzlawick, P., & Bodin, A. (1974). Brief therapy: Focused problem resolution. *Family Process, 13,* 141–168.

Weiner-Davis, M. (1985). Another useful intervention in brief family therapy. Unpublished manuscript.

Wilden, A. (1980). *System and Structure* (2nd ed.). London: Tavistock.

Chapter 5

The Galveston Family Institute: Some Personal and Historical Perspectives

Harlene Anderson, Harold Goolishian,
George Pulliam, and Lee Winderman

The story of the Galveston Family Institute is, at its core, the evolution of a small group of clinicians ranging from therapists practicing traditional psychoanalytic work with families in a medical school psychiatric setting to systemic therapists practicing and researching a distinctive and still evolving form of clinical work and theory now associated with the Institute. Each of us, having entered into this process at different times and at different points in our professional development, brings a distinct perspective to the telling of this story, but we believe that our varying experiences lend a richness of description that would be lost or muted in a single voice.

At the same time, we are aware that many perspectives are missing. Others—colleagues, trainees, visitors, and friends—who participated in the 35-year overlapping journey of first, second, third, and fourth generation family therapists in the Galveston community would have still different stories to tell. The story involves the intertwining influences of theories, clinical practices, clients, therapists, trainees, administrators, community agencies, other institutions, and the broader family therapy field in shaping and reshaping family therapy (Note 1).

Geographically, Galveston is a barrier reef island in the Gulf of Mexico 50 miles from Houston. Intellectually, Galveston is an island as well. Its isolation has encouraged two contradictory tendencies bearing on the development of family therapy in our community: the first a tendency to withdraw and interact exclusively with an intimate group of colleagues, the second to reach

---

The authors of this chapter are listed alphabetically; authorship is equally shared.

out to gain the interactive stimulation necessary for intellectual growth. There can be little doubt that Galveston's isolation contributed a context for us and for our clients that in time influenced our decision to use time and distance as key elements in the new therapy approach we were developing.

PHASE I: LOOKING BACK – OUR MEDICAL SCHOOL HERITAGE

Family therapy in Galveston was pioneered at the University of Texas Medical Branch, a large medical center, in the school's Department of Neurology and Psychiatry. The treatment of choice was primarily hospitalization, combined with various physical and psychopharmacological therapies for the identified patient. Although one would not have expected family therapy to have flourished there, the department was the more immediate context for our growth and significantly influenced our development of the theory and practice of family therapy.

The medical school's referral base represented a wealth of difficult presenting problems and clients as well as a variety of socioeconomic backgrounds, cultural groups, ages, and geographic areas. Impoverished, multiproblem families, juvenile delinquents, chronic schizophrenics, and other difficult populations pushed us constantly to think about our work context and our clients' needs, impelling us constantly to revise theory and practice to make a fit with our clients' unique situations. The journey took us from an initial position grounded in a psychoanalytic, disease model of thinking to our current systems position based on an epistemological and cybernetic definition of psychotherapy.

We were challenged to deal with multiple systems and to work with multiple realities because our client sources (the inpatient units, outpatient clinics, physicians, administrators, community agencies, back-home mental health professionals, referral sources, and others) were varied and often continued to be involved in the client's treatment. We learned to think differently about the "ownership" of patients. Because our patients were the clients of the medical school, they were not our private clients.

This perspective stimulated our capacity to vary format, style and approach and lifted the economic constraints typical of private practice settings. We could have the freedom to think in terms of cotherapists and teams as concurrently responsible for treatment. This was first expressed in our abandonment of the traditional view of confidentiality and the private, closed context of therapy. The team became the therapist. Thus, early on, we were not limited to one active therapist in the therapy room with others relegated to inactive supervisory roles. Of course, the value of teams is well established now, but then these ideas about team practice represented a radical break with traditional psychotherapy methods.

The luxury of university salaries allowed us to use multiple therapists and consulting teams and to immerse ourselves in our collaborative work to a far greater extent than would have been possible had we developed out of a private practice model where income-earning needs would discourage collaboration. Team practice saved us from the isolation of private practice and provided the enrichment of peer stimulation. Our parent department was fully engaged in extensive training and clinical programs. These activities permitted us to be ignored. Thus, this benign neglect provided uninterrupted time and opportunity for the growth and expansion of our ideas and work. Companion divisions (child psychiatry, psychology, and community psychiatry) provided major support through access to clinical populations and students. As a result, our teams were free to work with the difficult cases in whatever fashion felt clinically useful.

We did not appreciate the advantages of this neglect until the family therapy program was challenged and shut down in the late 1970s when a change in department administration resulted in the implementation of a restrictive medical model. It seemed wise to move our effort, the "Family Study Project," outside of the university and the Galveston Family Institute was created to continue the journey unhampered.

The family therapy effort at Galveston originated in the early 1950s in a manner similar to the origins of family therapy in other geographic regions. There was dissatisfaction with the capacity of current psychoanalytic theory to formulate a basis for work with difficult populations. For us the initial pivotal population were delinquents — acting-out, troubled adolescents. There was a secondary interest in the application of psychotherapeutic techniques to the treatment of schizophrenia. Many of these client problems did not respond well to traditional treatment. As we later would discover, some of the psychodynamic concepts used to explain the genesis of psychopathology were "family" in nature (e.g., schizophrenogenic mother, multigenerational origins of schizophrenia, inadequate parenting, and symbiosis (Hill, 1955). These and similar concepts were part of the heritage that spawned the family therapy movement.

In an effort to recapture the history of this time, we will rely on a story passed on through the generations of family therapists in Galveston. As we tell the story we are reminded that mythologies often combine realities which alter reality. This recursion is labeled history.

According to the story, the Youth Development Project of the Department of Neurology and Psychiatry, University of Texas Medical Branch, was formed in 1952. A small group of clinicians working on the project and committed to work with adolescents were frustrated by the impossibility of using the traditional therapy approach with this difficult population primarily because of the belief that the adolescent's inability to form a transference neurosis prohibited ordinary treatment approaches (Note 2). At this time the staff functioned in a traditional, interdisciplinary child guidance model. The psychiatrist or psychologist saw the child and the social worker saw the parents (usually the mother). Confidentiality was a strong theoretical and ethical issue because of professional and theoretical beliefs. Dialogue between disciplines was difficult. Consequently, to the extent that the clinicians communicated, they did so through charts and weekly case staffings at which each therapist reported to the others the progress of their clients.

The staff's dilemma intensified in these conferences as each therapist, in discussing the therapeutic progress of his/her client, described what seemed to be a different family, different family dynamics, different etiologies, different problem definitions, and different treatment strategies for the same identified patient.

Some therapists became painfully aware of what seemed to be a pattern: Many problems in treatment were attributed implicitly (at times explicitly) to colleagues' inability to work effectively with clients. After some time it appeared that the interaction of the members of the therapy team took the same form, or carried the same theme, as the core family struggle. It was as if the therapists had inherited or had come to reflect the family fight. This disturbing and powerful observation was a major impetus in the group's movement toward thinking about family systems and treatment systems, as well as about therapy systems encompassing both family and therapists.

These early understandings of the identified patient, family members, and therapy had stimulated the clinical group to think about systems rather than just about individuals and individual characteristics, although there was an absence of adequate conceptual tools for a systemic description. Differences in explanations of "change" and "no change" in families had led fortuitously to early thoughts and questions about therapist systems, as well as about the client systems. Thus began the group's questioning and building of ideas, theory, and practice.

In these early efforts, the staff invited family members to therapy to serve only as informants about the identified patient. Staff relied on observation and experience to guide their work since a vacuum in theory existed. In attempts to find justification for their changing observations and clinical practice, the group members read and re-read the works of Adler and Sullivan. In this early phase, the staff observed that client change was enhanced by two conditions: 1) Families in crisis, in a state of disequilibrium, were more amenable to change, and 2) adolescent development offered natural access to rapid therapeutic change. They also observed that with the momentum of adolescent growth, change could occur in a brief period of time and with minimum intervention. It was also noted that traditional treatment was often hampered by the obstacles of time, distance, and economics. Out of these novel observations and premises evolved a therapy that was designed to turn these handicaps into advantages, a therapy that focused on a sustained interest in brief therapies.

PHASE II: MULTIPLE IMPACT THERAPY

The Youth Development Project and the group's attendant struggles gave rise to Multiple Impact Therapy. The Multiple Impact Therapy Research Project began in Galveston in 1955 (Note 3). An interdisciplinary team collaborated in a quest for more fruitful ways to work with troubled adolescents who had been diagnosed as schizophrenic, neurotic, and personality disordered and with their families. The team's efforts evolved into a brief, problem-focused model called Multiple Impact Therapy (MIT). MIT was an innovative model in which multiple therapists and consultants worked with the adolescent, the family, and any other system relevant to the problem. Over time, the participants in this project included Robert MacGregor, Alberto Serrano, Agnes Ritchie, Eugene McDanald, Franklin Schuster, Harold Goolishian, and numerous staff, trainees, and visitors during the life of the project (Note 4).

Three major theoretical assumptions evolved from this seminal work:

1. "Recognizable patterns of parental interaction are apt to produce and maintain in dynamic equilibrium specific forms of developmental arrest in offspring which issue in various types of behavioral maladjustment in adolescence" (MacGregor, Ritchie, Serrano, Schuster, McDanald, & Goolishian, 1964, p. xvi).

2. "Certain types of interaction of the team with itself and the family in crisis may serve as model behavior with which the family may identify in its problem-solving efforts" (MacGregor et al., 1964, p. xvi).

3. "Certain messages of respect from the team to the family concerning the family's predicament and capacity for change may have favorable impact on the family's self-evaluative and self-revisory functions (family self-rehabilitative processes)" (MacGregor et al., 1964, p. xvii).

To operationalize these assumptions, teams were formed to work with whole families as well as relevant referring professionals such as school and social agency staff. Helping professionals currently involved or likely to become involved with the family were considered critical to the success of the therapy. The multidisciplinary teams met with the family and these relevant others over a two-to-three day period, using as many hours as needed, plus a follow-up six weeks later for one-half day. This agenda constituted the entire therapy. The team used a consultant to observe the proceedings from behind a one-way mirror and to intervene primarily at the team level through numerous scheduled and spontaneous team conferences initiated by either the consultant or any member of the active therapy team. The consultant could view from multiple rooms in the case of simultaneous interviews.

An important premise of this early work was that therapy should be an evolutionary process, blending therapist, team, and family data in a manner tailored to the particular family and problem. The group designed a structured format to guide the therapy toward this end by meeting with the consultant in a "briefing session" to familiarize themselves with the case material, to formulate an opinion, and to plan the initial interview. Next the team met with the whole family and relevant others to work toward the objectives agreed upon in the briefing session, while the consultant observed the meeting behind a one-way mirror. This meeting was followed by a team-consultant conference to review the family session and to plan the next step.

At this point, individual team members typically met concurrently with subsystems such as individual family members, parents, siblings, or community members. Later sessions included either the whole family, combinations of its members, or individual members. Team members were free to participate in any interview. Gregory Bateson, who was a consultant to the project, described these serial overlapping interviews as "crossmonitoring" (MacGregor et al., 1964, p. 191). Each step in therapy (for example, whom to see) evolved out of the team/consultant conferences and was based on the teams' decisions about intermediary objectives and overall goals, strategies for reaching those objectives and goals, and assessments of the family's response to the therapy.

The team always prefaced MIT's with an initial formulation, now more popularly known as a hypothesis (Selvini-Palazzoli, Boscolo, Cecchin & Prata, 1980). They continually refined and changed their original formulations (as well as strategies and goals) based on the feedback from the family and its members. As with current systemic thought, the team was "more interested in having the family entertain the idea that there are solutions than in advancing any particular remedy" (MacGregor et al., 1964, p. 188). Although the team considered all of their work as a continuous intervention, more explicit interventions were made in the form of "homework assignments" given at the lunch breaks and the end of each day. They carefully designed assignments for the end of the last day to be carried back to the home situation.

Families were understood in traditional terms: the father as the provider and leader of the household, the mother as the nurturing one, and the children each with their own responsibilities and boundaries based on age and sex. The primary therapeutic effort was to reestablish clear boundaries between the various generations within the family and to put the authority for the family back in the parents' hands, therefore establishing a healthier homeostasis or family balance.

Many strategies and techniques were used to accomplish these goals. Among these strategies and techniques were confrontation and interpretation of various family members' behaviors, along with attempts to facilitate communication between various family members. There was also direct asking for changes of behavior. In addition, the team attempted to interrupt the "unhealthy family" patterns by participating in family communications in a way that modeled "healthy" interpersonal interaction. There were always homework assignments during the breaks at mealtime and overnight for the family. Often the team would meet for an hour trying to plan a homework assignment that would precisely fit the dynamics they saw operating. The research project was a resounding success. Follow-up at six and 18 months revealed major change in over 75 percent of the adolescents and their families.

Interestingly, the original MIT work resembles, and is in some respects a forerunner to, what is today recognized as systemic family therapy. Families were viewed as possessing the capacity for change, as capable of finding the solutions for their problems. Great effort was devoted to what the MIT team called "protecting family members from losing face." In other words, the family's and its individual members' realities were respected. The teams wanted to minimize the opportunity for resistance to develop. Although they did not describe it as such at the time, they were working from a premise that resistance is an interactional phenomenon. There was an emphasis on what today is known as positive connotation. Therapy was considered an evolving process and a converging of family/therapist's strengths. The therapy process was also quite circular in that there was a continuing recalibration of therapist, consultant, and team behavior in response to the family as well as to each other.

Attention was paid to both team and family process. Therapist teams and consultants were viewed as useful for treating families and training therapists. In addition, the consultant's interventions were primarily at the team level, as in the Milan method (Selvini-Palazzoli et al., 1978). Thus, the role of the consultant was to introduce information and to perturb at the team level, creating context for therapist flexibility and creativity.

The MIT team was not yet thinking of differences (multiple views of team or family) in the manner described by Bateson (1979) as "news of a difference," but rather as a way of modeling "healthy differences" for the families. From a theoretical perspective, the group theorized that a developmental approach was sufficient to explain "family pathology." In general terms, the research team concluded that a child was at risk for developmental arrest and later symptom dysfunction if, at any time in the child's development, one or another of the parents related to the child in a fashion more appropriate to the adult relationship. The nature of the pathology was thought to be related to the developmental stage in which the generational violation occurred. This led to the major thrust of the MIT treatment — to restore family boundaries.

The similarities between this position and later structural family therapy are quite obvious. However, the Galveston group were not comfortable for long with organizational and structural descriptions of families and were to move beyond them as they wrestled with their dissatisfactions.

Beyond MIT

Some of the important outcomes of the MIT work were the formation of nontraditional psychotherapeutic formats. A discontinuous change had occurred in our thinking that made it impossible to return to the usual methods of clinical practice and theory. The customary issues of confidentiality in therapist-client relationship were altered by the opening up of the therapeutic process through the use of one-way mirrors, teams, and electronic equipment. The use of clinical dialogue between team members with the family observing, the flexible management of the frequency and duration of appointments, and the handling of differing opinions in a collaborative, as opposed to a hierarchical, supervisory fashion were all aspects which opened treatment to examination and change. Concepts from individual psychology and psychodynamic theory were no longer adequate to inform our work. A more responsive paradigm was demanded to understand the process more richly. The final, and most important, outcome of the MIT work was the shift into family systems thinking.

With the completion of the research project, the MIT team brought together for this work went separate ways. Agnes Ritchie and Harry Goolishian remained in Galveston at the University of Texas Medical Branch, where Agnes did therapy and supervised MITs. Goolishian struck out, more or less on his own, to search for new ways to understand, practice, and promote family therapy and interest people in the family approach (Note 5). When one considers that this was a very traditional Department of Psychiatry at a university hospital, it is amazing that the MIT project was even initiated, let alone completed.

In 1969 George Pulliam, who had a strong interest in innovative treatment techniques, joined the Division of Child and Adolescent Psychiatry. It was only natural that he and Goolishian recognized their kinship and quickly joined efforts. MITs were frequently conducted and organized as training events. During this time, Goolishian organized a family therapy seminar which he taught with Cameron McKinley and Agnes Ritchie. The seminar was a review of all the theoretical positions available at that time. Major emphasis was placed on the work of Bowen, Minuchin, Whitaker, Haley, Jackson, Watzlawick, and particularly *The Pragmatics of Human Communication* (Watzlawick, Beavin & Jackson, 1967). It should be noted that at no time during this period was training in family therapy given administrative recognition.

Concurrently, videotaping was used as a major tool for supervision with trainees. Gene Hornsby, the new Director of Child and Adolescent Psychiatry, solidly supported the use of videotape in supervision and practice. Although presentations were made of MIT work as early as 1957, the expanded use of videotaping increased teaching efforts outside the medical school. The first major videotape presentation was at an all-day workshop in Washington, D.C. at the American Orthopsychiatric Conference in the spring of 1971. The response from the workshop participants to actually seeing the MIT work was astonishing. The interest in family therapy was enthusiastic.

Shortly after this workshop, Peggy Sheely and George Pulliam participated in the seminar that Harry Goolishian was teaching and an important team was formed. Outside the seminar, the three of them studied the available literature, saw families together as cotherapists, and consulted with one another. The following spring they presented a workshop in Detroit, Michigan at the American Orthopsychiatric Conference on failures in family therapy which was an overwhelming success.

From that point until approximately 1974 there was a period of rapid growth and excitement for both teaching and learning family therapy from many different perspectives. Peggy Sheely, Harry Goolishian, and George Pulliam became the central figures in the family therapy training arena; they taught a family therapy seminar together which met twice weekly (one hour for seminar, one hour for practice). Workshops were conducted at national, regional, and state conferences; family therapy had become legitimate for the mental health profession. This was a period of high enthusiasm, camaraderie, and taking on the establishment in mental health, particularly those who were schooled in analytic and traditional points of view. Workshops were well attended and often resulted in great debates and discussions which continued formally and informally throughout the conference.

The workshops became an important context for our evolving ideas. We were energized by them, like a runner's high. This continuous process of debate, argument, and disbelief forged the shaping and clarification of our ideas. During this period we began to think of theory as an ever-evolving map; reality for us became fluid.

A Search for Theory

We did not continue to practice MIT solely in its original form. As Harry said then — and continues to say now — "Never be so in love with your theory that you carve it in stone." Instead, we continued to question and elaborate our current theory and clinical practice. To this end we read everything we could. When Ferber's *The Book of Family Therapy* (1972) was published along with the early writings of Auerswald (1968, 1971) and Hoffman (1971), we recognized a kinship with an ecological epistemology and a systems-oriented work. When Minuchin's book *Families and Family Therapy* (1974) came out, it was for a time one of our primary teaching texts.

It is interesting to note the recursiveness of the field. In 1958 the MIT research team consulted for a week with Minuchin and the staff at the Wiltwick School. Minuchin adopted variations of the MIT family therapy work as a primary tool for treating adolescent delinquents (MacGregor et al., 1964, p. 245). Simultaneously, we started to reread *Pragmatics of Human Communication* (Watzlawick et al., 1967) and to reread and rediscover Don Jackson's early writings (Jackson, 1957, 1960, 1961, 1974a, 1974b). We met one night a week for a year with a philosopher to study the logic behind the concepts contained in the *Pragmatics of Human Communication* (Note 6). In addition, we read everything we could lay our hands on and sought out personal contact with those therapists whose work either sounded similar to ours or whose theory and questions intrigued us. If we could not get them to come to Galveston, we went to them (Note 7).

In 1974, George Pulliam eased from the workshop circuit but continued to contribute to the training program; Peggy Sheely elected to pursue private practice in Houston; and Harry, with his unlimited and inexhaustible energy, continued to do workshops and to teach. By this time Paul Dell, who had been at the medical school as a psychology intern and stayed to do a family therapy fellowship, joined the faculty. Harlene Anderson, who had been at the University for a while and had participated in the early family movement, became a key member of the inner group. Harry, George, Harlene, and Paul became the core group and were a stable working team for the next six years. They continued and expanded the training at the medical school. Harry and Harlene began to work together doing workshops, even more training, and agency consultation (Note 8). They were particularly interested in behaving as trainers in a manner that reflected their theory. About this time, although all of us were interested in theory, Paul Dell began to put some papers together which he later published (1978, 1980). Paul was the first of the Galveston group since the original MIT group to put theory on paper.

In the mid-1970s we started our own faculty Family Therapy Study Project on Friday afternoons to practice and to think. At that time our clinical work was informed by an amalgamation of ideas from the MIT work, Bowen's family of origin work, Minuchin's structural family therapy, Haley's strategic therapy, MRI's interactional therapy, Bateson's cybernetic thinking, Whitaker's work, and Hoffman's writings. This was a time of tremendous debate and some stress within the group. Our ideas were different and we had to work out the boundaries of our responsibilities when working together. The glue that held us together was our general dissatisfaction with the theoretical underpinnings of many of these theoretical positions. In many ways the current art of family therapy still seemed too traditional for us.

We had evolved a clinical style which maximized the flow of information and creativity. Within the team, there were no hierarchical distinctions between the members, there was no single right answer to any question, and there was no one correct intervention to any clinical problem. The clinical style emphasized freedom of thought and action. Consultants (team members) behind the one-way mirror were free to consult (call in or enter the therapy room) in any manner they felt appropriate. Likewise, the therapist-in-the-room could process the consultation to the therapy in any manner he/she felt appropriate. We remember an interesting session when George Pulliam was the therapist and Paul Dell was the consultant. With consultative enthusiasm, Paul repeatedly interrupted the therapy session in an attempt to get the reluctant George to change his strategy. With good humor and a conviction that Paul misunderstood the requisite intervention, George defended his position and the sanctity of the therapy by unplugging the phone and locking the door. Recursively and persistently, Paul responded by knocking on the one-way mirror and talking loudly through the mirror.

This period (1975 to 1979) was a productive one. We continued to teach, to practice, and to understand and explain our work. This was a time when we were struggling with the concepts of homeostasis, positive and negative feedback, and the second cybernetics. The writings of Speer (1970), Weakland, Fisch, Watzlawick, and Bodin (1974), Watzlawick, Weakland, and Fisch (1974), and Hoffman (1971) seemed to offer hope for relief from the constraints of homeostasis and negative feedback as explanations for the dynamics of families. Harry, who always had provocative ideas for bumper stickers, suggested one that read "Outlaw Homeostasis."

Two events significantly influenced the direction of our thinking. In 1977 we learned of the work that had earned Ilya Prigogine (1978) the Nobel prize for his study of the thermodynamics of non-equilibrium systems and we first learned of the theories of autopoesis and structure-determined systems as proposed by Humberto Maturana (1975) and Francisco Varela (1976) (Note 9). We read their work with great excitement and intuitively knew that their conceptions fit with the way we viewed families, systems, and change. Dell and Goolishian described this fit in their paper *Order Through Fluctuation: An Evolutionary Epistemology for Human Systems* (1981).

At the same time we were struggling with what we later called a co-created reality. This notion developed out of our efforts to describe the interaction between client and therapist and what we were doing clinically with trainees. One of the most difficult concepts for trainees to grasp was the discursive process between the client and the therapist in the room. The trainees always emphasized the end-product interventions and the reframes as the important aspects of the therapy while we as faculty struggled to emphasize the phenomena of moving within and with the client's reality. We soon began to

describe this process in terms of a co-created reality, a therapeutic reality —
that is, a reality that is co-constructed by client and therapist in which they
both function and share meaning. We soon realized that we were moving away
from understanding therapy as a series of strategic interventions or as the
therapist changing the client or the client's reality to a conclusion where the
only person in the room that the therapist changes is the therapist. We believed
then, as we do now, that it is the slow and careful development of a co-created
reality that provides the context for change.

Training

In the early 1970s, the primary clinical teaching format consisted of a faculty member behind the one-way mirror supervising a therapist (or cotherapists),
with a group of trainees observing the process but not participating in the
actual clinical work. The major format for student participation in clinical
work was as a member of a MIT team. Beginning in 1975, as an outgrowth
of the faculty Family Study Project, which involved Anderson, Dell, Goolishian, and Pulliam, a new training format evolved consisting of clinical teams
whose members (faculty and trainees) actively collaborated as equals in the
clinical work (Note 10). These clinical teams usually consisted of six to eight
trainees and two faculty members. Trainees were assigned to a team for the
academic year; they saw families in front of the mirror, while other team
members consulted from behind the mirror. Teams always had planning sessions prior to seeing the cases and at least one break midway in which the
course of the session was discussed and an intervention strategy planned
(usually in the language of a "homework assignment"). The teams always had
an end-of-session conference to discuss the session and to make predictions
(hypotheses) about how the family might respond to the session and the
homework assignment.

These trainees were graduate and postgraduate psychology and social work
students, psychiatric residents, and medical school faculty and staff representing psychiatry, psychology, social work, nursing, internal medicine, pastoral
counseling, pediatrics, and occupational therapy. Team membership was not
limited by discipline, theoretical orientation, or level of experience. All trainees worked side by side. This live clinical work was coupled with a weekly
one-hour didactic seminar.

The groups were structured in the following manner: At the beginning of
the year, faculty maintained distinct boundaries with regard to team leadership. Around mid-year, team members (trainees) began to rotate into the consultant position. The faculty's position on the team was consultative rather
than supervisory. The basic distinction was that supervision required trainee
compliance with supervisory direction and consultation was simply informa-

tion to be used in whatever way the recipient felt useful. The goals were to avoid the notion of a more correct view (a right way to do it), to maximize trainee creativity, and to engender a sense of competence in trainees. This change in position of a trainee to consultant (blurring of faculty/trainee boundaries) enhanced the collaboration between trainees and faculty.

Learning was always a reciprocal process between trainer and trainees. Trainees' questions and challenges provided a stimulus for different thinking and learning on all levels. The training groups were a context where faculty were forced to explain what they were doing clinically. As the faculty continued to modify their explanations of their work, their clinical practice changed as well. This recursive process also continued to modify teaching and training.

Even though as individuals we had a formal status (faculty and administrative positions) within the medical school, we did not have a formally recognized training program. We had a large, viable training activity which on paper did not exist. However, we enjoyed a tremendous informal status and became a very popular group with students and referral sources. This nonofficial status permitted us the flexibility to accept referrals from both within and outside of ordinary channels and to see clients quickly without being delayed by clinic procedures. Consequently, some of the most difficult cases in the medical school were referred to us — a full range of presenting problems, crises, and treatment failures, e.g. schizophrenia, incest, and child abuse. We were able to maintain our collaborative working relationships with community agencies, such as child protective services, juvenile probation, and adult probation, that started in the early MIT days. This position of flexibility and respect allowed us to develop a "stuck case" clinic where we became the last hope (a dangerous position) as we modestly consulted with other therapists, from both within and outside of the medical school, on their therapeutic impasses. This activity became one of our most successful programs and the "stuck case" clinic concept was adopted by several other institutions and university training programs.

PHASE III: THE INSTITUTE

The Galveston Family Institute was formed because we thought that we had something of value which we had a professional commitment to pursue and nurture. In 1977 several events occurred which resulted in the Galveston Family Institute becoming an incorporated reality. A new departmental chairman instituted a shift in departmental organization and administration. The downgrading of all nonpsychiatric therapies and teaching programs (such as family therapy) no longer provided the benign neglect so historically important to our flexibility and development. Our work within the confines of a medical university had become an increasing struggle. We found it difficult to continue to change our ideas and practice to meet the needs of our clinical work because of mounting pressures to meet the traditions of the medical institution — fitting clients to clinical programs.

Harlene Anderson soon left the medical school to steer the Institute and to direct its training programs. Harry was to retire within the next couple of years; Paul Dell was to move to the University of Houston for a year and then on to Virginia; and George Pulliam because of health problems in 1979 remained with the medical school but participated as Vice President of the Board of the Institute and as a clinical supervisor.

In 1978 we rented a loft in Galveston's historical Strand District and the doors of GFI were opened as a freestanding, nonprofit research, clinical and training institution. In retrospect, this move continued our 35-year tradition of creativity and risk. The founding Board of Directors were Harry Goolishian, George Pulliam, Harlene Anderson, and Paul Dell. Harlene Anderson and two postdoctoral fellows, Rob Horowitz and Lee Winderman, literally opened the doors with paint brushes in their hands. Lee, after a postdoctoral fellowship in Pediatrics and a second GFI postdoctoral year in family therapy, became a faculty member. Harry Goolishian continued to work fulltime at the medical school while simultaneously donating full-time work to the Institute — practicing, teaching, and installing one-way mirrors and sound equipment.

The Institute was organized on what had become a familiar and workable model for us, the university model. Faculty did not maintain private practices; money from contracts, clinical services, and training went to the Institute. Faculty and postdoctoral fellows were on full-time salaries. This structure provided multiple advantages that maximized the opportunity for colleague interaction in the clinical (cotherapists, consultants, teams) and training domains (team teaching). We considered these elements essential to the development of new ideas and treatment techniques.

We steered away from a private practice model because we believed that the "private ownership of clients" isolated therapists into their own separate practices, placed a focus on maximizing income, minimized colleague interaction, and lessened (or prevented) the open flow of information. This model has largely contributed to our ability to provide quality training and a high degree of flexibility in our clinical work. We could afford the luxury of spending several hours on a difficult case. We had the freedom to focus on developing methods for therapy without the concern, or the necessity, of maintaining individual clinical incomes.

The clients referred to us in the beginning remained similar to that of the medical school — that is, mostly chronic treatment failures. Our reputation for success with "stuck cases" had followed us. The training program followed the model developed in the medical school and continued our strong focus on the importance of interfacing theory with live clinical work. The clinical studies seminar met weekly for three hours; the externship met weekly for five hours; and the commuter program met one day a month for six hours. These programs have basically remained intact from that time until now.

The externship program has evolved into our major training track. It is usually comprised of 24 trainees (i.e. agency staff, private practice, graduate students). In this 10-month program, all trainees meet together for a one-hour didactic presentation and then form three teams with two faculty members for clinical practice where they work with Institute clients. In addition, we have a variety of other programs such as seminars on "Epistemology" and "Order Through Fluctuation," "Clinical Dialogue with Senior Faculty," and "Stuck Case Consultation Clinic."

From its inception, the Institute took a rigorous theoretical position that can best be described as a *cybernetic, systems-oriented, strategic, brief psychotherapy* (Note 11). Our clinical work and our training programs were exclusively based on that model. This position forged a context, a clinical/training reality, in which the faculty and fellows were able to take the theoretical premises of strategic and systemic therapy to their uttermost limits. As faculty, we continued our own self-referential learning, a recursive process in which we attempted to formulate theory based upon our experiences in therapy and then to use this theory to inform our clinical work. Also to this end, we learned from others in the field. We brought to the Houston-Galveston area such theoreticians and therapists as Laing, Weakland, Watzlawick, Hoffman, Patton, Keeney, Boscolo, Cecchin, Maturana, and Von Foerster.

The simultaneous evolution of theory and practice was a fundamental task of the Institute. Institute faculty formed a tight collegial community which increasingly focused on interactions with each other in terms of the development of theory and clinical technique. We were less concerned with the wider family therapy community in terms of the politics of establishing a training Institute. We refused to design a training program to fit the requirements of an accrediting agency since those very requirements themselves ran contrary to our beliefs in a non-eclectic approach and to our increasing questions about the very concept of family therapy.

Members of the Institute had a strong sense of mission with regards to impacting the field of psychotherapy and improving methods of treatment in a manner which contributed to more humane clinical work. We considered ourselves client advocates, even to the point of being accused of "missionary zeal." All of us were originally trained in traditional psychiatry, social work, and psychology and we knew firsthand the worst face of our own disciplines. In addition, we were all frustrated by the limits tradition, politics, and credentialing placed on our work.

In our training programs we rigorously maintained a systemic perspective.

We held to a philosophy that though there are other ways of thinking about therapy and other ways of doing therapy, Institute trainees were there to learn and practice therapy as we could best explain it. We were never eclectic. Our tightly structured theoretical framework provided a powerful context in which trainees were able to experience the shift from an individual objective focus on "curing" pathology to a systemic focus which emphasized dealing with relationships.

Trainees continually talked about a sense of confusion when they first encountered the world of systems and relationships and then a sense of "opening-up" which occurred when they began to view the world from this new context. The emotional power of this experience was validated by the feedback from part-time trainees in their evaluation of the Institute training. They frequently acknowledged that the Institute was the most powerful training experience that they had encountered in their training and professional growth and that it compelled them to begin to think about their own personal beliefs and theories, particularly the relationship to their clinical work. We created a tight, non-eclectic, constantly shifting ecology of ideas in which we were all forced to examine our view of the world in relationship to ourselves and to practice.

In the period between 1979 and 1982, as we gained skills in these new approaches, we often practiced on each other. We experimented in changing our positions and views in daily conversation with each other to gain skill in working within someone else's view. We talked in terms of developing an ability to increase the therapist's flexibility and an ability to move within another person's world as well as the therapist's own. Our motto was, "Never utter in therapy anything you would not be willing to change." We talked in terms of becoming clearer about one's own theory and making one's assumptions more explicit so that we would know when those were impinging upon the world of the client. A common statement we often made in training had to do with speaking the client's language (Watzlawick, Weakland, & Fisch, 1974). Much of the work of the MRI group, Hoffman, Keeney, Bateson, the Milan associates, and Maturana was reading material for our courses. Although we saw ourselves as related to this body of work, we did not try to duplicate it, but rather to draw upon it as we wrestled with alternative theory and explanation.

The Institute grew rapidly and our activities expanded from the Galveston home base to three additional offices in Houston. In addition to the training activities described above, we developed contracts to train public agency professionals around the state, such as child protective service workers, juvenile probation officers, women's shelter counselors, and community mental health center staff. We also maintain two full-time, postgraduate fellows and six to ten graduate interns each year. The clinical activities are as important as the training activities: Great numbers of clients are seen each year by Institute faculty, staff, and trainees.

CURRENT POSITION AND DIRECTION

We have identified some of the history and assumptions that inform our present clinical work and guide us in our training activities at the Galveston Family Institute. We will now elaborate those ideas that we consider most relevant to the present direction of our work and to the broader field. All are concepts that have evolved through 35 years of growth and change, and characterize the Institute and its activities.

Treatment Versus Growth

We make a basic distinction between treatment and growth in our work. Treatment entails a problem-focused definition and resolution, in as brief and impactful a manner as possible, of specific dilemmas which clients bring to therapists. Growth entails those therapeutic processes that are long-term in nature. It often involves a process of introspection and learning through which the quality of life might be improved. Our assumption is that most clients come to treatment for the resolution of specific problems they are presently struggling with in their daily lives.

Though this distinction is arbitrary, we believe that many difficulties in psychotherapy are due to the therapist's failure to make this very distinction when engaging clients in treatment. For example, when clients come to a therapist seeking the resolution of problems and they are placed in a therapeutic context emphasizing the lengthy examination of many issues which do not impinge upon the resolution of the problem they came to solve, they often feel misunderstood and thus appear resistant or unmotivated. We view treatment as a present-oriented, co-created process which actively involves both the client and the therapist. We emphasize a non-pathologizing view of the origin, maintenance, exacerbation, and resolution of problems.

Training

We maintain just as strict a position in our training as we do in our clinical work. We attempt to be very specific about what we teach and what we ask of Institute trainees. We want trainees to develop an internally consistent view of treatment and the world of therapy. We demand that trainees be familiar with the theoretical origins of the field; however, we are not eclectic in how we operate nor in what we teach. We are extremely task-oriented in our work and place little emphasis on group process. Trainees are not required to engage in therapy themselves.

Just as the problem defines the system to be treated, our shared Institute task defines the quality of our boundary structures and interpersonal relationships. There is a high degree of openness between trainees and staff. Hierarchical boundaries (degrees, experiences) which often separate trainees from each other and from faculty are punctuations we do not find useful. Training groups and teams are composed of trainees with varying experience levels and representing multiple disciplines. The initial distinction between faculty and trainee quickly dissolves from an emphasis on supervision to one of consultation. Faculty interact with trainees with the same consideration we give our clients — that is, we respect their views, their differences, and their skills. The informality regarding degrees and disciplines places students squarely in the position of facing their own level of skill and competence. They are not protected by their diplomas. In the final analysis, we place emphasis on competency; this competency becomes the highest ethic.

Teams

For us, "team" refers to our shared Institute task. A team is not necessarily a group of people who meet together on a regular basis. Nor do we limit our thinking to a team behind a one-way mirror. Rather, "team" is a conceptual tool that keeps our thinking and our therapy open. The concept is built into the very fabric of the context in which we work. Since there are no private clients (clients are all Institute clients), all activities are open to observation. At the Institute, all facilities have one-way mirrors or video equipment. At any time any member (faculty or trainee) of the Institute may observe and consult or request observation and consultation from any other Institute staff. The responsibility and accountability for our work resides with the entire group; thus, the Institute is the team. This concept differs markedly from the usual practice of a closed team that erects tight boundaries around its membership and work. We believe that this open concept of team makes therapy a more alive, active, and responsive process that in turn maximizes the co-evolution of information needed to create realities for change.

In this regard, a constructivist notion of reality has greatly influenced our work (Watzlawick, 1984). In the early years of the Institute, we did not have the philosophical tools to understand our position as constructivist. We talked of multiple realities instead. This view demands that we define problem definition and treatment as epistemological in nature and that we abandon notions of systems in need of rehabilitation or repair. That is, we must not only consider alternatives to the concept of the family as the system to be treated, but also develop alternatives to the concept of the therapist as an agent of change.

Therapist Positioning

The concept of therapist positioning is a central theoretical concept in the training and clinical work at GFI. By therapist position we mean those epistemological maps through which the therapist relates to and organizes client data. Therapist positioning is viewed as an active ongoing internal process for the therapist. We teach our trainees to first join with the client's view of the problem — in essence, to create a common starting point for the building of the linguistic momentum necessary for change. We emphasize the necessity for the therapist to "fit" or "match" the reality of the client and those other broader systems involved in the problem definition.

Earlier we had framed this in more general terms such as "to go with or move with resistance." We now describe it as a semantic dance through which a reality evolves that permits change and movement in the definition and, therefore, the disintegration of the problem. This is to say that we understand "therapist positioning" as more than "therapist neutrality." It is more than the therapist's trying to not take sides or to not have an investment in therapeutic outcome. Rather, it is respecting and working within all those views simultaneously.

To accomplish the difficult task of working within multiple views simultaneously, it is necessary for the therapist to continually change. To this end, we tell our trainees that the only person they can change in the therapy room is themselves. What changes within the therapist is the therapist's map (theory) of the client. Within the context of training, we punctuate therapy as first, the self-recursive process of therapists' changing their behavior in relation to their changing map of the client; and second, the therapist's continually changing behavior is feedback to the client.

Therapeutic change is conceptualized as a rapid, active process that is discontinuous in nature. To participate in such a process requires of the therapist continuous and strenuous scrutiny not only of the therapist's own map but also of the recursive quality of client feedback. To quote Harry, "The best clue you have to what you are doing is based on what the client is doing back." And, "You need to listen recursively; each question is a modification of the answer to the previous question." Thus, the therapy is more focused on the evolving reality in the therapy room as opposed to inventing and designing interventions.

Co-evolution of Reality

We communicate to our trainees the idea that therapy consists not only of going with the client's reality (therapist positioning), but also of the building of a new shared reality unique to the problem being worked on by the therapist and the client together—the creation of a changing therapeutic system. The narrative developed in therapy is a co-evolved reality created out of the dialogue between client and therapist.

This new co-evolving reality is central to change. We work towards evolving new domains of experience through the co-invention of new linguistic patterns as explanations for the problems for which clients come to therapy. Keeney (1984) and Keeney and Ross (1985) refer to a similar concept when they talk about the cybernetics of cybernetics. The Milan team's discussion of circular interviewing also elaborates this notion of a co-evolved reality (Selvini-Palazzoli et al., 1980), a reality lived in the therapy room in a manner different from the reality of the family at home. We place a strong emphasis on beginning this process with the client's reality. It is the reality of the client, not the reality of the therapist, that is basic to evolving a context in which problems and solutions may be thought of differently.

At the Institute we do not work with clients around issues which they do not acknowledge as a problem. We do not take the diagnoses of others and proceed to work with that reality as a problem definition. Therapeutic work that operates outside of the client's view of the problem violates the client's sense of his or her own experience and fails to appreciate the richness or adequacy of the client's view and competency for dealing with life.

Problem-Determined Systems Versus Family Systems

The concepts of family systems and family systems therapy are considered punctuations that unnecessarily limit the parameters of therapy and handicap the thought and action of clients and therapists. Instead, we believe that a shared problem and the ensuing differences with regard to desired outcomes are the distinctions which realize an interpersonal human system that mark the boundaries of the system to be treated. Thus, we do not define the treatment system in terms of social, cultural, biological, or political punctuations. In our view, systems (e.g., families) do not cause or make problems, on the contrary, problems are the driving force that form systems. Thus we define ourselves as training therapists to work with problem systems that may be an individual, a couple, a family, a work group, an organization, or any combination of individuals organized by a shared problem.

From its inception, the Institute has conceptualized problems as including non-family others in the treatment process (MacGregor et al., 1964; Goolishian and Anderson, 1981; Anderson and Goolishian, 1985). From this perspective, we have always conceptualized problem-maintaining interactions as not limited by the arbitrary and narrow focus of the family as the "natural" object of treatment. Our therapy has always blurred and crossed so called family-system boundaries.

Traditionally in therapy and consultation the target of treatment has always been defined in terms of social role and social organization. Therapy and consultation are usually done with individuals, families, social agencies, communities, and sometimes institutions. The fields of psychotherapy and consultation are alive with considerable debate over which of these social units is the appropriate target of treatment. Family therapists, group therapists, individual therapists, and even political activists have much to say regarding this issue. All consider their view of the appropriate target for treatment as a central and major distinction between their and other views.

Central to this debate over who should be seen is the implicit assumption that social role and social organization, in some objective way, are the basic structures through which we can understand and treat disturbed and problem behavior. Although the various therapies disagree on which is the appropriate social structure to consider when doing therapy, they all share the common belief that one or the other of the various social structures is the prime locus or cause of problems. To this extent, most treatment theories are similar in that they focus on repairing the defects in those social structures thought to be the prime locus and cause of the presented difficulty. If the social structure is in some way the "container" of the pathology or defect, then this very social structure must be modified or reorganized through a treatment process that brings about an appropriate change in social structure.

The questions that theorists who engage in this debate ask are not the questions that we ask. In contrast, we maintain that systems distinguished through social, cultural, or political structure are not the proper descriptors of the system to be treated. We propose that traditional social system theory is not an appropriate descriptor of the system to be treated nor the proper context from which to understand those problems for which people come to therapy. We would substitute the concept of a *problem-determined system* as the appropriate descriptor for the target of treatment. The central proposition is: *"Systems do not make problems—problems define or make systems."* It is the definition of a problem that marks the context and, therefore, the boundaries of the system to be treated. This distinction allows us to avoid the task of current psychotherapies, that is, to repair defective social structure in a manner determined by the therapist's theoretical description of health versus pathology.

The work of Maturana (1975) gave us a new vocabulary to explain how we determine who or what is the system that defines treatment, as well as what we do in therapy. In particular, his concept of "linguistic domain" provided us with a powerful explanatory tool. It became clear that we were dealing with "meaning systems" and that much of the work of therapy had to do with the exploration of these systems of meaning. This is true whether we work with individuals (self-referential problems) or broader systems (relational problems). These "meaning systems" form an "ecology of ideas" that determines who does what with whom and what is the "interactional system" that is relevant to the problem being defined. These meaning systems determine the very behaviors and problems for which consultation has been requested.

This view is similar, in some respects, to the construct psychology proposed by Kelly (1955). It is a view that allows the distinction of the system of treatment concern to be defined by those who share in the communication that defines a problem. This view avoids all the controversial issues implicit in our maintaining predetermined ideas about the objective nature of social systems; in doing so, limit treatment and consultation to those predefined and supposedly objective systems.

As therapists, we are most concerned with systems that communicate rather than with fixed, objective, and predetermined, social structures. These communicating systems are complex, open, and in a constant state of evolutionary change. They are, in fact, an "ecology of ideas" that may be described as the shared cognitive and linguistic material out of which we derive meaning and create realities. In our view it is the definition of a problem in a communicating or cognitive-linguistic system that defines who must interact relevant to the problem. It is the communicated beliefs about a problem that define not only what must be changed, but who are the actors in this drama of struggle and change that we call therapy. All individuals actively involved in this communicated interaction form the membership of what we call the *problem-determined system*.

The core feature of a *problem-determined system* is alarmed objection or concern by an observer to what a significant person is doing, saying, or thinking. The person or situation complained about may be the observer or it may be someone else. The distinctions that an observer makes in response to what a significant person does, says, or thinks are the actions that mark and contribute to a *problem-determined system*. The contributions of the observer and the observed, the "ecology of ideas," constitute the membership, the realities, of the communicating system to be considered for treatment.

Membership in these communicating, *problem-determined systems* may overlap many different social roles and structures. Problem systems may be formed through communications based on relationships of loyalty and kinship. They may be formed through communications based on legislative mandate. They may be formed through communications based on accidental or chance relationships or they may be formed through any combination of the above. A *problem-determined system* may be smaller or larger than a family, individual or group. It is not distinguished by an arbitrary, ordinary social organization or role definition such as family. Rather, the system involves all those who communicatively interact around a common cognitive idea that has been mutually defined as a problem or something in need of change.

In assuming that a treatment system is no more than a problem-determined, cognitive-linguistic system, then the goals of treatment are set by those who communicatively interact around the problem definition. They themselves determine the system to be treated and for what. The challenge of therapy is to produce a context in which the concerned membership of a *problem-determined system* can think and talk of their shared problems differently. Through this process, change in therapy becomes the disintegration of the system bounded by a communicated problem definition. Communicative problem interaction can no longer exist if its cognitive-linguistic or language base changes. The goal of therapy is simply to provide a context wherein the actors in the *problem-determined system* can think and talk about the problem differently. It is the change in problem definition and related communication that produces a changed system, since communicative interaction must now be different.

Within this view the central concept is that problems do not exist in objective social structure but that problems exist only in language. Through language we can, and do, involve others in problems and this languaging around a problem defines those systems with which we work. The concept of a *problem-determined system* requires us to include in the treatment system all those who participate in languaging around a problem and thus all those who are relevant to a problem.

This view challenges much of what is sacred in the field. It is not an easy task to relinquish the use of psychological and social mechanisms, structures, and processes as explanatory concepts for our work. The proposition that problems exist only in language and communication forces us to challenge the validity of concepts such as individual therapy and family therapy and to substitute a definition of a treatment system that is not bounded by social role and function concepts.

Further, we are forced to develop concepts and practices that are epistemological and constructivist in nature. Once we define the object of treatment as only one of the multiple realities existent in the communicated world we call reality, we can no longer hold on to the notions of objective social role, structure, and function as the basis for understanding problem behavior. To fully grasp the extent of this challenge, it should be remembered that concepts of family and other social role concepts are part of the very traditions of the field and are a part of the economic and political fabric of our universities and professional organizations.

The concept of the *problem-determined system* challenges the data-driven or "objective" concepts of family, family therapy, health, and pathology, and places therapy squarely in the realm of human relationships, communication, and language. We work and live in a communicated reality and the systems we work with are determined by communication, not by social role. Meaning and knowledge in general, and thus in therapy also, are expressions of simple social exchange and communication. The systems we are concerned with can be distinguished only by a communicative process and this is what we refer to as the *problem-determined system*.

In the end, however, we are forced to remember the sobering remarks of Nietzsche who said, " . . . in the end we experience only ourselves" (Kaufman, 1954).

EPILOGUE

Who we are and what we have done are difficult to flatten onto the pages of this chapter. Like any group who have worked together intensively over long periods of time, our similarities and differences, our affections and disaffections, our loyalties and infidelities have all somehow enriched that which has driven us and kept us connected across time and distance.

We all have a driving intellectual curiosity which refuses to be bounded by professional constraints or social convention. We each have a strong sensitivity to social justice and equity which informs our work as theoreticians and therapists. We each have experienced alienation in the face of theoretical conformity and rigid professional dogma. We each value the importance of colleagueship and professional dialogue as a vehicle not only for our group task and work with clients, but also for our own personal development. Most of all we seem to possess a restlessness which is satisfied only through the adventure we find in the continued change and variation in our work and thinking. Sometimes we think of our journey as a kind of anabasis, where the chief foe was our own thinking.

Our journey began during those exciting times when we participated in the invention of family therapy. We now find ourselves seriously questioning the integrity of the concept of family therapy itself. Sometimes when we think of what we do and what we have done, we can only smile, shake our heads, and think of these closing lines . . .

> I see narrow orders, limited tightness, but will
> not run to that easy victory:
> > still around the loser, wider forces work:
> > I will try
> to fasten into order enlarging grasps of disorder, widening
>
> scope, but enjoying the freedom that
> Scope eludes my grasp, that there is no finality of vision,
> that I have perceived nothing completely,
> > that tomorrow a new walk is a new walk.

Corson's Inlet
A. R. Ammons (1977)

NOTES

1. We acknowledge that many people (in the Department of Psychiatry and Neurology and the Department of Pediatrics) too numerous to mention were involved in the evolution of this process and that they may have differing realities. Limitations of space and failing memory prevent their inclusion. We apologize for these omissions.
2. This group consisted of Harry Goolishian, Grace Jameson, Brook Mullins, and Eugene Mc-Danald.
3. This seminal work is described in the publication *Multiple Impact Therapy with Families* (MacGregor et al., 1964) and in several articles authored by members of the team (Goolishian, 1962). The work was initially supported by the Hogg Foundation for Mental Health and later funded through an NIMH, Mental Health Project Grant.
4. Bob MacGregor currently consults on team-family methods and MIT in Chicago; Agnes Ritchie, who practiced and taught until she was in her seventies, is deceased; Al Serrano practices and teaches at the University of Texas in San Antonio, Texas; Frank Schuster is in private practice in El Paso, Texas; Eugene McDanald is in private practice and a clinical teacher in Galveston; and Harry Goolishian is still carrying on multiple full-time jobs, one of which is the Executive Director of the Galveston Family Institute.
5. Although several people played major roles in the development of family therapy in Galveston, Harry Goolishian can be given the most credit for generating new ideas and creating an esprit de corps which was necessary to keep the family movement alive and growing. He has been the ever-present catalyst for change. His lust for knowledge, his uncanny creativity, and his unequaled personal energy combined to provide the triggering ingredients for an extraordinary context for change in what for others could have been a formidable environment. (Harry was the only author who voted against the inclusion of this footnote.)
6. The philosopher was Ed Erde, Department of Medical Humanities, University of Texas Medical Branch, Galveston, Texas.
7. In pursuit of understanding MRI's work, some of us flew to Chicago to hear Paul Watzlawick and John Weakland and several of us went to MRI. We have been significantly energized and influenced by their work. We went to see Bateson. We invited Carl Whitaker, Lynn Hoffman, and John Weakland to Galveston to discuss their theories and try to understand their thinking. Goolishian and Pulliam went to New York to visit with Lynn Hoffman for a day and listen to her ideas about the book which she was developing. They also visited with Peggy Papp to discuss a brief therapy project at Ackerman Institute which sounded similar to our own work. When we heard that a man named Brad Keeney had some ideas and questions similar to ours, we wasted no time and flew to meet with him in the Kansas City airport.
8. The consultation and training at the Hope Center for Youth have led to a continued and fruitful relationship with shared faculty, space and mutual support. Hope Center staff, Harriet Roberts and Phil Torti, are central in the Institute's endeavors.
9. Paul Dell first met Maturana at the Naropa Institute in Colorado and excitedly reported on his ideas to the Family Therapy Study Project on his return. Harry, George, and Harlene went to The Center for Statistical Mechanics and Thermodynamics at the University of Texas in Austin to visit with Prigogene's colleagues to try to understand their theory and what impact it could have on the social systems with whom we were working.
10. Daniel Creson and Israela Meyerstein also participated in the initial phase of the Family Therapy Study Project.
11. We have always found it difficult to find a label for our work because the field has multiple meanings for each label and our work seems always to be changing. By brief we mean the total amount of time a therapy takes, by strategic we mean planned, and by systemic we mean cybernetic. We sometimes refer to our work as interactional and "problem-determined system" therapy.

REFERENCES

Ammons, A. R. (1977). *The Selected Poems 1951–1977.* New York: W. W. Norton.
Anderson, H. (1984). The new epistemology in family therapy: implications for training family therapists. Doctoral Dissertation. University Microfilms Pub. No. 85-00,784.

Anderson, H., & Goolishian, H. (1985). Systems consultation to agencies dealing with domestic violence. In L. Wynne, S. McDaniel, & T. Weber (Eds.), *The Family Therapist as Consultant*. New York: Guilford.

Auerswald, E. H. (1968). Interdisciplinary versus ecological approach. *Family Process, 7*, 202–215.

Auerswald, E. H. (1971). Change and the ecological perspective. *Family Process, 10*, 263–280.

Bateson, G. (1979). *Mind and Nature: A Necessary Unity*. New York: Bantam.

Dell, P. F. (1978). The angel of doom. *Voices, 14*, 29–30.

Dell, P. F. (1980). The Hopi family therapist and the Aristotelian parents. *Journal of Marital and Family Therapy, 6*, 123–130.

Dell, P. F., & Goolishian, H. (1981). Order through fluctuation: An evolutionary epistemology for human systems. *Australian Journal of Family Therapy, 2*, 175–184.

Ferber, A., Mendlesohn, M., & Napier, A. (Eds.). (1972). *The Book of Family Therapy*. New York: Aronson.

Goolishian, H. (1962). A brief therapy program for disturbed adolescents. *American Journal of Orthopsychiatry, 62*.

Goolishian, H., & Anderson, H. (1981). Including non-blood related persons in treatment: Who is the family to be treated? In A. Gurman (Ed.), *Questions and Answers in the Practice of Family Therapy*. New York: Brunner/Mazel.

Hill, L. B. (1955). *Psychotherapeutic Intervention in Schizophrenia*. Chicago: University of Chicago Press.

Hoffman, L. (1971). Deviation amplifying processes in natural groups. In J. Haley (Ed.), *Changing Families: A Family Therapy Reader*. New York: Grune & Stratton.

Hoffman, L., & Long, L. (1969). A systems dilemma. *Family Process, 8*, 211–234.

Jackson, D. D. (1957). The question of family homeostasis. *The Psychiatric Quarterly Supplement, 31*, 79–80.

Jackson, D. D. (Ed.). (1960). *The Etiology of Schizophrenia*. New York: Basic Books.

Jackson, D. D. (1961). Interactional psychotherapy. In M. I. Stein (Ed.), *Contemporary Psychotherapies*. New York: Free Press of Glencoe.

Jackson, D. D. (Ed.). (1974a). *Communication, Family, and Marriage*. (Human Communication Vol. 1). Palo Alto: Science and Behavior Books.

Jackson, D. D. (Ed.). (1974b). *Communication, Family, and Marriage*. (Human Communication Vol. 2). Palo Alto: Science and Behavior Books.

Kaufman, W. (1954). *The Portable Nietzsche*. New York: Viking Press.

Keeney, B. P. (1984). *Aesthetics of Change*. New York: Guilford Press.

Keeney, B. P., & Ross, J. M. (1985). *Mind in Therapy*. New York: Basic Books.

Kelly, G. A. (1955). *The Psychology of Personal Constructs*, Vols. 1 & 2. New York: Norton.

MacGregor, R., Ritchie, A., Serrano, A., Schuster, F., McDanald, E., & Goolishian, H. (1964). *Multiple Impact Therapy with Families*. New York: McGraw-Hill.

Maturana, H. (1975). The organization of the living: A theory of the living organization. *International Journal of Man-Machine Studies, 7*, 313–332.

Minuchin, S. (1974). *Families and Family Therapy*. Cambridge, MA: Harvard University Press.

Prigogine, I. (1978). Time, structure, and fluctuations. *Science, 201*, 777–795.

Selvini-Palazzoli, M., Boscolo, L., Cecchin, G., & Prata, G. (1978). *Paradox and Counterparadox*. New York: Jason Aronson.

Selvini-Palazzoli, M., Boscolo, L., Cecchin, G., & Prata, G. (1980). Hypothesizing, circularity and neutrality: Three guidelines for the conductor of the session. *Family Process, 19*, 3–12.

Speer, D. C. (1970). Family systems: Morphostasis or morphogenesis, or is homeostasis enough? *Family Process, 9*, 259–278.

Varela, F. (1976). Not one, not two. *Co-evolution Quarterly, 10*, 62–67.

Watzlawick, P. (Ed.). (1984). *The Invented Reality: How Do We Know What We Believe We Know? (Contributions to Constructivism)*. New York: W. W. Norton.

Watzlawick, P., Beavin, J. H., & Jackson, D. D. (1967). *Pragmatics of Human Communication*. New York: W. W. Norton.

Watzlawick, P., Weakland, J., & Fisch, R. (1974). *Change: Principles of Problem Resolution*. New York: W. W. Norton.

Weakland, J., Fisch, R., Watzlawick, P., & Bodin, A. (1974). A brief therapy: Focused problem resolution. *Family Process, 13*, 141–168.

Section II

Expanding the Models

Chapter 6

Integrating System-Based Therapies: Similarities, Differences, and Some Critical Questions

J. Scott Fraser

Structural, Strategic, and Systemic approaches to family therapy have often been grouped together under the heading of Systems Based Approaches (Gurman & Kniskern, 1981). This classification is reasonable, considering that each approach itself claims to be based in General Systems Theory concepts, each describes problems in relation to current system transactions, and each attempts to facilitate change through altering system interaction. However, a closer look at both theory and practice among these views has not only raised questions about their similarity, but also raised a number of more fundamental questions for family therapy in general.

This chapter will be divided into four sections. The first section will address the general bases for similarity or integration among these views. The second section will then discuss dissimilarities, or bases for differentiation, which have been described. The third will turn to some of the critical questions in both theory and practice which have arisen from these attempts to integrate and differentiate among the approaches. Finally, the last section, *The State of the Art,* will note a number of preliminary attempts at resolving some of these issues with several limited metatheories.

For the purposes of this chapter, *Structural* will refer to the work of Minuchin and others at the Philadelphia Child Guidance Clinic (Minuchin, 1974; Minuchin, Rosman, & Baker, 1978; Aponte & Van Deusen, 1981; Minuchin and Fishman, 1981); *Strategic* will be separated into two groups representing the work of the Mental Research Institute (MRI) Brief Therapy Center (Watzlawick, Weakland, & Fisch, 1974; Weakland, Fisch, Watzlawick, & Bodin, 1974; Fisch, Weakland, & Segal, 1982) on one hand, and the strategic/structural approach of Haley and Madanes at the Family Institute of Washington, D.C. (Haley, 1976, 1980; Madanes, 1981, 1984) on the other; and *Systemic* will refer to the earlier work of Selvini-Palazzoli and others in Milan, Italy (Selvini-Palazzoli, 1978; Selvini-Palazzoli, Boscolo, Cecchin, & Prata, 1978; Tomm, 1984a, 1984b).

INTEGRATION

Concepts

As stated above, there are numerous points of similarity among these three perspectives. The most basic of these is the often implicit, but frequently explicit, reference of each view to its adherence to General System Theory assumptions. While these assumptions are often left only vaguely or broadly defined, generally, all of these views describe human behavior as embedded within multiple systems of interaction. These systems are seen to be relatively open to the exchange of information from both within and outside defined system boundaries. The system is said to be more than the sum of its component parts, and is thus best described by the emergent process which results from the interacting elements. Interaction among elements is said to be cyclical and reciprocal rather than linear and unidirectional.

The process of this interaction is described as feedback, which can be either positive or negative. Positive feedback tends to amplify differences or deviations, whereas negative feedback tends to reduce deviations. The emphasis on the feedback process directs attention away from historical causes for behavior, and instead toward current interaction for both an adequate explanation of a behavior and a locus to change it. This stance differs from more historical approaches to family therapy.

The nature of problems and the nature of change are also seen in relation to the system as described above. Each of these views see problems as generally resulting from an inflexible or repetitive process of interaction in the system, rather than from some inherent defect within a given system member alone. Such a rigidity of interaction is usually described as either a lack of an appropriate action which is needed or the repetitive process of an ineffective action. The broad goal of change among these views is to interrupt a rigidly repetitive and ineffective system process defined as a problem, and replace it with some new, more effective, and flexible set of interactions.

Insight, as traditionally defined, is not assumed to be necessary for therapeutic change. Instead, the individual and collective definitions of system members regarding the way they describe and order their lives are either used to support new action, or reframed or altered to facilitate new interaction. There is a general acceptance of multiple client world views, with a concomitant disavowal of any one particular description of reality as the one true version.

Practice

Therapy tends to be more present focused, active, and directive, with frequent and liberal use of homework assignments. Although these approaches tend to be quite active and deliberate, therapy interventions may be either direct or indirect. Direct interventions usually take the form of asking clients either to do something new or to deliberately engage in a current or former behavior pattern for a new purpose. Indirect interventions generally consist of the reframing of the actions, roles, or relationships of either clients, therapist, or therapeutic actions to facilitate a desired system change. So-called positioning moves may also be used, wherein the therapist deliberately takes a particular stand or position within the system which includes the family and the therapist in order to introduce a new set of interactions within the family as it is interacting currently within the session.

One of the most uniformly held stances to therapy across these views is a planned approach to change. The therapist's plan and approach to therapeutic change is most often *not* made explicit to the client system. The therapist's strategy is often distinct, and of a different order than that of the family, with the former frequently including the latter, but not vice versa.

Brevity in the length of therapy is also a generally shared stance to therapy, with the Milan Systemic and the MRI groups usually explicitly limiting their sessions to 10, and Haley (1980) reporting an average of 10 or 11 sessions. This stance appears to reflect the joint belief that the longer the therapist is engaged with a system, the less his or her therapeutic impact is likely to be. The emphasis across these approaches is more on solving problems than upon teaching new skills or providing insights which might lead to a supposed better life.

One other shared therapy characteristic across approaches has been the consultation group which is separate from the primary therapist(s), yet which is directly involved, one step removed, by observing the session through a one-way mirror. This consultation group frequently serves the purpose of offering a second-level perspective on both the client system and the client-therapist system, while helping to devise and often deliver interventions.

By way of summarizing these similarities, a recent Q-sort study (Rohrbaugh, 1982) emerged with a number of points of agreement among representatives of the Structural, Systemic, MRI, and Haley/Madanes approaches. In summarizing the items ranked highest (or as most reflecting their approach) by all eight raters, Rohrbaugh states that: "At the top were items about reframing, using the clients' 'language,' constructing workable realities, *not* sharing strategy with clients openly, promoting change without awareness, resolving the presenting problem, and arranging that the therapist be in charge of the case" (Rohrbaugh, 1982, p. 4).

Evolution

These general similarities are not surprising when one considers the similar roots, influences, and paths of development among these approaches and their authors. The work of Gregory Bateson (1972, 1979) has strongly influenced most of these authors, although their respective interpretation of his work differs somewhat. Both Haley and Weakland began their work in collaboration with Bateson. This was a fruitful collaboration which not only resulted in the original double bind theory of schizophrenia paper (Bateson, Jackson, Haley, & Weakland, 1956) among others, but also saw the establishment of The Mental Research Institute with Don Jackson, and of the Journal, *Family Process*.

Shortly after Paul Watzlawick joined the Mental Research Institute, Haley left to work with Minuchin at the Philadelphia Child Guidance Clinic. The Structural Family Therapy being developed in Philadelphia had an important influence on Haley's work, as did Haley's ideas on Minuchin during their 10 years together before Haley left to establish his own institute in Washington, D.C.

Turning to the Systemic view of the so-called Milan Group, much of their early work was guided by the consultation of Paul Watzlawick of MRI, the reading of the influential text, *The Pragmatics of Human Communication* (Watzlawick, Beavin, & Jackson, 1967), and by reading of some of Haley's early work, before turning directly to the work of Bateson. Similarly, the deliberate approach to instigating change and the use of indirection shared across approaches owes much to the influence of the work of the late Milton Erickson (Haley, 1973).

Despite all of these similarities in concept, practice, and evolution, however, the grouping of these four approaches under one heading as representatives of a shared perspective is probably unwarranted. Furthermore, a view which suggests that these perspectives represent different phases along an evolutionary continuum, with each successive stance representing an advancement toward some unified whole or paradigm, is probably also unfounded. Instead, each of these approaches developed in parallel at relatively the same time. In addition, a closer look at these respective approaches will show a wide divergence of not only practices, but also of models, concepts, and the way in which a number of fundamental questions about systems, problems, and change are answered. To address these differences, we will turn now to the literature on differentiation.

DIFFERENTIATION

The literature differentiating among Strategic, Systemic, and Structural approaches has grown mainly over the past five years. These works have ranged from distinguishing when and why to use alternate approaches (Andolfi, 1980; MacKinnon, Parry, & Black, 1984; Stanton, 1981a, 1981b; Coyne, 1984; Roberts, 1984), to distinguishing critical differences among and between the approaches (Duncan & Fraser, 1983; Fraser, 1982, 1984a, 1984b; MacKinnon, 1983; Rohrbaugh, 1982; Rohrbaugh & Eron, 1982), to analyses of the desirability or the possibility of mixing approaches (Colapinto, 1984; de Shazer, 1984; Duncan, 1984; Fraser, 1984b; Liddle, 1984; MacKinnon & Slive, 1984; Rohrbaugh, 1984). One of the best outline structures which helps to organize some of the major differences among these approaches is found in Rohrbaugh and Eron's chapter on "The Strategic Systems Therapies" (Rohrbaugh & Eron, 1982). In the interest of clarity and brevity, many of their categories for distinction will be used and augmented below.

Even though these four approaches have been grouped under the term of systems therapies, upon closer scrutiny, the definition of system, or what is important within a system is by no means clear or shared across views. Because our concepts help determine what we perceive and act upon and vice versa, such basic conceptual differences can have watershed differences among approaches as they are translated into therapeutic action. Watzlawick (1978) has stated that, "In therapy, the theory determines what we do." True to the self-fulfilling prophesy, what we choose to do in therapy subsequently shapes and reinforces our theory.

System Definitions

Because in social systems, as opposed to biological or physical systems, there are fewer apparent boundaries, the definition of what constitutes a system is much more dependent upon the observer. As one looks at these four approaches, there emerge at least two separate versions of a system model. Relating to a more process-based model of the study of self-regulating cybernetic systems, the MRI group focuses primarily upon the ongoing process of interaction among system members over time as their major definition of what is most important to observe within a system.

On the other hand, the Structural, Haley/Madanes, and Milan groups tend to be more organization-focused in present space. This focus tends to direct the Structuralist's attention toward the lateral structure of relationships in present space, with attention to such things as whether boundaries are rigid or diffuse, and so on. For the Strategic/Structural view (Haley), focus is directed to power differentials as they are distributed in vertical hierarchies, with attention being paid to how this affects a system's ability to negotiate the process of problematic life transitions.

In the Systemic (Milan) view, focus is directed toward overriding system rules and how these rules function to maintain system stability. These differences tend to create and perpetuate a problem-focused (MRI) versus an organization-focused (Structural, Strategic/Structural, Systemic) approach to the systems being dealt with; each approach assesses either the pattern of solutions around a defined problem (MRI), the current spatial positioning, roles, and subsequent interaction within a family group (Structural), the power differentials and interaction around disorganized hierarchies (Haley), or the subtle rules which stabilize a family system through the use of circular questioning (Systemic).

Breadth of Context

Following from the above distinctions, each of these approaches differs also in how broad or narrow the relevant context to be considered is, both in terms of the number of people needed to be involved and in terms of the amount and type of historical information needed. The MRI view has the narrowest potential context in that the approach reduces the system focus to the solution patterns and definitions which revolve around an identified problem. In this approach, a problem may be defined even as "self-referential," in which only one person may be seen. One or two persons may also be seen from a larger system as a preferred option in order to maximize therapist flexibility and influence. The information gathered focuses mainly on how relevant system members have attempted to solve the perceived problem currently and in the recent past. Symptoms are not seen as serving a function within the system, and thus the attention of therapy is directed to altering the pattern of transaction around the symptom, which, when altered, will be eliminated.

By contrast, the formulations of the Structural, and Haley/Madanes views assume that symptoms are functional in the broader context of system organization. Thus, dyads, triads, or even larger groups are seen in therapy, with a goal of assessing and altering the organizational structure to eliminate the function of the symptom. Much relevant information is gained by observing the positioning and interactions among system members as they transact within the session as an organized group dealing with a problem. History is relevant mainly as it relates to the development of the current structure and power differentials within the family's organization. A history of repeated cycles will often be used to speculate about the purpose or function of the symptom in maintaining the current family organization.

The broadest context is defined by the Systemic approach, whose practitioners usually intervene with triads or larger, extended families, and often see the symptom as serving a function of stabilizing a family pattern which may extend across generations. Large family groups are seen together as they are asked circular questions about their interrelationships, and the entire group is quite often included in systemic prescriptions and rituals. Historical and intergenerational traditions are seen as relevant information in the process of generating hypotheses about the major family myth or metaphor which perpetuates its current impasse.

Level of Inference

Another related difference among the approaches is the level of inference used to interpret the data or interactions among system members. This varies from the highly deductive process of sequential hypothesis generation and testing around the nature of major family rules of the Systemic view to the highly inductive approach of the MRI group, which deliberately avoids functional hypotheses, and hypothetical structures, and instead attempts to stick as closely as possible to observed and reported interaction patterns around a described problem.

The Structural and Strategic/Structural views occupy a middle ground in which they do speculate about symptom functions and metaphorical representations within organized family hierarchies and structures, yet many of their concepts of hierarchy, enmeshment, etc. are more concrete than the more abstract and general cybernetic system rules of the Systemic view.

The MRI view may be said to be parsimonious at the expense of an understanding of broader family context and overriding issues, whereas the other views may be said to capture the significance of human interaction within a systemic context at the expense of moving too far from the identified problem.

Problem Definition

As implied in the previous section, a main point of differentiation among these views is their respective position on whether the identified problem or symptom is assumed to serve a function within the larger system or organization. There is a clear distinction between the MRI approach and the others in that it assumes no function is served by the symptom, whereas all of the others assume that it does. The MRI view assumes that problems develop surrounding repetitive interactions around a perceived deviation or change within a system, and that they are perpetuated and amplified by these same solution patterns. With no presumed function served, a change in solution pattern is assumed to lead to an elimination of the problem.

In each of the other three approaches, the symptom is viewed as serving some stability function within the larger organizational context, and thus this context becomes the locus for change. For Haley/Madanes, the problem within the organization is most often an abnormality in hierarchical power differentials, including often covert crossgenerational coalitions needing realignment. Within the Structural approach, the horizontal dimension of organizational structure is emphasized, with attention being paid to the over- or underinvolvement of family members with one another, and with an assumption that the symptom is a function of an overly rigid family structure which the symptom serves to balance. Similarly, the Systemic approach focuses upon overriding general family rules within which a symptom is understood. The symptom is believed to exist in the service of a homeostatic imperative of a family system in danger of change. Such major family rule change is said to eliminate the stabilizing function of the symptom.

Feedback

As pointed out at the beginning of the chapter, a hallmark of a system-based view is its emphasis upon the process of feedback in a self-regulating system. However, closer scrutiny of these four approaches shows a great difference in the emphasis placed upon the role of positive versus negative feedback. As stated earlier, positive feedback is said to amplify deviations in a cycle of (the more of A, the more of B), whereas negative feedback is said to reduce deviations, linking increases in one variable with decreases in another (the more of A, the less of B).

Clearly, a major difference between the MRI view and that of the other three lies in the MRI emphasis on positive feedback cycles and the others' emphasis on negative feedback cycles upon which to base their approach to problems and their resolution. A fundamental assumption of the Structural, Haley/Madanes, and Systemic views is that the system with a problem is stuck in a negative feedback loop wherein the system is balancing itself against the possibility of change. This usually is said to take the form in which the more one element begins to change, the more other elements begin to act in a way to reduce that change. The system is seen as in the throes of attempting to remain stable in the face of change. On the other hand, the MRI view sees the system as stuck in the process of change. Problems are seen as vicious, positive feedback cycles, and resolution is cast as the initiation of a new, virtuous, positive feedback cycle.

These differences in emphasis on positive or negative feedback yield considerable differences in practice. Whereas a negative feedback view tends to see the task of change as the overcoming of a potent homeostatic balance or a rigidly organized organizational structure, a positive feedback-based view sees the task of change as the interruption of a vicious cycle with the introduction of a small change which may initiate new, positive ripples in the ongoing process. This point of differentiation is a major one, which raises fundamental questions regarding the process of social systems such as the family, and it will be dealt with in more detail later.

The Scope of Change

Following from the above differences in emphases, there are subsequent differences in how small or large a change is assumed to be needed. In the Structural view, change in the identified problem is predicated upon concurrent change in the structure of the relationship patterns which underlie the problem. Symptom change is predicated upon structural change.

In the Haley/Madanes approach, change of the identified problem is based upon realignment of confused hierarchies, resulting in new interactional patterns, and the elimination of the need for or function of the symptom. Symptom change is predicated upon hierarchical power realignments.

In the Milan approach, change in the symptom is based upon an overriding cybernetic rule change, produced often through a positively connoted statement of the family and a prescription for members to deliberately perform their current patterns of interactions. Symptom change is predicated upon major family rule change which enables the family to move on in its evolution.

As opposed to these large, organizational changes, the MRI approach usually targets very small changes in solution pattern around the identified problem, with the assumption that symptom change will be predicated upon a small but significant change in solution pattern.

Goal Setting

Although all approaches share the position that therapy strategy is rarely shared or made explicit with the clients, there are differences in how explicitly the therapy goals or contracts are made. The MRI and Haley/Madanes approaches are the most explicit in their agreements with clients to solve the presenting problem. Although these contracts are explicit, however, therapeutic action is then directed toward the respectively implicit goals of interdicting solution patterns or realigning hierarchies. Therapy actions toward these ends are often very indirect.

Although the Structural approach also will agree with clients to alter symptoms, practitioners also will frequently be explicit about the organization's structural anomalies which need change, as well as being direct in their therapeutic efforts to alter those structures. Direct action toward this goal of structure change is common, with the goal of symptom change being secondary.

The Milan approach is least explicit in both their contracting and actions. A position of therapeutic neutrality is maintained with respect to the family and the symptom. Whereas the symptom is acknowledged to be inconvenient, it is frequently cast as positive along with the family's rules of interaction; thus, both symptom and rules are often prescribed for the family. Whereas there is an overall contract to change the symptom and the family, it is most often extremely implicit, as are the therapeutic actions employed.

Group Size

Given the respective goals and subsequent tasks of each of these views, the size of the groups seen in therapy also varies. With the goal of introducing some small change in the solution pattern around the presenting problem, the MRI group will very often see only one or two system members, even when the problem is explicitly defined as a marital or family one.

With the goal of altering confused intergenerational hierarchies, the Strategic/Structuralists will often work with dyads or triads.

In attempting to change organization structure through in-session enactment, the Structuralists are likely to meet with large family groups or defined subgroups.

With the target of identifying and altering overriding cybernetic family rules or patterns, the Systemic approach most often attempts to engage as much of the system as possible in therapy, including multiple generations as needed.

Therapist Influence

Although all of these approaches believe in deliberate therapist influence, they differ among themselves in how direct or indirect they are in employing this influence.

By far the most direct approach is that of the Structuralists who will often give bold and explicit directions to family members to change seating arrangements, engage or disengage in actions within the session, take sides with a family member or subgroup, or confront other members. This approach is based strongly upon either family compliance with these directives or the precipitation of a crisis which enables family members to realign themselves, even if this alignment is against the therapist.

The Haley/Madanes approach also utilizes direct therapist influence to realign power differentials, yet frequently also uses explicit "symptom prescription," or other such similar directives by which clients benefit whether they choose to comply or defy.

Whereas the MRI approach is likely to give direct homework assignments to perform new and even unique behavior, and whereas they often engage in paradoxical looking therapy moves or prescriptions similar to Haley, therapist influence is frequently very indirect. The therapist is more often in a nonauthoritarian position and a major therapy activity is often an implied agreement with, and a subtle reframing of, clients' positions.

The Systemic approach is possibly the most indirect. Whereas the therapist may direct sets of circular questions to family members, and deliver broad systemic family prescriptions or rituals, these prescriptions are most often based on a subtle reframing and positive connotation of family patterns. The therapist attempts to maintain a position of ostensible neutrality with the family system. Overall, family rule change is based upon a position of either family compliance with or defiance of the therapist's prescriptions.

Therapist Engagement and Position

In pursuing these therapy actions, these approaches vary also in how actively engaged the therapist gets with the system, as well as how much of an authority position is taken by the therapist (one-up vs. one-down).

Clearly, the most actively engaged and one-up position is most frequently found in the Structural approach, in its attempts to join the family, direct its action, and precipitate change in session through the active impact of the therapist within the system.

Whereas the Haley/Madanes approach does not attempt to as actively join the system and create change from within as a member, it does at times take an authority position to direct power realignments or to deliver paradoxical looking prescriptions, or ordeals.

The MRI stance is much less engaged with the system and, indeed, may work only with one or two members, often getting only retrospective and indirect reports of system transactions. Another hallmark of the MRI approach is a characteristically nonauthoritarian or one-down position with clients to increase collaboration. A one-up position is taken deliberately mainly in instances where it might aid in desired client defiance.

Finally, the Milan group tend to be the most disengaged and deliberately neutral with respect to the system. This disengagement is maintained from a position of authority through spacing sessions as much as a month apart with strict limits on between session contacts, and deliberately delivering intervention messages at the end of sessions or by letter to limit further engagement of the family with the therapist which might reduce the impact of the intervention.

Locus of Change

A final difference among these approaches regards their positions on whether the focus of therapeutic change is in the therapy room or elsewhere.

Again, the active and directive approach of the Structuralists explicitly focuses upon in-session enactment as the main arena of change.

The Strategic/Structural (Haley) approach will attempt some in-session realignments of hierarchical power and control, yet they also rely heavily on directed homework assignments.

In both the Systemic and MRI approaches, the major locus of change is outside of the session and as a result of homework. In both approaches, the therapist is relatively disengaged. Whereas both approaches pay close attention to the in-session effects of therapist position and intervention framing and delivery, the expected impact of the intervention, and the initiation and amplification of change are assumed to occur elsewhere.

Empirical Comparisons

Many of the above differences are supported in the results of the same Q-sort study cited earlier (Rohrbaugh, 1982). Sixty statements referring to theory and practice were sorted into nine categories, ranging from least to most agree, by eight raters (two each representing each of the four approaches under consideration). The 16 items which clearly differentiated the models statistically divided themselves into two groups of eight, representing theory and practice respectively. Some of the greatest differentiations related to the broad versus narrow breadth of context of the Systemic and MRI views respectively. The Structural and Haley/Madanes views preferred a broad breadth of context with the system in the session, aligning with the Systemic view here; yet they aligned with the MRI regarding a more narrow historical focus. Similar differences were noted on items relating to level of abstraction and inference. As opposed to all of the other raters, the MRI raters ranked items on "homeostasis," "hierarchy," and the functionality of symptoms lowest.

Relating to technique, the Structuralists put significantly more emphasis on active engagement with the family in the session than did the MRI or the Systemic people. On the other hand, the Structuralists placed significantly less emphasis on paradox. The Systemic stance of therapist neutrality significantly differentiated them from both the Structuralists and Haley/Madanes.

Finally, the Haley/Madanes raters showed least preference for consultation groups and one-way mirrors, and the MRI group showed the greatest enthusiasm for the notion that therapy be brief. Two general, undesignated factors were found which grouped the Structural, Strategic/Structural (Haley), and Systemic on the first, and the MRI and the Strategic/Structural (Haley) approaches on the second (the Strategic/Structural was loaded equally and significantly on both).

Practical Integration Attempts

Turning to practical comparisons, most of the focus has been placed upon the integration of Structural and Strategic approaches. Stanton (1981a, 1981b) has been a major proponent of this sort of integration. He has suggested starting with a Structural approach, moving to a Strategic approach when impasses are reached, and then returning to a Structural stance once the impasse has been broached. Andolfi (1980) suggests a slightly different approach in working with families of severely disturbed adolescents. He recommends starting with a Strategic approach to broach initial impasses, and then moving to a Structural stance once these initial hurdles are overcome.

Others have cautioned about such practical integration of these two approaches. Pointing out the practical difference between the relatively "cool" or disengaged position of the therapist in a Strategic approach versus the more "hot" or actively engaged position of the Structural therapist, Coyne (1984) has noted a number of possible problems in moving between the approaches. Not the least of these problems is a possible narrowing of the therapist's range of maneuverability with clients, and a possible loss of client trust in the therapist after such shifts. Rohrbaugh (1984) suggests that the Structural, Strategic, and Systemic approaches have such different, and largely irreconcilable differences in what the focus of change should be, that an integrated approach will be likely to necessarily lose or diffuse therapeutic focus and result in longer and more complex treatment than necessary. While de Shazer (1984) has supported the added richness or depth of vision gained by conceptually using a Structural and a Strategic view in constructing a case, he does not recommend integration in practice because it would blur such distinctions.

Turning to the integration of the Haley version of Strategic/Structural therapy with the Milan Systemic view, Roberts (1984) points out some advantages of the sequential practice of the two, whereas MacKinnon & Slive (1984) found some significant conceptual confusion and practical paralysis in their attempted integration of the two approaches. Roberts suggests that the advantage of defining a clear model to begin with, and then deliberately switching to another may not only help to meet "a particular family's needs at a particular point in time," but also may add a variety of creative problem-solving benefits for the therapist and the family.

MacKinnon & Slive (1984), on the other hand, noted that while there were creative and practical advantages from a mixing of tactics, they found switching models in midstream very disconcerting because the definition of the problem and units of analysis of each implied great differences in what was to be done, when, and why, and what constituted success. These authors did find a great advantage to their exercise in integration in that it caused them to see how the respective constructions of each model led them therapeutically in different directions, which helped to create an emergent or constructed reality of the families in treatment which was not a reflection of some preexisting reality of those families alone.

Colapinto (1984) has reflected upon the merits of various versions of practical integration by discussing what he calls recipe-book, spontaneous, compromise, and model-building integration. He critiques a *recipe-book integration* which suggests that certain approaches be applied to certain "types" of problems or families compatible to them (such as MacKinnon, Parry, & Black, 1984), for overobjectifying a supposed external reality and overlooking the emergent reality created by action within each of the approaches. *Spontaneous integration* lacks such preplanned fitting of approach to family or problem type and adopts a flexible shifting among approaches in an attempt not to be narrowly dogmatic, but instead to search for "what works." However, such flexible eclecticism not only risks losing touch with guiding constructs on the nature of problems and their appropriate resolution, but also may run directly into stark contradictions on these questions, as well as on what kind of change is desired or appropriate, and how to measure it. Such tactical eclecticism can meet with unexpected practical problems due to unexamined assumptions.

A so-called *compromise integration* may result from a conflict between specific goals, practices, or assumptions of a particular approach and those allowed within a given context. Provocation may be undercut by an agency's wish to keep clients happy; therapist neutrality may be disallowed by peer review criteria; or a lack of evening hours may prevent all relevant family members from attending, and so on. Such compromise integration is probably the worst sort in that it is random in the parts of the approaches allowed for practice.

In contrast to the previous variations, *model-building integration* uses a conceptual core around which to organize the ideas and techniques of various approaches. While this form of integration probably holds the greatest coherence in guiding the selective actions of the therapist, most often the concepts and tactics used from another approach are given other meanings or are done for different reasons. This raises the question of whether this is truly integration, or whether one approach is merely usurping another rather than organizing both under a new, larger, overriding model. Nevertheless, something closest to the model-building version of integration is probably the best option for guiding future practice.

Theory Integration Attempts

Turning finally to the theoretical plane, Sluzki (1983) has suggested that the Structural, Strategic, and Systemic views actually represent different subviews or corollaries of the same basic general system theory viewpoint. One's focus upon system structure (Structural), process (Strategic), or world view (Systemic) is said to determine most subsequent differences among the approaches. The question of whether integration can or even should be attempted is left unanswered, yet the implication of shared system theory assumptions certainly leaves the door open.

Duncan & Fraser (1983), on the other hand, have suggested that the model of system theory employed among these approaches is actually *not* the same. In an analysis of these views in relationship to Walter Buckley's (1967) explication of levels of system description, it was concluded that all but the MRI view appeared to be based upon the implicit homeostatic and structural assumptions of a biological level of system description. The MRI view, however, appeared to share more with the process-based, deviation-amplifying assumptions of a social system level of description (see also Maruyama, 1963; and Speer, 1970). From this analysis, it was concluded that theoretical integration would be more easily achieved among views sharing the same level of system assumptions than among those sharing different levels, and that the assumptions of the higher level might be used to subsume those of the lower. Such an analysis as this further raises the question of what is meant by Strategic. As implied earlier, the approach of Haley/Madanes probably shares more in concept with that of the Structural view than with that of the MRI view. The term Strategic has become reified to often include both the MRI and Haley/Madanes views. Whereas some authors may find the integration of Structural and Strategic views quite easy (when Strategic is practiced in the Haley/Madanes mode), others appear to find it quite incompatible (when Strategic is translated MRI).

Fraser (1982) came to this latter conclusion in comparing Structural with MRI views. Noting that the Structural view was based upon structure-function and negative feedback concepts, and that the MRI view was based on fluid process and positive feedback assumptions, these differences were traced in part to the way in which each approach engages with the system. In essence, Fraser suggests that the Structural view is based upon close-range engagement with large segments of a system in repeated short-time samples of interaction in the here and now around critical issues. The MRI view is based, instead, upon often retrospective reports by separate system members about the pattern of solution processes over longer time spans surrounding a defined difficulty.

These two views might be compared to the observation of single frames or short segments of a family therapy video tape versus viewing an edited documentary of the ongoing process of the same system over a span of weeks or months. In the former case, spatial constructs of interpersonal distance, the structure of role relationships, and the apparent vying for a position of power in defining goals, rules, and the direction and nature of change emerge as most salient. In the latter case, spatial constructs give way to the process of patterns across time, in which each instance of seemingly homeostatic struggle is seen to escalate in a vicious cycle of positive feedback.

Although Fraser does integrate these two views in this way using some of Bateson's (1979) concepts on evolution, this integration places the two views on two different empirical and logical levels of analysis, which he suggests will make practical integration as difficult for a therapist as is second-order change for a family from within its own family system. Much of this argument suggests that from an initial choice of either concept or hypothesis or mode of engagement with the data, subsequently separate sets of experiences and observations are produced which often confirm and perpetuate a perspective through a process of self-fulfilling prophecy. Consequently, similar therapeutic actions are done for different reasons and their results are interpreted and acted upon in increasingly divergent ways. Such growing differences have eventually generated quite strikingly different definitions of a number of very fundamental concepts and assumptions like the nature of problems, the process of change, and the basic principles which guide the process of the systems with which we work. It is to these questions which we will now turn.

CRITICAL QUESTIONS

In order for the issue of integration among these system-based approaches to be adequately addressed, there are a number of critical and fundamental questions which must be considered. If it is true that the theory does determine what we can see and act upon, and that the nature of our subsequent actions tends to yield cyclical confirmatory reactions in a constructive fashion (cf. Watzlawick, 1984), then the nature of our basic assumptions can mark watershed differences in practice. The most primary of these questions relate to our assumptions about the guiding principles of system theory as they relate to the systems with which we work.

The Nature of the System

As stated earlier, there are a number of concepts of General Systems Theory (cf. Ashby, 1956; von Bertalanffy, 1968) upon which there appears to be tacit agreement among the system-based views. For example there are the concepts of *wholeness* or *nonsummativity*, meaning that the whole is more than and different from the sum of the parts. Other concepts are those of *equifinality* and *multifinality*, or more simply, that among systems, similar end points may be reached from a variety of different beginnings, and similar beginning points may result in a variety of different ends. These concepts place the greatest emphasis not upon beginning and end points (which are viewed as an artificial and arbitrary punctuation of an ongoing cyclical process), but instead upon the cyclical self-regulating process which intervenes. The focus of this self-regulating process is *feedback*, which may be either *positive* or *negative*. Whereas positive feedback amplifies deviations, negative feedback is said to minimize deviation. There is general agreement upon these basic concepts. However, beyond this general agreement there are broad differences in emphasis and use of these and a number of other concepts.

A primary example of these differences is the question of the relative importance of positive and negative feedback. Is the system a self-balancing one which maintains a steady state for long periods of time and is only interrupted by periodic crises which require a painful and reluctantly achieved recalibration to a new steady state? Some have suggested that the influential work of von Bertalanffy (1968) overly emphasized the role of negative feedback or homeostasis in self-regulating systems (cf. Dell, 1982; Elkiam, 1985; Maruyama, 1963; Speer, 1970), and that this overemphasis has unduly influenced the practice of family therapy. Yet, while system evolution is acknowledged, how can an adequate view of systems be based upon a positive feedback idea of morphogenesis? How can this view account for the perceived stability of systems and the difficulty observed in change?

Recently, the work of the chemist Prigogine (1978), the mathematician Thom (1975), and the anthropologist Gould (1982) have been cited as examples of how systems can undergo relatively rapid and catastrophic change in what appear to be relatively stable states. This position has lent support for the view that lasting system change can be rapid and discontinuous as opposed to gradual and linear. However, doesn't this position reinforce the idea that systems are relatively stable structures which may require catastrophic events to unbalance their naturally homeostatic state to move them to a new, relatively stable and balanced state? Furthermore, doesn't this lend more support for the position that it is often the therapist's job to enter a system and actively exacerbate a crisis state to agitate the system enough to move it far enough from equilibrium that it might leap to a new structure (like the rearrangement of a new crystal in chemistry), rather than to be inexorably pulled back to its stable state again? Doesn't this answer the critiques of how a family therapy approach based upon the concept of stable systems can deal with the idea of change (cf. Speer, 1970)? Given these observations, how can a view like that of the MRI reconcile itself to being so heavily based upon a positive feedback model of systems and problems? Such is the current dispute which seems to continue positions of rather irreconcilable differences.

Turning to the nature of system boundaries, structures, and power hierarchies, there are clearly differences in the emphasis and use of these concepts. Relating to structure and hierarchy, Minuchin and Haley turn more to the theory of organizations for the use of these spatial constructs than to general system theory, whereas the Milan and MRI views use these ideas sparsely, if at all. This raises the questions of how one can ignore natural system structures, such as (1) intergenerational groupings of grandparents, marital couples or parents, and children; (2) the subsequent power differentials among them; and (3) the nature of the boundaries among them, and between what is defined as the family and what is outside? How can an approach which emphasizes these concepts be integrated with another which ignores them?

On the other hand, are these structures, boundaries, and hierarchies inherent in the systems with which we work, or are they concepts applied by ourselves as observers and describers of those systems? Furthermore, are all systems in general alike, or do the concepts of structure, hierarchy, and boundary have more salience for relatively more tangible systems such as tables, buildings, biological structures, etc. than for the more amorphous systems of human interactions. Even the basic assumption that social systems are relatively open in their boundaries to exchange of information from the outside has recently been called into question by Dell (1985). Citing the work of the theoretical biologist, Humberto Maturana, he suggests that human social systems are essentially closed, coherent structures which simply react to perturbations from the outside according to the way the systems themselves are structured. Whereas this position is a challenge to ideas on the nature of the boundaries of social systems as relatively open versus essentially closed, it does reinforce strongly the concepts of boundary and structure themselves.

Given this reinforcement, the question again arises as to how the MRI or Milan approaches can overlook these concepts. Are these views looking at the same kind of system? Granted our concepts help determine what we see and act upon, yet can't this position lapse into pure solipsism—the view that nothing exists but ourselves, and that reality or the systems with which we work are entirely what we make them? How can views with such strikingly different concepts and emphases about the very nature of systems begin to be integrated?

The Nature of Change

Following from the relative positions of these views on the nature of the system, their positions on the nature of change differ as well. If, as implied above, the system is seen as in the process of balancing itself against the possibility of change, then change is viewed as a breaking of an homeostatic cycle. From this perspective, the system is seen as maintaining stability. Change is thus a process of overcoming this force for stable balance either through forceful rearrangement of the current system structure or through agitating the system enough to move it far enough from stability to allow a leap to a new organization, countering the force which might move it back to its former state.

Another variation of this theme is for the system to be directed to escalate its efforts to maintain stability so intensively that a "runaway" is created which again destabilizes the system and moves it so far from equilibrium that it may then shift to a new organization. Furthermore, viewing system process as a function of structure and hierarchy directs the emphasis of change toward altering these structures and rearranging hierarchies. Once such structures are altered, subsequent process changes are assumed to follow.

On the other hand, if the system is viewed as in a continual process of change, rather than in the process of maintaining stability, then the focus of change is in redirecting the process of change rather than in overcoming the system's inertia against it. If the system is seen as engaged in an overall process of growth and elaboration in a general positive feedback process, then problems in changing are approached as reverberating positive (rather than negative) feedback cycles which are vicious cycles to be broken. The process of change is thus focused upon the initiation of some small but significant new action, either cognitive or behavioral, which will interdict the vicious cycle solution pattern and hopefully serve as a "kick point" for a new beneficent cycle which will yield progressive benefits. This is a redirection of a process of change, rather than the interruption of a force towards stability. System pattern or process is seen as primary, rather than structure, and thus altering process is assumed to alter what might be described as system structure.

The Nature of Problems

Following from some of the basic differences in the way in which systems are defined, there are consequent differences in the way problems are viewed. The Structural and Structural/Strategic approaches view problems as a function of inappropriate organizational structure or hierarchy. Problems are described as a symptom of a malfunctional system structure, defined in either horizontal or vertical space. Based upon a view of systems as primarily self-balancing units passing between relatively long periods of stable states punctuated by brief transitional crises, problems or symptoms are often attributed the function of maintaining the current balanced state of the system against the prospect of system imbalance and change.

The Systemic approach takes a similar view of the system as engaged in the process of maintaining balance, and thus describes the problem or symptom as serving a central function in maintaining this balance against the force of change.

The MRI approach *does not* assume that the problem serves some *function* of maintaining balance within the system, mainly because it sees the system as caught in the ongoing process of attempting to change rather than to stay stable. From this perspective, problems are not seen as a function of an aberrant structure attempting to balance itself, but as the product of a vicious cycle of positive feedback around some system dissonance.

From these contrasts come the questions of whether symptoms are a function of structure? Also, do symptoms serve a function of balancing a system against the prospect of change, or are they simply a product of unproductive solution patterns? Furthermore, if such symptoms are functional in these ways, won't simple symptom removal without structure change yield the substitution of a new symptom in order to balance the system as it still stands?

Aren't there certain normative structures for family systems which will tend to yield positive family process, and aberrations of these normative setups which will produce symptoms? The answers to these questions have important implications regarding the nature and goals of therapy.

The Goals and Nature of Therapy

In accordance with the above differences, there is a broad split in the global goals of therapy. For those views which see the system stuck in an attempt to balance its stable state against change, the overall goal is to overcome the force for stability to allow for change. For the Structural approach, this means altering structures and boundaries to eliminate the function of the symptom. For the Haley/Madanes approach, this means realigning the power differentials in confusing hierarchies. For the Systemic approach, this means altering overriding family metarules to break the family's homeostatic tendency and free the symptom from its stabilizing function. On the other hand, for the MRI approach which sees the system as stuck in a process of attempting to change, the goal is to interrupt and/or redirect the process of change. A small change in the pattern of interaction around the defined problem will be the target, and the goal will be to eliminate the problem behavior.

It is not uncommon, however, for each of these approaches to employ the same therapeutic action. It is not inconceivable that each approach might deliver the same reframing or directive to the same system. Such perceived practical similarities understandably have led to presumptions that the approaches are very similar and/or easily joined. A closer look at their respective practices, however, will prove otherwise. Such similar actions may frequently be carried out for quite different reasons. Again, if we employ the increasingly common setting of a video tape view of a set of four therapy sessions representing each of the four views under consideration, one might see four very similar therapeutic interactions occur across four short tape selections. On the other hand, if the context for each of these brief vignettes is broadened to include the entire tape of each session, it becomes quickly apparent that the action both preceding and following the segments in question often diverges greatly.

Based upon a problem definition which revolves around inequitable power hierarchies, the Structural/Strategic therapist may have actively aligned with one spouse to balance power in a couple prior to a particular reframing, for example. The reframing itself may be done for the purpose of thwarting one partner's pattern of controlling the other and enabling the other to have the chance to more equitably control or define the activity in the relationship. Following the reframing, an assignment might be delivered as homework, to reinforce this designed power shift.

In the Structural session, the same reframing might have been preceded by a very active direction of a couple to change their seating arrangement in the session and to actively negotiate an agreement around a parenting task. The reframing itself might have been devised to facilitate a firmer boundary around the couple, and between them and their children. The action following the reframing again might include more in-session enactment of the targeted new couple interaction as orchestrated by the therapist. In both of these cases, the therapist will be seen as rather actively engaged with the clients within the session in the relative role of an authority figure.

In the Systemic session, the therapist may also be seen as an authority figure, yet one who is much less active or engaged with the system. The particular reframing in question may have been preceded by the bulk of the session which might have included an elaborate set of circular questions by the therapist directing the system members to reflect upon and describe the interactions and relationships among other family members while in the presence of these others. The reframing itself might have been devised to enable the perceived rules of the system to be described in a positive and thus more acceptable manner, and to support the delivery of a prescription for the system to deliberately enact prior interaction patterns outside the session. In this session, the action following the reframing might consist of a very brief and structured assignment of a ritual or deliberate practice to be performed, or the promise of a letter to be sent to the clients to this effect, followed by the rapid termination of the session with little or no further opportunity for any more questions or discussion.

Finally, with the goal of altering ineffective solution patterns around a defined problem, the MRI therapist might be seen as having preceded the same reframing with a set of questions to a single system member most interested in change. The position of the therapist is most likely to be nonauthoritarian and least actively engaged with the client in the session as the client is asked to define the problem and to describe the range of attempts which have been made to solve it. The reframing in question might be variously done for the purpose of redefining the situation so that the dilemma is seen as less of a problem and thus eliminating the need for the solution pattern, or redefining the situation to enable new or opposite action to be taken, etc. The action following the reframing may then focus upon the advisability or inadvisability of such an implied new course of action or inaction, and its possible consequences, along with an agreed upon homework assignment to test the effects of the new solution option.

Such divergences are not just limited to these brief, hypothetical options within a given session as described above, but are amplified in succeeding sessions not only to the effect of differing choices of group size and composition, therapist engagement, activity level, and focus, among other things, but also in the fundamental decisions as to whether the therapy has been a success or failure, and upon what criteria it should be decided to continue or stop.

For example, whereas the elimination of a child's defined problem behavior may be judged quite sufficient by an MRI view, it may be seen as quite insufficient by a Structural or Haley/Madanes view if the therapist perceives there to be a persisting marital problem, or various other anomalies in boundary, structure, or power. The nature and focus of therapeutic action and decisions regarding termination, among other things, all depend upon therapy goals. These goals, in turn, depend upon the way problems are defined, which relates back similarly to the way in which systems and system change are presumed to function. From frequently implicit differences in a number of basic assumptions, there grow a variety of practical divergences which, as in the criteria for success and failure and the choice for appropriate therapeutic focus and activity, are not always easily reconcilable.

The concepts of organizational structure or power hierarchies, of overriding systemic rules, and of the patterns of system process tend to lead to different therapeutic action. The choice of each of these concepts as primary tends to lead to the elaboration of a particular style, focus, and set of goals for treatment, while it gradually eliminates other options.

Nevertheless, while each of these approaches is different in style and goal, each claims a considerable degree of success. On what bases, if any, can the successes of each of these approaches be reconciled? Are there any reasonable bases for the integration of their often divergent practices? Are each of these views equally "correct" or useful and thus afforded mutual respect, or is this another instance of perpetuating a sort of uneasy pseudomutuality to preserve a professional peace?

Furthermore, if we are to make such judgments about these approaches and the assumptions upon which they are based, upon what set of criteria do we proceed? What is the most useful system model for describing human social systems such as the family? In pursuit of these questions and others, there has been a considerable amount of recent work toward advancing a set of metamodels to provide criteria upon which to build.

THE "STATE OF THE ART"

Currently in the field of family therapy, there are not that many writers asking the above questions; much less are there any definite answers. Probably, the best option in attempting to answer these questions lies in the pursuit of an organizing metamodel. In this respect, there are a range of recent alternatives. Each of these options reflects a slightly different approach to systems and often proceeds by borrowing from separate, and respectively different spheres of study, or by emphasizing different systemic or philosophical concepts to guide its organization.

There are, in fact, several preliminary models being developed and advocated for the description of social systems like the family, and for the explanation and direction of the process of change. Stanton (1984) turns to the physical sciences to put forth a geodynamic balance theory of family process. Dell (1985) turns instead to the concepts of the new theoretical biology to propose a biological foundation for the social sciences. Weeks (Weeks & L'Abate, 1982; Bopp & Weeks, 1984) and Liddle (1984) use the dialectical view from philosophy to organize their limited metatheories. Keeney & Ross (1985) use a set of cybernetic constructs to construct the similarities among systemic family therapies. Finally, Fraser and Duncan (Duncan & Fraser, 1983, Duncan, 1984; Fraser, 1984a, 1984b) combine a social system process view from sociology with the constructivist view from philosophy in proposing their process-constructive model.

Each of these models has been developed in response to a perceived need at this time for some broader reaching constructs to organize the current state of confusion among system-based approaches to family therapy. Each model is in a preliminary process of evolution. There are some areas of overlap among models and other areas of diversion. None, of course, is entirely right or wrong. In the long run, their relative success should rest upon their utility.

To further describe, compare, contrast, and analyze these preliminary models at this point would probably not only require an additional chapter, but might also be premature. None of these positions has, as yet, been fully elaborated. Each is struggling with its own attempts to define and integrate a systems approach. None of them has, as yet, addressed all of the critical questions raised above. This is the current "state of the art" in the area. As with the systems approaches which it attempts to organize and subsume, each metamodel will "create its own reality." At this point, it will be up to the authors, the reader, and the field to determine which answers are the most useful. What is clear at this time is that not all views referred to as systems approaches share the same assumptions on even some of the most fundamental questions. Thus, to attempt to integrate these approaches without adequately addressing these critical questions will be folly.

REFERENCES

Andolfi, M. (1980). Prescribing the family's own dysfunctional rules as a therapeutic strategy. *Journal of Marital and Family Therapy, 6*, 29–36.
Andolfi, M., Menghi, P., Nicolo, A. M., & Saccu, C. (1980). Interaction in rigid systems: A model of intervention in families with a schizophrenic member. In M. Andolfi & I. Zwerling (Eds.), *Dimensions of Family Therapy*. New York: Guilford Press.
Aponte, H. J., & Van Deusen, J. M. (1981). Structural family therapy. In A. L. Gurman & D. P. Kniskern (Eds.), *Handbook of Family Therapy*. New York: Brunner/Mazel.
Ashby, W. R. (1956). *An Introduction to Cybernetics*. London: Chapman and Hall.
Bateson, G. (1972). *Steps to an Ecology of Mind*. New York: Ballantine.
Bateson, G. (1979). *Mind and Nature: A Necessary Unity*. New York: Dutton.

Bateson, G., Jackson, D. D., Haley, J., & Weakland, J. (1956). Toward a theory of schizophrenia. *Behavioral Science, 1*, 251-264.

Bertalanffy, L. von. (1968). *General System Theory*. New York: George Braziller.

Bopp, M. J., & Weeks, G. R. (1984). Dialectical metatheory in family therapy. *Family Process, 23*, 49-62.

Buckley, W. (1967). *Sociology and Modern Systems Theory*. Englewood Cliffs, NJ: Prentice-Hall.

Colapinto, J. (1984). On model integration and model integrity. *Journal of Strategic and Systemic Therapies, 3*, 38-42.

Coyne, J. (1984). Introducing structural interventions into strategic therapy: A caution. *Journal of Strategic and Systemic Therapies, 3*, 23-27.

Dell, P. F. (1982). Beyond homeostasis: Toward a concept of coherence. *Family Process, 21*, 21-41.

Dell, P. F. (1985). Understanding Bateson and Maturana: Toward a biological foundation for the social sciences. *Journal of Marital and Family Therapy, 11*, 1-20.

de Shazer, S. (1984). Fit. *Journal of Strategic and Systemic Therapies, 3*, 34-37.

Duncan, B. L. (1984). Adopting the construct of functionality when it facilitates system change: A method of selective integration. *Journal of Strategic and Systemic Therapies, 3*, 60-65.

Duncan, B. L., & Fraser, J. S. (1983). *Systems of systems: Integration and disintegration among system views of family therapy*. Paper presented at the 41st Annual Conference of the American Association for Marriage and Family Therapy, Washington, D.C., October.

Elkiam, M. (1985). From general laws to singularities. *Family Process, 24*, 151-164.

Fisch, R., Weakland, J. H., & Segal, L. (1982). *The Tactics of Change: Doing Therapy Briefly*. San Francisco: Jossey-Bass.

Fraser, J. S. (1982). Structural and strategic family therapy: A basis for marriage, or grounds for divorce? *Journal of Marital and Family Therapy, 8*, 13-22.

Fraser, J. S. (1984a). Paradox and orthodox: Folie à deux? *Journal of Marital and Family Therapy, 10*, 361-372.

Fraser, J. S. (1984b). Process level integration: Corrective vision for a binocular view. *Journal of Strategic and Systemic Therapies, 3*, 43-57.

Gould, S. J. (1982). *The Panda's Thumb*. New York: W. W. Norton.

Gurman, A. S., & Kniskern, D. P. (Eds.). (1981). *Handbook of Family Therapy*. New York: Brunner/Mazel.

Haley, J. (1973). *Uncommon Therapy: The Psychiatric Techniques of Milton H. Erickson, M.D.* New York: W. W. Norton.

Haley, J. (1976). *Problem Solving Therapy*. San Francisco: Jossey-Bass.

Haley, J. (1980). *Leaving Home: The Therapy of Disturbed Young People*. New York: McGraw-Hill.

Keeney, B. P., & Ross, J. (1985). *Mind in Therapy: Constructing Systemic Family Therapies*. New York: Basic Books.

Liddle, H. A. (1984). Towards a dialectical-contextual-coevolutionary translation of structural-strategic family therapy. *Journal of Strategic and Systemic Therapies, 3*, 66-79.

MacKinnon, L. (1983). Contrasting strategic and Milan therapies. *Family Process, 22*, 425-441.

MacKinnon, L., & Slive, A. (1984). If one should not marry a hypothesis, should one marry a model? *Journal of Strategic and Systemic Therapies, 3*, 26-39.

MacKinnon, L., Parry, A., & Black, R. (1984). Strategies of family therapy: The relationship of styles of family functioning. *Journal of Strategic and Systemic Family Therapy, 3*, 6-22.

Madanes, C. (1981). *Strategic Family Therapy*. San Francisco: Jossey-Bass.

Madanes, C. (1984). *Behind the One-way Mirror: Advances in the Practice of Strategic Therapy*. San Francisco: Jossey-Bass.

Maruyama, M. (1963). The second cybernetics: Deviation-amplifying mutual causal processes. *American Scientist, 51*, 164-179.

Minuchin, S. (1974). *Families and Family Therapy*. Cambridge, MA: Harvard University Press.

Minuchin, S., & Fishman, H. C. (1981). *Pathways to Change: Techniques in Family Therapy*. Cambridge, MA: Harvard University Press.

Minuchin, S., Rosman, B., & Baker, L. (1978). *Psychosomatic Families*. Cambridge, MA: Harvard University Press.

Prigogine, I. (1978). Time, structure, and fluctuations. *Science, 201*, 777-795.

Roberts, J. (1984). Switching models: Family and team choice points and reactions as we moved from the Haley strategic model to the Milan model. *Journal of Strategic and Systemic Therapies, 3*, 40-53.

Rohrbaugh, M. (1982). Q-sort comparisons of the structural, strategic, and systemic family therapies. Paper presented at the APA Annual Convention, Washington, D.C.

Rohrbaugh, M. (1984). The strategic systems therapies: Misgivings about mixing the models. *Journal of Strategic and Systemic Therapies, 3*, 28-32.

Rohrbaugh, M., & Eron, J. B. (1982). The strategic systems therapies. In L. E. Abt & I. R. Stuart (Eds.), *The Newer Therapies: A Workbook*. New York: Van Nostrand Reinhold.

Selvini-Palazzoli, M. (1978). *Self-Starvation: From Individual to Family Therapy in the Treatment of Anorexia Nervosa*. New York: Jason Aronson.

Selvini-Palazzoli, M., Boscolo, L., Cecchin, G., & Prata, G. (1978). *Paradox and Counterparadox*. New York: Jason Aronson.

Sluzki, C. (1983). Process, structure and worldviews: Toward an integrated view of systemic models in family therapy. *Family Process, 22*, 469-476.

Speer, D. C. (1970). Family systems: Morphostasis and morphogenesis, or "Is homeostasis enough?" *Family Process, 9*, 259-278.

Stanton, M. D. (1981a). Marital therapy from a structural/strategic viewpoint. In G. P. Sholeval (Ed.), *Marriage is a Family Affair: A Textbook of Marriage and Marital Therapy*. Jamaica, N.Y.: S. P. Medical and Scientific Books.

Stanton, M. D. (1981b). An integrated structural/strategic approach to family therapy. *Journal of Marital and Family Therapy, 7*, 427-439.

Stanton, M. D. (1984). Fusion, compression, diversion, and the workings of paradox: A theory of therapeutic/systemic change. *Family Process, 23*, 135-267.

Thom, R. (1975). *Structural Stability and Morphogenesis*. Reading, MA: Benjamin.

Tomm, K. (1984a). One perspective on the Milan systemic approach: Part I. Overview of development, theory and practice. *Journal of Marital and Family Therapy, 10*, 113-125.

Tomm, K. (1984b). One perspective on the Milan systemic approach: Part II. Description of session format, interviewing style and interventions. *Journal of Marital and Family Therapy, 10*, 253-271.

Watzlawick, P. (1978). *The Language of Change*. New York: Basic Books.

Watzlawick, P. (Ed.). (1984). *The Invented Reality: How Do We Know What We Think We Know? (Contributions to Constructivism)*. New York: W. W. Norton.

Watzlawick, P., Beavin, J. H., & Jackson, D. D. (1967). *Pragmatics of Human Communication*. New York: W. W. Norton.

Watzlawick, P., Weakland, J., & Fisch, R. (1974). *Change: Principles of Problem Formation and Problem Resolution*. New York: W. W. Norton.

Weakland, J. H., Fisch, R., Watzlawick, P., & Bodin, A. (1974). Brief therapy: Focused problem resolution. *Family Process, 13*, 141-168.

Weeks, G. R., & L'Abate, L. (1982). *Paradoxical Psychotherapy: Theory and Practice with Individuals, Couples, and Families*. New York: Brunner/Mazel.

Chapter 7

An Evolving Model:
Links Between the Milan
Approach and Strategic Models
of Family Therapy

Janine Roberts

INTRODUCTION

In the last few years, the Milan model (particularly as evolved by Cecchin and Boscolo) has moved towards a position of less direct intervention with families, so families can find their own solutions to difficulties (Boscolo & Cecchin, 1982; MacKinnon, 1983; Parry, 1984). Imber-Black (Coppersmith) (in press, b) has written more explicitly about these ideas, describing a systemic resource model of family therapy that focuses on how to best tap and pull in family strengths in the areas of "(1) religious, cultural and racial identity; (2) inner language; (3) commitments and loyalties; and (4) interactions with the outside world" (p. 7). In the systemic resource model, the therapist always remains very open to what the family does with any new information or interventions, assessing how they are mobilizing their own strengths.

However, as I have worked with the Milan model over the past seven years in residential, outpatient and private practice settings, a number of issues have been raised for me about the adaptability of the Milan model across clinical situations. Each model of family therapy has its own views about change, about therapist-family-outside system connections, about how problems have evolved and how they can be solved; these views may or may not fit the family's own view of how they can be helped. As Brickman et al. (1982) pointed out, sometimes helpers are not able to aid people in need of help because they have very different ideas about how the problem arose and what should be done about it; thus, help givers and help recipients can be applying models "that are out of phase with one another" (p. 375). For instance, some families may think they need a more direct model of help than the Milan model typically uses, or the Milan positive connotation that the family problem is the best solution the family could come up with may fit too well the family view of their problem evolution. Other questions have arisen for me around the large temporal frame of the Milan model (it seems to me that it can become cumbersome at times), as well as around therapist neutrality. I wonder if it is really possible to be neutral to family dilemmas when larger social systems are involved and have already taken a non-neutral stance.

Parry (1984) also noted that perhaps the Milan model is not as effective for treating families with aggressive acting-out disorders. MacKinnon, Parry & Black (1984) stated that based on the historical model development of strategic and systemic models and the types of cases they have reported working with, the Milan methodology is less effective with families that have a centrifugal style of functioning (Beavers, 1977) characterized by elements such as open and intense conflict, diffuse external boundaries, and members who are more attentive to cues from the environment than from one another. They further stated that cases of leaving home present some real difficulties for the Milan model because of their involvement with other social control agencies.

To address these concerns, I have been working in my clinical practice to try to expand the Milan model by bringing in some of the techniques of the Mental Research Institute (MRI) and Haley strategic models without losing the basic overarching frame of the Milan approach. As family therapy models have evolved, they have defined more clearly their positions regarding problem evolution and change. These model positions can be used as a framework within which to ask families questions about their views about giving responsibility for and solving problems. Rather than accepting a model view of problem evolution and solution as *the* only map to dilemmas, several model views are used as a framework within which to collaboratively evolve with families a view of what both the helper and the help recipient need to do.

In the strategic and systemic family therapy field in the last few years, there has been a trend towards more collaboration in several areas: (1) training teams which highlight trainee resources (Roberts, 1983); (2) an emphasis on respecting the autonomy (and coherence) of systems (Keeney, 1983); and (3) models proposed for working conjointly with larger systems and families (Imber-Black [Coppersmith], 1983; in press, a). However, little has been written directly about collaborative processes between families, therapists, and therapeutic teams.

There are four main parts to this chapter. First, I explore the integration debate and give a rationale for the type of integration I am proposing. In the second section, after describing what I think are the clinical strengths of the Milan model, I move into illustrating, through four case vignettes, the major problems I have experienced using the model. Then, out of these problems,

I pull six treatment areas, where by comparing and contrasting the Milan, MRI and Haley models, I propose some new ways to work within the Milan model. In the last section, I present ideas on interviewing questions that can be used to work with the links between models.

THE INTEGRATION DEBATE

As models have become more defined, a debate has arisen as to the benefits of integration or differentiation of structural, strategic and systemic models. There appear to be two main reasons that this debate has arisen now. First, the models themselves have been more fully developed and delineated. Second, family therapy training has moved beyond the apprenticeship stage of each person training with a "master" in one approach. Practitioners are being trained in more than one model and with this background can compare and contrast more than one theoretical perspective.

Stanton (1981) first proposed an integration of strategic and structural approaches with the therapist initially working structurally and switching to strategic techniques if the first approach was unsuccessful. A structural approach was also recommended at the end of treatment as a way to consolidate changes. Other authors have critiqued his approach, stating that it is not really an integration but a switching of models that Stanton is recommending (Liddle, 1984), and that the two models work with differing units of analysis (Fraser, 1982).

There seems to be widespread agreement about the benefits to be gained from *conceptualizing* families from more than one model (Fraser, 1982; Grunebaum & Chasin, 1982; Keeney & Ross, 1983; Liddle, 1982). However, many difficulties have been brought up about utilizing this binocular vision in *practice*. As MacKinnon & Slive (1984) thoughtfully demonstrated through presenting in depth two cases in which they worked from the perspective of three models, each model brought up very different ramifications for data gathering and interventions for the families. Rohrbaugh (1984) questions whether the structural, strategic and systemic therapies are epistemologically consistent. Coyne (1984) cautions that a structural approach and a strategic approach have very different stances on the style of the therapist (one is more directive and active, the other low key and free of confrontation) and that shifts in models should be assessed not only for their short-range impact on the case, but also for the long-range consequences for the therapeutic contract.

Other authors (Gurman, 1978; Lebow, 1984; Pinsof, 1983) have outlined advantages gained by integrating models such as a broader theoretical base, ability to work with a wider range of clients, combining the strongest aspects of specific approaches, greater flexibility in treatment, providing an arena to adapt new techniques, and less likelihood of therapists becoming bound by their model's world view. Lebow (1984), however, cautions that integrative approaches may have difficulty with being inconsistent as well as too complex for people to readily master.

Colapinto (1984), Fraser (1984), Keeney and Ross (1985), Liddle (1984) and Sluzki (1983), have gone beyond the integration debate to propose paradigms that connect models and provide ways to find workable links. However, they have yet to propose a *clinical map* of how these models work. Thus, this paper is concerned with flushing out a beginning framework for clinical practice in linking models.

Sluzki (1983) proposes that different strategic and systemic models emphasize parts of a larger, connected paradigm where the MRI model is process focused; structural and Haley strategic models focus on structure; and the Milan model emphasizes world view. Keeney and Ross (1985) have described a cybernetics of cybernetics frame in which the different emphases the Haley, MRI and Milan models place on semantic (meaning) and political (organizational consequences) frames are presented. They tried to link their different emphases by showing how each model is dependent on second-order cybernetics, where information loops back upon itself.

Fraser makes the case that the MRI strategic model fits with Buckley's (1967) description of a sociocultural model of systems, while the structural model fits with Buckley's organismic model of systems. He proposes that one way to integrate the structural and MRI strategic models is to subsume the organismic (structural) level premises under the sociocultural process level, selectively choosing tactics and metaphors from the structural model to fit into the process level. But he does not present any clinical examples of how he has done this, nor does he provide a clinical framework for others to begin to do this.

Colapinto (1984) critiques various types of integrative efforts and offers that model-building integration is the most useful. "Model building typically proceeds by enriching an approach — primarily espoused by the therapist — through the import of elements from other approaches. In some cases, the meaning that the imported notions or techniques had within the original conceptual context is altered to make them compatible with the next context" (p. 40). Liddle (1984) proposes going beyond the integration debate not only to find compatible links between models, creating integrative models at more than just the level of technique, but also to integrate models around the notion that they have complementary theories of change.

It is in the spirit of Colapinto's and Liddle's writing that this article proceeds. I am working towards an extension of the Milan model in a way which finds compatible links with the strategic models.

QUESTIONS ABOUT THE MILAN MODEL

Clinical Setting

Over the past couple of years, I have worked with two peer teams with live supervision. These two teams have had different emphases in regards to the Milan model; each has informed my attempts to adapt the model to a wider variety of clinical settings. In my smaller team with Richard Whiting, we were trained together in a variety of models (structural, strategic and systemic). We are more likely to use a wider range of models, shifting them or mixing them. On my other team with Lynn Hoffman, Stuart Golann and Alexander Blount, we have been trying more specifically to put the Milan model in practice and work most often with families where there are multiple helpers involved, previous therapy, and difficulties over a number of years.

For myself, the many strengths of the Milan model of therapy far outweigh any deficits. Generally, the model seems to provide "stretch" in two dimensions clinically: the temporal by linking past, present and future; and the spatial dimension by including the therapist, treatment team and referring persons as part of the treatment context. The patterns and new connections that are generated both for the team and family with circular questioning are very powerful. Multigenerational issues are worked with in a way that is not a cause-and-effect description of events but rather a way to provide new relational information to the system.

In the model, I like very much the inherent esteem for the family's autonomy and problem-solving capabilities, and the respectfulness of the view that problems for families are often the best solution that could be found by them at that time. There is also not a strong pathological focus that says this or that organization is dysfunctional; rather, there is flexibility about the myriad ways a family can organize. There is an awareness of multiple realities, with the thought that the therapeutic presentation of a view about the problem is not "reality" but only another hopefully more useful view.

However, there have been cases where I felt the Milan model did not work as successfully as it could have. Four case vignettes drawn from the two team sites described above are presented here, and represent sample cases where issues about the Milan model were highlighted for me. It is impossible to explain all the variables that affected each case and I have chosen here to focus on how the model seemed to work for the family and team.

Case Vignette #1: The A-B Family

The A-B Family, a blended family with three teenagers, was referred to us by another therapist after he had worked with the mother individually for some time, with the mother and live-in boyfriend, and for a few sessions with the family with a cotherapist. The presenting problem was fighting in the home, particularly with two teenage daughters who were engaged in some acting out behaviors such as staying out with friends, drinking, and school difficulties. The girls' biological parents had divorced some 10 years earlier and they had been living primarily with their mother. Two years ago, mother's boyfriend moved in with them at the same time that he and the mother opened up a business together. The biological father had regular contact with the children, but lived quite a different lifestyle as a "minimalist." He apparently did not have discipline problems with the children and was currently living with a girlfriend and her children. Other issues in the family included the level of commitment of mother and boyfriend to each other, and an older daughter who was off working part-time, but who had not really left home (she was living with grandparents and came home frequently to visit).

As we worked with this family, I think we did some good work through circular questioning and prescriptions at the end of sessions, linking several issues. We were struck by how the current issues about adult-child relationships in the home kept bringing biological father back into the picture and provided a way to rework some of the issues that had never gotten resolved about father's way to parent and mother's way to parent. This served to keep the boyfriend on the periphery, while always keeping the family membership boundaries open. The issue of whether this blended unit could really live together as a family was always up in the air, so that no one had to accept a definition of the end of one family and the beginning of a new family.

However, over time, things seemed to get worse with this family, not better. Initial presenting problems escalated. One daughter ended up in the hospital after a very severe drinking binge and was failing in school. Mother and boyfriend were more and more distant in both their personal relationship and business arrangements.

Model problem. There were three ways in which using the Milan model did not seem to help us. First, it seemed that the model was too isomorphic with an already dysfunctional pattern of finding and linking many explanations (parents had both had some training as therapists)—that it was easier to focus on these explanations than it was to make some concrete changes. Also, in gathering data, with the family connected to a number of households and with so many different crises, it seemed that as we tried to find patterns between the crises and number of people and households, we spun off in too many directions. The larger temporal and spatial frame of the Milan model gave us perhaps too much data.

Second, as more and more outside social control systems started to get involved, the family therapy lost its position as a primary relationship. In part, this happened because we were not a crisis team and were not available every day of the week, but it also happened because the Milan model regards calls for help in crises as feedback to interventions that can weaken the impact of ongoing work if they are responded to too readily (Selvini-Palazzoli et al., 1978). Eventually, I felt as if we lost this family to outside systems—they connected with other systems more and more and we never really terminated with them.

Third, longer intervals of time between sessions, described as necessary for too richly cross-joined systems so as to be able to process new and complex information (Selvini-Palazzoli, 1980) seemed to have the effect of diffusing interventions, rather than allowing them to influence family patterns in some way. In three weeks, a month, the family had gone on to a new crisis in which the end of session prescription was lost.

This case raised two questions for me in regards to the Milan model:

1) Would we have been able to slow things down and prevent some of the escalation of presenting problems if we had narrowed our focus instead of opening up more and more connections over several households, problems and generations?
2) What would have happened with this case if we had had more flexibility around working with the crises of the family? Would we have "lost" them to the other social control agencies?

Case Vignette #2: The K Family

The K family was referred to family therapy by the school counselor after the oldest daughter had flunked most of her previous year in high school. The parents had been separated for three years and there was one other child, a son a year younger than the daughter. As the family started in therapy, the father agreed to participate to see what he could do to help the children.

Shortly after therapy began, the presenting problem shifted to the son who had now started to do poorly in school (while his sister was doing reasonably well). In addition, the parents openly acknowledged that they had many issues and hurts between each other because of their very difficult marriage.

As we worked with the family, everyone agreed that it would be good for the father to be more connected to the children, especially spending more time with his son; for the mother to be off on her own more; for the son to be more disciplined about his studying (both self-disciplined and disciplined by his parents); and for the daughter to be supported in her quest to be more involved with her peers. They also described shifts in their overall organization in that they wanted father to be more of a parent and mother less of a sibling and more responsible for the overall running of the household. But as these things were discussed in terms of why they should not happen, who would be the most affected if they did happen, what other relationships would change, how this would affect the quasi separation of the parents, etc., things did not change in the family that much.

We also tried with little effect a ritualistic thanking prescription where each member of the family thanked the others for specified behaviors which kept things the same (e.g. the mother thanking the son for not moving on with his life as it protected her by keeping her close to home and concerned more with his life than with her own changes).

We started to ask family members how they would be most likely to do some of the things they had said they wanted to do and several members said, "If you tell us to do it directly." In fact, we had some evidence for this. When we had asked them to gather data outside of the session, they had done it very thoughtfully and thoroughly. (All had been asked to write down which dyadic relationship would be easiest to change, and which one would be hardest to change. Mother and father were also asked to write down the advantages and disadvantages of parenting each child in the ways they had been parented by their own mother and father.)

Model problem. This case raised the following three questions for me:

1) Where and how does the Milan model take into account the importance of the family view of change and how the therapist-family relationship can facilitate working with their views of change? For example, some families seem more concrete than others in how they approach change, others seem more metaphoric, and yet others are more able to begin to change if "directed" from outside.
2) What are some ways to gather data from families about how they would like to see the therapist-team-family interface around change?
3) How can you work with the family picture of how their organization and hierarchy should be if your model talks more about reflexive relationships?

Case Vignette #3: The Q Family

The presenting problem with the Q family was behavioral difficulties with the oldest son who was eight years old. The mother clearly believed that his worsening behavior was linked to the murder of the mother's lover by her estranged husband and father of her four-year-old daughter. Her husband was currently in jail. Given that the mother's lover was a woman and that she lived in a relatively conservative community, the mother had borne the brunt of a lot of negative feedback from the town which considered that she had brought this whole situation upon herself.

Her husband's family and her own family were also very intertwined. Her only sister had been engaged to her husband's brother for 10 years, her father had had an affair with a member of her husband's family, and all of her husband's siblings had come previously to the family home to try to remove the mother's lover after her husband had moved out.

The mother felt that she must move the family after the murder because of the community's attitude and the bad feelings between her husband's family and her and her two children. When the mother moved, she left behind any support network of (1) extended family, (2) neighborhood, and (3) school and peer friends for the children. As her husband was in jail, she also was receiving no parental support in regards to the children.

Model problem. The two questions this case raised for me about the Milan model were:

1) The Milan model calls for therapist neutrality, yet this is a situation where the woman and her family need a new support network. Is it appropriate for therapy to temporarily become part of the support network — for the therapist to be in closer proximity?
2) If the therapist is in closer proximity for a time, how can the therapist regain neutrality at some later point?

Case Vignette #4: The Z Family

The Z family was brought into treatment with the team after one of the team members had worked with the family alone for some sessions and felt there had been little change. The presenting problem was the daughter's not leaving the house for anything except her individual therapy session once a week. Some marital difficulties were also acknowledged between stepfather and mother and the couple had been seen alone for a few sessions.

We met with the mother, stepfather and daughter once and decided to enlarge the spatial frame of therapy by inviting in the mother's parents. We decided to do this because there appeared to be many issues about mother's separation from them (she had moved back home with them after leaving her abusive first marriage when her daughter was two), their acceptance of the stepfather, and the daughter's relationship with them. We worked with these three generations over a period of several months and came to see many powerful links. Mother had had a special relationship with her mother because of a long childhood illness which resulted in a disabled limb. The daughter also had a special relationship with the grandmother who had taken care of her granddaughter for a number of years after the mother moved back home and went back to work. The grandfather had a history of long hours of work away from the home, the biological father had disappeared, and the stepfather seemed on the periphery of intense relationships between grandmother, mother and daughter.

The daughter's symptom of not going out seemed to mirror the theme of independence/dependence which had been an issue in the previous two generations with (1) grandmother wanting more independence out of the home but being afraid to take it with grandfather very independent from the home; (2) mother having difficulty leaving home because of her special relationship with her mother around her illness and the debt she owed to her; and (3) the daughter's biological father taking complete independence from the family.

We positively connoted how the daughter's symptoms kept these issues alive, allowing all the generations an arena in which to work them out. The daughter's symptomatology remained the same with little change over a period of months. Some changes in the family occurred, with people speaking more directly to each other and a wider range of emotions being expressed. Everyone seemed more open about sharing information generally. However, the positive connotation of the daughter's symptom seemed too isomorphic with the family's own view of the problem not really being a problem. It did not bring to the fore that side of the family that would every once in awhile say, "What a shame it is to see a young woman wasting her life like this." Rather, the positive connotation highlighted the family view that said, "There are good reasons for this problem and we need to sit and understand it more."

Model problem. The questions this case raised for me about the Milan model were:

1) If we had focused more on the specific presenting problem of the daughter, would there have been more and faster change in her symptoms?
2) What happens with families when a positive connotation is too isomorphic to their existing view of the problem?

Summary: Six Model Problem Areas

In these case vignettes, a number of model problems occur. First, there is the question of *neutrality* and how it works as a therapeutic stance when many outside systems are involved; or when judgments are being made for and about a family by other systems; or when it seems appropriate for therapy to temporarily be part of the support system for the family. Second, there is the issue of the stance of the therapist and team towards *outcome and change* in treatment. Does being neutral to outcome work for all families? Third, do all families change the same way in therapy or do some families work better with a more *directive* stance, others with a more *co-evolutionary* process or even with a more *open-ended* approach that emphasizes their own problem solving? Related to this question is another query: "Are all families stuck in the same ways? If they are stuck in different ways, do you offer change in different ways?"

A fourth question that is raised is whether always seeing a problem as a *positive solution* limits some of the possible therapeutic strategies. A fifth theme clusters around what the family view is of how *hierarchy and reflexivity* work within their unit. Whom do they hold responsible, whom do they see as having power, etc.? Finally, is the *larger temporal frame* of the Milan model needed at all times for families or does it sometimes introduce too much information and too many diffuse issues?

As MacKinnon (1983) has pointed out, the Milan associates "sacrifice some strategic flexibility in order to maintain rigor and consistency within their systemic theory and methodology" (pp. 435–436). The question for me becomes how to maintain the consistency within the Milan model while giving it more adaptability with some stances of the MRI and Haley models, which provide another alternative to address the model problem areas.

In the third section of this chapter, these six model problem areas will be addressed by (1) describing what I see as the Milan, MRI and Haley positions on the six areas; (2) proposing a new model link that would address the problem area; and (3) concluding with a chart which presents a synopsis of the model position and the proposed change.

MODEL POSITIONS ON ISSUES AND LINKS TO THE MILAN MODEL*

I. Therapist-Family-Team and Outside System Connections

MILAN MODEL POSITION	MRI MODEL POSITION	HALEY MODEL POSITION
Neutrality towards connections, with therapist, team and referring persons all seen as part of therapeutic suprasystem.	Utilize client world view and language especially to connect with "complainant," little emphasis on therapeutic suprasystem.	Planfully join individuals and subsystems with emphasis placed on outside systems coming under control of therapy.

With the *Milan model*, the therapist and team are to remain neutral to individual positions in the family, to the referring person(s), and to other outside systems. This provides the therapeutic team with a metaperspective on the family difficulties that protects against inadvertently creating alliances or coalitions or seeing things from only one perspective.

The Milan model is the first systems model to really actualize premises that consider the therapist and team as part of the therapeutic system. In that sense, the spatial context for therapy is expanded. Also, referring persons and

---

*See chart on pp. 168–169.

extended family are often considered as an integral part of the family system. Therefore, other people will often be invited into sessions and the therapist/team will be included in therapeutic loops that are examined.

In the *MRI model*, there is more emphasis on utilizing world view and language of people for connection to clients, especially the "complainants." MRI focuses on as small a unit as possible. There is little discussion about working at the interface of larger systems and families and little attention paid to the formation of a new therapeutic suprasystem.

With the *Haley model*, individuals and subsystems are joined with the intention of using these alliances as positions from which to unbalance and restructure the family. This strong connection with the therapist is not interfered with by the team members or supervisor coming out from behind the mirror and there is not as strong a family/team connection as there is in the Milan model. The deliberate joining by the therapist is seen as a way to engage the family in treatment as well as to create energy for change.

The *Haley model* is more likely to emphasize the hierarchical nature of family relationships with outside systems and the control of those relationships by the therapist. For instance, he (Haley, 1980) recommends not working in situations where the therapist does not have control of issues such as medication of an individual or rehospitalization. The focus is on outside systems *fitting into the family therapy*, with this focus seemingly providing a way to limit the field of family-outside support-therapy interactions.

Discussion: Problem and proposed change. The Milan model has been critiqued for sometimes not engaging people in treatment because of the therapist's more neutral stance (Pirrotta, 1984). Also, as Miller (1984) has pointed out, neutrality in response to a family dilemma may not be neutrality at all in the sense that not taking a position about an issue then allows a larger societal position on the issue to take priority. This becomes a difficult issue to address when you are doing therapy in a situation that reflects the oppression of the larger society, e.g., the Q family presented earlier where the mother's woman lover was murdered and much of the community turned against her. To be neutral to her dilemma is to indirectly condone the reaction of her community.

The benefits of neutrality — not being pulled inadvertently into coalitions or alliances and being able to keep a metaperspective — seem to far outweigh the deficits of a neutral position. But how can the concept of neutrality be modified to work better in situations of engagement of families and where the larger society has made a stand which is not neutral in regards to the family?

Both in relationship to the initial engagement in treatment and to nonneutral stances made by outside systems, I would like to propose two changes in the Milan model. First, the therapist should remain neutral as to the assignment of responsibility for the family problem, and neutral as to how to solve the problem (unless as described later, "experimentally" the therapist does otherwise), but not neutral to the pain, hurt and anger that the dilemma causes each individual and the family as a whole. Affectively, one can connect with each member without losing the overall neutrality of not siding with the ascriptions of blame and/or responsibility given by family members. The thought would be not to join each person to create a base from which to restructure the family. Instead, one engages all members of the family "equally" as a means of keeping them in treatment

Second, the therapist and team would not remain neutral to the fact that non-neutral stances from the outside have impact on the family. Rather, questions would be asked in therapy about how positions of outside systems impact upon them and work done explicitly with the family around ways to make these relationships better. The family themselves would be encouraged to take a stand that was not necessarily neutral.

II. Change in Therapy and Stance Towards Outcome

MILAN MODEL	MRI MODEL	HALEY MODEL
Neutral to change and outcome.	Advocate change but often from go-slow, one-down, no-change position of therapist.	Advocate change, often from a one-up expert position. Work towards particular outcome.

The *Milan model* is neutral to change in that they do not have a picture of exactly how the family should be after they have solved their problem. Rather, they feel that the family themselves will work out how they will be. Interventions more often keep balancing stability and change at the same time rather than as interventions that are given in one mode and then the other. Stability is usually positively connoted and change often worked with in the hypothetical future arena, as opposed to "do this change now."

The *MRI and Haley models* are both more likely to espouse change in a particular direction, or else as a tactic to espouse no change (but because they think they will get more change if they do this).

MRI is more likely to go one down and look at the no-change position and talk about all the ways things should remain the same and how things work for people so therefore should not be changed. The Haley model is more likely to remain in a one-up expert position, directly promoting change.

Both models have a non-neutral stance to change in the sense that even when they take a no-change position, they are taking that position because they think it will bring about change in a particular direction.

Discussion: Problem and proposed change. All three models emphasize a stance on change which may or may not be the family's view of how they change with outside help, or reflective of the way that the family has successfully changed in the past. In the MRI and Haley models, change is helped along (either overtly or covertly) in a specific direction which the therapists judge is the best, while the Milan model evolves with the family what things might look like in the future.

Yet none of the models takes into account that just as individuals have learning styles, so do families have unique problem-solving styles. Ways need to be created to gather this information and design therapist-family-team fits that work with the family style.

Rather than assuming that each model's underlying assumption about how families change in therapy is the only way families are transformed, I propose using each model's map of change as a guide to ask circular questions of the family about how they problem solve. This assumes the view that families change in different ways, such as: (1) by being told what to do; (2) by understanding how the present situation works for them and is no longer a problem; (3) by enlarging their temporal time frame and gaining a multi-generational perspective both past and future; (4) by going against therapists; (5) by changing in spite of therapists; and (6) by brainstorming a number of new solutions.

Circular questioning provides a vehicle to ask hypothetical questions about change. For instance, with a family where the parents were having trouble disciplining a young child, questions might be asked such as:

1) If we were to ask you to parent your child differently, what do you think we would ask you to do?
2) Who would be most likely to listen to us?
3) Who would find it easier to change if we told you to directly do some things?
4) Whom would it be harder for?

III. Directiveness/Indirectiveness of Team and Therapist

MILAN MODEL	MRI MODEL	HALEY MODEL
Coevolutionary stance.	Directiveness masked as indirectiveness.	Directiveness.

The *Milan model* takes the position that families will find their own different solutions in therapy if the therapists introduce "news of a difference" and comment on relationship patterns. They do not particularly ask people to change relationships in a way that says, "This is the way this family should be."

The *MRI model* tends to work more indirectly, with some commonly used strategies such as the therapist going one-down, working in therapy with all the reasons not to change, and solving one problem by linking it with another problem.

In the *Haley model*, clients are told directly what to do based on underlying assumptions on what is the current family organization. People are asked to do things that put them closer to a picture of a properly functioning hierarchy.

Discussion: Problem and proposed change. With the Milan approach, it seems that some families are not able to sufficiently focus their energies on different solutions and things either keep escalating as the team introduces more "news of a difference" (A-B family) or redundantly repeating (K family, Z family). A possible way to bring more focus around change issues but not to move to the Haley end of the continuum and direct people in a particular way is to ask the family themselves about how they might change. One can "experiment" with directiveness and indirectiveness. In other words, in the same way that the Milan group sometimes asks people to gather information as part of an experiment to provide additional data, people might be asked to do specific tasks (if they choose a directive approach) not with the frame that if they do that task, they will be a "better" family, but rather with the frame that in doing the task they will generate useful information about how they work. In reverse, if a family felt that they would prefer a more indirect approach to change, the therapeutic system could "experiment" with this. Circular questions would then be asked about each experiment. In a sense, the therapeutic team remains neutral to specific change, but does not remain neutral to the issue of discussing change, experimenting with it, and analyzing what happens. This is all done in the spirit of collaboration, not a spirit of tricking or pushing people into change.

IV. Problem and Solution Ascription

MILAN MODEL	MRI MODEL	HALEY MODEL
Problem as the solution. Connoting problem positively.	Solution as the problem. People are doing the best they can.	Problem as reflection of wrong social organization. Connoting problem both positively and negatively.

The *Milan model* views the problem as the best solution that the family could come up with in trying to solve another difficulty. Therefore, in the Milan approach, the solution is positively connoted, while other possibilities are introduced through circular questioning, prescriptions, rituals, etc., without necessarily directly trying to shift the problem-solving cycle.

MRI views the attempted solution as often then becoming a problem in and of itself and therefore tries to interdict that problem-solving cycle.

Haley sees the problem as reflective of dysfunctional social organization and therefore tries to realign the structure of the family through changing interactional patterns.

Discussion: Problem and proposed change. Rather than assuming the model view of the problem-solution cycle is the only way to view it, I propose that the three models' different positions be used to both discover and enhance the family's possible views of the problem-solution cycle. As noted earlier, Brickman et al. (1982) have emphasized that helping systems sometimes are not able to help those in need of aid because they have very different ideas about how the problem arose and what should be done about it.

The converse is also a problem at times — where the therapist-team view of the problem-solution cycle is so close to the family's that no "news of a difference" is introduced (e.g. the Z family described earlier in the case vignettes). By finding out what the family problem-solution cycle is, the therapy team can avoid presenting a view which fits the family view either too closely or not enough. But while the therapy team is clarifying the family position by asking questions from each of the models, they can be teaching the family about other kinds of ways to work with the problem-solution cycle.

For instance, in the Z family where the young woman had the problem of not being able to leave the house, she tried to solve it by going to individual therapy. Her grandmother tried to solve it by saying she wanted to get closer to her, get her more interested in things. Mom and stepfather tried to solve it by not putting pressure on her, supporting her therapy and talking with her. Once the kinds of solutions have been detailed, questions can be asked about them which inform both the family and the team, such as:

1) Which of these solutions worked?
2) Which of them became problems?
3) In what way did they become problems?
4) How did these solutions impact on your family structure?
5) How did these problems impact on your family structure?
6) Which solutions are likely to succeed in one year? Not succeed?
7) Which one would most people support?
8) If you tried this solution for five years, what would happen?

V. Hierarchy and Reflexivity

MILAN MODEL	MRI MODEL	HALEY MODEL
Relationships are reflexive; greater responsibility or influence of members not emphasized.	Family hierarchy not important. Do not work from pathological view of family structure.	Map of what is correct family hierarchy.

The *Milan model* sees the "members of the family as elements in a circuit of interaction. None of the members has unidirectional power over the whole, although the behavior of any one member inevitably influences the behavior of the others" (Selvini-Palazzoli et al., 1978, p. 5).

The *MRI model* does not work with a view of there being a pathological family structure. Rather, they focus on sequences of interaction and problem-solving behavior, ignoring the issue of whether someone has more or less power or influence over someone else. They are not interested in the question of motivation or why someone does something.

The *Haley model* implicitly has within it a view of who has more influence and responsibility in a family. People higher in the hierarchy (and a correct hierarchy is built around age differences in the home) have more power and responsibility for the turn of events in family situations.

Discussion: Problem and proposed change. Each model has within it a different view of how members influence each other and how hierarchy works or does not work. What seems more important than holding fast to each model's view of how all families are structured and influence each other is to question each family and ask them how they perceive their family. The descriptions of the importance or non-importance of hierarchy and reflexivity given by the models can be used as a resource in therapy, as descriptive information that can be the anchor point for questions to discover the family's view of their organization. Some possible questions are:

1) How would the family compare and contrast their family organization with other families?
2) Who has the most influence in the family? Least influence? Who would like to have more? Less?
3) If they wanted the family organization to look different, how would it look?
4) Have each family member sculpt how they view the current organization and ask questions about similarities and differences between each sculpt.
5) Inquire about past family organization (previous marriages, families of origin) and compare and contrast them to current family patterns.

There may also be cases where the family cannot or does not have as much choice about how they would like to work with or reorganize their family. For instance, when social control issues arise (such as abuse, delinquent behavior), the outside society may dictate how the family hierarchy must work by saying who will be held accountable and responsible for certain actions. In situations like this, it seems that the Haley model provides a map of who influences whom most in the family that fits with societal notions of responsibility.

VI. Temporal Frame in Therapy

MILAN MODEL	MRI MODEL	HALEY MODEL
Focus on linking past, present and future time.	Focus on interactional sequences in the present to discover dysfunctional sequences.	Focus on interactional sequences in the present to discover dysfunctional sequences and structure.

In the *Milan model*, the past, present and future are all linked through circular questioning. An important part of building a systemic view in therapy seems to be these cross connections in time. Current issues are explored in relationship to how past events give them meaning, as well as what meaning might be given to them if they continued into the future.

In the *MRI model*, little history is gathered (except history of the problem), nor is there much emphasis on future ramifications of problems. Rather, the temporal frame stays focused on the present. Given that any number of different past events could have led to the current problems (equifinality of systems), it is not considered important to uncover the past events, but rather just change the present dysfunctional patterns.

In the *Haley model*, again there is little emphasis on the historical or future frame. Rather, current dysfunctional sequences of behavior are focused on in order to shift a dysfunctional structure.

Discussion: Problem and proposed change. At times it seems that the Milan model can get bogged down in too much data, and that the "largeness" of the data can overwhelm smaller important sequences of interaction. On the other hand, it seems that with the MRI and Haley models, the historical and future meaning that is given to interaction by family members does not seem to be very fully explored. In these models, changes are tried at times in small sequences of behavior, but are unsuccessful because concomitant changes in world view of the problem are not made.

The most useful way to view the temporal frame would seem to be as a series of concentric circles within which therapists can work their way out as need be, or then go back in to a smaller temporal cycle frame.

SUMMARY

I propose to expand upon the Milan model by combining this model's notions about how problems evolve and families find solutions with the MRI and Haley model ideas about problem evolution and change. None of the model positions is seen as more "true" for all families; rather, each model

Model Positions on Issues and Links to the Milan Model

Milan Model	MRI Model	Haley Model	Model Links
I. THERAPIST-FAMILY-TEAM-OUTSIDE SYSTEM CONNECTIONS			
Neutrality towards connections with therapist, team and referring persons all seen as part of therapeutic suprasystem.	Utilize client world view and language to connect, especially with "complainant." Little emphasis on therapeutic suprasystem.	Planfully join individuals and subsystems with emphasis placed on outside systems coming under control of therapy.	Connect to family members affectively (with equal "air" time). Make explicit outside systems impact on the family while remaining neutral as to what to do re that impact.
II. CHANGE IN THERAPY AND STANCE TOWARDS OUTCOME			
Neutral to change and outcome.	Advocate change but often from go-slow, one-down, no-change position of therapist.	Advocate change, often from a one-up expert position. Work towards particular outcome.	Use three model positions to help discern family stance to change as well as what kind of change relationship with helpers in the past has worked for them.
III. DIRECTIVENESS/INDIRECTIVENESS OF TEAM AND THERAPIST			
Coevolutionary stance.	Directiveness masked as indirectiveness.	Directiveness.	"Experimental" directiveness.

	Milan Model	MRI Model	Haley Model	Model Links
IV. PROBLEM AND SOLUTION ASCRIPTION	Problem as the solution. Connoting problems positively.	Solution as the problem. People are doing the best they can.	Problem as reflection of wrong social organization. Problem connoted both positively and negatively.	Use three model positions to help discern family view of problem and solution ascription.
V. HIERARCHY AND REFLEXIVITY	Relationships are reflexive; greater responsibility of influence of members not emphasized.	Family hierarchy not important. Do not work from pathological view of family structure.	Map of what is correct family hierarchy.	Use the three model positions to help find out family view of how they think they should be organized.
VI. TEMPORAL FRAME IN THERAPY	Focus on linking past, present and future time.	Focus on interactional sequences in the present to discover dysfunctional sequences.	Focus on interactional sequences in the present to discover dysfunctional sequences and structure.	Make specific decisions to narrow the temporal frame to smaller interactional sequences.

is seen as offering a possible framework by which to find out how the *family views* their problem-solving capabilities.

The Milan model is proposed as the larger theoretical position from which to work for a number of reasons:

1) Its important technique and intervention, circular questioning, offers a rich way to ask questions about all the model positions.
2) It has a larger temporal frame, so that the therapist can contract and expand as need be into the past, present and future.
3) It has a larger spatial frame that includes the therapeutic team as part of the observing system as well as other important outside people (such as referring persons), so that the positions of these people "outside" the family can be examined as part of the loops of the family dilemmas.

Some of the ways that I am proposing to expand the repertoire of the Milan model include:

  I. While remaining neutral to the family dilemmas, join with individual members around their anger, hurt, sorrow, as a way to engage the family in treatment. Equal air time should be given to each person's affective responses. Explore with families the effects of being neutral or taking a stand in relation to various other social control agencies. Neutrality may not always be neutral and may, in fact, inadvertently end up supporting a position.
 II. Use different model positions about change and outcome to therapy to discern family stance to change as well as what kind of change relationship with helpers in the past has worked for them.
III. Use experimental directiveness as a way to have access to the various directive techniques of the strategic models without coming from the position that if you do things in this way then your family will be better.
 IV. Use the different model maps of problem and solution ascription as a guide to discover family members' views of the problem and solution cycles.
  V. Use the different model positions on hierarchy and reflexivity to find out family view of how they think they should be organized.
 VI. Make specific decisions to narrow the temporal frame at times when it appears the larger temporal frame is too isomorphic to the family's stuck patterns or that too much information is being introduced.

Here are some sample questions of the kind of things that might be asked of families to coevolve this picture of what model's framework would be most useful in working with them. First are some general questions about responsibility for the problem and solutions for the problem. Then there are questions for each of the three models.

General Questions:

Traditional questions around who/what/where/when, then into:

• Who/what events are given responsibility for the problem?
• What have you tried to solve it?
• Who has been most invested in solutions/least invested?
• What have you solved successfully in the past?
• Who was most instrumental in that successful problem solving?
• What skills in that situation can you use in this situation?
• What are advantages to current situation?
• What are disadvantages?
• How is this problem linked to other problems (if at all)?
• Who has changed the most in this family over time?
• Who has changed the least?
• How do you learn?
• Who thinks they could come up with a better solution than coming to therapy?

MRI Model Questions:

• How has the solution become a problem?
• Who is hurting the most?
• Who is most invested in family therapy?
• How is the problem a problem?
• If therapists were to work with just those most upset/hurting, who would be most comfortable with this? Least?
• If the therapist were to work with you indirectly, who would be most comfortable? Least comfortable?

Haley Model Questions:

• How do you view the family organization?
• How has this organization changed over time?
• If you were to change that organization, how would it look?
• If we were to tell you directly to do things, who would be most comfortable? Least?
• Who would be most likely to do it? Least?

Milan Model Questions:

- If we were to work indirectly with you linking past, present and future events, connections between this family and other families, who would be most comfortable? Least?
- Who would be most comfortable working with extended family? With referring persons?
- Who would think working this way is the most useful?
- If we were to tell you that we do not know *the* answer for this family, but we can work together to help experiment with some new ways with you, who would be most comfortable?

REFERENCES

Beavers, R. (1977). *Psychotherapy and Growth: A Family Systems Perspective*. New York: Brunner/ Mazel.

Boscolo, L., & Cecchin, G. (1982). Training in systemic therapy at the Milan Center. In R. Whiffen & J. Byng-Hall (Eds.), *Family Therapy Supervision: Recent Developments in Practice*. London: Academic Press.

Brickman, P., Rabinowitz, V. C., Karuza, J., Coates, D., Cohn, E., & Kidder, L. (1982). Models of helping and coping. *American Psychologist, 37* (4), 368–384.

Buckley, W. (1967). *Sociology and Modern Systems Theory*. Englewood Cliffs, NJ: Prentice-Hall.

Colapinto, J. (1984). On model integration and model integrity. *The Journal of Strategic and Systemic Therapies, 3*(3), 38–42.

Coyne, J. C. (1984). Introducing structural interventions into strategic therapy: A caution. *The Journal of Strategic and Systemic Therapies, 3* (3), 23–27.

Fraser, J. S. (1982). Structural and strategic family therapy: A basis for marriage or grounds for divorce? *Journal of Marital and Family Therapy, 8*, 13–22.

Fraser, J. S. (1984). Process level integration: Corrective vision for a binocular view. *The Journal of Strategic and Systemic Therapies, 3* (3), 43–57.

Grunebaum, H., & Chasin, R. (1982). Thinking like a family therapist: A model for integrating the theories and methods of family therapy. *Journal of Marital and Family Therapy, 8* (4), 403–416.

Gurman, A. (1978). Contemporary marital therapies. In T. Paolino & B. McCrady (Eds.), *Marriage and Marital Therapy*. New York: Brunner/Mazel.

Haley, J. (1980). *Leaving Home: The Therapy of Disturbed Young People*. New York: McGraw-Hill.

Imber-Black (Coppersmith), E. (1983). The family and public service systems: An assessment method. In B. Kenney (Ed.), *Diagnosis and Assessment in Family Therapy*. Rockville, MD: Aspen Publications.

Imber-Black (Coopersmith), E. (in press, a) The systemic consultant and human service provider systems. In L. Wynne (Ed.), *Family Therapist as Consultant*. New York: Guilford Press.

Imber-Black (Coopersmith), E. (in press, b). Toward a resource model in systemic family therapy. In M. Karpel (Ed.), *Family Resources*. New York: Guilford Press.

Keeney, B. P. (1983). *Aesthetics of Change*. New York: Guilford Press.

Keeney, B. P., & Ross, J. M. (1983). Cybernetics of brief family therapy. *Journal of Marital and Family Therapy, 9* (4), 375–382.

Keeney, B. P., & Ross, J. M. (1985). *Mind in Therapy: Constructing Systemic Family Therapies*. New York: Basic Books.

Lebow, J. (1984). On the value of integrating approaches to family therapy. *Journal of Marital and Family Therapy, 10* (2), 127–138.

Liddle, H. A. (1982). On the problems of eclecticism: A call for epistemologic clarification and human-scale theories. *Family Process, 21*, 243–250.

Liddle, H. A. (1984). Towards a dialectical, contextual, coevolutionary translation of structural-strategic family therapy. *The Journal of Strategic and Systemic Therapies, 3* (3), 66–77.

MacKinnon, L. (1983). Contrasting strategic and Milan therapies. *Family Process, 22* (4), 425–441.

MacKinnon, L., Parry, A., & Black, R. (1984). Strategies of family therapy: The relationship to styles of family functioning. *The Journal of Strategic and Systemic Therapies, 3* (3), 6–22.

MacKinnon, L., & Slive, A. (1984). If one should not marry a hypothesis, should one marry a model? *The Journal of Strategic and Systemic Therapies, 3* (4), 26–39.

Miller, D. (1984). Therapeutic neutrality as a primary distinction between models in systems-oriented family therapy. *The Journal of Strategic and Systemic Therapies, 3* (4), 55–62.

Parry, A. (1984). Maturanation in Milan: Recent developments in systemic therapy. *The Journal of Strategic and Systemic Therapies, 3* (1), 35–42.

Pinsof, W. (1983). Integrative problem-centered therapy: Toward the synthesis of family and individual psychotherapies. *Journal of Marital and Family Therapy, 9* (1), 19–35.

Pirrotta, S. (1984). Milan revisited: A comparison of the two Milan schools. *The Journal of Strategic and Systemic Therapies, 3* (4), 3–15.

Roberts, J. (1983). The third tier: An ignored dimension in family therapy training. *The Family Therapy Networker, 7* (2), 30–31, 60–61.

Rohrbaugh, M. (1984). The strategic systems therapies: Misgivings about mixing the models. *The Journal of Strategic and Systemic Therapies, 3* (3), 28–32.

Selvini-Palazzoli, M. (1980). Why a long interval between sessions? In M. Andolfi & I. Zwerling (Eds.), *Dimensions of Family Therapy.* New York: Guilford Press.

Selvini-Palazzoli, M., Boscolo, L., Cecchin, G., & Prata, G. (1978). *Paradox and Counterparadox.* New York: Jason Aronson.

Sluzki, C. (1983). Process, structure, and world view: Toward an integrated view of systemic models in family therapy. *Family Process, 22* (4), 469–476.

Stanton, D. (1981). An integrated structural/strategic approach to family therapy. *Journal of Marital and Family Therapy, 7*, 427–439.

Chapter 8

The Strategic Use of Hypnosis in Family Therapy

Howard Protinsky

The map or framework that forms the basis for this approach to hypnotic interventions in family therapy has several major components. First, symptomatic behavior is understood as being maintained by the interpersonal patterns that surround it. That is, symptoms are anchored in redundant sequences of behavior that occur between people. This notion has been written about in detail by Fisch et al., (1982); Haley (1976); and Watzlawick et al., (1974). Hypnotic interventions from this part of the framework are aimed at the interruption of these symptom maintaining recursive loops.

For example, in a family where the presenting problem was the psychogenic headaches of a 15-year-old daughter of a single-parent mother, the rigid sequence around the manifestation of the daughter's headaches involved the following. Daughter would come home from school and talk about her pain that was, in her view, due to school stress. Mother would become worried about her daughter's headache and feelings of stress. She would question her daughter in detail about her headache and about the various stresses that the daughter might be experiencing. This questioning would last from 15 to 30 minutes, and then daughter would go to her room with extreme pain. Mother would feel helpless and busy herself with dinner preparation. Much of the remainder of the evening would be spent with mother checking on the daughter's condition and attempting ineffective solutions for the headaches, such as aspirin, cold compresses, massage, and further discussion of what could be troubling the daughter. Despite all of mother's efforts, the daughter's headaches became worse throughout the evening. The more mother tried to help, the more the daughter's headaches increased.

Treatment consisted of teaching the daughter the use of self-hypnosis for

174

pain reduction. Anytime the daughter complained of headaches, mother was to send her to her room so that she could practice her self-hypnosis. The content of the self-hypnotic trance was particular to the daughter's situation and involved the use of suggestion and imagery in a way that would help the daughter deal with her stresses and alleviate pain. The process of the daughter's headaches being the cue for the mother to send the daughter to her room for trance was sufficient for interrupting the pattern of interaction of mother and daughter around the symptom. The fact that the mother was convinced by the therapist that self-hypnosis would be the most effective treatment for her daughter enabled the mother to disengage from the typical sequence so that the daughter could be alone for her trance work.

Another part of this framework is that symptoms are also a part of redundant sequences of behavior that are intrapersonal in nature. O'Hanlon has written about the internal processes that accompany symptomatic behavior. These processes involve the sensory-perceptual systems, internal processing systems, physiological response systems, and motor behavior systems. All of these may be used as points of hypnotic intervention so that internal pattern interruption may occur (O'Hanlon, 1982).

For example, in the treatment of a recently divorced mother and her acting-out teenage son, it was determined that the son reminded mother of her ex-husband, especially of his negative traits. When the son would begin to misbehave, mother was not able to take effective action due to her extreme emotional response to him and his behavior. She would then become an emotional reactor rather than an effective actor in that situation.

The therapist decided to use a hypnotic intervention with mother that would deal with her internal response pattern to her son's behavior in a way that would lead to a different way of interacting with him, i.e., external pattern interruption. In trance work over several sessions, mother was taught to use effectively the trance phenomenon of negative hallucination. This phenomenon refers to the ability not to see what is actually there. She was able to use this ability to overlook or not see those parts of her son that reminded her of her ex-husband and that increased her irrational emotional reactions to him. In addition, she was taught in trance to be able to focus upon her son's positive qualities. In fact, certain behaviors that had been defined by her as negative would be the cue for her to experience positive feelings about her son. As she accomplished this first in trance and later transferred the ability to the waking state, her behavior toward her son changed and their negative pattern of interaction was abolished.

It is also assumed in this framework that these pathological sequences of interaction may be understood to form certain interpersonal structures. Patterns of interaction may be analyzed from the viewpoint of boundaries (who participates with whom) and hierarchy (who is in charge of whom). These ideas, of course, have been greatly expounded upon by Minuchin (1974) and Haley (1976). For this framework, what is important is that the modification of boundaries and hierarchy that are associated with symptomatic behavior will have an impact in terms of pattern interruption. Thus, the boundary and hierarchy component of this framework offers another guideline for the planning and implementation of hypnosis as an intervention strategy.

As an example of the above, a family consisting of an overinvolved mother and a distant father was referred because of the night fears of their 10-year-old son. This family represented the recognizable structure of the stable coalition (Haley, 1976). The treatment strategy involved activating father and disengaging mother by having father learn to use hypnotic trance with his son in order to help him with his fears. Mother was not taught these skills, so only father and son could work together on the problem. Improvement could be understood as the result of the restructuring of the family, in addition to the specific hypnotic strategy employed.

The final aspect of the framework is that such repetitive, pathological sequences between people and the structures these sequences form may also be understood in a functional context. The functions of symptoms in marriages and families have been written about by Haley (1976) and Madanes (1981). For example, sometimes a symptomatic child may be understood as serving the function of detouring marital conflict. Or, a symptom in one family member may be protective of or helpful to another.

An example would be the way in which a child's encopretic behavior may help his recently divorced mother who forgets her pain as she focuses on his problem. Successfully dealing with this protective function of the child's symptom may be accomplished in trance in different ways. One method would be to suggest to the child the substituting for his present symptom of a less debilitating symptom that could also serve to help mother. Thus, it could be suggested to the child in trance that refusing to do his chores would be just as effective as his encopresis in his efforts to protect his mother. Another way would be to suggest to the child in trance that the therapist will take over the function of helping mother so that his symptom would no longer be needed.

HYPNOTIC FRAMEWORK

In this approach, hypnotic trance refers to a state of heightened altered awareness and concentration where attention focuses inward on thoughts, values, memories, and feelings. In this state, the client can make use of the learnings that he/she already has and apply these learnings in different ways. This essentially describes the utilization approach of Milton Erickson. It is based upon the client's ability to utilize in a creative way resources he/she already possesses. From an Ericksonian perspective, therapeutic trance is useful because it helps people go beyond their own learned limitations and more fully use their potential.

In interpreting Erickson's work, Rossi has written (Erickson & Rossi, 1979) that therapeutic trance involves the temporary alteration of one's usual frames of reference and beliefs so that the client can then become more receptive to other patterns of association and functioning on a mental level that are conducive to problem solving. The hypnotherapist helps clients to find their own unique way of experiencing the trance state.

Erickson and Rossi have published a paradigm for the induction of trance and the use of suggestion within trance. The first step is to fixate attention either upon an external or internal point. For example, the client can be encouraged to focus upon a spot on the wall or upon certain bodily sensations. Also, interesting stories or conversations can be used as fixation points. Thus, anything that absorbs a person's attention can be classified as hypnotic. Erickson and Rossi point out that trances occur throughout the day for all of us as we focus upon or become preoccupied with something to the exclusion of awareness of our outer environment.

Another aspect of trance is that of depotentiating learned frameworks and belief systems of the client. In fixating attention, client belief systems are suspended temporarily, consciousness has been distracted. During this time unconscious patterns of association and experience can be manifested in a way that produces trance. Also, an unconscious search for new solutions to the problem may occur. Metaphor, puns, and analogy are ways of interrupting habitual patterns and creating an unconscious search for a new frame of reference. Thus, for example, indirect suggestions given in the context of a metaphorical story fixates attention, suspends habitual frameworks, and produces an unconscious search for a new perspective.

Direct suggestion may be effective while the client is in the trance state and this may be successful in removing the symptomatic behavior. However, from this framework, it is believed that symptom removal will be more permanent if it is the result of a reorganization and reassociation of resources. For example, for a client who is unable to assert herself in her marriage and predictably occupies a one-down position, she may reexperience within trance times in her past when she was assertive. This cognitive and emotional reexperiencing may then be reassociated to her present situation with her husband. Thus, the potential to be assertive which already resided in the client is activated and utilized for solving her present problem.

It is assumed that people have the necessary resources or potentials available to them to construct new patterns of intrapersonal and interpersonal interaction that do not include the symptomatic behavior. The use of trance is one way to activate these potentials. Also, as Wilk (1982) has commented, these potentials can become activated by abolishing the limiting interpersonal patterns that cause people to operate under the "illusion of limitations." Once the intrapersonal and interpersonal patterns are abolished, resources may be realized and new systems of interaction can take place.

HYPNOTIC INTERVENTION WITH SYMPTOM FUNCTIONS

As previously stated, one understanding of the creation and maintenance of symptoms in children is that they are related to the purpose that the dysfunction serves for the family or for individual family members. Specifically, the disorder may serve some helpful or protective function for the family system. Those behaviors that often seem as though they are self-destructive, hostile, irrational, or antisocial on the part of the child are understood as an attempt at helpfulness by the child. For example, a child's acting-out behavior may be helpful to his father who is experiencing some type of stress at work. As the child becomes symptomatic, father becomes preoccupied with his problem and allows his work stress to fade into the background.

The same process may occur with a couple experiencing marital stress. As the child becomes symptomatic, the parents submerge their conflict and focus on the child. As the child's behaviors provoke a concerned response on the part of the parents, they become organized around the child's problems, feel needed, and are provided a reason to overcome their own difficulties or to table them for the present. In this way, the marriage may be preserved.

If the therapist believes that the child's behavior is somehow protective of members of the family, an hypothesis must be formed as to the details of this act of helpfulness. This hypothesis is derived from family interviews in which the therapist discovers when, how, where, and with whom the symptom occurs; how the symptom becomes alleviated; who is most upset by the child's behavior; what is the level of functioning of each family member; who is closer to whom as a result of the problem; and what can be avoided by the family members when the child is symptomatic. As the answers to these and other questions are ascertained, then the therapist forms an hypothesis as to who and what are being protected by whom.

After the protective function of the symptom has been formulated, the therapist arranges an individual session with the symptomatic child in order to decide upon the best method of hypnotic induction. It is believed that by age seven most children are good subjects and that between the ages of nine and fourteen hypnotic susceptibility reaches its peak. For the school-age child and the adolescent there are a variety of induction procedures that are useful, especially if tailored to the individual child (Gardner & Olness, 1981).

For example, visual imagery induction techniques are often useful with children. The child is asked to close his/her eyes and focus upon a favorite place as the hypnotherapist enhances the image with details. Another visual imagery technique is that of having the child close his/her eyes and watch a favorite movie or television show. The therapist can then, of course, intersperse therapeutic suggestions indirectly within the context of the image or movie. For example, for a girl who had been referred for temper outburst, the therapist described how she could experience the sense of calm that she felt while in her favorite place whenever she felt the tension in her chest that preceded her temper outburst.

Some children are more oriented auditorily; therefore, an induction is useful in which the child imagines singing a favorite song, letting the words run through his/her mind. Stories which are tailored to the developmental age of the child and to the child's interests are also useful in producing a trance state. Within such stories, suggestions for change can easily be embedded as illustrated in a later section of this chapter.

Eye-fixation techniques are sometimes appropriate in which the child focuses his attention on a spot. It is common in child hypnosis to draw a picture on the thumbnail of the child and have him focus upon it or to fixate his eyes on a quarter held between the thumb and forefinger, with the quarter dropping to the floor as the child enters trance.

When the child has been able to achieve some level of trance, the therapist may make use of both indirect and direct suggestion for helping the child give up the protective symptomatology. If it is believed that the child's behavior is protective of the marriage, the therapist might directly suggest to the child under hypnosis that such protective behavior on his/her part is no longer needed since the therapist will now be helping the parents with their marital problem. Instead of a direct suggestion to give up the symptom entirely, the therapist could suggest to the child that some other less destructive behavior might also accomplish the same protective function. For example, a child could substitute a mildly negative behavior like refusing to do chores for a more serious behavior like enuresis. Such direct suggestions seem to work best with cooperative children who have a desire to please.

For those children who do not respond to direct suggestion, the use of metaphorical suggestions can be used. Metaphorical stories are indirect and, thus, stimulate less resistance. According to Erickson, metaphor is useful for seeding ideas of change and creating positive expectancy (Zeig, 1980). At the same time, directives can be embedded in the metaphorical story. The directive can be highlighted by a change in voice tone or location which takes the phrase out of context, thus marking it for the child. For example, in using a metaphorical story with an overly dependent child about how puppies someday grow up and leave their mothers, thus progressing to future developmental stages, the phrases "grow up" and "leave their mothers" might be underscored for the child.

Having the metaphorical story match or mirror the child's present situation builds rapport and leads to suggested changes for the child. The metaphor should include, in some form, the idea that the child's behavior is not needed to protect her parents. It could also include some suggestions for symptom substitution that would involve a less severe behavior taking the place of the present one and for developmental stage progression.

Concurrently, the parents may be seen together by the therapist. In these sessions, the theme centers around the protective function of the child's behavior. The therapist attempts to help the parents understand how children with the level of caring and perception that their child has often make a mistake in believing (unconsciously) that one or both parents need his/her help in some way. The emphasis at this point is not on resolving the personal or marital issues that may be revealed, but rather on just how the parents may convince the child that his/her protection is not needed. The therapist directs the discussion to specific behaviors that the parents may emit that will prove to the child that the protection is not needed. For example, if it is the marriage that is being protected, the therapist would encourage the parents to engage in certain behaviors that would convince the child that they can deal with their marital problems without his/her help. This might include presenting a unified front to the child concerning discipline or it might include the spouses' spending time together and discussing their marital issues in private.

Throughout the work with the parents, marital or personal issues may come up. It is best to first focus on the child and the plan for alleviating the symptom in the child. When there is improvement in the child, then the therapist can contract with the parents for marital or individual help (Haley, 1976).

Case Examples

Case 1. An 11-year-old oldest daughter with a two-year history of stealing was seen with her parents. In the initial interview it was determined that the child's stealing started during the parents' first marital separation three years ago. The stealing behavior seemed to increase during times of marital stress. The child was currently stealing items from the parents and from various stores. The parents related that there was marital stress present, but they had tabled dealing with it until they could get their daughter straightened out. The parents were divided on how to deal with the daughter, with the mother being seen by the father as too lenient and the father seen as being too strict by the mother.

The individual sessions with the daughter revealed that she was a very creative child who liked to paint and draw. She expressed a desire to stop her stealing. The therapist explained to her that she could use her creative mind to help her with her problem, and that in order to do that she would need to be relaxed and listen to what the therapist would tell her. The method of induction chosen was an eye-focus technique in which she was asked to stare at an abstract painting and imagine all the possible things she could see in it. She was given suggestions for eye closure and trance deepening.

Because she was a cooperative child with a desire to please, it was decided to use direct suggestion. She was seen three times over five weeks and told under hypnosis that there was no need for her to continue to try to help her parents with their marital problems because the therapist would do that. If she wanted to help the therapist help her parents, she could do so by choosing some minor misbehavior such as not going to bed on time at night. She was told that she would be surprised to learn how quickly she could change her behavior, and that certainly by the time she graduated from the fifth grade (six weeks in the future), her childhood stealing behavior would not be a problem.

The parents were helped to understand their daughter's behavior as an unconscious attempt on her part to be helpful to them. Because they had raised a daughter with a well developed sensitivity to people's feelings and a high degree of caring, they could expect her to continue her protective behavior until they could somehow convince her unconscious mind that it was not necessary. It was then explained that while the conscious mind might be convinced with words, the unconscious mind can only be convinced with behavior. Therefore, the parents were directed to devise a plan in which they would behave in such a way as to convince their daughter that her stealing was not necessary in order to help them divert their marital problems. With input from the therapist, the plan included the parents being united on discipline, no longer arguing in front of their daughter, and a regularly scheduled time each week in which they would go to a restaurant as a couple for a discussion of their marital difficulties.

The parents were told that as they changed their behavior they should watch for any small signs of behavior change on the part of their daughter. They should specifically watch for an increase in rather insignificant negative behaviors such as refusing to go to bed on time. They were also asked not to spend time with her discussing her stealing as this would reinforce her unconscious belief that they were being helped by that behavior.

As the child's stealing behavior improved and her misbehavior around bedtime increased, the parents asked to be seen for marital therapy. The therapist assured them that he would be willing to work with them but only after the daughter's behavior was no longer a problem. As the daughter was due to graduate from the fifth grade in another few weeks, the therapist asked the parents to plan a graduation party that would not only celebrate that event but also mark her growth from a child to an adolescent. In addition to understanding the protective function of the stealing, the parents as well as the child were told that the stealing behavior was associated with childhood and, along with the bedtime problem, would probably stop completely when she became a young adolescent.

The child's stealing did stop the week before graduation from the fifth grade. The parents did not follow up on their request to have marriage counseling. A follow-up at the three, six and 12-month intervals revealed that the child remained symptom-free and that the parents were still together despite continuing periods of marital stress.

Case 2. A 14-year-old boy who is an only child was brought to therapy by his parents because of his refusal to attend school and his suicidal gesture when his parents tried to force him to attend. His parents related that he had very poor peer relationships and that he spent most of his time watching television. Several interviews with the family revealed that the mother was involved with her son's life to the exclusion of a relationship with her husband and that she actually had no other important interests. Father was highly involved with his business and was content to criticize from a distance his wife's involvement with their son. The therapist conceptualized the son's behavior as being helpful to the mother as it filled a void in her life by providing her a place to be involved and as being helpful to the father in that it freed him from the relationship demands of his wife and allowed him to be very competent with his work.

In the individual sessions with the son, he expressed a desire to have more friends and wanted his mother to give him more space. He also presented a somewhat passive-aggressive attitude. Since his favorite activity was watching television, the therapist decided to use a trance induction that involved the boy closing his eyes and imagining his favorite program. After he had watched a shortened episode of the program from beginning to end, the therapist asked him to "stay tuned" to a new show that the therapist would narrate. The therapist then related a metaphorical story that involved a forest ranger (therapist) who watched over many different families of trees. There was one particular family (clients) in which the roots of the young tree were entangled with the roots of the mother and father trees to the extent that the growth of the younger tree was stunted.

Although the story lasted about 20 minutes, the main point was that the forest ranger tried to help the younger tree untangle its roots from the parent trees but was unsuccessful because the younger tree was afraid that the parent trees, especially the mother tree, would be too lonely. Only after the parent trees convinced the younger tree that they would be all right if he moved away from them a little did the younger tree allow the forest ranger to transplant him a little distance from the parent trees. There the younger tree grew and flourished and the parent trees who at first were lonely also became happier in time.

Throughout the course of several individual sessions over two months time, other metaphorical stories were used, some of which had embedded directives in them. For example, in telling a story about a young lion cub who worried about growing up and leaving his mother, the therapist used a change of voice intonation to underscore words like "grow up," "get friends," and "mother will be all right."

Work with the parents centered around the behaviors they could show that would demonstrate to their son that they did not need him to refuse to grow in order to be of help to them. Mother decided to become involved in activities outside the home and to spend less time with her son. Both parents were directed to spend more time with each other and strengthen their relationship in order to demonstrate to their son's unconscious that his sacrifice was not needed. They also presented to him a united front on the issue of school attendance.

The sessions took place over the summer vacation. When fall arrived, the son, who had not attended the last three months of the previous school year, not only attended school regularly but had greatly improved his peer interactions and no longer relied on television as his primary activity. The parents entered marital therapy for the stress that resulted between them when they stopped using their son to avoid marital dissatisfactions.

Case 3. A divorced mother brought her 13-year-old son in because of his encopresis. He had refused to have bowel movements on the toilet for the past two years (several times weekly he "leaked feces" in his pants). Medical treatment, including hospitalization, had failed. The encopresis started around the time of the initial separation of his parents, and the mother related that she had spent so much of her time and energy worrying about her son's problem that she had not had time to adjust to being a single woman. The therapeutic hypothesis was that the son's encopresis protected the mother from the pain of the divorce and the anxiety of adjusting to a new life. The mother was congratulated on raising such a fine son, and the therapist related the theme of his unconsciously believing that she needed him to help her with her adjustment. Several sessions were spent with the mother around that theme and how she might behave differently in order to prove to her son's unconscious that his view was erroneous.

The son was seen for two sessions in which an induction was used each time that made use of the son's interest in creative writing. After the therapist read several of the son's short stories written for school, he asked the boy to close his eyes and begin to write a story in his head. When the boy was through, he signaled the therapist who then asked the son to listen to his story. The therapist then related a metaphorical story of a volcano that kept its gasses inside. Every day the pressure felt greater and greater, but the volcano wouldn't let go. The volcano feared that if it did let go then people that it was close to would be hurt. The story progressed with the ending being that the volcano felt so much pressure from inside that it finally "erupted," "let go," "felt relieved," and was surprised to learn that the people to whom it was closest were not hurt at all, but rather took shelter with a kind stranger (therapist).

The second session with the boy two weeks later made use of a similar metaphor of a boy holding back the water in a dam by keeping his finger in the small crack. The following week the mother reported that her son had used the toilet for a bowel movement several times during the week. Each week there were more frequent movements until there no longer seemed to be a problem. The mother was seen in future sessions to help her deal with the pain of divorce and for help with her new life. Six-month and ten-month follow-up reports revealed no return of the symptomatic behavior of the child.

HYPNOTIC UTILIZATION STRATEGY

People operate out of their own models of the world which, as Erickson points out, are as "unique as a thumbprint." One's world view is based upon the person's own genetic make-up as well as life experiences. It is the person's internal map of reality and not reality itself that determines experience and behavior, i.e., one's model of the world governs one's behavior as opposed to one's sensory experience. For example, if one's view of the world is through the eyes of the lifestyle of a "victim" who believes that others are always out to take advantage of him, often the behavior of those in this client's environment will be interpreted in terms of being victimized. Even behaviors that were intended to be helpful to this person may be interpreted as "taking advantage of me." In order for therapeutic change to take place, the client's world view must be accepted and then utilized in the treatment process rather than confronted or debated.

The process of establishing rapport with a client by accepting his/her model of the world is often referred to as pacing. This concept is not new and, as the Lanktons (1983) point out, goes at least back to Biblical times as evidenced in Romans 12: 15–16: "Rejoice with them that do rejoice, weep with them that weep. Be of same mind one toward another." What Erickson adds that is new, however, is the utilization of that world map as the basis for altering behavior.

One of the more quoted case studies of Erickson that illustrates these principles is that of the paranoid patient in the psychiatric hospital who believed that he was Jesus Christ. Erickson responded to this patient that he understood he had experience as a carpenter (pacing) and led the patient into using these skills to build needed bookcases (utilization) which led to his improved functioning.

In working with a rural couple who both agreed that it is important for men to be "real men" and to show leadership in the family, the task of the therapist using the utilization strategy was to find a way to incorporate the "real man" world view into a change strategy. The wife's major complaint about the husband was that he would not allow her to have interests such as a job or hobbies that took her away from the home. After pacing this importance for the man to be the leader in the family, the therapist carefully expanded the definition of the term "real man" to include men who were secure enough to let their wives work. Thus, since it was important for the husband to be a "real man" and since real men were secure enough to grant freedom to their wives, the husband agreed to his wife's request to work outside the home.

This utilization approach is especially useful in hypnotically treating the fears of young children. Developmentally, it is not unusual for preschool children to develop fears of fantasy objects, such as monsters, or of real objects, such as animals. It is also not unusual for well-meaning parents to attempt to solve these fears in their young children in such a way that the solution makes a problem out of this normal developmental difficulty. As Watzlawick et al. (1974) have so well described, there is a positive feedback loop established within the system of interaction where there is a solution attempted for a difficulty in such a way that the difficulty continues and worsens which leads to a further application of the same solution which leads to an escalation of the difficulty into a major problem. In terms of children's fears, a most common parental solution to such a difficulty is for the parents to try to convince the child that there is nothing to be afraid of. Thus, the child's model of the world is challenged rather than accepted, which may stabilize both the fears and the pattern of family interaction around the fears.

This particular hypnotic strategy with children's fears involves several aspects. The child's fear must be accepted and paced rather than challenged. This process establishes rapport and sets the stage to use the child's fearful internal map as the means of changing. The method of pacing the fear is idiosyncratic to the individual case. For example, if an adolescent is afraid that he will faint as a result of facing a certain fearful situation, the therapist might agree with that possibility. The therapist may then encourage the adolescent to face the fearful situation in the office, perhaps in a fantasy situation, to see if he would indeed faint since it would be best to faint in the presence of the therapist who could then take care of the client. Or perhaps, a child with a fear of a dog could be told that indeed it is important to have a healthy fear of dogs, but that there are also those dogs who are afraid of humans. The therapist could then instruct the child to find a fearful dog and teach him not to be afraid of him. Presumably, this contact would help diminish the child's fear of dogs. An excellent example of this process is found in Haley's (1976) writings.

It is important, however, not only to accept the child's fear, pace it, and then utilize that fear process to eradicate the fear itself, but also to utilize the fear in such a way as to eradicate the interactional pattern or family structure that supports the fear. One way of doing this is to elevate into the status of cotherapists with the therapist those parents who are enmeshed with the child or who are divided between themselves about how to deal with the child. This creates a united parental subsystem and a firmer boundary between the child and the parental subsystem. If one parent is disengaged, uniting the parents into a cotherapy subsystem also creates involvement between the parents and between the child and the disengaged parent. Then, the parents in cooperation with the therapist carry out the utilization plan developed by the therapist for the purpose of interrupting the problem-maintaining pattern of interaction.

Case Example

A clinical example might best illustrate this process. A four-year-old boy was referred by the director of his day care center because she was aware that he had developed night fears during the past six months. When the parents were interviewed, it was learned that John had developed an extreme fear of "moos," which was his term for cows. He was afraid that these "moos" would come into his room at night and harm him. This fear led to either one of his parents sleeping with him or his sleeping with both of them in their bed. The fear and the sleeping arrangements had been going on for the past six months.

A story was told to John in such a way as to capture his attention and produce a trance state. The tone of the therapist was soft and the rhythm of the therapist's storytelling was at first geared toward matching John's breathing rate and then toward slowing down so that John's respiratory tempo also slowed down. As John focused intently on the story, the therapist observed some of the common indicators of the trance experience. John's respiration rate slowed, his movements stopped as he became very still in his chair, his facial features became smooth and relaxed, his eye-blinking reflex slowed considerably, as did his swallowing reflex, and he fixated his attention upon the therapist to the exclusion of his parents who were in the room. Thus, the therapist felt confident that a conversational trance had been induced.

The story told by the therapist paced John's dilemma as it concerned a herd of cows that began running toward a boy who did not know that it was feeding time for the cows. The cows thought the boy was bringing the grain. The boy had images of the cattle stampedes in the old westerns. John could relate to that as he, too, liked to watch old cowboy movies on T.V., and he certainly could relate to that boy's fears at that moment. The therapist told him, however, that the boy had learned something really important about "moos" from that experience. Now that the therapist had sufficiently paced John's fear and had John's intense interest in trance, the utilization tactic was employed.

The therapist told John that the important discovery that the boy had made about "moos" was that if you fed them, they were your friends for life. Thus, the therapist suggested that he put some "moo" food in a box in his room and if they came they would eat it, become his friends, and, therefore, not harm him. His idiomotor response to this utilization indicated to the therapist that this made sense to John in a therapeutically effective manner. So the therapist called his parents into the session (the therapist had previously told them of the plan), and John set about making the arrangements for buying grain and getting a feeding box for his room.

Three days later, the family returned. John reported that on the first night he put the food in his room and slept all night. In the morning upon checking the feeding box he discovered that no food was missing, and, therefore, no "moos" had come. He then decided to put the box in his parents' bedroom instead of his. Once again the next morning he discovered that no food was missing and concluded that the "moos" had not come. At that point, the idea came to him to put the "moo" food on the porch, lock the door, and let the "moos" eat outside if they came.

John's parents reported that John had slept through the night those three nights; they too enjoyed their restful nights. A two-week, one-month and six-month follow-up revealed no recurrence of the presenting problem or of any other symptomatology.

The effectiveness of this type of intervention may be explained in various ways. From a structural view, perhaps change resulted from a clearer marking of parental/child boundaries. As the parents were united on a plan and disengaged somewhat from their involvement with their son's fear, the problem behavior stopped. The MRI approach might understand the intervention at the level of the solution so that something new replaced the "more of the same" solution. Thus, the positive feedback loop was interrupted, the pattern was abolished, and a new pattern could then become operational. Ericksonian hypnotherapists could explain the results as successful intrapersonal pattern interruption. The child was able to decrease his fearful ideation and find a new solution to his problem. It seems most likely that the effectiveness of this type of intervention is overdetermined, and that all of these explanations have some validity. Thus, the intervention might be described as multilevel.

CHALLENGING REFRAMES AND EMBEDDED DIRECTIVES

In using this approach, the therapist first identifies the aspects of the client's behavior that need to be changed in order for the client to meet his/her stated goals. Next, the therapist ascertains some strong value that the client holds. The therapist accepts this value, agrees with its importance, and makes a connection as to how this value is not being realized due to the client's behaviors that are not goal-producing. In this way, the motivation behind the client's behavior is reframed in a conceptually aversive way that indirectly challenges the client to change. Thus, the motivation to change on the part of the client comes from the client's desire to escape or refute the challenging rationale given by the therapist. For example, a teenager who highly values being a "man" may be told that his fighting with his mother is an indication that he is still an immature boy. Such a reframe of his behavior may motivate him to prove that the therapist is wrong. Of course, the therapist must first have the necessary rapport with the client so that this challenge is accepted.

By challenging the client first through a frame that is aversive, the client is motivated to make a change. However, since the change is being at least partly motivated by the client's desire to move against the therapist and prove him wrong, suggestions for how to go about this change are best given in an indirect manner. Otherwise, such suggestions may be rebelled against in the same manner that the client rebels against the aversive frame. One manner of giving indirect suggestions is through the inducement of conversational trance with suggestions for change embedded within the context of metaphorical stories. Such an indirect method reduces the chance of setting up client resistance to the change directives.

Case Example

Sally, age 10, was referred because of enuresis and poor school performance. Her mother was very upset about her behavior. Sally's mother was a divorced, single parent and was socially isolated. She withdrew from friends and maintained a highly involved relationship with her daughter. It seemed that Sally's symptoms served to help mother have some legitimate means of remaining highly involved with her while remaining underdeveloped in her own social life.

Sally and her mother were seen together for a total of five sessions. In the initial session, Sally's mother demonstrated a high level of involvement in her daughter's symptoms and reported a variety of failed attempts to solve the problem. She had sought the advice of mental health and school counselors and had placed Sally on restrictions, as well as trying several behavior modification programs.

In a subsequent session, the therapist reframed the problem as one in which Sally had somehow believed that her mother did not want her to grow up. The therapist related that many children get crazy ideas like this — of parents needing them to remain young. Also, the therapist told Sally and her mother his idea that even though Sally was 10, she was acting like a child of four or five. After all, bedwetting is most often a symptom of young children.

This reframe produced a change in context about the problem. If mother's overinvolvement continued, it would be an admission that she did need Sally to remain young. Moreover, this reframe indirectly suggested to Sally that thus far she had chosen to behave like a young child and not as a 10-year-old. Both Sally and mother were challenged to begin the process of change.

In each of the last two sessions, the therapist told an analogical story to mother and daughter that had as its theme the overinvolvement between two people that led to the lack of growth of each. The stories were told with great detail in such a manner as to induce conversational trance. Each story was designed to match or pace the mother and daughter's pattern of interaction and within each story were embedded directives for changing the pattern.

One story had to do with an older sister (Sally's mother was the oldest of three) who had a very close relationship with her younger sister. At first glance, this was a wonderfully loving and satisfying relationship for both. The story went into detail about all the ways that the older sister made life easier for the younger one. Also described were the specific behaviors that the older sister did that were positively motivated but that had the unfortunate result of keeping the younger sister young and immature. Such behaviors included cleaning the younger sister's room for her, doing her chores, intervening in disagreements that the younger sister had with others, and, in general, solving any problem that the younger sister encountered. The younger sister became more and more dependent upon the older one.

This relationship was fine until it was time for the older sister to graduate from high school and leave for college, which coincided with the younger sister's starting high school. The younger sister was too afraid to leave the protection of the older sister, and the older one discovered she was too frightened to leave home. She used the fears of her younger sister as an excuse to stay home, i.e., she needed to be there to take care of her.

Suggestions for changing such an unfortunate situation were given within the context of the story. Each of the sisters would have to learn to make it without the other. Both would have to draw on strengths that they already had but were not using in order to separate from each other and grow and develop. Each sister was asked to recall times in her past when she had acted with personal strength and independence. They were asked to use in the present situation those abilities that they already had. It was very difficult for the older sister to let go, but she had to for her own sake and especially for the sake of her beloved sister. The specific actions that the older sister took were left rather vague so that the mother might fill in the content in a way that would be most meaningful for her. What was made clear was that it was up to the older sister to take the necessary steps for change since that was the responsibility of the oldest and most mature. Somehow the oldest sister would have to control her own anxieties for the sake of her sister, especially since the sister believed that she should remain dependent in order to help her older sister.

Sally's mother reported in the fifth session one month later that she had thought of these stories often. She added that she would never have guessed that Sally believed that "I didn't want her to grow up." However, she was able to think of instances in which she had treated her as if she were still a young child and was currently changing these behaviors. It was evident here that Sally's mother had been challenged by the reframe offered by the therapist and was following suggestions given in trance. In order to refute the frame that she wanted Sally to remain young, mother had looked for ways to prove that she wanted Sally to grow up. The embedded directives had provided a map for change.

The client's symptoms of enuresis and poor school performance stopped by the end of the fifth session. A six-month follow-up with the mother revealed that there had been no more behavioral problems on Sally's part and no return of the presenting problem.

The intervention in this case centered around the initial reframe of Sally's misbehavior, followed by embedded suggestions for change offered in a metaphorical framework. Because Sally and her mother were effectively joined and challenged in this reframe of their problem, their level of cooperation with subsequent embedded directives was probably heightened.

PARENTS AS HYPNOTHERAPISTS

Sometimes a useful way to abolish a repetitive cycle of pathological interaction and at the same time rearrange a certain family structure is to enlist the help of one or both parents as cotherapist. The therapist then teaches the parents how to use trance work with their child for the presenting problem. Often, under the guise of having the parents experience hypnosis with the therapist so that they might best be able to use the procedure with the child, the therapist can engage the parents in effective hypnotherapy themselves.

For example, in a family with an over-involved father and a distant mother, the therapist might use hypnosis as a means of getting mother more involved with the child. Mother and child might schedule regular sessions at home in which the mother uses trance with the child to help him/her with the presenting problem. On the other hand, the father's interaction with the child might be confined to only trance work times with the child each day in an effort to create more distance for him from his child's problem. Thus, the family structure is being rearranged.

Another example of the use of this strategy might be the case where one parent has an enmeshed but hostile relationship with a child around a certain problem. If the usual pattern is for this parent to react to a certain behavioral cue on the part of the child with anger, this pattern can be interrupted by having a child's behavior become a cue for a hypnotic "session" and not for an angry response.

Case Example

In working with a family in which the parents believed that their 12-year-old son's acting-out behavior was due to his low self-esteem, the therapist joined the parents in their diagnosis and suggested that one way to raise self-esteem was through the use of hypnosis. The family atmosphere was extremely negative, and the parents perceived the son as having few positive qualities. The parents were united in this view of the son and seemed to look for behaviors to support that view.

After explaining to the parents and child how hypnosis could be used to raise his self-esteem and that the parents could be trained in this technique, the therapist emphasized that the parents should experience trance so that they could then learn to use it with their son more readily. The therapist then proceeded to induce trance in mother, have her go back into time when her son was young and remember when he had done something that had made her feel very proud of him and proud of herself for being his mother. When her ideomotor behavior indicated that she was doing this, the therapist asked her to open her eyes and see her son in a new way. Thus, the positive feeling experienced in trance was linked to her son in the present. The next session, the father was "trained" in hypnosis in the same way, and during his trance the therapist noted that mother also experienced trance.

The following session, the therapist induced trance in the son with the parents observing. The therapist had the son recall times in his past when he had accomplished something that gave him a good feeling. As he was experiencing this in trance, the therapist asked him to memorize that good feeling and take it with him the coming week. The therapist then had both parents put the son in trance, using the same experience.

The family was then sent home with the directive that any time the son misbehaved it must be due to his low self-esteem, and his parents were not to react to him as they normally did but rather were to put him into a trance. In that trance, they were to have the son recall some past positive feeling until he felt good about himself in the present. Trance would then be terminated with the son, and they were to return to their normal activities. Each night, each parent was to put the other into trance and have the hypnotized parent recall positives about their son.

The use of trance in this family was successful in interrupting the cycle of negative perception and angry interaction between parents and child. In addition, the son was able to become more aware of his strengths as a person, as were his parents. In this way, the presenting problem was solved in five sessions with no reoccurrence reported at a six-month follow-up.

RESOURCE RETRIEVAL AND PATTERN INTERRUPTION

One method of abolishing pathological patterns of interaction is to find a way for one of the participants in that pattern to make the necessary behavior change that will lead to pattern interruption. The Bowen family therapy approach has a well developed theory concerning the "coaching" of an individual family member to make the necessary moves toward differentiation which lead to the interruption of triangular patterns of interaction. The MRI school is also well known for working with the most motivated member of the family in a strategic way so that the client can make the changes necessary in his/her behavior to interrupt problem-maintaining feedback loops. The use of Ericksonian hypnotherapeutic strategies offers the therapist, who is working with an individual while thinking systems, another method of encouraging behavior change in one family member that can lead to a change in the behavior of others.

Erickson often told his clients that their unconscious minds contained a "vast storehouse of learnings and resources" (Erickson & Rossi, 1979). Erickson and Rossi also have described hypnotherapy as a process in which clients make use of their potentials, remembrances, and internal mental associations so that they can achieve the therapeutic goals they have set for themselves. Previous failures to achieve these goals are seen as a result of untapped or underdeveloped life learnings, skills, and experiences. Since, as Erickson has stated to his clients, "you know more than you think you know," trance is useful for having the client recall and reexperience abilities and learnings that are out of his/her level of awareness. This reexperiencing of such resources can then be associated to solving the present therapeutic problem.

A simple example of the process of resource retrieval would involve first having the client experience the trance state, followed by the therapist's describing in detail the experiences that the client is most likely to have in his/her personal history. These experiences should contain within them the resource(s) that the client needs for making an effective behavior change that would lead to pattern interruption. For a wife who occupies the one-down position with her overfunctioning husband, one resource that she might need in order to make a personal behavior change within their pattern of interaction is self-confidence. Within trance, the therapist might then ask her to recall times in her past when she felt real good about certain accomplishments such as learning to write, ride a bicycle, swim, etc. As these experiences are retrieved from her unconscious, she then reexperiences that feeling of self-confidence that accompanied those accomplishments. This resource is then available to her for use in her interaction with her husband.

This calling forth of the resource with the concomitant reexperiencing of it is only half the intervention. Next, the therapist must somehow associate that resource to the current problem. In this example, the therapist could have the client, while she is indeed experiencing that sense of self-confidence, form a detailed image of herself interacting with her husband with that sense of self-confidence. The therapist would have her imagine in detail how her behavior would be with him when she felt that way. She would also imagine the specific ways that their pattern of overfunctioning/underfunctioning would then change. It would also be possible to anchor (Grinder & Bandler, 1981) that resource of self-confidence to some specific thought or behavior on her part. For instance, while she is experiencing in trance that sense of self-confidence, she could touch her forefinger to her thumb so that the feeling of self-confidence could then be reexperienced whenever she made that particular movement in the future.

Case Example

A 36-year-old single parent (Mrs. B.) came to therapy seeking help in managing her two teenage sons who were both acting in rebellious ways. She had been divorced for five years, and the boys did not have contact with their father. While their behavior problems had been in existence since the divorce, they had increased significantly within the past year. The sons were so rebellious that they refused to attend therapy sessions. The mother described the typical pattern of interaction around both the sons' misbehaviors as one in which they would engage in an unacceptable behavior; she would meekly ask them to stop; they would continue and usually escalate; she would then begin to cry and leave the scene while the boys continued their behavior. She described herself as becoming increasingly depressed over her ineffectiveness. She was especially despondent over the fact that while she could think of appropriate consequences for her sons' misbehaviors, she was unable to implement them.

The therapist asked this client what personal characteristic or ability she would need that she did not possess now, in order to deal effectively with her sons. She responded with a list that included the feeling of self-confidence, the ability to be assertive and persistent, and the ability to provide leadership for the family.

For each of the traits that this client had indicated that she needed in order to effectively deal with her problem, the previously described resource retrieval and association process was used. The first two hypnotic sessions focused upon the development and deepening of the trance state. Once this subject achieved trance, she was able to move from a light trance state to one of more depth through the use of imagery. Since she enjoyed walks in the woods, the client was asked to visualize herself walking on an autumn afternoon through a very beautiful forest. A link was made between her walking and her deepening trance. With each step that she took, she was to feel herself sink deeper and deeper into trance.

As Mrs. B became able to experience a therapeutic trance state, the therapist had her visualize herself during her younger years of adolescence and childhood. She first was asked to recall particularly pleasant experiences and then to search through her past until she found three instances where she exhibited strong leadership behavior. Mrs. B was then instructed to experience in detail those leadership behaviors, with careful attention to how she was thinking, feeling, and behaving. She then was told to climb inside each of those remembrances and reexperience them in the present trance state. As the therapist observed Mrs. B's facial expression and body posture changes that indicated she was indeed experiencing that sense of leadership in the present, he associated that experience to a tactile cue. Mrs. B was asked to slowly make a fist with her right hand and trap in that hand those feelings, behaviors, and thoughts that go with leadership. In the future, whenever she wanted to experience leadership, she would simply slowly close that right hand into a fist.

The next step in the process was to link these leadership behaviors to the current problem. Mrs. B was asked to picture a typical problem interaction between her and her sons in which she would like to show a leadership response. While imagining that interactional sequence, Mrs. B was told to close her right hand slowly and experience leadership; then she was to see herself behaving in a leadership fashion with her sons. She was asked to be very detailed in her image by including all the behaviors, thoughts, and feelings that she would have as a leader. She was then asked to imagine future scenes in which she effectively dealt with her sons due to her newfound leadership behavior.

The above process was also used for the behaviors of self-confidence, assertiveness, and persistence. Mrs. B scanned her past until she could come up with three instances where she had exhibited these traits. She then reexperienced those traits in trance, was given a tactile cue for each, and then the reexperiencing of those traits was linked to the problem sequence. Mrs. B was successful in manifesting different behaviors that were useful in interrupting the rigid pattern of problem-maintaining behaviors with her sons. As the pattern was successfully interrupted, the acting-out behaviors significantly decreased. Mrs. B reported that her depression had subsided, and that she had the pleasant experience of finding herself acting with more self-confidence, assertion, and leadership in her work and social life.

TRANCE PHENOMENA AS RESOURCES

There are certain phenomena that are associated with the trance state that are usually understood as being of significance to the use of experimental hypnosis. The Lanktons (1983) have an excellent discussion as to how Erickson made use of such phenomena for therapeutic purposes. These phenomena include age regression, dissociation, negative hallucination, and pseudo orientation in time.

As the client experiences a trance phenomenon, the particular mental and emotional mechanisms involved in that experience may be associated to the solving of the present problem. For example, in the case discussed in the previous section, as the client experienced regressing in age to points in her past where she experienced leadership behaviors, she then reexperienced the mental and emotional process of leadership. This experience was linked to solving her problem situation and to interpersonal pattern interruption.

The trance phenomenon of dissociation refers to clients' ability in trance to experience a part of themselves as separate from their total being. For example, a client could experience a levitated arm as being separate from his/her body. It is also possible to have a client remain in trance from the neck down while coming out of trance from the neck up. In this way, the client experiences his/her body as being detached from the mind. The following case example illustrates the use of this phenomenon of dissociation.

Case Example

A 20-year-old college student presented herself for therapy with the complaint of obesity. Further discussion of her problem revealed an anxiety about leaving home for graduate school, overinvolvement with her mother, and several unsuccessful attempts to leave home while an undergraduate. The specific pattern around her overeating involved acting in such a way as to involve her mother in an interaction where the daughter felt hungry and would eat high calorie foods; mom would get upset and encourage her to eat less; the daughter would then binge. The pattern around the inability to leave home was similar. Daughter would make some arrangements for leaving, then become anxious; mother would try to soothe her; daughter would leave temporarily and become anxious; mother would encourage her to stay at home; and daughter would become dysfunctional and return home.

After several sessions, the client decided to work on the leaving home problem first and save the eating change until later. The therapist hypothesized that the daughter needed a way out of the enmeshed pattern of interaction with her mother. The therapist also believed that the daughter needed to be able to feel separate from her mother, to experience enough confidence so she could differentiate and move to the next developmental stage of life.

In subsequent trance sessions, one major focus was upon having the client recall the successful progression through previous developmental stages and the specific behaviors and skills and sense of accomplishment that went with them. For example, in trance the client recalled leaving successfully for the first day of school, moving from elementary school to junior high school and from junior high to high school. Many other childhood accomplishments were brought back to life in trance, such as learning to write, walk, swim, etc. When the client fully experienced these in trance, they were then linked to the task at hand—namely the progression through the next developmental stage of leaving home. Recalling those past abilities in detail evoked prior learnings and feelings of esteem, and these were associated to solving her present problem.

In addition to using the above process of resource retrieval and association, the client was given suggestions for arm levitation which she readily achieved. While she was in this levitated state, the therapist asked her to allow her arm and hand to remain in trance but for the rest of her to wake up and experience the arm and hand as being separate from the remainder of her. She was told that this would be an interesting and pleasant experience. She was successful in this and was next instructed to go back into trance with her entire being. She was then instructed to wake up from the neck up while her body remained in trance. As she was accomplishing this, she was told that her unconscious could remember this process of separating one part from another, and that this same process that she was experiencing in trance could be used to aid her efforts to differentiate from her mother.

She was then asked to return her total being to trance and to experience what it would be like to be able to separate from her mother in the same way that she could separate from parts of her body. Then, the therapist had her imagine in great detail how the pattern of interaction between her and her mother would be different now that she knew how to be truly separate. Specific suggestions were given by the therapist as to how she could accomplish a successful move away from home because of her newfound ability to individuate. In this way, the trance phenomenon of dissociation was experienced, and the internal processes that accompanied the dissociation were linked to her present problem situation in such a way that the typical pattern of rigid interaction between her and her mother could be interrupted. Thus, the presenting problem of failure to leave home was resolved.

Another trance phenomenon that is useful as a resource for pattern interruption is that of pseudo orientation in time, which refers to orienting the client to the future. In trance, it is possible to have clients imagine and actually experience behaving in the future. The purpose of this in a therapeutic sense is usually to have the clients project themselves to a time in the future when the present problem no longer exists and to experience in detail the feelings, thoughts, and behaviors that would be present when they were free of the present problem of concern. Then, the client is instructed to review in trance all the specific behaviors that he/she manifested that were successful in producing the problem-free situation in that future time.

In working with a family consisting of mother, father, and two sons ages seven and nine, the therapist decided to use pseudo orientation in time as a major intervention. This decision was made in part because in the first two sessions it was observed that when the therapist spoke to the family about his impressions of their situation, the family members listened intently and demonstrated the signs previously discussed in this chapter of entering into the trance state. Also, there were multiple complaints from all the family members about others in the family, and it was very difficult for the therapist to conduct a "normal" interview due to interruptions and loud disagreements.

The therapist used a conversational trance induction with the family in which a series of metaphorical stories were told that had embedded within them suggestions for trance. For example, since the family loved vacationing at the beach, a detailed story was told about a therapist in Florida who conducted family therapy sessions at the beach. The description of the family receiving these sessions at the beach matched this family. The therapist then described what the family experienced as they sat in the sun with their muscles feeling very relaxed and their minds clear.

As the therapist observed the family members slipping into trance, he described the type of treatment that the family in Florida experienced while at the beach. That particular family was asked by their therapist to imagine themselves in the future being very happy, with the family members enjoying themselves and with none of the present problems in existence. The therapist then described how each of those family members was asked to imagine and experience what each must have done to contribute to the solving of their problems.

In each of the next three sessions, the therapist told analogical stories similar to the one above. These sessions were scheduled every two weeks, and the family reported improvement in the presenting problems each week. After the end of the fifth session, the family treatment was terminated. A six-month follow-up revealed that the family was functioning much better, with no return of the original problem interactions nor any substitution of new difficulties.

The ability not to notice something that is actually present in the internal or external environment is referred to as negative hallucination. As the Lanktons (1983) have noted, not noticing certain stimuli can lead to an increased awareness of other stimuli. Negative hallucination is experienced by many people in common everyday trances. For example, as one becomes absorbed in or is actually entranced by reading a book, that person may not notice that someone is calling his/her name or may even not notice hunger cues from within. If a client can experience negative hallucination in trance and the accompanying mental mechanisms, then that process can be used as a resource for helping that client to change his/her behavior so as to lead to interpersonal pattern interruption and, thus, to a change in the marital or family interaction.

Negative hallucination was used as a primary intervention in the following case. A single mother was involved in a pattern of interaction with her seven-year-old son that resulted in his hitting and kicking her. When the mother would request a certain behavior from her son, he would immediately respond with a "look that could kill." Then before he could actually carry out her request, she responded to that look by losing control and hitting him. He responded by kicking her in the shins and sometimes hitting her. At that point she would leave the scene in tears. The mother requested of the therapist a different way of handling the problem interaction. The therapist gave her many suggestions, none of which worked due to her not being able to control her emotional reactivity to that "look" that her son would give her.

The therapist explained to the mother the importance of responding differently to her son's facial expression and suggested hypnosis as a means of helping her to find the resources necessary for that. The mother experienced trance through an induction that required her to focus her eyes on a spot in a picture on the wall and to concentrate on her breathing. Suggestions for eye heaviness and closure were given and trance was achieved. Within trance, the therapist told several anecdotal stories about common experiences of not seeing things that were actually there. These included missing highway signs while driving, being absorbed in a movie and not noticing the audience, looking for one's glasses while they were right there, etc. These were designed to activate the processes of negative hallucination that the client had already experienced so that this trance phenomenon could then be used as a resource.

Since this client was able to form visual images in her mind, the therapist asked her to imagine a typical scene where she might receive that look from her son. He then asked her not to notice that look but instead focus upon some other aspect of his being, such as the frightened little boy who was underneath all that aggressiveness. While in trance, she was asked to imagine many different scenes in which she would ask him to do something and then notice only the frightened little boy behind the mask of aggressiveness. The suggestion was given that in the future she would respond to the frightened little boy when she asked him to stop his misbehavior.

In the next two weeks, the mother was able not to notice that "look," but rather to be very sensitive to the frightened little boy. That perception change led to a change in her behavior with him which in turn led to a change in the problem interaction between them. The therapist conducted a six-month follow-up interview in which both mother and son reported no further difficulties with that particular problematic interaction nor with any problematic interaction taking its place.

CONCLUSION

Certainly, the strategies of hypnotic-strategic intervention presented here do not constitute a comprehensive therapy approach. Nor is it necessary to use these strategies only within the procedural framework presented in this chapter. It does seem useful, however, to enhance the effectiveness of hypnotic intervention by embedding it within a systems framework while at the same time recognizing that trance strategies may greatly enhance the effectiveness of strategic-systemic therapy.

REFERENCES

Erickson, M., & Rossi, E. (1979). *Hypnotherapy: An Exploratory Casebook*. New York: John Wiley.

Fisch, R., Weakland, J., & Segal, L. (1982). *The Tactics of Change*. San Francisco: Jossey-Bass.

Gardner, G., & Olness, K. (1981). *Hypnosis and Hypnotherapy with Children*. New York: Grune and Stratton.

Grinder, J., & Bandler, R. (1981). *Trance-formations*. Moab, UT: Real People Press.

Haley, J. (1976). *Problem Solving Therapy*. San Francisco: Jossey-Bass.

Lankton, S., & Lankton, C. (1983). *The Answer Within*. New York: Brunner/Mazel.

Madanes, C. (1981). *Strategic Family Therapy*. San Francisco: Jossey-Bass.

Minuchin, S. (1974). *Families and Family Therapy*. Cambridge, MA: Harvard University Press.

O'Hanlon, B. (1982). Strategic pattern intervention. *Journal of Strategic and Systemic Therapies, 1*, 34–44.

Watzlawick, P., Weakland, J., & Fisch, R. (1974). *Change*. New York: W. W. Norton.

Wilk, J. (1982). Context and know-how: A model of Ericksonian psychotherapy. *Journal of Strategic and Systemic Therapies, 1*, 2–20.

Zeig, J. (1980). *A Teaching Seminar with Milton Erickson*. New York: Brunner/Mazel.

Chapter 9

Testing the Limits in Milan Systemic Therapy: Working with an Individual

Mary-Jane Ferrier

The view that is held in common by the Strategic and Systemic therapists is described as "the interactional view" by Bateson. From such a perspective, one looks at the "patterns that connect" rather than at the inner fantasies, feelings, dreams, and motives of the various individuals who may make up a family or any other significant group. It is a systemic view, conceptualizing the family as a human system which is more than the sum of its parts. It is a cybernetic view, paying close attention to complex feedback loops within the family and between the family and the therapist. It is a view which looks at human behavior contextually and, as a consequence, pays close attention to behavior as communication, searching out the persons in the significant system for whom the message is intended and/or to whose communication it is a response.

A number of different methodologies have grown out of this commonly held view. Yet, the field is so new, developing so rapidly, that it is difficult to classify them accurately. The structuralists lay claim to this base, too, emphasizing the hierarchical organization of the family as a system. The strategic therapists emphasize more the interactional sequences that perpetuate the more-of-the-same-wrong-solution behavior that has become the problem. Milan-style systemic therapists tend to emphasize the belief systems which give meaning to behaviors. Of course, these are but the broadest and sketchiest of distinctions, but they do capture the distinguishing characteristics that most practitioners would recognize today.

It is interesting to note that, although all of these therapies have had their beginnings and their development as *family* therapies, not all of them today would be comfortable with an exclusively "family" designation. Certainly, strategic practitioners make it clear that the unit for treatment need not be the family, even though the conceptualization of problems remains an interactional one (cf. Fisch, Weakland & Segal, 1982). It seems to me that the increasing use of the term "systemic" rather than "family" when referring to a number of these therapies suggests a tendency to think about these approaches more as true alternative conceptualizations than as modes of therapy in some generic sense. If, indeed, they do represent an alternative way of thinking about human problems, then questions immediately arise about the range of applicability of this way of thinking and the consequent therapeutic methodologies.

The work of the Milan group shares a common root with the Palo Alto strategic therapists (MRI), since Selvini-Palazzoli and her colleagues originally worked very closely with Paul Watzlawick for a number of years. When they did cut themselves off to develop their own methodology, a systematic operationalizing of some of Bateson's concepts, they focused exclusively on families. In recent years, there have been some interesting developments of their methodology which go beyond work with families, e.g. with larger systems (Imber Coppersmith, 1982, in press.)*

Others have explored the limits of applicability in terms of what *types* of families can be most usefully treated in this model (MacKinnon, Parry & Black, 1984). The question that has intrigued me has been the possibility of using this approach with individuals. Certainly, there are plenty of available methodologies for such work, including at least one with a shared systemic or interactional view (cf. Weakland, 1984). Virtually all of them would accept the truism that every individual exists within some significant system and that an individual's problem behavior is somehow related to that system. The strategic therapist would work quickly and discretely with the individual's "problem solution." Most, if not all, other individual therapies would arrive at similar final results, but would be likely to take much longer, would range much further into the internal and external events and phenomena of the client's life, and would address the relationship to the significant system through the transference process.

A Milan systemic approach might cast a wider net than the strategic therapist would, emphasizing as it does belief systems that have developed over generations in a family, but it would do so within the shorter time frame that has become familiar to family practitioners. But if one were to adapt this approach to work with an individual what would it look like, and how would one do it? Would such an adaptation offer yet another useful alternative to

---

*Even more recently the Milan team has split into two groups that focus on different emphases of this original work (cf. Pirotta, JSST, Winter 1984). The emphasis in this chapter will be on the work more characteristic of Boscolo and Cecchin.

work with individuals? And, finally, why would a family therapist want to make such an adaptation? Before attempting an exploration of some of these questions, it will be useful here to outline what I understand to be the salient features of the Milan systemic model.

THE SYSTEMIC INTERVIEW

Hypothesizing

It seems to me that the systemic interview itself is the best approach to an understanding of both theory and practice in this model. This should be no surprise, since the methodology of the Milan interview is a self-conscious effort to operationalize the interactional view, Bateson's idea of mind as "the patterns that connect" (Bateson, 1979).

In the systemic interview the therapist comes armed with explicit hypotheses which guide the inquiry in relational terms. The inquiry itself is conducted in a circular fashion, creating within the session itself the circular/reflexive reality of the family's own experience of interacting with each other over time. Moreover, the therapist adopts the stance of an explorer in this reality, accepting all the family members' opinions as valid, holding to no one of them more than to another, as, indeed, he/she holds onto no hypothesis past the point of its usefulness. Each systemic interview is an "experiment" where the therapist tests hypotheses with a view to accepting, rejecting or modifying them. Each systemic interview is, for the family, an opportunity to hear some "news" about their own shared reality and so to see it somewhat differently.

For sure every therapist uses hypotheses. Those of the systemic therapist are of a particular kind, flowing as they do from the interactional view of human behavior. In this view, the observed behavior of an individual can be most usefully understood as part of a series of transactions with other members of a significant system. Consequently, hypotheses about one or another "problem" behavior attempt to answer this question: In what system would this behavior (symptom) make sense? Implicit in this question is another: What *is* the significant system in this particular case? These are fairly simple formulations from which to begin developing hypotheses. However, they are comprehensive enough in their scope to guide the therapist into considerations that can range across generations and out into the work, social service, or professional network that may be the context for this family.

The development of these systemic hypotheses also implies some assumptions about how behaviors develop and are maintained in human systems, and, therefore, by implication, the way they change. If the observed behavior of an individual leads us to look for the relationship network within which it is embedded, then we shall also have assumptions about how it got to be that way and how it continues that way, especially if the behavior in question is reported to be a "problem". Behavior is dynamic, always changing. It is guided by beliefs about what works, what is right, what fits, i.e. by an epistemology, however informal and implicit. Patterns of behavior develop in trial and error recursive loops — successful action leading to a nascent belief about its efficacy, aptness, rightness. Further successful action guided by these beliefs in turn strengthens the belief, and so on.

In the normal course of events new information, news of difference, enters this recursive process, from the ever-changing, developing behaviors themselves or from people and events outside the family, so that the guiding belief system, or "map," is subject to modification over time. When, however, for a variety of possible reasons, new information does not enter this recursive process, behavior will continue to change while the maps that guide it remain unchanged, becoming less and less useful guides in the new "territory" of newly developing behavioral patterns.

The important point here is that no matter how "stuck" a family may appear to be in its behavior patterns the apparent point of stuckness is not principally on the level of behavior, which is always changing, but rather on the level of the constraining belief which is guiding the family's action (cf. Tomm, 1984 a, b). Hypotheses organize the therapist's thinking about the current information available in terms of these levels of action and belief. They will guide the therapist's inquiry into repetitive, or redundant, patterns of behavior around the apparent point of stuckness, with the purpose of discovering the family's beliefs that guide them in this pattern.

It is in this context, then, that systemic therapists think of change and how it comes about. If a problem behavior pattern can be accounted for in terms of some failure to incorporate appropriate news of difference, then the goal of therapy will be to facilitate the introduction of news of difference that will make a difference for them. In this sense, the systemic therapist will not have any other specific or concrete goals, nor opinions about how exactly this family should or should not be. The manner and direction of change will be unpredictable and idiosyncratic. Accordingly, the therapist remains neutral, respectful of the family's own solutions when they come, i.e. the change of its current ways of changing such that it can continue to develop freed from the constraining beliefs that have been guiding the problem behavior pattern (cf. Tomm, *supra*).

Circularity

From this it should be apparent that the systemic therapist works in a world of information in the Batesonian sense of "news of difference," or in the sense used by Keeney and Ross (1985) and derived from communications usage of "meaningful noise." It is the circular interview which is the vehicle *par excellence* of emergent information in both these senses. A therapist making use of circular questions, based on carefully constructed hypotheses, creates for the family the experience of "double description" and "binocular vision" of their own consensual reality (Bateson, 1972; cf. de Shazer, 1982).

Family members, hearing the observations and opinions of other family members about shared family experiences, and especially those that surround the problem, become in turn observers of their own reality. In a well conducted circular interview, family members release into the awareness of other family members "news" about that reality, making new punctuations of patterns and events possible, either by themselves or through the therapist's interventions. The therapist in the circular interview is an explorer who asks many questions but offers no answers. She assesses her hypotheses in the light of the patterns that begin to emerge, continually monitoring the feedback loop between herself and the family, adjusting or discarding hypotheses, and forming new ones based on that feedback. As Tomm has so aptly described it, the circular interview is an *enactment* of the family's systemic reality (Tomm, 1985). It is, in my opinion, the most significant contribution that the Milan group has made to the practice of family therapy.

Neutrality

Integral to the practice of Milan style systemic therapy is the notion of *neutrality*. The systemic therapist strives to maintain neutrality towards the opinions of family members, towards the feedback from interventions and towards her own hypotheses or punctuations of the family patterns. Neutrality is at one and the same time both a pragmatic positioning of the therapist and an epistemological position. From a pragmatic point of view, a neutral stance is maximally useful to the therapist in his efforts to understand *this* family's way of being and to respect its integrity. It is also useful in the way that it offers the therapist the greatest flexibility for moving in the family system, *allied with all and allied to no one*. As an epistemological position, neutrality flows naturally from a set of assumptions that includes the one that there are a number of valid alternative constructions of reality and that it is *only* constructions of reality that we ever know directly.

These notions — hypothesizing, circularity, neutrality — are the title words of the landmark article by the then Milan team in 1980 (Selvini-Palazzoli et al., 1980a) and subsume within themselves some of the key concepts and practices of systemic therapy. However, there are one or two other ideas it would be important to look at before entertaining some of the considerations about the application of this model to work with individuals.

Time — Past, Present, Future

Time plays a very important role in systemic therapy. This is evident in the practice of planning relatively long intervals between sessions, what has been referred to as "long-brief" therapy. Not only does this practice dramatize and enact the assumption that change will take place outside of the therapy session, back where the family lives its life, but it also demonstrates that it *takes time* for the "news" of the session to reverberate through the family system. Systemic therapists, by staying out of the system for long intervals, allow the family to deal with new information in their own way and so to change in their own way. As a corollary to this, when the family comes back for the next session, the therapist approaches the family in the same spirit of exploration as she did in the previous encounter, for, in a very real sense, this is a slightly different system to be understood. For human systems are always changing and developing through time. Change is not only unpredictable, it is inevitable.

Anyone witnessing a circular interview would quickly become aware of the importance of time in the therapist's conceptualizations. Questions range across generations, from the past into the future. This is not history-taking in the classic sense, but a carefully focused examination of history that is active in the present relationship — the "rules" and "maps" which have brought this family to this point. It is also an exploration of how the imagined future is active in shaping present behaviors and beliefs.

Teams

Although the use of teams has been associated with a number of family therapy models, it is worth noting here the principal ways in which such teams are used in the systemic model. Perhaps the most important function of the team is to offer the benefits of what de Shazer (1982) calls "polyocularism," i.e. multiple views of the family-therapist system. The benefit, of course, following Bateson's observations of binocular vision, lies in the bonus obtained from the *difference* in these views, the difference that will make a difference and be news for the system. The team occupies a position *meta* to the family-therapist system and so can offer a conceptualization of what is going on at a higher level of organization than that of either the family or the therapist. From this *meta* position, they can quickly see when the therapist is slipping from neutrality and so intervene to help him to regain it. In practice, also, the team plays an important role in assisting the therapist to formulate hypotheses both before and during the session and to design end-of-session interventions based on the current hypothesis that seems most useful.

End-of-Session Interventions

End-of-session interventions differ markedly from the rest of the systemic interview. At this point the therapist consciously abandons neutrality for a brief time. From among all the possible punctuations of the family's reality as it has emerged in the session, one is selected, and it is this which forms the basis of the interventions, whether it be in the form of an opinion or a prescribed ritual.

Not just any punctuation will do, of course. It must take into account the "facts" as they are currently known, as well as the language and beliefs of the family itself, while at the same time containing some element of the unexpected which can provoke the release of news into the system. In systemic therapy these opinions and rituals, representing as they do the taking of one position by the therapist, are always offered to the family as the opinion or suggested action *for today, for now*. Even at the point of offering them, the therapist prepares to reposition herself in the neutral stance relative to whatever feedback may be stimulated by the intervention over the following weeks before the next session.

It should be evident from this necessarily brief and compressed overview that Milan-style systemic therapy represents a coherent and tightly organized model for work with families. Given a choice, most therapists trained in this model would choose to work with the family present and would make considerable efforts to ensure that family members would come in for sessions. However, in any general practice there are bound to be cases where the available "family" consists of one person. Single adults, living at some distance from their families, are not unusual applicants for treatment. Nor is it uncommon to have single parents with very young children, also at some distance from their families, who, at least for the purposes of therapy, will be the only effective interlocutor. It has been out of this context that my questions about the applicability of the systemic model to work with individuals has arisen.

INDIVIDUALS IN THE SYSTEMIC PROCESS

Thinking about individuals from a systemic perspective poses no problems. As mentioned earlier, any individual coming to therapy with a problem can be thought about in terms of the significant system in which that person and that problem behavior are embedded. Hence, framing useful relational hypotheses for work with an individual is a fairly simple procedure. However, just as the Milan team has operationalized this systemic perspective in work with families, the challenge that confronts a therapist who wants to adopt this view in work with individuals will be in the area of operationalizing it.

To begin with, when working with families a therapist can usually assume that at least an important part of the significant system will be present for the interview and therefore immediately and concretely available to the inquiry. When there is only one person present, the first task will be to discover the significant system, as well as to evoke it within the therapeutic situation itself in the most effective way possible.

The circular interview—to my mind the core of the systemic methodology—poses a considerable challenge in the individual situation. The principal effect of the circular interview, i.e. to make participants observers of their own reality, will be necessarily limited when there is only one interlocutor. It will take considerable ingenuity to adapt the questions themselves to this somewhat confined situation.

Finally, the context of a therapist with a single client poses some real difficulties for a therapist who wishes to practice neutrality. In the family context, the therapist joins with everyone by allying with no one. Joining with a single client is usually thought of as allying with that person with the faint, or not so faint, implication of being on that person's side rather than on the side of anyone else in the system. If the therapist hopes to maintain both neutrality and engagement with an individual, she will have to exercise not only a lot of "systemic discipline," but a lot of creativity as well.

At least this much can be foreseen without actually plunging into work with an individual. The original questions still remain to be explored: What would this work look like? How would you actually carry it out? To attempt an answer, the best course is to take a close look at a case treated this way and from that to draw some conclusions, and possibly some further questions.

CASE ILLUSTRATION

Joan applied to the clinic for help in handling her three-year-old son, Andy, an only child. Joan was a single parent, separated and subsequently divorced from her husband since the birth of Andy. Little further information, other than of a demographic nature, was collected at time of application. Accordingly, this looked like a very ordinary child-oriented case. The first session was arranged for mother and child to come in together, and just happened to be scheduled at a time when the therapist's team would also be present.

The Client's View of the Problem

From the very start of the first interview, Joan formulated the problem that brought them to therapy in terms of her own fear and anxiety in the face of repeated threats from her ex-husband, Gary. She attributed her troubles

with her son to her shortness of temper when anxious, tense, or tired from
lack of sleep. In addition, she thought Andy probably picked up her tensions
and responded with cranky, oppositional behavior, perhaps to divert her or
to get her attention. However, of paramount importance to Joan was her own
abiding fear of a man who had beaten her up at the time of their first separation, had shot an object through her window (probably with a slingshot), and
who, periodically, kept watch on her house from a parked van.

Joan had come for therapy on the recommendation of a supervisor at
work. Apparently, her performance had been deteriorating in the past few
months ever since Gary had reappeared to keep watch on her house after a
quiet interlude of some months. The manner of the referral confirmed the
impression that Joan saw the therapy as being for herself rather than for the
child as it had seemed at the time of application.

The Therapist's View of the Problem

The therapist and team saw the problem presented as a fragment in a pattern of interactions. If the therapist was to discover how this fragment fit,
she would have to find ways to become familiar with Joan's significant system
and with the patterns of interaction in it. This task seemed particularly important since at the first session it looked as if one of the effects of Joan's
increased fear and anxiety in the face of Gary's reappearance was to narrow
her circle of interactions. The therapist learned that she had been cut off from
her two brothers, the only members of her own family who lived anywhere
near her. She was afraid to maintain friendships with people who had been
friends of the couple lest that provoke further contact with Gary. She was
increasingly fearful of going out with her own friends lest she meet her ex-
husband, as she once had in a restaurant. As a consequence, she was spending more and more time brooding in her own home, with the result that her immediate and unavoidable relationships were deteriorating, e.g., with Andy, with
her fellow workers, and with the woman she had invited to share her house.

The team consultation ended with a decision to address this narrowing circle by attempting, through a task, to involve Joan in some kind of structured
interaction with members of her circle. It was made clear to her that the team
had really understood the danger of her situation and the anxiety it provoked
in her. Because of the reality of this danger, the team told her that they were
reluctant to move ahead with therapy. They were reluctant to help her overcome her fear until they knew whether her fear was a necessary and important safeguard against this very real danger, or whether she might have allowed her fear to work overtime and so be an unnecessary drain on her, as
her supervisor had apparently thought. In order to find this out, she was asked

to consult with anyone of her choice, e.g. family, friends, coworkers. She was to ask them this question: Is my fear reasonable and necessary to protect me, or is it working overtime? She was then asked to bring one or several of the people she chose to be her consultants to the next session to help the therapist understand better what the task of therapy would be.

A Developing Hypothesis

The second and subsequent sessions were conducted by the therapist working without the team actually present. However, as will become apparent, that was not the end of the team's role. At this second interview, there were two adults present along with the child, for Joan had brought with her one of the friends she had consulted. Consequently, this was a fairly straightforward systemic interview, making full use of the friend as a consultant whose opinions about Joan's situation helped to widen the circle of inquiry. During this interview the therapist tested an hypothesis the team had formulated after the first session: Joan was in a bind which was connected in some way not only to her own opinions about her situation, but also to the opinions of some other significant people in her network.

The friend whom Joan had brought had been very influential in urging her to come to therapy, agreeing with the supervisor's implicit opinion that Joan's fear was getting in the way of her functioning and that it should be "cured." On the other hand, since this friend had known Gary and had been Joan's confidante and support through some of the times when Gary's threats had been escalating, she also agreed with Joan that he was dangerous, crazy, and unpredictable, and that she could never be too careful. Our hypothesis seemed to be borne out. At least one of her friends was communicating contradictory messages to her, i.e. your fear needs to be cured/your fear protects you from a madman. Since this session had been framed as a consultation, no intervention was made at the end other than to thank Joan's friend for being so helpful.

Adaptations of Practice

It was at this time that the technical problems of keeping subsequent interviews truly systemic began to emerge most clearly. As noted before, there was the difficulty for the therapist of maintaining a neutral position toward a family system that would be known only through the perceptions and opinions of this one adult. There was, too, the tricky task of maintaining engagement while at the same time maintaining this neutrality. It is difficult enough to do in a family group where it is possible to elicit differing views from the various family members. It would be doubly difficult to keep this position when the only source of information would be this one person.

One of the major attractions of circularity in questioning techniques is the possibility of having one member of a family "gossip" about two or more others in their presence, with the oft-noted result of activating those others to elaborate on the differences in family perception (Selvini-Palazzoli et al., 1980a). "News of difference" elicited in this way can have extraordinarily powerful effects on the subsequent organization of the family, often without any other intervention on the part of the therapist (Tomm, 1984b; Parry, 1984). Obviously this technique would not be available to the therapist without her insisting on the presence of at least some members of Joan's family system, her friend, or the woman who shared her house. By the end of the second session, it looked as if insisting on their presence in any regular way would lead to endless and unavailing struggles over attendance and to therapy petering out as a result. Accordingly, it was decided that Joan alone would be the regular client in this therapy. The possibility of inviting other "consultants" was left open at this time.

As a consequence, during subsequent interviews it would be necessary to adapt circular techniques to this situation. Although the sessions were marked by substantial segments of ordinary assessment questions by the therapist and by some "storytelling" on Joan's part, the inquiry characteristically focused on Joan's relationship system: her son, her friend who had come to the second session, her supervisor and colleagues at work, her brothers, her ex-husband, Gary, and his family, her housemate, and Ken, a man with whom she had what she reported to be a casual relationship. Invoking this system of relationships took the form of questions that asked her about these people's opinions of her situation, their reactions to a variety of events, and the advice they would give her about one thing or another. For example, in the third session, the therapist was exploring with Joan what it would be like if Gary should move far away:

Therapist: What would happen, for instance, between you and your brothers?
Joan: I don't know—I haven't talked with them since then—probably would go to visit them—do the first step anyway.
Therapist: So you'd take the first step. What's your best bet, do you think it would work? Would they accept you, welcome you back?
Joan: I suppose so—mainly because one went through a divorce. He's the one that reacted worst. . . .
Therapist: Which one of your brothers, do you think, would be most likely— if you took the first step—would be most likely to welcome you back?
Joan: That one, I suppose . . .
　　　Later, in the fourth session:

Therapist: If Gary's mother were here with us today—and she knew about some of the things we've talked about—what do you suppose she would say? What advice would she give you?

Joan: —uh—she would probably be very upset.

Therapist: Would she be upset with you? with Gary?

Joan: With everything that happened really—I talked with his brother—his sister—but I couldn't talk to her.

The original team was never again actually present behind the mirror. However, they continued to play an active role at one remove. Throughout the treatment, the therapist consulted them and frequently reported their opinions to Joan. In addition, all the sessions were videotaped. This made it possible for the consulting team to see parts of sessions. It also offered the therapist the advantage of reviewing the tapes and so enjoying a kind of *meta* position to the therapy itself.

Working with the Hypotheses

In the third session the therapist reported to Joan an opinion offered by the team: Joan and Gary were really still married, i.e. the divorce had not "taken". By introducing the team's opinion, the therapist also introduced the team as a continuing presence in the sessions. The opinion itself then became the focus of an exploration of what the people in her relationship system would make of it. In this context of a continuing unusual marriage, Joan was given a further opinion at the end of the session. She was told that the therapist was still in a dilemma about whether to carry on treatment. As things stood now, it looked as if her fear protected her from getting on with a new life, which activity might show Gary she could get on without him. In this way her fear and paralysis helped to satisfy what she had described as Gary's desire for revenge. The price for this was, of course, that her life was crippled. On the other hand, if treatment reduced her fear, helped her to cope with the threats in such a way that she was doing well without him, he would not be satisfied in his quest for revenge, and he might well escalate the threat to even more dangerous proportions. She was asked to consult with her friends about this dilemma and to come back and report responses. The session ended with this interchange:

Therapist: So I'm in a big dilemma. If we do therapy, then maybe you're going to have a better life, maybe that will get him mad enough to threaten you some more, to escalate things. On the other hand, if we don't do therapy, and we say your fears are justified—and that's just right—you're going to live a crippled life, and he may be satisfied. So that's kind of a Catch 22 isn't it?

Joan: Well, yeah — if you put it that way I can see it — but I can't live the rest of my life like that.

Therapist: But you can see the dilemma, can't you?

Joan: (*tears beginning to form in her eyes*) Uh-huh

At this point she burst into tears, stood up and left the room, repeating that she could not continue to live this way.

This intervention can be conceptualized at two levels. The first was that of the dilemma in her life in relation to her ex-husband whom we had observed was still married to her. The fear of which she was complaining was connoted as possibly a good thing. It kept her from stepping out of her ever-narrowing circle and so her behavior reassured Gary that he was still the determining influence in her life. This was the unusual marriage in which she was a partner and which appeared to keep Gary satisfied. On the other hand, she was experiencing the unusual marriage as crippling her life and that of the child. If she were really to divorce Gary and begin a new life without his overriding influence, he might be provoked into increasing the level of threats to bring her back into the marriage with him.

The second level was that of the therapeutic system. Joan's dilemma was framed as dilemma for the therapist. Implicitly, therapy was connoted as a powerful force for change, specifically change of Joan's and Gary's unusual marriage. However, the message that the therapist was reluctant to make use of that powerful influence for change and was holding back on doing therapy lest she meddle in some finely-tuned relationship served to highlight and dramatize the bind that Joan was in herself. In addition, by taking the dilemma on herself, the therapist implicitly empowered Joan to be the decisive factor in breaking out of the dilemma. The intervention might be diagrammed as shown in Figure 1.

Joan returned several weeks later, reiterating that she was not going to go on living this way. However, she was still vague about what she might do or what might happen to make things different. She had thought about it and had talked with her friends about whether she should ask for a job transfer to another part of the country and move away, but it was not clear what either she or her friends thought about these proposals. Accordingly, most of the session focused on the central question: If this unusual marriage were to end, as she kept repeating she wanted it to, how was it most likely to happen — by some action she might take, by some action Gary might take, or by some action someone outside the couple might take? Underlying these questions lay the hypothesis that Joan was acting congruently with some important beliefs in her significant system, beliefs that appeared to take a form something like

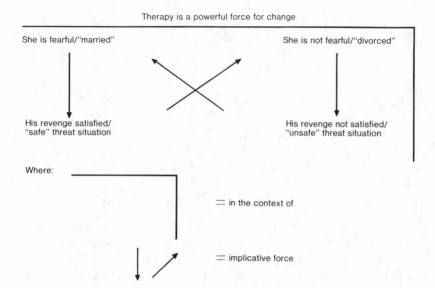

Figure 1. Diagrammatic representation of a stange loop adapted by Karl Tomm, M.D. (cf. Pearce & Cronen, 1980).

this: Men are the active agents and determine how things shall be and women react. This form of questioning about the hypothetical future is based on the assumption that change is a natural and expected event in human systems and, hence, inevitable. These questions are not unlike what Tomm calls embedded suggestion or reflexive questions that are only minimally neutral (Tomm, 1985).

As expected, Joan's responses tended in the direction of someone else taking the initiative, possibly a member of Gary's family. Consequently, considerable time was spent exploring who might most want this unusual marriage to end, who in his family would have the most influence in this regard, and what advice various people in Joan's network would give her if it were to end.

One of the better-known end-of-session interventions familiar to systemic therapists is the odd-days/even-days ritual (Selvini-Palazzoli et al, 1978b). It is particularly useful, indeed designed for, situations where there is a pattern of behavior that seems to revolve around two conflicting but simultaneous injunctions. The form of the ritual is to split the two injunctions and prescribe a behavior consonant with one for the odd days and another behavior consonant with the other for the even days, leaving one or more days free for the person or family to "do what they usually do." The effect of the ritual is to separate in time the two conflicting injunctions so that the stuck behavior that usually obtains in such a situation can be unravelled, allowing the behavior appropriate to each of the injunctions to be acted upon in the clear, so to speak.

In Joan's case she was subject to conflicting injunctions at a number of levels. The dilemma these represented for her and for the therapist had been outlined in the opinion at the end of the third session. At this point it was also clear that her "systemic rules" decreed that change, if it were to happen at all, should come from someone acting upon her. On the other hand, the very act of coming to therapy implied that on some level she saw herself as the agent of change. With change as the fulcrum, Joan was now given an odd-days/even-days ritual to perform for the next few weeks. On the odd days, in the evening after Andy had gone to bed, she was to write down on a slip of paper one thing that could happen that would end the unusual marriage, then put the paper in a box. On the even days she was to write down one thing she could do that would be sure to keep it going, and put that in another box.

By this time, of course, therapy had shifted from the dilemma itself to the possibility that there could be an end to it. The ritual was an attempt to dramatize for her the two sides of the dilemma, while at the same time introducing the possibility that she might consider it within a framework that assumed it could end.

Middle Moves

At the outset of the fifth session, a few weeks later, Joan announced that although she had not performed the ritual as prescribed, she had done a lot of thinking. She had decided she would not pursue Gary for child support payments, which he had ceased paying a few months earlier. She had decided that, although she had every right to child support, this was one powerful link that kept the unusual marriage going and she was going to sever that link. The rest of the session was devoted to exploring the consequences of her decision, with special emphasis on the opinions and attitudes of the significant people in her life—who would try to persuade her to do otherwise, who would support her decision. Without direct access to these people, and well aware of their influence in her life, it was important for the therapist at this point to take her through this exploration of how they might view her action. In a sense, it gave her the opportunity ahead of time to be an observer of potential, and likely, interactions with these people.

It is worth noting here that the therapist remained neutral towards Joan's decision, neither commending her for it nor taking a position with regard to her right to child support. This does not mean that the therapist does not have a personal position or set of values concerning women's rights in this regard.

What it does reflect, however, is the therapist's acceptance of Joan's immediate solution to this particular problem. Joan's view of the events surrounding child support must be seen in the light of the larger dilemma with which the therapy had been dealing so far.

At the end of this session, Joan was given another ritual to perform in the intervening weeks. She had begun reporting going out a great deal more with her friends, but was still terrified that she would meet Gary on one of these occasions. Accordingly, she was to spend a few minutes each evening rehearsing some alternative responses to him if such a meeting should occur, including the imagined dialogue that would ensue.

Working Through to the End

At the next session, Joan reported that she had not been able to do the ritual task. During the intervening weeks, her "casual" boyfriend had broken up with her and she was devastated. She had hardly been able to think of Gary, let alone carry out the ritual of conjuring up a meeting with him. This had been a great surprise to her, although not to her friends, who had seen her as much more involved with Ken than she had seen herself, or reported herself to be. The session closed with the following opinion:

> It looks to me as if you have been much closer to ending your unusual marriage with Gary than either you or I had realized, since you were so surprised to find how emotionally involved you had become with Ken. Your friends seem to be pretty reliable observers and they have been much more in touch with how that relationship was developing than either you or I have been. In circumstances like this, a breakup of an important relationship, some people would return to the older, more familiar one, in your case the unusual marriage with Gary, so I will not be surprised if that happens.

Joan and Andy went on vacation at this time. Five weeks later, she reported that they had had an excellent vacation together, although the return had been marred by his cranky and provocative behavior for the first few days after they got home. However, Joan talked of her handling of this in a matter-of-fact way. She also reported that she had surprised her friends by failing to plunge into a deep depression over the breakup with Ken, as they had predicted she would do. She was sad and grieving, but she was not notably depressed. She was continuing to go out with her friends and had decided she would not stay at home to wait for him to call her as she had at first been tempted to do, which would have been more consonant with the systemic rules under which she had been operating up to now. There had been no further encounters with Gary, although she had seen his van outside her house once. Apparently, he drove away as soon as he caught sight of her standing in her doorway.

At this point it appeared that, although Gary was still an element in her life, he did not represent the crippling factor he had been six months previously. Accordingly, Joan was asked to do another task. The therapist had consulted with the team again and reported their suggestion to Joan that she should consult with her friends as she had after the early sessions.

Therapist: Ask your friends if they think that your present level of caution is right, reasonable, the way it ought to be. Or, do they think you've been too incautious, taking too many risks — by having too good a time, by looking so great, by getting involved with another man to the point where you're really upset when he leaves.

If that's so, do they think you need to practise being a little more afraid, or a little more cautious, so that you won't take these kinds of risks in the future?

So, you would ask them first of all: Is the level of my caution just right, or do you think I've gone too far and maybe I need to pull back and be a little more cautious, a little more frightened, a little more fearful?

You might want to talk with them about this and then when we meet in about a month you can tell me their opinions.

Joan returned about a month later to report that she had not felt she could consult her friends and housemate because they were all dealing with troubles of their own. She spoke about this in a detached, almost amused, manner, like someone observing the vagaries of human existence. This attitude extended to her own situation. She seemed to be more interested in telling the therapist about recent difficulties in placing her son in the preschool of her choice than in discussing whether she was being cautious enough with regard to her ex-husband. However, when pressed, she indicated that she had no intention of restricting her social life. Moreover, she went on to say that her supervisor had especially commended her for her work recently.

During this session Joan volunteered the following observations from a conversation with a friend:

> After that time I was here — when I was home — she was wondering what was wrong with me that night — that I was kind of crazy — and I told her I was in therapy. She really shocked me. She said, well, she said — it was going back to that funny kind of marriage you were talking about — she said, it looks like the more you're going to be after him — the whole thing's going to go on. It really shocked me — that's the first one that said something similar to you.

This sounded very much like the kind of "news" that family members hear when they become observers of their own reality in the classic circular interview.

Towards the end of the session the therapist observed that it looked as if she had found her balance between appropriate caution and being able to come and go as she pleased. The problems that she still faced sounded like the usual life problems that anyone, including the therapist, faces, and there did not appear to be any further reason for coming to therapy. Joan agreed with this view and therapy ended with this interview. At the three-month follow-up routinely done in the clinic, Joan reported that all was going well and that she was very satisfied with the treatment.

Reflections on This Case

This case illustrates one way in which systemic family therapy can be applied to work with an individual. Throughout the course of treatment, the working hypotheses attempted to conceptualize Joan's problems in interactive, systemic terms. The exploration of these hypotheses was consistently carried out in terms of the client's relationship system. Moreover, the therapist located the course of therapy itself in a context larger than the dyad meeting in the therapy room. Two major strategies contributed to this: 1) the therapist consulted repeatedly with members of the original team and then introduced their opinions into the ongoing treatment; 2) she assigned consultation tasks several times for Joan to do outside of the treatment sessions. End-of-session interventions drew heavily from the repertoire of those developed in work with families.

One of the original questions had been: What would systemic therapy with an individual look like? In some ways, in this case, it looked a lot like therapy with a family. It was characterized by interviews in which extensive use was made of adapted versions of circular or triadic questions. Careful attention was paid to the formulation of hypotheses to be explored in these interviews. Therapy team opinions played an important role in the treatment. Sessions were held at fairly long intervals and the therapy was completed in eight sessions. Finally, the client was given tasks to do between sessions, the most important of which were to consult with significant people in her network.

Throughout the treatment the therapist maintained a consistent systemic approach. It was assumed that change was natural and to be expected, that the goal of treatment was change of this woman's current way of changing. As a function of the further assumption that whatever change that would occur would be idiosyncratic and unpredictable, the therapist paid close attention to whatever the client brought to each session, accepting her way of doing or not doing the tasks and accepting her formulations of what she would do to make changes in her life. Further, the therapist actively entertained a variety of alternative punctuations of events (a way of organizing sequences of events or exchanges — cf. Watzlawick, Beavin & Jackson, 1967) and adopted a neutral stance towards these, as well.

This case illustrates well a number of challenges which are common in systemic work with individuals. The most obvious is that of adapting the actual circular interview techniques developed in work with families. However, apart from constructing the hypotheses, as well as the questions to test them, in a relational or systemic perspective, the therapist has to counteract or deal with the very strong pull to form a close dyad with the client and thus begin to see the client's predicament in her terms only. In this case it became apparent very early that to do this the therapist would have to be rigorous and disciplined in her thinking about the case while at the same time maintaining engagement with Joan herself so that Joan would be able to accept whatever "news of difference" might be introduced into the therapeutic system. In this regard, sessions were marked by humor and by the use of many metaphors and fantasies, or hypothetical instances, in which it was possible to frame serious or frightening material in a lighthearted way, and so to entertain constructions of the future that had not been accessible before. For example, the repeated reference to her relationship with Gary as an "unusual marriage" was a reframing that served to introduce a novel and somewhat lighter tone to the deadly seriousness of her initial descriptions.

A retrospective view of the case also reveals how important the assignment of tasks is, whether they are performed or not. One of the hazards of working with an individual is the narrowing of the field of inquiry as client and therapist exhaust the avenues of information. The tasks at the end of each interview serve to provoke the emergence of new information from one session to the next and so to keep the field of inquiry sufficiently open.

One important factor in helping to strike this balance between neutrality and engagement seems to be the periodic use of a consultation team. This works on at least two levels. At the therapist level, even a brief consultation with a colleague from the team serves as reinforcement of the commitment to a rigorously disciplined systemic perspective, as well as providing for another view of what is going on in the case. These periodic consultations can function a little like Bateson's double description for the therapist (Bateson, 1979). At another level, the consultation team becomes an additional presence in the interviews themselves — a presence to which startling, novel, or potentially unpalatable opinions can be attributed without committing the therapist to these views. This is, of course, similar to the use often made of collaborative teams in family therapy situations, but in this case the team also serves the crucial purpose of widening what could easily become a very narrow context.

In any case, where an individual is the client, there is probably already a tendency towards the narrowing of context. This serves to cut the person off from new information which could help in evolving new options. Perhaps the most powerful aspect of a systemic treatment like this one is the insistence on framing the situation in a context wider than that which is initially presented. Over and over, the person is confronted with the therapist's questions about other significant people's reactions and opinions, along with tasks that are designed to provoke consideration of connections with these people and their potential for being a resource for the person. Whenever the client is asked to consult with others, the questions are designed to work on two fronts: to provoke the individual's own consideration of novel ways of looking at the situation while at the same time involving observers in these same questions. A systemic therapist's insistence on opening up what is usually a narrowing field by locating the person and the therapy in a larger context can have a very powerful effect in removing systemic constraints and leaving the client better able to make use of his/her own resources (Imber Coppersmith, in press b).

Comparison with Strategic Approach

Inevitably, one wonders how this work would compare with what a strategic therapist might have done in this case. In some sense, both would deal with solution behavior — the strategic therapist with the more of the same wrong solution behavior, the systemic therapist with the current way of changing and the redundant interactions that have developed. However, the former would focus discretely on patterns and processes in the present, while the work we have described ranged further into the past and the future. It is this matter of focus that is one of the most notable differences to be remarked.

It is my surmise that a strategic therapist in this case would have, as it were, zoomed in on the threat-withdrawal sequences of behavior so that the lens would bring these into sharp focus, leaving much of the field on the periphery. In the systemic work, on the other hand, the lens was zoomed in the other direction, so that the threat-withdrawal sequences took their place in a field which included family, friends, and colleagues in the past, present and future.

As mentioned above, this zooming in on the attempted wrong solutions by the strategic therapist contrasts sharply with this systemic work, which emphasizes, rather, the underlying epistemology, i.e., the belief system which gives rise to what looks like rigid rules. As a consequence, the intentions of the therapist would be quite different. The strategic therapist would seek explicitly to alter the solution behavior, would set specific and concrete goals, and project the desirable outcome with the client. In this case, a strategic therapist might have negotiated with Joan a goal of going out with her friends a specified number of times, or of having her accost her ex-husband safely in his waiting van, thus reversing the threat-withdrawal sequence. In the systemic work, however, no such goals were negotiated. The therapist's intention was to introduce new information, to avoid any outright challenge to the existing situation, and to remain neutral to the outcome, thus accepting whatever solution Joan would come up with herself once the new information had had its effect.

There are a number of aspects of the systemic work which would be familiar to a strategic therapist, notably the extensive use of reframing and of restraint from change. The use of teams and tasks, as well as the brief time span within which the work was carried out would be familiar, too. Yet, there is a very different feel to the two approaches, some of which can be attributed to the different pictures the therapist gets using the different lenses. Additionally, as MacKinnon points out, the strategic model is a pragmatic model, concerned principally with getting things done, whereas the Milan systemic approach tends to be an aesthetic one, concerned with purity in systemic thinking and with uncovering the patterns that connect, in this way allowing the system itself to develop how it will (MacKinnon, 1983).

At this time we do not appear to be in a position where we can make valid claims about the advantages and disadvantages of these treatment models, even with families, let alone with individuals. Useful work has been reported by the practitioners of all the systems-based therapies. There are some suggestions that one approach may be useful with one type of family or client, while another may be more useful with a different type of family or client (MacKinnon, Parry & Black, 1984). Strategic practitioners have done more exploring of the use of their model with individuals and/or parts of families, while the systemic therapists have tended to widen the field even further than the family to include social service systems and professional networks, and to develop consultation models for the therapist-family system (Imber Coppersmith, 1982; von Trommel, 1984). Up to now, however, little attention has been paid to the possibility of adapting the Milan systemic model to work with individuals. As a consequence, to make meaningful comparisons on an axis of effectiveness or usefulness is simply not as yet possible.

If there is any advantage to be offered by this adaptation of Milan-style work, it is the advantage of an alternative methodology (cf. Wilcoxon, 1985). Therapists need to have more than one string to their bows, for sure. We should be skilled in a range of approaches to problems so that we can match the work of therapy to the needs of clients. By the same token, we also need to be able to apply firmly established skills in as wide a variety of cases as makes good clinical sense, so that we work from our strong suit, so to speak.

It is fairly well accepted that one of the major factors that distinguishes successful from unsuccessful therapy, whatever the complexities of outcome research, is the person of the therapist working confidently within a model that makes sense to him/her. The work outlined here offers some promise to the therapist who moves freely and confidently in the systemic model with families that those skills can be applied and adapted to work with individuals.

The work of adaptation is, and continues to be, an adventure in testing the limits of the Milan systemic schema.

REFERENCES

Bateson, G. (1972). *Steps to an Ecology of Mind*. San Francisco: Chandler.
Bateson, G. (1979). *Mind and Nature*. New York: Dutton.
Dell, P. F. (1982). Beyond homeostasis: Toward a concept of coherence. *Family Process, 21* (1), 21–41.
de Shazer, S. (1982). Some conceptual distinctions are more useful than others. *Family Process, 21* (1).
Fisch, R., Weakland, J. H., & Segal, L. (1982). *The Tactics of Change*. San Francisco: Jossey-Bass.
Hoffmann, L. (1981). *Foundations of Family Therapy*. New York: Basic Books.
Imber Coppersmith, E. (1982). The place of family therapy in the homeostasis of larger systems. In M. Aronson & L. R. Wolberg (Eds.), *Group and Family Therapy: An Overview*. New York: Brunner/Mazel.
Imber Coppersmith, E. (1985). We've got a secret: A non-marital marital therapy. In A. S. Gurman (Ed.), *A Marital Therapy Casebook*. New York: Guilford.
Imber Coppersmith, E. (in press). The family and public service systems: An assessment method. *Family Therapy Collections*.
Keeney, B., & Ross, J. (1985). *Mind in Therapy: Constructing Systemic Family Therapies*. New York: Basic Books.
MacKinnon, L. (1983). Contrasting strategic and Milan therapies. *Family Process, 22* (4), 425–441.
MacKinnon, L., Parry, A., & Black, R. (1984). Strategies of family therapy: The relationship to styles of family functioning. *Journal of Strategic & Systemic Therapies, 3* (3), 6–22.
Parry, A. (1984). Maturanation in Milan: Recent developments in systemic therapy. *Journal of Strategic & Systemic Therapies, 3* (1), 35–52.
Pearce, B. W., & Cronen, V. E. (1980). *Communication, Action and Meaning: The Creation of Social Realities*. New York: Praeger.
Selvini-Palazzoli, M., Boscolo, L., Cecchin, G., & Prata, G. (1978a). *Paradox and Counterparadox*. New York: Jason Aronson.
Selvini-Palazzoli, M., Boscolo, L., Cecchin, G., & Prata, G. (1978b). A ritualized prescription in family therapy: Odd days and even days. *Journal of Marriage & Family Counseling, 4*, 3–10.
Selvini-Palazzoli, M., Boscolo, L., Cecchin, G., & Prata, G. (1980a). Hypothesizing — circularity — neutrality: Three guidelines for the conductor of the session. *Family Process, 19* (1), 3–12.
Selvini-Palazzoli, M., Boscolo, L., Cecchin, G., & Prata, G. (1980b). The problem of the referring person. *Journal of Marriage & Family Therapy, 6* (1), 3–9.
Tomm, K. (1984a). One perspective on the Milan systemic approach: Part I. *Journal of Marriage & Family Therapy, 10* (2).
Tomm, K. (1984b). One perspective on the Milan systemic approach: Part II. *Journal of Marriage & Family Therapy, 10* (3).
Tomm, K. (1985). Circular questioning: A multifaceted tool. In D. Campbell & R. Draper (Eds.), *Applications of Systemic Family Therapy: The Milan Method*. New York: Academic Press.
von Trommel, M. (1984). A consultation method addressing the therapist-family system. *Family Process, 23* (4).
Watzlawick, P., Beavin, J., & Jackson, D. (1967). *Pragmatics of Human Communication: A Study of Interactional Patterns, Pathologies and Paradoxes*. New York: Norton.
Watzlawick, P., Weakland, J. H., & Fisch, R. (1974). *Change: Principles of Problem Formation and Problem Resolution*. New York: Norton.
Weakland, J. (1984). Family therapy with individuals. *Journal of Strategic and Systemic Therapies, 3* (1).
Wilcoxon, A. (1985). Systemic intervention in university counseling center: A population that falls between the cracks? *Family Therapy News, 16* (2).

Chapter 10

The Relationship Between Individual Psychologies and Strategic/Systemic Therapies Reconsidered

Barbara S. Held

INTRODUCTION: THE DILEMMA

We systemic therapists face a dilemma. On the one hand, the systems revolution has taught us to look beyond the individual so that we may perceive the patterns of current interpersonal interactions which contextualize and thus define all behaviors. On the other hand, however, we cannot seem to resist acknowledging the importance of understanding the individual as a system within larger systems and therefore as a valid focus of intervention in his/her own right. Our prior training in individually oriented models of psychotherapy, as well as our own life experiences, has certainly persuaded us of that, and we are usually reluctant to relinquish the notion of "the individual." We may, therefore, ask on what grounds systemic therapists may interpret the individual as a system in itself when the essence of the systems revolution has suggested otherwise.

To define this question further, we could ask whether it is even possible to "see" both the individual and the systemic whole simultaneously. To focus on the system is to risk losing our vision of the individuals who comprise it,

I wish to thank Professor Edward Pols and Dr. Richard D. Flanagan, with whom I collaborated in the past on projects which contributed to some of the ideas developed in this chapter. Additional gratitude is extended to Professor Pols for his editorial comments and helpful suggestions on an earlier draft of this chapter. I also wish to thank Robert Mower for his assistance in the preparation of the manuscript itself.

while to focus on the individuals could preclude the broader perspective our movement has struggled so hard to attain. This latter focus could certainly make us appear "guilty" of being nonsystemic in our thinking, a conclusion reinforced by the many warnings our leaders have given of the dangers to a true systemic view posed by training and thinking in terms of concepts derived from individual therapy models (Held & Flanagan, 1984a, 1984b). To put the matter differently, we will encounter difficulties when we try to "think systems" and "think individuals" simultaneously (cf. Dell, 1980, 1982a, 1984a; Kerr, 1981; Sluzki, 1974, 1981).

Despite these admonitions, the importance of considering the level of the individual and the consequences of failing to obtain a cogent theoretical understanding of the individual have emerged as appropriate concerns of systemic therapists (Dell, 1982b, 1984b; Duhl & Duhl, 1981; Framo, 1983; Gurman, 1978; Hare-Mustin, 1980; Lagos, 1984; Reamy-Stephenson, 1983; Ziffer, 1983). Gurman and Kniskern (1981) express this sentiment in an editorial note.

> In our view, most of the major family therapy approaches that have been strongly influenced by general systems theory, cybernetics, and the like . . . have too often deemphasized organismic factors that influence family process, i.e., variables *within* individual family members. (Gurman & Kniskern, 1981, p. 500)

Three points about this emerging realization may be noted: (a) It seems to have coincided with the attainment of professional legitimacy by systemic therapies and may thus be a sign that the field has progressed to a point where we may now stop and assess those aspects of human behavior which were minimized when we were trying to distinguish ourselves from individual models (Framo, 1983; Ziffer, 1983); (b) It raises the "depth vs. surface"(Note 1) controversy in systemic therapy, which Dell (1984a) has argued is one of the foremost problems facing the systems movement; and (c) Finally, it suggests that if we believe that psychology has provided valid (or at least useful) information at the individual level—and most systemic therapists seem to believe so—then we must decide how we can use this information within a systemic framework.

In this chapter I examine the possibility of including within a systemic framework a viewpoint that takes the individual seriously. The problem is to determine how we can "see" the individual without contradicting or losing the systemic perspective which has so enriched our work. I begin with a hard look at the fundamentals upon which our operative principles are based, turn then to an illustrative case, and end with an exploration of the implications of this discussion for strategic/systemic theory and practice.

PHILOSOPHICAL AND HISTORICAL ISSUES:
THE EPISTEMOLOGY DEBATES

The "Epistemology" Debates (Note 2) (circa 1980–1983) in the systems movement seized upon the supposed distinction between linear and circular (or nonlinear) causality (Note 3) and used it to define a fundamental difference between two types of psychotherapy models. The individual and more traditional models were defined as linear, and a variety of newer systemic models were defined as circular. Thus, individual and systemic models were and are assumed to be philosophically, if not historically, incompatible, and it was therefore concluded that to *be* systemic we must abandon models that *are* linear (Held & Flanagan, 1984a; 1984b).

There are several reasons for questioning this assumption. The most significant one asks whether the "linearity" or "circularity" resides *in the model or construct itself* (and we may substitute for the word construct the notion of "level of description" – e.g., individual vs. interpersonal) or, alternatively, in the *way* the therapist employs the construct. If, say, psychoanalytic or developmental concepts and hypotheses *require* that a linear perspective be taken, it may indeed be impossible to use these concepts within a circular framework. If, however, the "linearity" resides in how the constructs of a model are viewed and used, then the "linearity" or "circularity" resides in the attitude of the therapist (or viewer) and not in the construct or model. It is argued here that no construct or description *inherently* imposes that a linear or circular perspective be adopted.

To illustrate this point, consider Dell's (1980) article on schizophrenia in which he demonstrated how systems (i.e., interpersonal) level descriptions or constructs could be used linearly (e.g., parental/marital problems *cause* schizophrenia). Sluzki (1981) similarly addressed this problem when he distinguished between interpersonal "processes of symptom production," which he believed to reveal a more traditional, linear orientation, and interpersonal "patterns of symptom maintenance," which revealed a system or circular orientation. It was thus demonstrated that a therapist was not automatically circular and hence systemic in his/her thinking simply because he/she attended to interpersonal (e.g., family) relationships. Several others (e.g., McNamee, Lannamann, & Tomm, 1983; Parry, 1984; Reamy-Stephenson, 1983) have reinforced this distinction by noting the disadvantages of "pairing . . . the 'unit of treatment' [i.e., individual vs. interpersonal] . . . with epistemology ["epistemology" here referring to linear vs. circular orientation]" (Reamy-Stephenson, 1983, p. 61).

Now, if we can use concepts from circular/systemic models linearly, then can we not, by the same logic, use concepts from individual or "nonsystemic" models circularly? For example, cannot "individual" concepts – such as splitting-defenses, concrete operational thinking, Oedipal struggle, self-concept, obsessive-compulsive behavior—be "disembedded" from causal ("linear") hypotheses and instead be utilized to assist our understanding of the components which comprise the "circular" patterns within individuals that appear to surround or maintain symptoms (Note 4)? It can therefore be argued that *any* useful construct from *any* level of system description (i.e., individual or interpersonal) may be seen and therefore used as part of a "circular loop" that is potentially system maintaining.

For example, consider the components or elements of the circular feedback loop in Figure 1 that comprise a system defined at the level of the individual; that is, the elements may be seen as aspects of an individual. While these elements certainly can be connected (by an observer) to other elements of an interpersonal nature, they also have the potential to be sufficient in themselves for a successful intervention.

What makes the therapy "linear" or "circular" is therefore not the particular *content* or constructs used to describe patterns at individual vs. interpersonal levels, but rather the *process* of thinking that permits the organization of the therapist's observations (cf. Keeney, 1983). The therapist is then free to use any level of description (i.e., intrapsychic, individual, intrapersonal vs. interpersonal) that seems relevant to the formulation of a pattern and, therefore, an intervention. The question is not, "How many other people is the problematic behavior connected to?" Nor is it necessarily concerned with the time dimension (past vs. present interactions) of the elements in the pattern. The question, rather, is how to employ all sorts of constructs in "systemic" terms. These questions will be discussed more extensively in the section, "What is Systemic?"

A Challenge to the Linear/Circular Distinction:
A Logical Contradiction

The argument presented above is based on an assumption about the implicit clarity of the linear/circular distinction. That assumption can be challenged (Dell, 1982a, 1982b; Held & Pols, 1985), particularly with regard to using this distinction as a means to explain how relationships *really* operate.

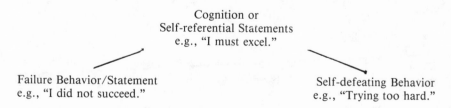

Cognition or
Self-referential Statements
e.g., "I must excel."

Failure Behavior/Statement
e.g., "I did not succeed."

Self-defeating Behavior
e.g., "Trying too hard."

Figure 1.

But that question is beyond the scope of this discussion. Rather, let us turn our attention to a logical problem which I believe our field needs to confront and which has arisen from the use of the term "epistemology" as it has appeared in our literature. This problem is more dramatic than the matter of the clarity of the two terms "linear" and "circular" and has put our field in danger of falling into a logical contradiction. To show just why this is so, I must first summarize some terminological distinctions made with a collaborator in a recent article (Held & Pols, 1985).

The systems field has employed the term "epistemology" with two distinct meanings, one correct and usual, the other incorrect and unique. Unfortunately, the incorrect meaning is the one that seems to have prevailed. The first and correct use of the term—we have called it epistemology (meaning 1)—concerns the nature of knowledge, but most important for our field is the question whether the knower is capable of attaining a reality that is independent of the knower, or whether the act of knowing creates its own reality. We called the first kind epistemology (meaning 1)-R and the second kind epistemology (meaning 1)-NR, where "R" stands for "independent reality attainable" and "NR" stands for "no independent reality attainable." The two kinds are sometimes described as objective and subjective respectively in systems literature, and although those descriptions do not always accord with philosophical precedents, I will sometimes use them in this chapter.

The second and incorrect meaning—we called it epistemology (meaning 2)—concerns what characteristics the knower ascribes to the thing known. The characteristic most discussed in the systems literature is that of causality. One can sum up the discussion in this question: Is causality linear or nonlinear? We called epistemology (meaning 2) an incorrect meaning because the question whether the thing studied is characterized by this or that kind of causality has classically been called a *metaphysical*, or *ontological*, question rather than an epistemological one.

Now systemic therapists have clearly indicated a preference for an epistemology (meaning 1)-NR (or a "subjective" epistemology) doctrine, that is, a doctrine that reality is not independent of, but rather made by, the knower (e.g., Dell, 1982a, 1984a, 1984b; Keeney, 1983; Reamy-Stephenson, 1983; Selvini-Palazzoli, Cecchin, Prata, & Boscolo, 1978; Sluzki, 1974; Watzlawick, 1976, 1984; Watzlawick, Weakland, & Fisch, 1974). And this would not be a problem in itself, except that at times we also seem to advocate an epistemology (meaning 1)-R, that is, the view that the knower *does* attain an independent or "objective" reality. This occurs, for example, in the debate about linear and circular causality when it is assumed that circular causality *really* (or *correctly*) characterizes the thing known and is not merely imputed to it by the act of knowing.

Putting aside for a moment our questions about the precision of the linear/circular distinction, we find a startling logical dilemma, namely, that we cannot logically argue for *both* a "subjective" epistemology (meaning 1)-NR and a circular basis of causality in the real world. That is, we cannot logically argue on the one hand, "There is no objective or independent or true reality (available to us)," and on the other hand say, "Circular causality is the true or objective reality." Put differently, an epistemology (meaning 1)-NR provides no grounds for knowing what any true or objective reality is (really) like. If we have no way to obtain an independent reality, how can we argue any position about the true nature of that reality, including the nature of causality (Held & Pols, 1985)?

What are the implications of this problem for the question here under consideration, namely, the use of an individual view in systemic therapies? When we consider that contributions from individual models are often rejected on the basis of their purported adherence to an "objective" epistemology – an epistemology (meaning 1)-R – (e.g., sexual and aggressive instincts are the *true* [objective] cause of neurotic behaviors), as well as their adherence to a linear causality, the relevance of this problem emerges (Note 5). So that until we become clear, or at least consistent, about our position on the question whether our knowledge can or cannot attain an independent or objective reality, it would be presumptuous to reject implicitly any concept or hypothesis from any therapy model on the basis of this argument.

While it would similarly be presumptuous on my part to propose an ultimate solution to this dilemma, I am willing to hazard a guess at one possible direction in which to proceed. First we must accept the well-established (e.g., Goldfried, 1980; Strupp, 1981; Watzlawick et al., 1974) premise that therapy or change is based, at least in part, upon the ability of the therapist to assist the client in creating or framing a new vision of "reality." (This activity, of course, demands the freedom to create multiple "realities" from the same events or data.) Then, we can still argue quite logically, as has been done in our field, that *construing* the relevant components or elements of the problem in "circular" terms, regardless of how these components are "really" or objectively related, is more efficacious for the reframing and hence the change process.

Put differently, therapy works better when we treat events (at any system level) *as if* they occurred in circular terms, regardless of how causality "really works" in the "real world." This last statement raises the question of whether we seek the true or objective basis or cause of problems through our constructs, or whether we seek efficacy (i.e., while our constructs may not objectively explain the causal basis of problems, they may nonetheless help us to change behavior). Furthermore, the efficacy of a "circular approach" can certainly be put to an empirical test (Note 6).

To summarize this section, neither considerations of linear/circular causality, nor "objective/subjective epistemologies," impose a rejection by systemic therapists of concepts and hypotheses derived from or used at the individual level of description. If anything, we can conclude that, in the therapy situation, the linearity or circularity of an event should be a matter of the perceptions, choices of description, attitudes, or thinking processes of the therapist, regardless of the particular concepts used to describe behavior.

The Differentiation and Evolution of a Therapy Movement

If the systems movement's own philosophical positions provide no clear rational basis for rejecting any notions derived from individual models, neither do some of its most pervasive theoretical positions about the basis for healthy development or "differentiation" (see Bowen, 1978; Minuchin, 1974). In particular, as I have argued with another collaborator, Bowen's concept of "the differentiation of a self within the family of origin" may serve as a useful metaphor for the differentiation of the strategic/systemic movement within its family of origin—the field of psychotherapy (Flanagan & Held, 1983; Held & Flanagan, 1984a, 1984b).

If we accept this metaphor, then we must notice that to become "differentiated," or achieve its own "solid" identity, a new movement must not engage in "emotional cutoffs" from its "family of origin." Following from Bowen theory, there are two basic ways to be cut off and hence undifferentiated: (a) never leave home, and (b) never return home. In the case of systemic therapists, the two ways to be cut off emotionally are (a) to accept the past *indiscriminately* (i.e., be totally aligned with any model in an uncritical way or never leave home), and (b) to reject the past *indiscriminately* (i.e., eliminate all "old" concepts in an uncritical way or never return home).

Thus, to differentiate ourselves as individuals or members of therapy movements, we must be able to incorporate the past into our new identity *on our own terms*, which then, of course, changes the way the past is viewed and acted upon. An implication of this analysis is that if we believe that some ideas, concepts, hypotheses, or assumptions from individual models of therapy, and the field of psychology in general, have merit (e.g. ego defenses, self-concept, cognitive style or level) (Note 7)—and I perceive that most systemic therapists hold this belief—then it is imperative that we find ways to think about and use these concepts so that we can subsume from the past what is useful and therefore evolve in a differentiated way (Held & Flanagan, 1984a, 1984b).

There is an interesting paradox which emerges, however, when we examine by means of Bowen theory the question of the place of the individual within the systemic perspective. For of all of the systemic theorists/therapists, it seems to me that Bowen has paid the closest attention to the individual while still considering his/her relationship to both the present and past interpersonal context. Bowen theory thus grapples directly with the depth vs. surface controversy precisely because of its attention to the past (Note 8). Bowen theory further makes deliberate use of a variety of individual concepts, many of which seem to have psychoanalytic origins (e.g., fusion, self-differentiation, projection), although they become systemic by virtue of being related to both *present and past* interpersonal contexts.

The paradox arises when we consider two distinct tendencies of Bowen theory. On the one hand, Bowen theory has three features which are compatible with some individual theory: (a) it assesses the degree of fusion between emotional and intellectual systems; (b) it attends to the development of the individual within the interpersonal system; and (c) it may be seen to view unresolved problems from past generations as, in some ultimate sense, "causal" of present symptoms. On the other hand, this theory is more vehement than most about the rejection of thinking and training in concepts derived from individual theories. Consider the following statements on "Bowen theory" in Michael Kerr's chapter in the *Handbook of Family Therapy*:

> People were initially seeing what they had been long trained to see, namely, individual psychopathology. To become observers of the family as a unit, they literally had to *untrain* themselves. This remains the major thrust of our family training program, namely, *untraining* people from *individual concepts*. (Kerr, 1981, p. 229) (all italics added)
>
> *Individual and systems thinking are two distinctly different ways of conceptualizing human behavior and attempts to mix them reflect a failure to appreciate their difference.* (Kerr, 1981, p. 234)

This sort of indiscriminate rejection strikes me as a rather undifferentiated position, and although it perhaps was necessary for the establishment of our theory's beginnings, it can potentially thwart our attempts to refine and develop systemic theory and therapies according to Bowen's own assumptions (cf. Framo, 1983; Held & Flanagan, 1984a, 1984b; Ziffer, 1983). Hence, we are confronted with another contradiction. A closer examination of Kerr's two statements does, however, hint at a possible and partial solution to the problem. Notice that Kerr equates *individual concepts* (i.e., content) with *individual ways of thinking* (i.e., process) as the two targets for elimination. This equation—not uncommon in psychotherapy, as will be elaborated upon later—thus confuses the "content level" with the "process level" of therapy.

While a clear consensus about how exactly to distinguish therapeutic process from its content is by no means apparent, this distinction may nonetheless provide us with some assistance for the problem at hand. First, however, we must distinguish as best as possible between process and content aspects or "levels" of psychotherapy. In general, clinicians seem to agree that therapeutic

process refers, at least in one sense, to one's theory of *how* change occurs —
the "how to's," mechanisms, or procedures used to enhance change regardless
of the specific content to be changed. The content then refers to the *what* or
that which will be changed—the "object" of the change process (Kaufman,
DeLange, & Selfridge, 1977; Prochaska & DiClemente, 1982).

With this distinction in mind, we can then argue that the problem is not
in the use of individual concepts (concepts that describe at the individual level;
e.g., self-esteem) as opposed to systems concepts (concepts that describe at
the interpersonal or "system" level; e.g., diffuse boundaries), but in the *way
any* of these concepts are employed in the conceptualization and intervention (i.e., change) process. So that, if we use our descriptions or concepts
systemically and strategically in both our thinking (theorizing) and our actions (interventions), we are then free to pick and choose, in a conscious,
deliberate (i.e., differentiated) manner, which sort of description (individual
or interpersonal) is relevant to a particular case.

In conclusion, if the strategic/systemic movement is to differentiate itself
within the field of psychotherapy, and thus evolve in a positive manner, we
must redefine and use family-of-origin themes (e.g., individual concepts) on
our own terms; that is, we must use them systemically and strategically. The
fundamentals of what it means to "function" systemically and strategically
are thus the next topic of discussion (Note 9).

STRATEGIC AND SYSTEMIC PROCESS

What Is Systemic?

Within General Systems Theory (GST), a system has been defined as "sets
of elements standing in interaction" (von Bertalanffy, cited by Gray & Rizzo, 1969, p. 7). It is thus clear that any entity which contains elements "in
interaction" may constitute a system. GST has also been defined as a theory
which seeks to describe relationships between elements in the empirical world
in such a way as to determine the *general* principles which explain these relationships in all systems or "organized wholes." The term "structural isomorphism" has also been used to describe the position that the principles of relationship and organization that define one system also apply to many other
or to all systems. (Hence, perhaps, the origin of the recent attempt to relate
observations at the quantum level in physics to family interaction—a dubious
endeavor at best.) As von Bertalanffy states,

> The *organismic trend* starts with the trite consideration that organisms are
> organized things; we have to look for general principles and laws concerning
> "organization," "wholeness," . . . "growth," . . . and others. These traits are
> common to biological, behavioral, psychological, and social phenomena; there

are, as it is called, *isomorphisms* between biological, behavioral, and social phenomena and sciences. Therefore, we should try to develop a "general theory of systems." Interaction among many variables and free *dynamic order* may be indicated as central notions. (1969, p. 37)

Thus, "thinking systemically" has come to mean the search for relationships or patterns which describe or explain the "system as a whole." As long as we attempt to understand the pattern of relationships, rather than to view each of the elements in isolation from the total context, we may then be said to be thinking systemically. Circular causality is, of course, a natural enough result of the realization that if elements are defined only in relationship to each other — a relationship which by definition must recur in order to establish pattern or "self-regulation" — they must then be in some sense mutually influential.

Systemic theorists (e.g., Levenson, 1978; von Bertalanffy, 1969) have argued that GST is not a theory of specific content. It is instead a "theory of theories" that posits the importance of understanding relationships between elements in the empirical world *apart* from the content of (i.e., the particular elements in) those relationships. It is thus more a theory of "process" (Note 10) than of this or that content. As von Bertalanffy states, "General systems theory . . . emphasizes the commonalities in modern developments of fields which otherwise are different in content" (1969, p. 38).

If systemic therapies are rooted philosophically in GST (and this statement can be, and has been, debated), then the above discussion suggests that we can think systemically at any system level of description (e.g., within one individual or between individuals) as long as we seek patterned or recurring relationships between the elements which comprise the whole. The "elements standing in interaction" then provide the pattern or "context" for the behavior of any one element.

Many family therapists believe, of course, that the family is the relevant context for system definition, and that a therapist is not thinking systemically if he/she does not consider the interpersonal relationships between all the family members or elements in the system. There is nothing in GST, however, which specifies the sorts of elements to be considered and, if anything, family therapists are now considering broader social contexts (e.g., school systems, juvenile justice systems) as relevant system components (e.g., Schwartzman, 1985). In fact, our systemic theorists, who hold a subjective epistemology (meaning 1), have argued that the therapist must recognize that *he/she* defines the boundaries of the system or "the whole" as a result of his/her own subjective punctuation of events (Dell, 1984b; Keeney, 1983; Sluzki, 1985). The obvious implication of this line of reasoning again is that the "systemic whole" can constitute any unity which is comprised of elements or subsystems, whether that whole be an individual or a group of individuals (see Note 11).

Now it seems to me that, since we continually make therapeutic decisions about whom or what to include as members (i.e., elements) of the system, most systemic therapists already know this fact. Yet we seem to forget it when confronted with concepts from individual therapy models that threaten to invade our theory's territory. Consider the following statements which define systemic theory or the "systems model":

> This model challenges our everyday experience. We all tend to experience ourselves as the unit of our lives. When psychiatry, therefore, deals with transactions among people as introjects in the individual's experience, it is merely validating the common reality. The systems model demands a quantum jump: acceptance that dependency and control, attraction and aggression, symbiosis and avoidance, are more than introjects. They are interpersonal interactions in the *present* [italics added]. The psychological unit is not the individual. It is the individual in his significant social contexts. (Minuchin, Rosman, & Baker, 1978, p. 21)
>
> The systemic paradigm which underlies family therapy is fundamentally relational or interactionist. That is, the behavioral "traits" of an individual must always be understood in terms of the behavior of the other members of the system. Similarly, the behavioral "traits" of the system-as-a-whole must always be understood in terms of the behavior of extra-systemic others (e.g., the therapist, extended family, courts, schools, etc.). This, in fact, is the essence of the systemic paradigm: *individuals and families do not have inherent traits or properties* (e.g., passive-aggressive, narcissistic, dependent, symptomatic, resistant, homeostatic, etc.). . . . Instead, such apparent traits manifest themselves in *some* contexts, but not in others. When we fail to remember this context-dependent nature of behavior, then we will be convinced that we are observing traits or properties which are inherent (e.g., homeostasis). . . . On the other hand, *when we remember that "traits" are actually context-dependent, then we will think systemically.* (Dell, 1984a, p. 354) (italics added)

Thus, when Dell and Minuchin argue that to "think systemically" we must consider the *present or ongoing social interaction between two or more people* as the smallest unity or whole, they seem to be confusing the content of the theory (or unit of analysis) with "process" (or the act of making connections or determining relationships between elements). For example, the problem of insomnia has often been described in self-referential (i.e., *intra*personal rather than *inter*personal) terms (e.g., Fraser, 1984; Watzlawick et al., 1974). This sort of description nonetheless meets the criteria of a systemic approach because it considers the recurrent interactions between the elements which define the systemic whole or context.

In the intrapersonal system in Figure 2, the thoughts (a) and behaviors (b) of the individual comprise the interacting elements of the system, and thus each provides a context for the other; the thoughts are a context of the wakeful behavior, which contextualizes the thoughts. No additional people (as elements) *need* be considered to formulate an intervention which alters this systemic pattern. Of course, it can always be argued that change will be bet-

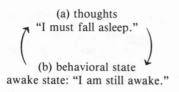

(a) thoughts
"I must fall asleep."

(b) behavioral state
awake state: "I am still awake."

Figure 2.

ter served if the therapist considers more (or fewer) elements of an intrapersonal or interpersonal nature, but this is a question of what is efficacious or parsimonious or strategic, and not one of defining what is systemic.

The point of this example is to illustrate the notion that individual or "nonsystemic" models of psychotherapy may provide concepts which help us to see patterns or recurrent processes within, as well as between, individuals, and so may expand the repertoire of systemic therapies (Held & Flanagan, 1984a, 1984b). What then is the difference between traditional/individual models and strategic/systemic models? Three distinctions come to mind: (a) Even though other models may define problems in recursive or circular terms (D. Efron, personal communication, January, 1985), these models do not necessarily capitalize on and so fully realize the implications of a "circular" approach. This is because most individual models still adhere to the ("linear") notion of a *true* or *correct* component or element in the pattern at which to intervene (e.g., the "internalized object-representation" must be altered before "splitting-defenses" will diminish). They therefore may lose the flexibility and adaptability – the "fit" with the client – of strategic/systemic therapies, which permit intervention or interception at *any* point in a problem cycle. (b) More obvious, traditional models do not consider carefully enough the *current* interpersonal context or pattern when, as we certainly know by now, this may be relevant to the change process. It should be noted, however, that while all therapy models (to my knowledge) at least consider the therapist-client interpersonal system as an aspect of treatment, strategic/systemic therapies emphasize this dyad by paying maximum attention to the feedback loops between client and therapist. In this sense, strategic/systemic therapies always operate on an interpersonal level. (c) Thus, while many other models may consider the therapeutic relationship, by emphasizing an *intra*personal view they may not be strategic. These points invite the conclusion that both individual and interpersonal patterns may be of (strategic) consequence to therapeutic intervention, and that to deny or ignore uncategorically either level of analysis would therefore be limiting, if not foolish.

We can summarize this section by reiterating the point that "thinking systemically" or "interactionally" is the process, *on the part of the observer*, of determining relationships between the elements of a system that recur over time and so form a pattern. This process further imposes no restrictions on the elements, including the number of people who determine the whole, the time frame of the elements, or any other such qualities. At least one question, of course, remains: Why should we bother to think in terms of intrapsychic concepts, or elements within one person, that define the whole? To put the answer as squarely as possible, because it may, given the facts of some cases, be more strategic to do so (Held, 1984). (And just as important, we need not fear that attending to intrapersonal concepts or components will transform us instantly into psychoanalysts). We therefore now turn to a discussion of what is meant by the term "strategic."

What Is Strategic?

To answer this question, it is only reasonable that we turn first to the advice offered by Haley, who stated that "therapy can be called strategic if the clinician initiates what happens during therapy and designs a particular approach for each problem" (1973, p. 17). Hoffman reinforced this definition when, in reference to Haley, she defined strategic therapy as "any therapy in which the clinician actively designs interventions to fit the problem" (Hoffman, 1981, p. 271). *The American College Dictionary* defines strategy as "skillful management in . . . attaining an end" and thus introduces the notion of parsimony, which perhaps explains why most strategic approaches are also "brief" (e.g., Rabkin, 1977).

While *all* therapies probably attempt to "fit the problem" and achieve their ends "skillfully," strategic therapies have capitalized on general "strategies" and more specific "tactics" to deal parsimoniously with resistance. They thus do not adhere to strict (linear) notions of the "true" cause of the problem (e.g., aggressive instincts, poor self-concept) which *must* be the focus of the therapeutic intervention in all cases. Rather, strategic therapies, as exemplified by the Mental Research Institute (MRI) group, attempt to interrupt "faulty solutions" to problems — *whatever* their nature or content — that serve as elements in the perpetuation of the problem or symptom cycle (Watzlawick, Weakland, & Fisch, 1974).

As is well known by now, the primary intervention of the strategic therapist is "reframing," which is the alteration of clients' perceptions or experiences of a problem, so that either their cognitions or behaviors or both, as "elements" in the problem cycle, may shift and thereby eliminate the problem. The reframe offers a new way of perceiving/acting upon the problem; hence, many have begun to write about the importance of introducing some form of "novelty" into the change process (Keeney, 1983). Of course, this novelty must "fit" (be meaningful to) the client system, or it will not be useful (Keeney & Ross, 1983); to put the matter differently, it will raise "resistance."

Now it is true that while strategic therapists usually endorse working direct-ly with the smallest, or most parsimonious, unit of change (defined both by the *number* of people seen in therapy and the *goal* of therapy), they consider their approach to be interpersonal since they recommend that symptomatic behaviors always be conceptualized with regard to the relevant social con-text (e.g., Madanes, 1981; Watzlawick et al., 1974). Some strategic case reports do, however, contradict this interpersonal stance by presenting in-terventions which address elements comprised only of the individual's own perceptions and behavior. Thus, for example, these reports deal with such problems as insomnia and procrastination, where at times a social context (beyond the therapy relationship, that is) is not at least readily apparent (Note 11).

Nevertheless, it strikes me that the very strength of the strategic model resides in its ability to offer guidelines for interrupting and thereby chang-ing self-defeating or problematic cycles of behaviors, whether conceptualized in individual or social terms. It therefore seems reasonable to conclude that a concept, derived from an hypothesis or model of psychotherapy and aimed at a system level, can be used within a strategic framework.

By now it should be rather obvious that a strategic approach is *by defini-tion* systemic and thus shares the following components of systemic therapy: (a) It is a process or way of thinking and intervening which does not specify the content of therapy, that is, the focus of discussion and exploration (e.g., Oedipal concerns, family-of-origin themes). Rather, the content is always determined, as much as possible, by what the client brings as the problem focus. (b) It is concerned with delineating circular patterns or relationships between the elements that comprise the system or relevant context. (c) Final-ly, it permits the therapist/observer to choose or define the relevant elements of the system that are the potential "targets" of an intervention.

While these three points define a "systemic" view, and therefore are neces-sary components of a strategic view, they are not sufficient to achieve a strategic approach. A systemic view becomes strategic when it can be trans-lated into an intervention which introduces novelty into the problem cycle in such a way that change results. (It is therefore possible to be systemic in one's approach without being strategic — i.e., without being "skillful" in "fit-ting the intervention to the problem." To be strategic, however, by defini-tion entails a systemic process.) Recall, of course, that this "something new" or novel must fit the case (e.g., the client's belief system) well enough to be considered by the client as a viable alternative to "what is," but not fit so well as to be identical to what is. De Shazer (1982) discusses this question of fit in terms of "isomorphism", while Keeney (1983) discusses it in terms of pro-viding information (or "something random") which is "meaningful" to the client. Keeney calls this information a "meaningful Rorschach."

Not just any Rorschach will do; the client must assume that there is meaning or order in it. His search for meaning will then generate new structure and pattern. A part of therapy must always be presenting meaningful Rorschachs which clients (and sometimes, therapists) believe to contain "answers" and "solutions." These Rorschachs may be constructed from family history, cultural myth, psychobabble, religious metaphor, stories about other clients (fictional or not), and so forth. The explanations clients propose or request usually provide a clue for what form of Rorschach will be useful. A student of Eastern thought might be given a reading from the *I Ching*, whereas a deacon of a Baptist church may require some obscure Biblical reference. A client who happens to be a family therapist, however, may have to be given a theoretical mythology, such as Bowenese, Whitakerese, or Weaklandese. (Keeney, 1983, p. 170) (Note 12)

According to Keeney (1983), as well as most strategic therapists, however, the key to successful interventions resides in the ability of the therapist to convey simultaneously messages supportive of both stability and change (i.e., fit). The MRI's "tactics" are most notable for achieving this end (Note 13).

It has been argued that *all* psychotherapies create change (at least in part) by providing a new vision of experience (for both therapists and clients), which then destroys old patterns. Yet, unlike strategic/systemic therapies, most therapies, as stated previously, do not articulate clearly either the circular nature of the patterns they are employed to alter, or the various possibilities for introducing novelty into any of these cyclical patterns. Again, this is due to premises, found in many nonsystemic therapies, concerning the objective or true causes of the problem which *must* be addressed in some sequential (i.e., "linear") fashion. In other words, the notion of producing the one "correct" reframe or interpretation (e.g., Oedipal strivings, cross-generational coalitions) as a prerequisite to change may not be helpful to the achievement of change.

It is, however, possible (and sometimes desirable) to utilize the very concepts and hypotheses from these "nonsystemic" therapies in order to produce a strategic intervention or reframe. These concepts and hypotheses would expand our range of potential reframes (i.e., our available content), and it follows logically that the more ways in which we can reframe a problem, the greater the likelihood of our being strategic (i.e., of finding a reframe that fits the problem), which then enhances the possibility for new behavior sequences or solutions to emerge (Held, 1984).

It is here that I wish to argue for a significant point, namely, that knowing alternative systems of explanation (i.e., models of psychotherapy) at both individual and interpersonal levels of description also helps therapists to avoid a belief in the *objective* and *exclusive* truth of any one reframe or explanation (Held & Flanagan, 1984a, 1984b). It is precisely the rejection of this belief, a rejection widely advocated in our field, that permits the therapist to fit the explanation (reframe, interpretation, or intervention) to the specifics of a case at an appropriate system level and so to be strategic in the truest sense (Note 14). These statements are based on observations – of my own as well as others' work – of the strategic use of reframes derived from various "individual" models that appeared to be as effective as any "family-oriented" explanation. As long as we function within the limits of a strategic (and therefore systemic) framework, we need not fear a blurring of our theory's boundaries due to the use of any content (Note 15).

The *freedom* to choose explanations that provide good fit (and thus produce change) is what I believe distinguishes strategic therapists from other therapists, including therapists from those "systemic" orientations which appear to posit a true or objective explanation for all problems. For example, advocates of Bowen theory usually consider "family-of-origin work" to be relevant to a case, whereas structural theorists search for breaches in hierarchical boundaries, role-reversals, triangulations, and so forth to explain a problem and so to be a focus of intervention (cf. Fraser, 1984). Based on the argument presented here, an "individual" intervention (e.g., a psychodynamic reframe) could possibly be more strategic than would be an "interpersonal" intervention (e.g., reversing a role-reversal) by virtue of its providing a better fit for a particular situation. Consistent with this line of reasoning, I would like to add that the most strategic position I have taken in training strategic/systemic therapists in a variety of contexts has been to suggest that trainees need not abandon concepts, hypotheses, and interpretations from individual models that they have found to be useful; rather, it is only their *exclusive* belief in these ideas as providing "the one true solution" to *all* problems that must be modified.

To summarize this section, the concepts derived from systems theory which we have examined thus far – circularity, differentiation, systemic, and strategic – rely on process or ways of conceptualizing and intervening and not on the content or intrapersonal vs. interpersonal levels of behavior. The question of "levels" is, however, relevant to this discussion in another sense, and it is to this question that we now turn.

"Levels of Description"

The fact that many strategic/systemic therapists have resisted establishing a process for incorporating into their work a systematized knowledge of concepts from individual therapies and theories can be attributed to a confusion of "hierarchical levels." It is my observation that strategic/systemic therapists have been using individual constructs, many of which are rather similar to those found in traditional (even psychoanalytic) models. Yet we have not, with some exceptions, *systematically* and *deliberately* included this "level of system description" in our theories and explanations, in part because of (what

I take to be) a fear of being "nonsystemic" — a fear which has mysteriously worked its way into our theory "consciousness." In other words, to return to our original question, how can we think at the level of the individual and the larger system simultaneously?

If we recall that, as many strategic/systemic thinkers have suggested, the individual is a system comprised of elements and subsumed by larger systems, which then represent more encompassing categories, the dilemma disappears (Parry, 1984). Using a similar line of logic, it can be (and has been) argued that the *process* of thinking strategically can subsume any case content or description *because* it exists at a different "level of analysis" (Fraser, 1984) than the specific explanations, reframes, or interpretations selected by the therapist. Again, a strategic process must change the way we think about individual descriptions (i.e., we cannot take them — as well as interpersonal descriptions — to be exclusive truths), but it does not by any means erase the strategic utility of these descriptions (Colapinto, 1984; Duncan, 1984; Fraser, 1984) (Note 16). The "real" question for me thus is *how* to make useful connections between individual and interpersonal approaches, a much too infrequent activity to date for reasons already discussed. The following statement illustrates an active engagement with this process:

> Model building typically proceeds by enriching an approach — primarily espoused by the therapist — through the import of elements from other approaches. In some cases, the meaning that the imported notions or techniques had within the original conceptual context is altered, to make them compatible with the new context. For instance, the phenomenological descriptions of personality styles elaborated by psychoanalytic writers can be selectively blended into structural family therapy as a way of enhancing one's joining skills, while at the same time preserving the integrity of the structural model from infiltration by psychoanalytic ideas about etiology, the unconscious or the transferential relation. (Colapinto, 1984, p. 40)

The notion of therapeutic process existing at a higher level than content will be examined more carefully at a later point in this chapter.

CASE EXAMPLE

The case illustration which follows is important to me for several reasons. First, it was one of my earliest "strategic" cases, and in some ways is responsible for my "conversion." Second, I initially approached it from a psychodynamic framework, and therefore I believe this case has contributed to the thinking evident in this chapter. Third, it was one of my most difficult and taxing cases, and so it stands out in my mind as a developmental milestone in my career.

The client was a young woman who had a long history of psychotherapy and a diagnosis of borderline disorder at the time I began to work with her. She had been in several foster homes and had been hospitalized as an adolescent. Since that time, she had seen — and often "defeated" — several therapists, most of whom were female. There was a history of alcohol and drug abuse, self-mutilations — most notable was her cutting her hands — and severe "splitting-defenses" (Note 17).

As a trainee faced with my first "borderline" client, I approached this case with fear and excitement; after all, I might be able to make a difference. Working from an "object-relations" perspective, I reasoned that since this woman's relationship with her mother was perceived by her to be particularly depriving, she must have a poor maternal "object-introject" and thus a "split" or "weakened ego," which could account for the symptoms. Being rather inexperienced, I believed that I could provide what, according to object-relations theory, was the needed remedy and what the previous therapists presumably could not supply: a good maternal object to be internalized and so to "mend the split ego." In this initial stage, I could map my thinking as indicated in Figure 3.

Needless to say, the client "defeated" me in this approach. The more I "gave" as the good object (e.g., taking phone calls at 3 A.M. — notice that my therapeutic limits were not very clear), the more regressive, needy, and symptomatic she became, and thus the more frustrated and angry I became. In fact, it dawned on me that I could very well be experiencing the "counter-transference" that the previous therapists presumably had endured. My thinking thus began to shift from the "linear" model outlined in Figure 3 to a more "circular" (i.e., systemic) dynamic, which I now perceive to be Phase II of the case (see Figure 4).

My perception of a circular feedback loop or problem *cycle* at this point, although seemingly inadvertent, was probably not entirely accidental; I was simultaneously learning of the MRI model. While Phase II involved essen-

A. Etiology

"Poor Maternal Object-Introject" ⟶ "Split Ego" ⟶ "Borderline" Behavior

"Depriving" or "Rejecting" Therapist/Maternal Objects

B. Remedy

"Good Therapist Object-Introject" ⟶ "Mended Ego" ⟶ More Adaptive Defenses

Figure 3. Phase I.

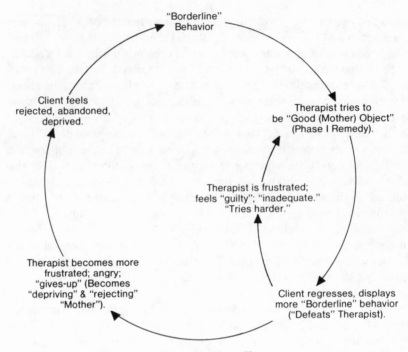

Figure 4. Phase II.

tially the same elements in the system ("depriving" mother, "depriving" therapists, client's behavior, my behavior), these elements were now reorganized
so that they formed a recurrent pattern. I had created or defined a system,
but was not sure what to do with it. Certainly, being a "good mother," my
Phase I remedy, was not strategic (nor was it indicated by an object-relations
approach, which called for clearer therapeutic limits/boundaries) and, in fact,
my "solution" was contributing to a "more of the same" dilemma, as indicated
by the subloop in Figure 4. But what were my other alternatives?

Ironically, it was my client's timing of a crisis that assisted my shift from
a systemic to a strategic/systemic conceptualization. I received a phone call
from my client informing me that she had once again mutilated herself by
cutting her hands, and inquiring, "What would I do to help her?" Realizing,
with the help of my supervisor, that I needed to *do something different* (i.e.,
inject novelty), I resisted my impulse to "take care of her" in the usual sense
and instead explained that if she could call me, she could call an ambulance;
that if she refused to do so, I would call one for her and make sure it got
there but would not go to the hospital with her; that perhaps we needed again

to reconsider psychiatric hospitalization (Note 18); and that we would discuss the matter at our next appointment a couple of days later.

I then found myself unable to finish dinner; nor could I sleep that night. I did, however, manage to formulate a novel reframe, that is, one which I was certain had not been suggested by prior therapists. I might add that the reasoning behind the reframe described below has certainly become more finely articulated than it was at the time of the reframe's presentation, no doubt due in large part to the luxury of analyzing this case with a perspective afforded by time. I nevertheless believe it to be the basis of the reframe I offered at that time. What follows constitutes my understanding of this reframe.

My client's acting-out behavior toward her prior therapists and me could be seen from a psychodynamic perspective as an attempt to express her rage toward, and so in a sense "defeat," her mother. This was accomplished by inducing the therapists — unlike her mother — to give more and more of themselves, which resulted in the client's regression to the condition of a child in need of constant care. This regression could be construed as "defeating the therapists," since as the therapists "gave more," the client became less self-sufficient. Since I had become aware of my own limits in this process, it was clear to me that I could never "give enough" and thus was doomed to be yet another "bad mother."

It struck me, however, that if this client's need was to get back at mother via the transference — and being a difficult client was a frequently articulated point of pride for her — then the *last* thing she would (consciously) want was to be perceived as helpful and altruistic toward her "therapist mothers." This line of reasoning may be seen as the basis for a reframe which I hoped would be strategic by seeming novel and yet "toxic" to the client. It would, that is, be so repugnant to her — yet make so much sense and thus be so compelling or meaningful (i.e., it would fit) — that she would be unable to dismiss it, and hence her old premises and patterns would be rendered untenable. When my client appeared at the next session (with stitches which she readily displayed), I delivered a version of the following message with more than a little trepidation.

> I must apologize to you. For the past few months I have been somewhat misguided in your treatment because, as I now realize, I was operating out of an erroneous assumption. I had assumed that you were very angry at all your past therapists and me for not being able to give you what your mother did not give you (Note 19). I had interpreted your self-mutilation as your attempt to show me your anger and so afford me the opportunity to show you how much I cared. And while you agreed with this interpretation, you have continued to get worse, culminating in this weekend's crisis. Yet as with many bad things, there is often a positive side, and there is one to this crisis, which is that I now understand the real issue with which you are struggling. Even though I predict

that you will find what I am about to say crazy, I must be honest with you.
    Despite all that you have said and done, I now see you as one of the most caring, giving, and altruistic clients I have ever had. *While I certainly want and hope for your improvement* and will continue to work with you toward positive goals, I now realize that staying miserable is, in part, an act of self-sacrifice. For by failing to improve, you continue to teach new therapists like myself how to handle cases such as yours, and you do so at your *own expense.* At the end of this year I will leave here having learned a great deal from you, and you will, by remaining miserable, go on to teach yet another new trainee.

My client's response was one of shock, disbelief, and then anger. She told me under no circumstances was she an altruistic person, and I had certainly revealed my ignorance by thinking so. I responded by agreeing that this may well be the case, but whether right or wrong it was how I now saw her. Furthermore, even if she disagreed with my perception, she could not deny the *fact* that one effect of her behavior *was* to train people like me. She left the office less than convinced, but returned regularly for her sessions. We terminated therapy several months later when I left this traineeship, at which time I referred her to a new therapist. The self-mutilation was eliminated during that time and, according to my client's self-report, in the several years since termination. In addition, she seemed to improve especially in the area of social relationships. While she might still be considered to be "borderline" in some aspects of her functioning, I consider my treatment to have been successful.

Discussion of Case

How might we understand this case in relation to this chapter? While there certainly are *many* alternative explanations for the dramatic shift that occurred, it is now apparent to me that I became unstuck at least partly as a result of my shift from a "linear" dynamic to a "circular," systemic orientation. The crucial component of this shift to me was not in a consideration of a broader social or interpersonal context by which to define the problem. Whereas some might argue differently, I would argue that the elements or components that comprised this system were perfectly compatible with those discussed in object-relations theory (e.g., mother's "behavior," client's feelings and behavior toward mother, prior therapists' behavior, client's feelings and behavior toward me and prior therapists, my feelings and behavior toward client). Thus, any good object-relations therapist would take those elements into account in treating the client (Note 20), and they were evident in my earlier formulations.
    Rather, I believe the basis for the change was in my connecting these elements in a way that created a feedback loop or pattern of relationships that "freed" me from the dictates of *where* (at what element) to intervene.

By altering my own problematic behavior and reframing what I took to be the client's operating premise from one of "my actions defeat therapists" to "my actions help therapists," novelty was introduced in a way that evidently fit—hence I was strategic. (At least one way to construe the effects of this reframe is that it imputed an unacceptable meaning to her self-destructive actions—they no longer served their intended purpose—so that they had to be abandoned. In any case, MRI and Milan advocates would probably note the strategic use of the "one down position" and "positive connotation" to enhance change.)

If anything, my hypothesis concerning the client's operating premise (i.e., client expresses rage toward mother through transference with therapists) was psychodynamic. I will of course never know whether I would have arrived at this or another intervention that fit as well without these ideas from an "individual model." For that matter, I will never know whether *my reframe caused* or contributed to the shift that took place. We psychotherapists certainly work with a tremendous amount of ambiguity, which is why I believe we feel a need for specific content (i.e., objects of change), or something more substantial than "process notions" of change, in order to survive. With this problem in mind, let us now address some practical considerations.

"PRACTICAL" IMPLICATIONS

The Eclectic Paradox

The central premise of this chapter is that, both in terms of where practitioners seem to be headed and in terms of the fundamentals of strategic/systemic therapies, the systems movement must find ways to understand the individual as well as his/her "larger contexts" by allowing interpersonal (previously referred to as "systemic") explanations to subsume individual psychologies and, similarly, systemic processes to subsume any content. Since this suggestion may seem to resemble what is now a rather prevalent topic of controversy within psychotherapy, namely, the question of eclecticism, we should consider the implications of this discussion for that question.

It is probably prudent to begin by stating outright that eclecticism in the "technical" sense is not what is being advocated. Lazarus (1967) defined "technical eclecticism" as the combined use of "effective technique[s], regardless of . . . [their] theoretical origins" (p. 415). He further distinguished this from a "theoretical" form of eclecticism, which was defined as the attempt to integrate "bits and pieces from divergent theories" for the purpose of "theoretical *rapprochement*," an attempt which Lazarus believed to be doomed to contradiction, confusion, and hence futility (p. 416).

Contrary to Lazarus, a technical eclectic approach to the problem at hand would probably be the quickest route to disarray, since it would provide the therapist with no clear map or conceptual framework to guide the selection and combination of techniques. It is not clear to me, however, that the solution resides in the form of theoretical eclecticism, at least not insofar as Lazarus defined it. Rather, as indicated throughout this discussion, I believe the answer to the dilemma facing systemic therapies resides in the creation of models which operate at higher levels by virtue of dictating processes for enhancing change, but not specific contents or targets of the change process.

To illustrate the distinction I am attempting to draw, I refer to a position I took in a previous article (Held, 1984). In this article I advocated combining the MRI's strategic tactics for reducing resistance with the therapy models of one's choice, to enhance the change as defined, in part, by the chosen models. Thus, for example, one could be strategic *and* psychoanalytic by providing an analytic interpretation but suggesting that the client be cautious about accepting it. I now believe this approach to fall somewhere along a continuum of "theoretical/technical" eclecticism: the chosen model provided the theoretical or conceptual framework, and the strategic tactics or techniques provided the means (i.e., processes) by which to accomplish the specific goals defined by the selected theory, the therapist, and the client.

If not a simple summation of two theoretical approaches, my suggestion at best had the strategic tactics *subsumed by* the selected model. In contrast to this approach, I have come to construe the strategic/systemic model described in this chapter as the conceptual framework which can subsume or incorporate the content or descriptions that any other model may have to offer. Furthermore, this framework has the potential to provide a process or means of selecting concepts from various models through the concept of "fit." (As an aside, I should mention that this subtle shift in my thinking makes me wonder how I will view the arguments put forth in this chapter in the future.)

This shift in my thinking also is consistent with the trend toward "convergence" which has begun to appear in the psychotherapy literature. This trend has been reflected in attempts to define models which exist at higher levels by virtue of describing processes which can subsume any content. Prochaska & DiClemente (1982) note that while "divergence has dominated the past decade of development within the field of psychotherapy" (p. 276), "there is a *Zeitgeist* emerging in which theorists and therapists [dissatisfied with the limitations of their models] . . . are searching for common principles of change. Perhaps this is a move toward a higher level of convergence to balance out and integrate the divergence of the past two decades" (p. 277). Two examples of such "higher order" models are "Prescriptive Eclecticism" (Dimond,

Havens, & Jones, 1978) and "Transtheoretical Therapy" (Prochaska & DiClemente, 1982). The distinction between these sorts of "process" as opposed to "content" models is described by Prochaska & DiClemente (1982).

> The processes of change are the contributions unique to a theory of therapy. The content that is to be changed in any particular therapy is largely a carryover from that system's theory of personality and psychopathology. Many books supposedly focusing on therapy frequently confuse content and process and end up describing primarily the content of therapy with little explanation about the processes of therapy. As a result, they really are books on theories of personality rather than theories of therapy.
>
> Those systems of therapy that do not contain theories of personality . . . are primarily process theories and have few predetermined concepts about what will be the content of therapy. . . .
>
> The transtheoretical model is much more a process than content theory of therapy. That is, rather than assuming that all presenting problems will eventually lead to conflicts over sex and aggression [or, triangulation] as the critical content of therapy, the transtheoretical model assumes that the content of therapy will vary considerably from client to client. . . . The client can initially serve as the expert on the content to be changed while the therapist serves as the expert on the processes that can produce change. (p. 282)

According to this description, strategic/systemic therapy, like transtheoretical therapy, may be considered to be a "process model," which provides the means of organizing any information at the content level.

A "process model" can be thought of as a "meta-model" in that it can incorporate and thus reexplain aspects of other models. Again, such a model dictates processes or procedures that are at a higher level than any of the content they subsume. Furthermore, by changing the way any content may be used, "process models" alter the meaning of that content (e.g., the "transference hypothesis" in the case example above acquired new implications in light of the strategic process: the goal no longer was to interpret the client's "transference" behavior "accurately" per se, but rather to reframe or interpret it in a way that was "novel," "meaningful," and "toxic" to the client, regardless of the "true" source of her problem). To return to the question of eclecticism, once a therapist attains this sort of "meta-model," a new model emerges which, if it achieves a degree of coherence and consistency, is no longer eclectic in the true sense of the word.

Thus, if we believe that *all* therapists have their own personal guiding principles of process and content that they employ with consistency—whether explicitly or implicitly, consciously or unconsciously, and regardless of how many models of therapy they draw from (Note 21)—then eclectic therapy is *logically impossible*. To quote an old chestnut, "One cannot not have a theory" (Liddle, 1982, p. 244). The therapist who integrates many theories in a unique way, and so defines his/her own process (and content), is no longer functioning eclectically. The more we consciously integrate, the less likely we are to be eclectic in the true sense of the word. This is the paradox of eclecticism: In actual practice, eclecticism may not exist, even though (in theory) it certainly appears to.

The Ultimate Paradox?

But there is a "paradox" which is far more ironic, especially to the strategic/ systemic therapist, which is that it may be more likely for a strategic (and hence systemic) approach to incorporate the concepts or content described by the "individual" rather than by the various "systemic" (i.e., interpersonal) (Note 22) models. This situation is due to the confusion between the process and content aspects of therapy — a confusion which, as discussed above, appears to pervade all or most schools of psychotherapy.

Since the content of the systemic models has been articulated in the literature as interpersonal in nature, and since most systemic therapists seem to agree that interpersonal systems subsume intrapersonal systems, then it follows logically that the larger interpersonal system can readily incorporate the smaller intrapersonal system. In fact, according to this line of reasoning, individual descriptions can be used "systemically" as long as their interpersonal context is always considered (Note 23).

A problem arises, however, when we consider the implications of integrating the systemic models, all of which advocate an interpersonal level of analysis. This fact appears to place the various systemic models at the *same* "level of system description." This being the case, how can one interpersonal model subsume or incorporate the descriptions or content of another interpersonal model the way any interpersonal model can incorporate descriptions at the level of the individual? To put the matter yet another way, if one model is to incorporate or subsume ideas from another model, do they not need to exist at different "hierarchical levels" (e.g., process (higher) vs. content (lower), or interpersonal content (higher) vs. individual content (lower)) (Note 24)?

If, however, we again accept the premise that a strategic model is at a higher level than other systemic models, the dilemma may then disappear. This argument is founded on the premise that the strategic model — to the extent that it is possible — suggests only processes to achieve change and therefore can subsume any content, whether at the individual or interpersonal level. Since other systemic models are each defined by specific content (e.g., role-reversals, triangulation, emotional cut-off, etc.) which coexists with the therapeutic process (or procedure) and which defines the "true maintainer" of the problem, at least in this regard they may be said to exist at a lower level than the strategic model. Their descriptions can therefore be incorporated by such a "process model" (cf. Duncan, 1984; Fraser, 1984).

But an obstacle to such incorporation still remains, and it may have less to do with logic and this or that theory regarding levels of analysis than with questions of "loyalty." To incorporate and use individual concepts strategically, we must, as previously discussed, change the *way* we think about and employ these concepts; we cannot attribute the exclusive or true source or focus of the problem to them. To use "systemic" or, rather, interpersonal concepts strategically requires the same process. We must abandon any pretensions we may have about the exclusive validity of these concepts with regard to source or maintenance of the symptoms, and instead see them as tools to organize experience and so to "create" patterns which (in some way fit the case and thus) contribute to the formulation of novel interventions. This is easier said than done; that is, we *say* we do this, but do we?

We strategic/systemic therapists, who became caught up in the systems revolution, seem not only to have abandoned the individual models on which we were raised, but also to display great loyalty to the particular systemic model that was the basis for our conversion. This loyalty may make us "resistant" to changing the way we think about and use the concepts from our preferred models. It is a similar circumstance, for example, to that of a psychoanalytic therapist who "resists" using his/her concepts from a strategic frame of reference. So that while we no longer believe in the exclusive or objective truth of individual concepts — thus leaving us more willing to "play with," alter, or change the way we think about and employ these concepts — we seem to be more protective of our "systems" level concepts.

In other words, while we have given great lip service to the "subjective epistemology" behind our systemic theories (e.g., acknowledging the nonexclusivity of our concepts, the coexistence of many possible descriptions, and the limits of our ability to know an "objective reality" which reveals the ultimate causes of problems), many of us (and I here include myself) are often quick to defend our faith in the (relative) validity of the concepts from our favorite theory. The absence of clear empirical evidence and the position that, given a subjective epistemology, "objective" evidence will never be possible certainly compound the problem. Indeed, the fear — expressed in the Fall 1984 *Journal of Strategic and Systemic Therapies* "Issue on Integrating the Models" — that we stand to lose the meaning or "crispness" of our constructs if we integrate the systemic models suggests to me that we believe our concepts are reflective of *something* "real," and therefore we should not tamper with them. If this is the case, we are back to our original dilemma: on the one hand arguing that there is no objective reality available to us, and on the other hand believing — or sometimes *behaving as if* we believe — our constructs reflect reality.

Now What?

If we accept: (a) the distinction between process and content aspects of psychotherapy; (b) that "process models" (which capitalize on means to achieve change rather than the content to be changed) can subsume any other model's content; and (c) that the strategic/systemic model is just such a "process model," then implications for both the individual practitioner and the field as a whole become readily apparent.

First, however, we must clarify our understanding of the process/content distinction by distinguishing not only *between* process and content models but also the process vs. content components *within* any one model. Recall that "process models" are defined in terms of offering theory and techniques (the processes that produce change) which allow the use of whatever content to describe the problem. The strategic model, by virtue of its grounding in systemic theory and its methods ("tactics") for change, is a "process model." In contrast, "content models" also offer theory and techniques but, as Prochaska & DiClemente (1982) suggest, they limit the specific content to be acted upon in the change process. In fact, sometimes they appear to stress the content more than the mechanisms employed to change it. Thus, while most "content models" also offer, at least to some extent, procedures to enhance change, their implication of the correct content to be addressed in *all* cases places them in the "content model" category.

It is my belief that the attempt to articulate this distinction (as imperfect as it may be) will permit more deliberate decisions about how (in what way — process or content) to modify our own therapeutic positions in response to our clients' behaviors. It will also assist in our much needed efforts to enumerate, define, and refine those processes (techniques, methods, interventions) that enhance the possibility for change to occur regardless of the particular content of a case (Note 25).

Thus, this distinction can help us determine the most effective (i.e., "fitting") ways to shift frames of reference and so to alter behavior, achieve compliance, interrupt a behavioral sequence or, even more primary, to define a pattern that can become the basis for a direct intervention. Put differently, my suggestion is that we get the "*hows*" figured out more precisely before we immerse ourselves in the detail of particular "*whats*" (although both aspects merit attention). To do this, however, we must distinguish, as best as possible, between the hows and whats.

It is precisely in reference to this problem that I believe strategic/systemic models to have a decided edge over other "process models." To put it as simply as possible, the strategic/systemic models — especially those based on the MRI and Milan models — do the best job of offering both general processes or approaches designed to assist change, regardless of the content involved, and more specific interventions given certain client responses. Whereas other "process models" may tend to become somewhat vague when it comes to the question of how *precisely* to achieve this or that goal, the MRI "tactics," along with, for instance, the Milan Associates and Ackerman Project approaches (e.g., the "Greek Chorus," systemic prescriptions, circular questioning, therapeutic neutrality), really offer processes or hows that direct the therapist in most if not all contexts (Papp, 1980; Penn, 1982; Selvini-Palazzoli, Boscolo, Cecchin, & Prata, 1980). This *is* our strength; we utilize a "process model" that is by definition flexible with regard to content (the elements that are seen to comprise a system) and yet manages to be both general and specific with regard to process. It is the best of both worlds; we can have our cake and eat it too.

Still, there is always room for improvement, namely, to capitalize on our strength by refining and enhancing the strategic process, activities in which many members of our field appear to be actively engaged. I would venture to guess that we might even learn a thing or two by assessing the successful and hence "strategic" process aspects of the so-called "nonstrategic" models (e.g., humanistic, gestalt, analytic). To conjure up some wisdom from Maslow (whom most of us would probably consider to be as far as possible from a strategic approach), "I suppose it is tempting, if the only tool you have is a hammer, to treat everything as if it were a nail" (Maslow, 1966, pp. 15–16).

Marvin Goldfried (1980), another "nonstrategic" therapist who has spent considerable time on the problems of eclecticism and theoretical convergence and *rapprochement*, offers the following sane advice with regard to the change process:

> I would suggest . . . that the possibility of finding meaningful consensus exists at a level of abstraction somewhere between theory and technique which, for want of a better term, we might call *clinical strategies*. . . . In essence, such strategies function as clinical heuristics that implicitly guide our efforts during the course of therapy. . . . I would like to offer as examples two such strategies that may very well be common to all theoretical orientations: (a) providing the patient/client with new, corrective experiences, and (b) offering the patient/client direct feedback. (p. 994)

Goldfried (1980) went on to observe,

> There exist certain "timeless truths," consisting of common observations of how people change. These observations date back to early philosophers and are reflected in great works of literature. . . . These observations have also been noted by most experienced and sensitive clinicians. *To the extent that clinicians of varying orientations are able to arrive at a common set of strategies, it is likely that what emerges will consist of robust phenomena, as they have managed to survive the distortions imposed by the therapists' varying theoretical biases.*

Although it is clear that a systematic and more objective study of the therapeutic change process is needed to advance our body of knowledge, it would be a grievous error to ignore what has been unsystematically observed by many. (p. 996)

Though he is not a strategic/systemic therapist by title or admission, Gold-fried's position should sound familiar to those of us who are.

But as a remedy to unbridled optimism, I wish to temper this discussion by noting a problem which I have yet to find addressed systematically in the "process literature," although I believe it to be of import to all therapists. It is another paradox of sorts, namely, that while "process models"—because they dictate no specific content to be altered—offer the most promise for solving the broadest range of problems, they also are the most frustrating to therapists. They do not tell us what specifically to change, only how to enhance change, and it seems that in the thick of therapy we mortals need some specific "what" to cling to. Process seems not to be enough, especially for those of us who are beginners, or middlers, or who are not Watzlawicks, Weaklands, Cecchins and Boscolos.

I know of no "process model" that directly acknowledges and thus adequately confronts this problem. We seem to need content to hang our therapeutic hats on, and I fear that all "process models" will be doomed to extinction unless they address this problem openly. A symptom of this dilemma may be observed in the proliferation of articles which suggest how various therapeutic contents may be used within a strategic framework. Berger and Daniels-Mohring's (1982) article, "The Strategic Use of 'Bowenian' Formulations," is an example of this trend.

So while we strategic/systemic therapists are working on the "hows," what do we do about the unspecified "whats"? If the "process" suggestion—that the "what" be determined solely on the basis of each unique case (i.e., *whatever* the client brings into therapy)—leaves most therapists feeling too ungrounded to determine the basis (content or elements) for pattern creation and interruption, then how shall a "process" therapist proceed? There obviously is no simple answer to this question, for as soon as we introduce formalized content into a model, it, by definition, ceases to be a "process model" (Note 26).

While I have no definitive wisdom to offer on this matter, some possibilities do spring to mind. It seems to me that an answer to this dilemma rests in the ability of a therapist to walk the tightrope between "pure" process and restricted content. And it is precisely on this line that the question of individual vs. interpersonal content returns. What if each therapist were to clarify, for him/herself, his/her own "warehouse" of concepts to be employed in the pattern description and hence reframing process? In other words, we could so observe our formulations and interventions that before long we would determine easily enough what concepts we *tend* to use to organize our observations (i.e., define elements and patterns between elements) at a variety of system levels (e.g., individuals, couples, families, larger social systems).

The idea, of course, is to be able to draw a variety of patterns at as many system levels as possible for any given case. Such activity promotes choice about where—at what system level—to intervene, which is, to recall our previous discussion, at the heart of the strategic/systemic model. In other words, we can fit the conceptualization and intervention as closely as possible, given our warehouse, to what the client brings. Thus, as has been noted ad infinitum by now, the family may not always be the most appropriate (i.e., strategic) system level for pattern conceptualization and intervention; it could be smaller, meaning fewer people, or larger.

It would, of course, be perfectly legitimate for us now to ask *how*, on what *basis*, we choose our warehouse of concepts. This question obviously subsumes the question of how we choose concepts to fit a specific case, which is the essence of the strategic process itself. At the risk of sounding less than profound, I suggest it be on the basis of pragmatism; we tend to rely on those concepts or descriptions that we have come to trust, those that have assisted our efforts at change. And I suspect that we all have our favorites—for example, reframing a self-defeating behavior as a sign of loyalty to the family of origin.

Our faith, belief, or trust in the utility of a concept also presents us with another tightrope. We must place *enough* stock in the meaningfulness and fit of our concept or description that it makes good sense to us and our client, but not so much that we end up believing it to be the *exclusive* and *objective* basis of the problem for this case (and worse, for all or most cases) (Note 27). Once we fall off the tightrope to the latter side, we are then in the domain of traditional or "nonstrategic" therapy which posits the "correct" content to be altered in all cases. This domain certainly provides a comfortable safety net, but, as we have seen, it limits the change process. While some might consider this type of conditional faith in our choice of content (and perhaps process as well) to be just another form of "placebo effect," I see it as the very stuff of psychotherapy (cf. O'Connell, 1983).

It is precisely because of the individuality of each therapist—the unique experiences that determine which concepts at different system levels (i.e., individual vs. interpersonal) make sense or help to organize observations at each level—that consensus *between* therapists will never exist at the level of content. Goldfried (1980) was correct. There also will and even should be variation in the choices of concepts at any one system level made by *each* therapist as he/she responds to or tries to fit each unique case and so evolves in his/her therapy approach.

Furthermore, I suspect that the longer each of us practices, the more finely tuned and unique to ourselves our theory of change becomes, especially with regard to content. If we consider, for example, the increasing appearance of systemic models which attempt to integrate individual psychology concepts (e.g., Duhl and Duhl's (1981) "Integrative Family Therapy," which utilizes concepts from Piaget; Lagos (1984), who incorporates Otto Rank's ideas into structural theory), we may realize that these efforts are the result of years of specific experiences, which have created the right amount of "faith" in the value of certain concepts to describe human behavior. This realization should remind each of us that we cannot buy ready-made products off the shelf and expect them to fit; we must wear them for a long time so that they mold to our unique forms.

In contrast to the tendency for therapists to become over time more unique in their choice of content, and consistent with Goldfried (1980) and Strupp (1981), it seems to me that the opposite is true of process (i.e., the general maxims that guide our interventions): Seasoned clinicians become more alike in this regard. I know of few therapists of any theoretical orientation who would argue, for example, against the notion that altering, as effectively as possible, a client's point of view or experience of events (whatever those events may be) is basic to the change process.

So what does this mean about our limitations as therapists? Mainly that we need to admit to them. Despite an armament of concepts descriptive of various system levels and the processes or strategies of change by which to employ them, our cognitive limitations alone preclude any one therapist from having an unlimited supply of concepts or descriptions available at any given time. This means that we will not be able to fit (precise reframes to) all cases equally well. Thus, it is highly unlikely that, either as individual practitioners or as a field, we will ever find The Theory—at both process and content levels—which *always* works. If the psychotherapy "process and outcome" research has taught us one thing, it is an appreciation of the complexity—in terms of sheer number of variables, not to mention the artistic or creative component—that makes quantifying change such an elusive process (Kiesler, 1971; Strupp & Bergin, 1969).

What we can do, however, is be flexible and intelligent in our therapeutic (strategic) process. If we find ourselves "stuck" in a case, with a knowledge of the process vs. content distinction we could change our own behavior in several ways. We could, for example: (a) change our strategy or "tactic" and leave the content relatively intact (e.g., take a "one down position" with regard to an offered reframe); (b) expand our vocabulary of concepts and thus offer a new reframe at the same system level to fit better "what the client brings"; (c) switch to a new level of system description (e.g., move from a couples analysis to a nuclear family analysis or vice versa); (d) seek consultation; and (e) admit limitations and secure a cotherapist. To offer another metaphor, we must be able to stretch (our concepts) enough (to fit the client and so to be strategic), but not stretch so much as to break the rubber band (i.e., lose our coherence or systematic framework).

As should be evident by now, the question of whether to use individual vs. interpersonal concepts and descriptions may be seen to be a moot point in light of the strategic process. With a warehouse of concepts to describe at different system levels on the one hand, and a strategic process which grants the flexibility to change concepts and levels in response to a client on the other hand, we can venture walking the fine line of trying to fit ourselves as much as possible to each case while still having enough focus, guidance, and coherence to stay on the tightrope. It is, of course, a deliberate compromise, a balance between the promise of the all-encompassing (but potentially vague or unfocused) theory of the "process model," and the limited (but precise and focused) theory of the "content model." While not speaking directly to the problem of process vs. content models of therapy, Hoffman (1981) well expressed this tension in reference to systemic models when she stated, "If the structuralists need to admit to their knowledge of process, the strategists need to admit to their knowledge of form" (p. 278).

The "Real" Thing

If our original question about the role of the individual within a systemic framework is not the "real" dilemma confronting the strategic/systemic paradigm, then what is? While there are probably many problems that our field must address, it will at this point be no surprise to the reader if I implicate the "epistemology question" (meaning 1) as a prime candidate. As we have seen throughout this chapter, our field's increasing fondness for philosophical solutions in general, along with its appeal to a "subjective epistemology" in particular, has led us into a quandary: how we can arrive at any conclusion about how things *"really"* work — and based on our journals we certainly *behave as if* we are indeed attempting this feat when we consider such questions as the "validity" of linear vs. circular causalities, more and less effective strategies of change, the "correct" level for system conceptualization and intervention, and so forth — if we are to adhere to the rather extreme subjective epistemology position *as it has been expressed in our literature.* Put differently, how can we argue that there is no objective or independent reality or, if there is, that there is no way for us to know it (since we each create what we perceive) while we continue through our research questions to quest for knowledge of how the world of behavior "really" works, a quest which I can only assume we hope will tell us something beyond our own individual creations?

Based on an argument previously made with a collaborator (Held & Pols,

1985), I believe we have adopted the notion of "subjective epistemology" rather cavalierly—that is, without examining as closely and clearly as possible the variety of positions such a notion can embody, and the implications of these positions—so that we end up contradicting ourselves. It seems to me that we have two rational choices. We can either really "dig in" and come to grips with the question of epistemology (meaning 1)—as, for example, some physicists have attempted to do—or we can decide that such issues are beyond the limits of our expertise and therefore simply stop addressing them altogether.

The latter suggestion raises the question why we have gotten into such a muddle in the first place and why we continue to be in that muddle (e.g., the "epistemology" debates). I propose that it is, at least in part, due to a sense of guilt, an interpretation which I realize has a terribly psychodynamic tone to it. The strategic (i.e., reframing) process is based on the premise that we do not believe our reframes to be "Truth," "Reality," or the "Ultimate Cause" of the problem. Yet we sometimes deliver them to our clients as if they are or at least could be. This element of our model has left us open to (self) criticisms about our misuse of power and the ensuing manipulation of clients.

For instance, the "aesthetic/pragmatic" debate within the epistemology debates is a prime example of this situation. If we are able to argue that *there is no objective reality*, however, we can then *justify* our attempts to reframe events in *any way* which is strategic to the case without the anguish of feeling controlling, devious, misleading, manipulative, and so forth. After all, how can we be deceitful if there is no basis for truth *in reality*? Reamy-Stephenson (1983), in her article, "The Assumption of Non-Objective Reality . . . ," confronts this dilemma rather openly when she states, "The complex process of reframing so central to the work of strategic therapists depends on the assumption of non-objective reality. Without this assumption, reframing is indeed a clever technique with which the therapist manipulates the client" (p. 55).

My relentless return to our field's flirtation with questions of epistemology is not a needless digression into philosophy—this issue has very "real" implications for the evolution of the field. As I hope has become evident by now, how we view our therapeutic process (and content) in relation to the problem of "objective reality" provides not only a basis for a distinction between us and traditional therapies, but also affects how we do research as well as how we view research (e.g., What constructs can our research validate? What does the term "validation" mean? How do we feel about what we do in [therapy and] research?). The recent debates in *The Family Therapy Networker* over an appropriate research paradigm for the "systemic epistemology" (meaning 2) is a manifestation of this problem and certainly reinforces my concerns (Kniskern, 1983; Tomm, 1983).

Since we are, at this point, really addressing the question of the evolution of a paradigm, it seems only proper to conclude with some popular Kuhnian wisdom, namely, that when established paradigms are confronted with anomalies, contradictions, or paradox, a period of "crisis" which alters the course of research emerges. To quote Kuhn's own words,

> Confronted with anomaly or with crisis, scientists take a different attitude toward existing paradigms, and the nature of their research changes accordingly. The proliferation of competing articulations, the willingness to try anything, the expression of explicit discontent, the recourse to philosophy and to debate over fundamentals, all these are symptoms of a transition from normal to extraordinary research. (Kuhn, 1970, pp. 90–91)

The above statement is reinforced by the following:

> It is, I think, particularly in periods of acknowledged crisis that scientists have turned to philosophical analysis as a device for unlocking the riddles of their field. (Kuhn, 1970, p. 88)

Judging from our own and other mental health journals over the last five years, it seems clear that the strategic/systemic "paradigm" has achieved legitimacy within the mental health establishment, and that we have certainly produced the symptoms of crisis reminiscent of those described by Kuhn.

Kuhn further argued that "all crises begin with the blurring of a paradigm and . . . close in one of three ways": (a) The existing paradigm is "able to handle the crisis-provoking problem despite the despair of those who have seen it as the end of an existing paradigm." (b) "The problem resists . . . radical new approaches" and so it is "labelled and set aside for a future generation with more developed tools." or (c) A new paradigm (or at least a "candidate" for one) emerges (p. 84).

Although Kuhn's prediction (echoed by Minuchin [Simon, 1984]) that paradigms are displaced not so much by new evidence as by the simultaneous emergence and acceptance of a new paradigm is certainly ominous, we can only speculate about which of the three routes, if any, our field will take. The one thing we can count on, however, is that our wait will be anything but subdued.

NOTES

1. This controversy may be characterized by asking whether systemic interventions are so "surface" or present/behavior-oriented that they preclude lasting or "real" change. It was last expressed in the debates between the behaviorists and the psychoanalysts over the question of "symptom substitution." According to Dell (1984b), the current version may be seen as a "battle" mainly between psychoanalytic/transgenerational and strategic (family) therapists.
2. The use of quotation marks around the term "epistemology" in this case indicates the author's

conviction that those debates are improperly so called. For a full discussion of the matter, see Held and Pols (1985).

3. Some readers may find an elaboration of this distinction as it has appeared in the family systems literature to be helpful. Linear causality has been characterized by the notion of simple, deterministic, isolated (i.e., not contextualized) cause and effect sequences of events. For example, Event A causes Event B, which causes Event C, which culminates in Event D (Watzlawick, Beavin, & Jackson, 1967, p. 30). In contrast, nonlinear or circular causality is characterized by the idea of a system being "self-regulating"; thus, feedback from output is introduced back into the input as "information" (von Bertalanffy, 1969; Watzlawick, Beavin, & Jackson, 1967) so that now, as Penn (1982) states, "D loops, and is fed back to A . . . [in a way that] makes a continuous line or event impossible. . . . A now has a context (A, B, C, and D) and is a part of a system in which it both acts and is acted upon by the components of its system" (p. 270). In this chapter, "circular causality" is used to indicate a therapist's way of *thinking* about the relationships between events or elements in a system, and *not* as a description of how the "real world" operates (see Held & Pols, 1985).

4. Dell (1984a, p. 354) has argued that we must abandon the notion of (individual) traits because all traits are "context-dependent" and therefore are not to be seen as "inherent" qualities of the individual (or system). As will be argued in this chapter, the "context" can be another aspect of the individual as well as the interpersonal environment (or, of course, both). Thus, the appearance of the trait can still be seen as dependent upon other elements "in the system," thereby eliminating the problem. This question will be addressed more fully throughout the chapter.

5. Some rather prominent systemic therapists (e.g., Gurman, 1983; Minuchin et al., 1978) have in fact argued that we must make *some* linear assumptions in order to function effectively as therapists. In this regard we may not always be so different from "traditional therapists."

6. The discerning reader will detect a subtle "paradox" which is confronted here. That is, the change process entails using the notion of "subjectivity" to permit shifting constructions of reality in therapy. This statement, however, exists within a more "objective epistemology" in that it assumes we can "know" what best accounts for change (i.e., changing perceptions of events). The question, "What is the relationship between the etiology of a problem and the nature of changing it," may also be raised here.

7. I disagree with Dell (1984a) and Minuchin et al. (1978), who hold that in order to be truly systemic we must define such individual qualities only in relation to a *current interpersonal* context. As stated previously, and as will be elaborated upon in the forthcoming section, other aspects of the individual, and past interpersonal contexts, can certainly serve as relevant system components. This position is consistent with the "interactionist model," which is currently espoused in the field of psychology and which emphasizes the relationship between Person ("enduring" individual characteristics) and Environment (social/interpersonal context) explanations of behavior.

8. In fact, Dell (1984b) believes that transgenerational (depth) models are enjoying a new preeminence, perhaps as some family therapists appear to have become dissatisfied with a "present-only" (surface) orientation.

9. Again, I would like to emphasize my perception that all family therapists use *in practice* concepts that describe at the individual as well as the interpersonal level, but that we are more formally aware of and comfortable with the latter in our *theorizing*. As Gurman and Kniskern (1981) point out in their editorial response to Kerr, "Most distinctions between individuals and systems are arbitrary and probably even artificial, in that, from the view of general systems theory (which is not equivalent to family systems theory), individual persons are *sub*systems of the family, and these subsystems themselves contain subsystems, e.g., levels of awareness, such as conscious and unconscious experience" (p. 234).

10. Here the term "process" can be taken in the sense that Yalom (1975) proposed in reference to "group process": the "relationship implications [arising out] of interpersonal transactions" (p. 122).

11. One can always argue that all (psychological) components of the individual, such as perceptions or behaviors, always occur in reference to *some* significant other, past or present, real or imagined. If this is the case (and the argument does have merit), then I am unaware of any model of psychotherapy which is not, in this sense, interpersonal.

12. I might add that a client who happens to be a psychoanalytic psychotherapist would probably respond well to a psychodynamic "mythology," which, in this case, would be a strategic reframe.

13. Another way to state this (although I am aware that some would object) is that an intervention is strategic when it considers *all* potential sources of "resistance" at both interpersonal and intrapersonal levels.

14. One point that continues to plague me is the question of how a therapist's *belief* in the "truth" of his/her explanation/intervention relates to the change process. While systemic theorists argue that "marrying" one's hypotheses can lead a therapist to become rigid and then stuck, which then of course impedes change, others argue that therapy works by virtue of the therapist's and client's *belief* in the method (i.e., the "placebo" effect) (O'Connell, 1983). Perhaps the process vs. content distinction is useful here, in that therapists need to "believe" only in the particular therapeutic process, and not in specific content, to be effective agents of change.

15. McNamee et. al. (1983) illustrate this point in stating, "Participants in the workshop were impressed by Cecchin and Boscolo's willingness to gather information about the family using concepts from various frames of reference, including structural and psychoanalytic models. They endeavor to be consistently systemic and use other concepts within the context of an overall systemic view" (p. 60).

16. Fraser (1984), by applying Buckley's classification scheme to his analysis of the different systemic models, has recently provided an excellent discussion of how strategic therapy can be understood to operate at a "higher level of system description" than structural therapy. The reader is referred to this article for further elaboration, including Fraser's use of the term "process."

17. Splitting has been defined as the separation of good and bad qualities in the self and others such that the integration of these qualities is avoided. Abrupt reversals in feelings about the self or other are a primary manifestation of splitting-defenses (see Kernberg, 1977, p. 108).

18. A note of caution is indicated here. I had, in the course of treatment, hospitalized this client once, which may have contributed to her increased dependency and regression. Like other clients with similar symptoms, this client often argued that she would become worse if we tried to hospitalize her, thereby placing the therapist in a profound double bind (e.g., "I will mutilate myself if you do not hospitalize me, and I will mutilate myself more if you do hospitalize me."). Nonetheless, had I (and my supervisor at that time) been convinced of a suicide danger (whether deliberate or not), we would have proceeded immediately with (if necessary, involuntary) hospitalization. The "strategic" use of hospitalization in cases of threats of self-mutilation and suicide is an area where I feel more exploration is indicated.

19. The client and I had spent several months discussing her problems concerning her mother. She revealed in these discussions (based on insights from prior therapy, no doubt) that she sought female therapists because they were her "substitute mothers" whose lives she could then make miserable. Hence, there was a groundwork laid for this reframe.

20. This suggestion again illustrates the point, made earlier, that *all* behavior *can* be seen as directed toward someone or something (e.g., the self, or real or imagined others). In this sense, all psychotherapies "deal" with the "interpersonal" event. Furthermore, an object-relations therapist might argue that my intervention could be interpreted within the realm of object-relations theory as helping to change the maternal introject.

21. Of course, it is always better to be able to articulate consciously and deliberately our therapy approach in order to be truly systematic in our work.

22. The use of the term "systemic" within quotation marks is meant to indicate the essential point of this chapter, namely, that an interpersonal perspective neither defines nor is necessary for a systemic approach. The quotation marks thus convey a different meaning of the term "systemic" than has been offered in this chapter.

23. Recall once again that this is a prevalent argument in the field, although it is contrary to the argument concerning the fundamentals of systemic thinking put forth in this chapter.

24. I perceive the debates about the feasibility of integrating the "systemic" models and the loss of model "integrity" and potential dilution of concepts which could ensue as reflecting, in part, this dilemma (see *Journal of Strategic and Systemic Therapies*, Fall 1984 issue).

25. I should mention that one reason for the imprecision of the process/content distinction may

reside in the fact that certain "processes" (strategies, methods, means) to achieve change may be more appropriate for (i.e., fit better with) certain kinds of clients. This, of course, implies that clinical strategies may vary along a continuum of generality; that is, there are general approaches which may apply to all cases, while some "tactics" are warranted only in specific instances. For example, the essence of the strategic/systemic "process" — defining the elements of a case in circular terms; introducing new information which, by virtue of its fit, changes the pattern — is a process that, as is here argued, applies to all cases. Similarly, suggestions about how best to achieve fit (e.g., positive connotation), or how to maintain "therapeutic maneuverability" (Fisch, Weakland, & Segal, 1982), are more general in nature. In contrast are the specific methods which are employed only if the specific situation warrants their use, that is, only if they "fit" the client's responses to us (e.g., "discuss the danger of improvement"). I believe it would serve our field well to put some effort into distinguishing our more basic processes from those which are more situation specific, including an elaboration of which strategies work better in (fit) which situations (see Goldfried, 1980).

26. Don Efron (personal communication; March 14, 1985) has suggested (and quite correctly, I believe) that many systemic therapists seem to deal with this problem by specializing in a particular content area (e.g., alcoholism, eating disorders). They may become so immersed in the content of their area of specialization that they lose perspective on the process vs. content distinction and hence their systemic framework. Efron believes these therapists then to be in danger of a return to a "content-based" model.

27. This issue arose during a conversation with Richard D. Flanagan in 1983.

REFERENCES

American College Dictionary (1957). New York: Random House, s.v. "strategy."

Berger, M., & Daniels-Mohring, D. (1982). The strategic use of "Bowenian" formulations. *Journal of Strategic and Systemic Therapies, 1,* 50–56.

Bowen, M. (1978). *Family Therapy in Clinical Practice.* New York: Jason Aronson.

Colapinto, J. (1984). On model integration and model integrity. *Journal of Strategic and Systemic Therapies, 3,* 38–42.

Dell, P. F. (1980). Researching the family theories of schizophrenia: An exercise in epistemological confusion. *Family Process, 19,* 321–335.

Dell, P. F. (1982a). Beyond homeostasis: Toward a concept of coherence. *Family Process, 21,* 21–41.

Dell, P. F. (1982b). Family theory and the epistemology of Humberto Maturana. In F. W. Kaslow (Ed.), *The International Book of Family Therapy* (pp. 56–66). New York: Brunner/Mazel.

Dell, P. F. (1984a). Why family therapy should go beyond homeostasis: A Kuhnian reply to Ariel, Carel and Tyano. *Journal of Marital and Family Therapy, 10,* 351–356.

Dell, P. F. (1984b, March). *Whither family theory?* Workshop presented at the Seventh Annual Family Therapy Network Symposium, "Getting Unstuck," Washington, D. C. Recorded by Creative Audio, Highland, IN.

de Shazer, S. (1982). *Patterns of Brief Family Therapy: An Ecosystemic Approach.* New York: Guilford Press.

Dimond, R. E., Havens, R. A., & Jones, A. C. (1978). A conceptual framework for the practice of prescriptive eclecticism in psychotherapy. *American Psychologist, 33,* 239–248.

Duhl, B. S., & Duhl, F. J. (1981). Integrative family therapy. In A. S. Gurman & D. P. Kniskern (Eds.), *Handbook of Family Therapy* (pp. 483–513). New York: Brunner/Mazel.

Duncan, B. L. (1984). Adopting the construct of functionality when it facilitates system change: A method of selective integration. *Journal of Strategic and Systemic Therapies, 3,* 60–65.

Fisch, R., Weakland, J. H., & Segal, L. (1982). *The Tactics of Change: Doing Therapy Briefly.* San Francisco: Jossey-Bass.

Flanagan, R., & Held, B. (1983). What next? [Review of "Family systems over time: The fourth dimension." Sponsored by the Ackerman Institute for Family Therapy, New York, N.Y., May 20–21, 1983.] *The Family Therapy Networker, 7,* 51–53.

Framo, J. (1983). The state of the art. *The Family Therapy Networker, 7*, 19–20.

Fraser, J. S. (1984). Process level integration: Corrective vision for a binocular view. *Journal of Strategic and Systemic Therapies, 3*, 43–57.

Goldfried, M. R. (1980). Toward the delineation of therapeutic change principles. *American Psychologist, 35*, 991–999.

Gray, W., & Rizzo, N. D. (1969). History and development of General Systems Theory. In W. Gray, F. J. Duhl, & N. D. Rizzo (Eds.), *General Systems Theory and Psychiatry* (pp. 7–31). Boston: Little, Brown.

Gurman, A. S. (1978). Contemporary marital therapies: A critique and comparative analysis of psychoanalytic, behavioral and systems theory approaches. In T. J. Paolino Jr. & B. S. McCrady (Eds.), *Marriage and Marital Therapy* (pp. 445–566). New York: Brunner/Mazel.

Gurman, A. S. (1983). Family therapy research and the "new epistemology." *Journal of Marital and Family Therapy, 9*, 227–234.

Gurman, A. S., & Kniskern, D. P. (Eds.). (1981). *Handbook of Family Therapy*. New York: Brunner/Mazel.

Haley, J. (1973). *Uncommon Therapy: The Psychiatric Techniques of Milton H. Erickson, M.D.* New York: W. W. Norton.

Hare-Mustin, R. T. (1980). Family therapy may be dangerous for your health. *Professional Psychology, 11*, 935–938.

Held, B. S. (1984). Toward a strategic eclecticism: A proposal. *Psychotherapy, 21*, 232–241.

Held, B. S., & Flanagan, R. D. (1984a). *An "epistemologically correct," strategic, family-of-origin prescription for the field of family therapy.* Unpublished manuscript.

Held, B. S., & Flanagan, R. D. (1984b, March). *What next for family therapy?* Workshop presented at the Seventh Annual Family Therapy Network Symposium, "Getting Unstuck," Washington, D. C.

Held, B. S., & Pols, E. (1985). The confusion about epistemology and "epistemology"—and what to do about it. *Family Process, 24*, 509–517.

Hoffman, L. (1981). *Foundations of Family Therapy: A Conceptual Framework for Systems Change.* New York: Basic Books.

Kaufman, R., DeLange, W. H., & Selfridge, B. D., Jr. (1977). A system approach to psychotherapy. *Psychotherapy: Theory, Research and Practice, 14*, 286–292.

Keeney, B. P. (1983). *Aesthetics of Change.* New York: Guilford Press.

Keeney, B. P., & Ross, J. M. (1983). Cybernetics of brief family therapy. *Journal of Marital and Family Therapy, 9*, 375–382.

Kernberg, O. F. (1977). The structural diagnosis of borderline personality organization. In P. Hartocollis (Ed.), *Borderline Personality Disorders: The Concept, the Syndrome, the Patient* (pp. 87–121). New York: International Universities Press.

Kerr, M. E. (1981). Family systems theory and therapy. In A. S. Gurman & D. P. Kniskern (Eds.), *Handbook of Family Therapy* (pp. 226–264). New York: Brunner/Mazel.

Kiesler, D. J. (1971). Experimental designs in psychotherapy research. In A. E. Bergin & S. L. Garfield (Eds.), *Handbook of Psychotherapy and Behavior Change: An Empirical Analysis* (pp. 36–74). New York: John Wiley.

Kniskern, D. P. (1983). The new wave is all wet. *The Family Therapy Networker, 7*, 38, 60–62.

Kuhn, T. S. (1970). *The Structure of Scientific Revolutions* (2nd ed.). Chicago: University of Chicago Press.

Lagos, J. (1984, March). *The Individual Within the Family.* Workshop presented at the Seventh Annual Family Therapy Network Symposium, "Getting Unstuck," Washington, D. C. Recorded by Creative Audio, Highland, IN.

Lazarus, A. A. (1967). In support of technical eclecticism. *Psychological Reports, 21*, 415–416.

Liddle, H. A. (1982). On the problem of eclecticism: A call for epistemologic clarification and human-scale theories. *Family Process, 21*, 243–250.

Levenson, E. A. (1978). Two essays in psychoanalytic psychology: II. General Systems Theory: Model or muddle? *Contemporary Psychoanalysis, 14*, 18–30.

Madanes, C. (1981). *Strategic Family Therapy.* San Francisco: Jossey-Bass.

Maslow, A. H. (1966). *The Psychology of Science: A Reconnaissance.* New York: Harper & Row.

McNamee, S., Lannamann, J., & Tomm, K. (1983). Milan clinicians and CMM theoreticians meet: Was it a fertile connection? *Journal of Strategic and Systemic Therapies, 2,* 57–62.

Minuchin, S. (1974). *Families and Family Therapy.* Cambridge, MA: Harvard University Press.

Minuchin, S., Rosman, B. L., & Baker, L. (1978). *Psychosomatic Families: Anorexia Nervosa in Context.* Cambridge, MA: Harvard University Press.

O'Connell, S. (1983). The placebo effect and psychotherapy. *Psychotherapy: Theory, Research and Practice, 20,* 337–345.

Papp, P. (1980). The Greek Chorus and other techniques of paradoxical therapy. *Family Process, 19,* 45–57.

Parry, A. (1984). Maturanation in Milan: Recent developments in systemic therapy. *Journal of Strategic and Systemic Therapies, 3,* 35–42.

Penn, P. (1982). Circular Questioning. *Family Process, 21,* 267–280.

Prochaska, J. O., & DiClemente, C. C. (1982). Transtheoretical therapy: Toward a more integrative model of change. *Psychotherapy: Theory, Research and Practice, 19,* 276–288.

Rabkin, R. (1977). *Strategic Psychotherapy: Brief and Symptomatic Treatment.* New York: Basic Books.

Reamy-Stephenson, M. (1983). The assumption of non-objective reality: A missing link in the training of strategic family therapists. *Journal of Strategic and Systemic Therapies, 2,* 51–67.

Schwartzman, J. (Ed.). (1985). *Families and Other Systems: The Macrosystem Context of Family Therapy.* New York: Guilford Press.

Selvini-Palazzoli, M., Boscolo, L., Cecchin, G., & Prata, G. (1980). Hypothesizing—circularity—neutrality: Three guidelines for the conductor of the session. *Family Process, 19,* 3–12.

Selvini-Palazzoli, M., Cecchin, G., Prata, G., & Boscolo, L. (1978). *Paradox and Counterparadox.* New York: Jason Aronson.

Simon, R. (1984). Stranger in a strange land: An interview with Salvador Minuchin. *The Family Therapy Networker, 8,* 20–31, 66–68.

Sluzki, C. E. (1974). On training to "think interactionally." *Social Science and Medicine, 8,* 483–485.

Sluzki, C. E. (1981). Process of symptom production and patterns of symptom maintenance. *Journal of Marital and Family Therapy, 7,* 273–280.

Sluzki, C. E. (1985). Foreword. In J. Schwartzman (Ed.), *Families and Other Systems* (pp. vii–x). New York: Guilford Press.

Strupp, H. H. (1981, August). *Some implications of psychotherapy research for training.* Paper presented at the symposium, "Towards an Empirically Based Eclecticism," American Psychological Association Annual Convention, Los Angeles, CA.

Strupp, H. H., & Bergin, A. E. (1969). Some empirical and conceptual bases for coordinated research in psychotherapy: A critical review of issues, trends, and evidence. *International Journal of Psychiatry, 7,* 18–90.

Tomm, K. (1983). The old hat doesn't fit. *The Family Therapy Networker, 7,* 39–41.

von Bertalanffy, L. (1969). General Systems Theory and psychiatry—An overview. In W. Gray, F. J. Duhl, & N. D. Rizzo (Eds.), *General Systems Theory and Psychiatry* (pp. 33–46). Boston: Little, Brown.

Watzlawick, P. (1976). *How Real is Real? Confusion, Disconfirmation, Communication.* New York: Random House.

Watzlawick, P. (Ed.). (1984). *The Invented Reality: How Do We Know What We Believe We Know? (Contributions to Constructivism).* New York: W. W. Norton.

Watzlawick, P., Beavin, J. H., & Jackson, D. D. (1967). *Pragmatics of Human Communication.* New York: W. W. Norton.

Watzlawick, P., Weakland, J. H., & Fisch, R. (1974). *Change: Principles of Problem Formation and Problem Resolution.* New York: W. W. Norton.

Yalom, I. D. (1975). *The Theory and Practice of Group Psychotherapy* (2nd ed.). New York: Basic Books.

Ziffer, R. (1983). Notes from a family therapy partisan. [Review of "Creativity in Therapy, Families and Therapists," sponsored by the Family Institute of Philadelphia, Nov. 11–12, 1982.] *The Family Therapy Networker, 7,* 51.

Chapter 11

Intervening in the Medical Community: A Prescription for Applying Strategic Therapy in Family Medicine

*Cheryl L. Storm
and John McFarland*

Other authors suggest that brief, problem-focused therapies are applicable to family medicine (Bishop, Epstein, Golbert, van der Sprey, Levins & McClemont, 1984; Bullock & Thompson, 1979; Fosson, Elam & Broaddus, 1982; Weakland & Fisch, 1984). The purpose of this chapter is to propose that the brief, problem-focused strategic model is particularly applicable to family medical practice. First, we discuss why we believe this is so. Second, we review the experiences, both successes and difficulties, of others who have applied these ideas. Third, we suggest that successful application may depend on strategically intervening in the wider context of the medical community. And, finally, we describe one family physician's experiences in considering and intervening in the medical community as he applied strategic ideas in his practice and in his position as a teacher of family medicine.

THE FIT BETWEEN STRATEGIC THERAPY AND FAMILY MEDICINE

We propose that there is an especially good fit between the strategic model and the practice of family medicine for several reasons. Strategic therapy and family medicine share the same conceptual foundation. Each claims a systemic (i.e., Batesonian) epistemology (Stanton, 1981; Ransom & Vandervoort, 1973). Specifically, both recognize the importance of context, particularly home life, and of relationships, particularly familial, in the creation, maintenance, and solution of problems. Consequently, in each there is a movement away from reductionism to holism (Auerswald, 1968; McWhinney, 1981).

261

Haley (1976) notes that the strategic view focuses on "the social situation rather than on the person" (p. 2) and the therapist's "place in the social situation" (p. 7). Thus, a unique therapeutic strategy is required for each case. Similarly, McWhinney (1981) states that the holistic view of family medicine

> . . . recognizes that illness is closely related to the personality and life experiences of the patient, and that man cannot be understood in isolation from his environment. The holistic view acknowledges that every illness is different, and that the physician himself is an important aspect of the healing process. (p. 24)

Strategic therapists and family physicians have looked toward the family life cycle to understand family development and problems. Strategic therapists believe problems evolve in families when they are having difficulty making the transition from one stage to the next (Stanton, 1981). Family physicians have noted that physiological changes in family members often impact families' successful accomplishment of appropriate developmental tasks (Geyman, 1977; Medalie, 1979). For both, their role is to assist families in their movement through the stages of the family life-cycle.

Many of the problems treated by strategic therapists and family physicians are the same. Recent studies of the content of family practice indicate that from 30 to 50 percent of patients present psychosocial complaints (Rakel, 1977; Stumbo, Del Vecchio-Good & Good, 1982). The most common of these are depression (Cassata & Kirkman-Liff, 1981; Kirabey, Coulton & Graham, 1982; Stumbo et al., 1982), anxiety (Rosenblatt, Cherkin, Schneiweiss, Hart, Greenwold, Kirkwood, & Perkoff, 1982), obesity (Cassata & Kirkman-Liff, 1981), marital discord (Cassata & Kirkman-Liff, 1981; Poole, Morrison, Marshall & Simmons, 1982), sexual problems (Cassata & Kirkman-Liff, 1981), insomnia (Kirabey et. al., 1982), parent-child problems (Cassata & Kirkman-Liff, 1981; Poole et. al., 1982), hyperactivity (Poole et. al., 1982), and suicide (Cassata & Kirkman-Liff, 1981; Poole et. al., 1982).

No empirical analysis of strategic therapists' practices has been done. However, in an assessment of the treatment applicability of strategic therapy, Stanton (1981) concludes that strategic therapists have "seen a plethora of problems" that range "widely in age, ethnicity, socioeconomic status, and chronicity" (p. 368). Stanton cites the presenting problems that have been approached strategically; all of the previously mentioned problems are included in his list. (For a more detailed account of problems that have been approached strategically see Stanton's (1981) chapter in the *Handbook of Family Therapy*.) Some people seem to experience symptoms, e.g., headaches, frame them as emotional, and seek out a therapist. Others experiencing the same symptoms, frame them as physical, and call their family doctor.

A major tenet of strategic therapy is an emphasis on the patient's current complaint in the present. The strategic approach differs from other family therapy approaches because it does not require an extended history nor family data from all members. As Weakland and Fisch (1984) state, " . . . other family approaches are very time-consuming for a busy practitioner and much of the information gathered may be of little relevance to the particular medical complaint at hand" (p. 128). In contrast, because the strategic approach is "more narrowly focused on how the family is involved in the current problem and its treatment, in the here and now" (p. 128), it is more applicable to family practice.

Current family physicians' methods are consistent with the strategic approach. Family physicians, similar to strategic therapists, routinely define their patients' symptoms behaviorally. They commonly ask the who, what, when, where, and how of the presenting complaint (Haley, 1976; McWhinney, 1981). Each negotiates contracts with patients. Each is accustomed to taking responsibility for patients' treatments and telling them what to do to alleviate their complaints. Family physicians write prescriptions and give instructions. Likewise, strategic therapists give directives and assign tasks.

Because family physicians' current methods are consistent with the strategic approach, they can use their current skills with personal ease and without challenging their patients' view of what should occur in their doctors' office. The problem experienced by strategic therapists working in hospital settings of their presence being seen "as an indication by the families that the problem was extra-medical" (Freidrich & Copeland, 1983, p. 297) is thus avoided. Family physicians working strategically accept their patients' complaints as legitimate. Thus, they can fulfill their patients' expectations and avoid engendering "resistance."

The strategic approach, unlike most other family therapy approaches, can be applied even when only one family member is accessible. The approach developed at the Mental Research Institute (Watzlawick, Weakland & Fisch, 1974), in particular, has focused on working with the "customer" — whether a concerned family member or the person exhibiting the symptom. Studies show that family physicians see all members of the family only some of the time (Detchon, 1985; Fujikawa, Bass & Schneiderman, 1979) and have difficulty convening families even when they are committed to doing so (Bishop et. al., 1984). Thus, strategic therapy can be valuable to physicians who most frequently see only parts of families.

In conclusion, we contend that the strategic model shares a similar conceptual foundation as family medicine and treats many of the same complaints. The strategic model is consistent with family physicians' present methods and meets patients' expectations. This results in a good fit between strategic therapy and family medical practice.

EXPERIENCES OF OTHERS USING STRATEGIC IDEAS IN MEDICINE

The strategic approach has been applied to typical family medical problems by innovative family physicians, several physicians in collaboration with family therapists, and numerous family therapists working alone. The experiences of these individuals are briefly discussed below.

Applying strategic ideas during their day-to-day practice offers family physicians a response that lies between family therapy and providing care to individuals that ignores the impact of their relationships (Massad, 1984). Weakland and Fisch (1984) outline how the strategic model of the Mental Research Institute can be used by family physicians in their daily practices for problems that baffle physicians. These problems "that don't make sense" (p. 125) include: 1) symptoms that persist after standard medical treatment is applied successfully, 2) complaints of significant others that continue after treatment indicates the symptom should disappear, and 3) puzzling complaints in which information presented by patients and family members is vague and contradictory, or conflicts with physicians' observations and medical knowledge. They present a variety of case examples in which a family physician applies the strategic model during routine medical visits. Similarly, Massad (1984) reports using the strategic model during a forty-minute office visit to treat a teenager complaining of headaches. The initial experiences of family physicians adapting the strategic model for use in their day-to-day practice seems promising.

Some physicians have collaborated with strategic family therapists. One physician teamed up with two family therapists to treat a family that presented a child's migraine headache (Keeney & Ross with Silverstein, 1983). In the Family Heart Project (Hoebel, 1976) physicians identified nine heart patients who failed to follow their advice to alter lifestyle after a heart attack. A family therapist, using the Mental Institute Research model of strategic therapy, met with the patients' wives for a maximum of five sessions with the goal of altering the wives' attempts to modify their husbands' behaviors. The physicians continued their routine care of the husbands. Seven out of the nine wives changed their behavior, followed by some change in their husbands' lifestyle. A collaborating pediatrician and family therapist (Frey & Wendorf, 1984) found strategic and structural family therapy interventions to be effective in common behavioral problems of children (i.e., aches and pains, teen-age depression, school problems, and hyperactivity). Although collaboration is not yet widespread, family physicians and strategic family therapists who team up are reporting positive experiences.

Strategic family therapy has been used by family therapists in a variety of inpatient medical settings. Bartholomew (1984) reports using strategic therapy to successfully treat a teenager hospitalized for anorexia nervosa. Freidrich & Copeland (1983) present a case in which strategic therapy was used with a child refusing treatment on a pediatric cancer unit to gain the child's co-operation. Aldridge and Rossiter (1983) report their experiences of applying this model to patients exhibiting suicidal behaviors in general, psychiatric, and day hospitals. And finally, Jesse and L'Abate (1980) describe their use of paradox for stealing, hyperactive behavior, and destructive play of hospitalized children. As can be seen, strategic therapy appears to have proved useful to those working in inpatient settings.

There are numerous accounts by family therapists who are employed in medical settings, mental health centers, and family service agencies of their experiences in working strategically with symptoms typically encountered by family physicians. Several articles describe the work of The Chronic Illness Project at the Ackerman Institute in New York. In this project a group of family therapists practice the Milan systemic team approach (Selvini-Palazzoli, Boscolo, Cecchin & Prata, 1978) to treat families that have one or more chronically ill member. They have treated over 30 families with symptoms ranging from psychosomatic to organic and genetic illness (i.e., hemophilia, brain tumor, leukemia, etc.). Penn (1983) discusses how a chronic illness affects the organization of the family and how to therapeutically intervene in such systems. Walker (1984) describes the caretaker-parent/ill-child coalition that often forms in these families and the use of positive connotation and relabeling as effective interventions in these cases. Sheinberg (1983) writes how the team has observed how marked improvement in health frequently corresponds with improvement in related family problems.

Other strategic therapists cite successful therapeutic outcomes with symptoms often presented to family physicians, including low sexual desire (Penn, 1982; Storm, 1982), obesity (Harkaway, 1983; Moley, 1983), depression following a stroke (Watzlawick & Coyne, 1980), depression (Coyne, 1984), dizziness (Rohrbaugh, Tennen, Press White, Raskin & Pickering, 1977), paranoia (Frazer, 1983), stomach aches and vomiting (Erickson, in Haley, 1973), sleep disturbances (Madanes, 1980), and anxiety (Watzlawick et al., 1974). Thus, family therapists who work with symptoms seen daily by family physicians seem to obtain beneficial results.

As can be seen by this review, strategic family therapy has infiltrated medical practice. However, the effectiveness of strategic therapy in medical settings and with typical medical symptoms has yet to be demonstrated. Until then, the positive experiences and enthusiastic writings of these individuals who have applied the strategic model in this context are encouraging.

DIFFICULTIES IN APPLYING STRATEGIC IDEAS

The interface of strategic family therapy and family medicine is not without problems. Weakland and Fisch (1984) conclude that although the strategic model seems "simple in principle, its application to (medical) practice is a different and more complex matter . . . " (p. 136, parenthesis added). We summarize below the difficulties encountered by us and others who have applied this approach in family medicine.

The most pervasive difficulty seems to be gaining acceptance within the medical community for a psychosocial view of problems. A "nonmedical" approach such as strategic therapy is not seen as viable. Freidrich and Copeland (1983), applying the strategic model on a pediatric cancer unit, noted a problem with "the attitude of attending physicians to consider behavioral and family variables only after all other 'medical' options have been exhausted" (p. 297). A questionnaire study of family practice patients indicated that while 64 percent of patients perceived problems in their family lives, only 26.5 percent had psychosocial notes and 3.5 percent had a psychosocial diagnosis recorded in their charts by their physician (Goldstein, Snope & McGreehan, 1980). Another study found that physicians respond negatively to common psychosocial complaints (Klein, Najaman, Kohrman & Munro, 1982). Merkel (1983) further states:

> . . . the physician who finds a rate, verifiable disease that his colleagues have overlooked or dismissed as "probably emotional" is a diagnostic hero, acclaimed by peers and teachers. A psychosocial diagnosis (including familial considerations) is usually made after clinical hunches are played out and high tech medicine has failed. (p. 861)

Thus, the strategic approach with its psychosocial view of symptoms is at odds with the general practice of the medical community.

Consequently, to apply strategic ideas in this context individuals must first strategically intervene to gain acceptance and credibility for their view. Freidrich and Copeland (1983) set the stage for acceptance of their strategic approach by first providing the more traditional psychological evaluations and developing relationships with physicians by working jointly on research projects. In essence, they modeled Erickson (in Haley, 1973) and first accepted the medical community's position before introducing an alternative view.

A second major problem is convincing medical personnel to change their behavior. Because the strategic approach views patients' significant others, including helpers, as contributing to and maintaining symptoms (Selvini-Palazzoli et al., 1980; Watzlawick, Weakland & Fisch, 1974), the well-meaning efforts of the medical community may need to be altered. Several authors have observed that medical personnel's responses to patients had become part of patients' problemmatic patterns (Bartholomew, 1984; Hoebel, 1976; Simon, 1983). Hoebel (1976), in fact, recommends using strategic ideas to intervene in the doctor/patient relationship when physicians have made numerous unsuccessful attempts to treat patients and now may need to change their behaviors.

Particular difficulty may arise when medical personnel are asked to change their behavior in ways typically unfamiliar to them. Many strategic therapy interventions such as restraining patients from changing, positive connotation, and prescribing the symptom are foreign in the medical setting. As Candib and Glenn (1983) point out, physicians "are used to telling patients what they want them to do, not what they do not want them to do" (p. 777).

Finally, physicians applying strategic ideas may find it hard to assume the one-down position, a common stance in strategic therapy (Fisch, Weakland & Segal, 1983). A study of the content of physician/patient communication showed that physicians contributed over one half of all communication with patients, reflecting their authoritarian role (Bain, 1979). Physicians are accustomed to being the "captain of the ship" with others, including patients and nurses, carrying out their orders. Abdicating their position to patients and becoming "first mates" may seem initially uncomfortable.

Although family physicians may have an easier time than family therapists to gain medical community acceptance for the strategic view of problems and treatment, even they experience difficulties. We have found that family physicians using the strategic approach have to maintain credibility as a "real doctor practicing real medicine" or find themselves being discounted by other medical personnel. In the next section, we describe how the second author, a family physician, intervened in the medical community to gain acceptance and credibility for his strategic approach to patient care.

STRATEGIC INTERVENTION IN THE MEDICAL COMMUNITY

In a review of the status and future of medicine, the Royal College of General Practice (1973) notes "the days of the do-it-all-himself doctor are over" and current patient care requires "a team or group of doctors and their nursing and other colleagues working together, each adding their skills and expertise to the best way of helping the patient" (p. 42). Consequently, introducing a new approach to patient care into the medical context, such as the strategic approach, may require intervention at the broader level with the other doctors, nurses, and other health care providers. We describe examples in which a family physician intervenes during day-to-day practice when a specialist is asked to consult and during his attending responsibilities at a teaching hospital.

Case Example 1

The physician, John, hospitalized one of his patients, Charlie, for suspected intestinal obstruction. A surgeon was called in to consult and he recommended surgery. Charlie was hesitant to consent to the surgery. His wife was undecided. She wanted Charlie to do what he felt was best and at the same time she wanted to make sure he received the best medical care. However, both their parents were insistent that something be done immediately. The more the family members demanded action, the more passive Charlie became about his desires in the presence of his wife and family and the more vehement he became with John about not wanting surgery. John was concerned that if Charlie felt pressured by his family, the surgeon, and himself to have surgery and reluctantly consented, he would later be angry at his family and the medical community. He intervened in the following ways.

Intervention with the surgeon. After establishing that the patient was not in any immediate danger and time could be allowed to see if the surgery was necessary, John asked the surgeon to join him in supporting Charlie's hesitancy and recommend to the family that the decision be made in the morning. The surgeon agreed.

Intervention with the patient. John first agreed with Charlie that making a decision then may be too hasty and that he was wise to wait until morning. He then instructed Charlie to find a way to reassure his wife that he *wanted* to wait until morning to decide. John explained to Charlie that if he was convincing to his wife then she could be convincing to their family.

Rationale. First, John was hoping that when he matched Charlie's hesitancy Charlie would view the medical community as on his side and be more willing to hear their advice should surgery become absolutely necessary. Second, by asking Charlie to convince his wife of his desires, Charlie would become more active and his wife, who wavered in her support when he was quiet, could get the family to back off. If Charlie felt less pressure from his family and doctors, the pattern would be changed and he would be in a better position to consider his alternatives.

Results. Charlie became more verbal with his wife and his wife with their family. Everyone agreed to wait until morning.

When John arrived the next morning to check on his patient, Charlie, the family, the nurses, and the surgeon were embroiled in conflict. Charlie continued to not want surgery. The family, anxiously awaiting some action, had demanded the nurses call the surgeon and tell him they wanted to see him immediately. The surgeon, who was performing emergency surgery on another patient, told the operating room nurses to tell the nurses on Charlie's floor that he would talk to them later. The family, viewing the surgeon as unresponsive and uncaring, became angry and more demanding. The nurses were upset that they had to deal with the angry family members, the irritated nurses in the operating room, and the surgeon who wasn't responding to their messages. The surgeon, in turn, was upset that he had followed John's advice the night before and not done surgery, and was angry at the family's demands and interruptions. He told John to call in another surgeon.

After obtaining information about the conflict, John decided to intervene with the surgeon, the nurses, and the family.

Intervention with the surgeon. John called the surgeon, reemphasizing his concern that if they had gone ahead and pushed for the surgery Charlie would have been dissatisfied with his medical care. In fact, he may have been critical of them in the community or even sued. He assured the surgeon that Charlie trusted him and wanted his care (which was true for Charlie, but not his family). John pointed out that Charlie was just having trouble with his overinvolved family. Further, he argued that calling in a new surgeon would be unwise, as well as costly to Charlie, something he knew the surgeon would not want. Consequently, he was asking the surgeon to stay involved.

Intervention with the nurses. John empathized with the nurses and told them he didn't think it was their job to deal with the problem. He asked that they not deliver any messages between the surgeon and the family, but instead call him.

Intervention with the family and patient. John apologized for not meeting with the family earlier and suggested that there was a communication gap that could have been avoided had he made his hospital rounds earlier. He told the family that he had talked to the surgeon who would do whatever was necessary to insure that Charlie had the best medical care, including referring him to another physician. However, he believed that calling in another surgeon would not be in Charlie's best interest since this surgeon was familiar with the case and had already seen Charlie. Also, Charlie's medical condition had remained stable and surgery might be avoided. But, he would do whatever *Charlie* wanted.

Rationale. John decided to break the dysfunctional pattern in several ways. With the family he 1) took a one-down position by sincerely apologizing for not coming earlier and by taking the blame for the conflict, and 2) reframed the surgeon's instructions for the family to get another surgeon as a concern that Charlie get the best medical care possible. With the nurses, he asked them to reverse their behavior and not relay messages from the family to the surgeon and vice versa. And finally, with the surgeon he reframed his asking the surgeon to support Charlie's decision to wait as his concern for the surgeon's good reputation and doctor/patient relationship. He reframed the situation as a nice patient who just had a difficult family.

Results. The family decided to listen to Charlie's desires, the nurses removed themselves from the situation, and the surgeon agreed to stay on the case. After reexamining Charlie shortly thereafter, the surgeon stated that Charlie would not need surgery and that waiting had been a wise decision. In the end, what Charlie wanted was best for him!

Case Example 2

Barbara, an 18-year-old Black woman was admitted to the hospital by a family practice resident because of unexplained "seizures." She described her seizures as "bad spells" in which she "didn't feel real" and like she was "on the outside looking in." During the previous six months, the resident had been conducting a variety of tests and had not yet uncovered an explanation. Barbara had suffered a particularly bad spell during one of her college classes, thus precipitating the hospitalization.

John, as the attending physician, was to review the resident's treatment of the case, act as a consultant to him, and supervise the young woman's hospitalization. First, he met with the woman briefly and found out she was the youngest child and still living at home with her divorced mother. By asking contextual questions, he discovered most of the spells occurred when she was away from home and that she immediately returned home when she experienced one. He empathized with her about how disruptive these spells had been in her life. Just as John was leaving, Barbara whispered in a conspirator's voice, "Excuse me, but do you think these could be psychological? I've been reading my psychology text and I think I may be manic-depressive, experiencing anxiety attacks, or schizophrenic."

In reviewing the case, John concluded the resident had been very thorough in his medical work-up. However, he seemed to be operating from the common beliefs identified by Williamson, Beitman, and Katon (1981) that prevent a consideration of psychosocial factors: "I must rule out organic disease before I can focus on psychosocial problems"; "if I do not my patient may die or my colleagues may laugh at me"; "my patients want me to rule out organic problems." Overall, the resident was ignoring her family and wider social context.

John identified the following resident/patient dysfunctional pattern. Barbara has a "bad spell" and seeks medical care. The resident assures her there is an organic explanation and orders tests. The tests come back negative but the symptoms persist. The resident orders additional tests with the same results. He becomes frustrated and begins to question her sincerity. Barbara has another spell, worse than the previous one. The resident, convinced she's really sick, becomes more determined to find an organic cause and orders even more sophisticated tests and consultations with medical subspecialists (which are also negative). The cycle repeats. John decided to intervene in this resident/patient pattern.

Intervention with the resident. He complimented the resident for thoroughness and tenacity in sticking by his patient. The resident had obviously done an exhaustive workup when many doctors might have dismissed the woman's complaints as not serious. John then suggested considering other psychosocial factors. By doing so they would be considering all possibilities and be even more thorough. The resident responded by saying "perhaps it is all in her head," to which John replied that Barbara had asked the same question. He and the resident decided to meet with the family.

Rationale. Based on prior experiences with the resident, John felt if he questioned the resident's handling of the patient, the resident would become defensive and more invested in finding an organic cause. The resident had done what he was trained to do well. Instead, he asked the resident to change his behavior by defining it as "an extension, really quite a minor one, of the way he already is" (Erickson in Haley, 1973, p. 125).

Results. John and the resident made an agreement to talk with the woman and her mother to get more information about the spells. Before they could meet, the resident announced that the results of more tests and consultations had arrived and that the young woman had "idiopathic hypotension" or low blood pressure of unknown cause. (Although the resident did not acknowledge it, one possible cause is bedrest and Barbara had been confined in the hospital for five days.) The resident responded again by ordering additional tests, prescribing medication for a trial period, and discharging Barbara from the hospital because they finally knew what was wrong with her.

During the discharge meeting with the family and the resident, John told the family, "I'm glad you and the resident found your answer. It must be comforting to know what is wrong with Barbara." Barbara and her mother agreed. However, Barbara wanted to know when John could meet with them to talk about her anxiety about college.

Soon thereafter, the tests the resident ordered returned normal. There were no further abnormal blood pressure readings even though Barbara had quit her medicine. Yet, she was still complaining of bad spells. The resident decided he wanted to be thorough and asked John to try his "soft" medical approach. John met with the family for six sessions, applying the strategic approach with the resident's full support. The bad spells disappeared and the resident, pleased with the results, concluded that there was no organic cause after all.

As can be seen from these examples, John effectively used common strategic techniques to intervene in the wider context of the patient/medical community system.

CONCLUSION

In conclusion, we offer a prescription for those who wish to comfortably and competently use the strategic model in family medicine. Most importantly, individuals, whether family physicians or family therapists, must be willing to intervene strategically in the patient/medical system to allow them the maneuverability (Fisch, et. al., 1982) needed to work strategically. Held (1982) describes effective strategies (e.g. avoiding triangulation, proceeding slowly, etc.) for systemic therapists to use in gaining acceptance of their approach when entering traditional mental health systems. As family physicians and family therapists intervene, they may wish to adapt these, use those described in this chapter, or discover their own.

In any case, family physicians must use their ingenuity to mold a model developed in a therapy setting to their medical practice. This requires accepting a psychosocial view, learning interventions that indirectly rather than directly ask people to change, and at times assuming a one-down position with patients and other medical personnel. Then, using this new style, the physician must actively intervene to gain the help and support of other medical personnel applying this new approach to patient care.

Strategic therapists must refrain from acting as missionaries converting the heathens. Rather they must accept and join the medical community, practicing the strategic art of "blending and bending; not defending" (Saposnek, 1980) their point of view. Hence, they must learn to talk a new language, perhaps momentarily accept the same values, and defer to the organizational hierarchy. Only by doing so can they gain the maneuverability and credibility to introduce a different approach to patient care.

REFERENCES

Aldridge, D., & Rossiter, J. (1983). A strategic approach to suicidal behavior. *Journal of Strategic and System Therapies, 2,* 49–62.
Auerswald, E. (1968). Interdisciplinary versus ecological approach. *Family Process*, 202–215.
Bain, D. (1979). The content of physician/patient communication in family practice. *Journal of Family Practice, 8,* 745–753.
Bartholomew, K. (1984). I would eat for her if I could. *Journal of Strategic and System Therapies, 3,* 57–65.

Bishop, D., Epstein, N., Golbert, R., van der Sprey, H., Levins, S., & McClemont, S. (1984). Training physicians to treat families: Unexpected compliance problems. *Family Systems Medicine, 2,* 380-386.

Bullock, D., & Thompson, B. (1979). Guidelines for family interviewing and brief therapy by the family physician. *Journal of Family Practice, 9,* 837-841.

Candib, L., & Glenn, M. (1983). Family medicine and family therapy: Comparative development methods, and roles. *Journal of Family Practice, 16,* 773-779.

Cassata, D., & Kirkman-Liff, B. (1981). Mental health activities of family physicians. *Journal of Family Practice, 12,* 683-692.

Coyne, J. (1984). Strategic therapy with depressed married persons: Initial agenda, themes, and interventions. *Journal of Marital and Family Therapy, 10,* 53-62.

Detchon, T. (1985). *Family physicians' acceptance of family systems theory and exposure to and acceptance of family therapy.* Unpublished master's thesis, Auburn University.

Fisch, R., Weakland, J., & Segal, L. (1982). *The tactics of change.* San Francisco: Jossey-Bass.

Fosson, A., Elam, C., & Broaddus, D. (1982). Family therapy in family practice: A solution to psychosocial problems. *Journal of Family Practice, 15,* 461-465.

Frazer, S. (1983). Paranoia: Interactional views on evolution and intervention. *Journal of Marital and Family Therapy, 9,* 383-392.

Freidrich, W., & Copeland, D. (1983). Brief-family focused intervention on the pediatric cancer unit. *Journal of Marital and Family Therapy, 9,* 293-298.

Frey, J., & Wendorf, R. (1984). Family therapist and pediatrician: Teaming-up on four common behavioral pediatric problems. *Family Systems Medicine, 2,* 290-297.

Fujikawa, L., Bass, R., & Schneiderman, L. (1979). Family care in a family practice group. *Journal of Family Practice, 8,* 1189-1194.

Geyman, J. (1977). The family as the object of care in family practice. *Journal of Family Practice, 5,* 571-575.

Goldstein, H., Snope, F., & McGreehan, D. (1980). Family emotional health: A survey of family practice patients. *The Journal of Family Practice, 10,* 85-90.

Haley, J. (1973). *Uncommon Therapy.* New York: W. W. Norton.

Haley, J. (1976). *Problem-solving Therapy.* San Francisco: Jossey-Bass.

Harkaway, J. (1983). Obesity: Reducing the larger system. *Journal of Strategic and Systemic Therapies, 2,* 2-14.

Held, B. (1982). Entering a mental health system: A strategic-systemic approach. *Journal of Strategic and Systemic Therapies, 1,* 40-50.

Hoebel, F. (1976). Brief family interactional therapy in the management of cardiac-related high risk behaviors. *The Journal of Family Practice, 3,* 613-618.

Jesse, E., & L'Abate, L. (1980). The use of paradox with children in an inpatient setting. *Family Process, 19,* 59-64.

Kenney, B., & Ross, J., with Silverstein, O. (1983). Mind in bodies: The treatment of a family that presented a migraine headache. *Family Systems Medicine, 1,* 61-77.

Kirabey, D., Coulton, C., & Graham, A. (1982). How family practice patients view their utilization of mental health services. *Journal of Family Practice, 15,* 317-323.

Klein, D., Najaman, J., Kohrman, A., & Munro, C. (1982). Patient characteristics that elicit negative responses from family physicians. *Journal of Family Practice, 14,* 881-888.

Madanes, C. (1980). Protection, paradox, and pretending. *Family Process, 19,* 73-85.

Massad, R. (1984). Brief treatment of a headache: A case report. *Family Systems Medicine, 2,* 53-54.

McWhinney, I. (1981). *An introduction to family medicine.* New York: Oxford University Press.

Medalie, J. (1979). The family life cycle and its implications for family practice. *The Journal of Family Practice, 9,* 47-56.

Merkel, W. (1983). The family and family medicine: Should this marriage be saved? *The Journal of Family Practice, 17,* 857-862.

Moley, V. (1983). Interactional treatment of eating disorders. *Journal of Strategic and Systemic Therapies, 2,* 10-28.

Penn, P. (1982). Multigenerational issues in strategic therapy of sexual problems. *Journal of Strategic and Systemic Therapies, 1,* 1-13.

Penn, P. (1983). Coalitions and binding interactions in families with chronic illness. *Family Systems Medicine, 1*, 16–25.

Poole, S., Morrison, J., Marshall, J., & Simmons, R. (1982). Pediatric health care in family practice. *Journal of Family Practice, 15*, 945–952.

Rakel, R. (1977). *Principles of Family Medicine.* Philadelphia: W. B. Saunders & Co.

Ransom, D., & Vandervoort, H. (1973). The development of family medicine: Problematic trends. *Journal of the American Medical Association, 225*, 1098–1102.

Rohrbaugh, M., Tennen, H., Press, S., White, L., Raskin, P., & Pickering, M. (1977). Paradoxical strategies in psychotherapy. Symposium presented at the American Psychological Association, San Francisco.

Rosenblatt, R., Cherkin, D., Schneiweiss, R., Hart, L., Greenwold, H., Kirkwood, R., & Perkoff, G. (1982). The structure and content of family practice: Current status and future trends. *The Journal of Family Practice, 15*, 681–722.

Royal College of General Practice (1973). Present state and future needs of general practice. *General Practice, 3*, 16.

Saposnek, D. (1980). Aikido: A model for brief strategic therapy. *Family Process, 19*, 227–338.

Selvini-Palazzoli, M., Boscolo, L., Cecchin, G., & Prata, G. (1978). *Paradox and Counterparadox: A New Model in the Therapy of the Family in Schizophrenic Transaction.* New York: Jason Aronson.

Selvini-Palazzoli, M., Boscolo, L., Cecchin, G., & Prata, G. (1980). The problem of the referring person. *Journal of Marital and Family Therapy, 6*, 3–9.

Sheinberg, M. (1983). The family and chronic illness: A treatment diary. *Family Systems Medicine, 1*, 37–47.

Simon, R. (1983). Issues in the referral for family therapy. *Family Systems Medicine, 1*, 56–61.

Stanton, M. D. (1981). Strategic approaches to family therapy. In A. Gurman & D. Kniskern (Eds.), *Handbook of Family Therapy.* New York: Brunner/Mazel.

Storm, C. (1982). Sexual problems: An opportunity to work strategically. *Journal of Strategic and Systemic Therapies, 1*, 14–23.

Stumbo, D., Del Vecchio-Good, M., & Good, B. (1982). Diagnostic profile of a family practice clinic: Patients with psychosocial diagnoses. *Journal of Family Practice, 14*, 281–285.

Walker, G. (1984). The pact: The caretaker-patient/ill-child coalition in families with chronic illness. *Family Systems Medicine, 1*, 6–29.

Watzlawick, P., & Coyne, J. (1980). Depression following stroke: Brief, problem focused treatment. *Family Process, 19*, 13–18.

Watzlawick, P., Weakland, J., & Fisch, R. (1974). *Change: Principles of Problem Formation and Problem Resolution.* New York: W. W. Norton.

Weakland, J., & Fisch, R. (1984). Cases that "don't make sense": A brief strategic treatment in medical practice. *Family Systems Medicine, 2*, 125–136.

Williamson, P., Beitman, B., & Katon, W. (1981). Beliefs that foster physician avoidance of psychosocial aspects of health care. *Journal of Family Practice, 13*, 999–1003.

Chapter 12

Strategic Parenting

Donald E. Efron,
Bill Rowe, and
Brenda Atkison

INTRODUCTION

Parents struggle with many frustrating situations in rearing their children. Usually these problems are not serious enough to warrant engaging in professional therapy, yet they are bothersome enough that parents consult parenting literature, public health nurses, teachers, family life educators, etc. Traditionally, the advice given them directly or through the literature has been loosely based on psychotherapy or educational models. It is usually difficult to directly discern the links between the many "how-to" parenting books and the theories currently being used in psychotherapy.

What is proposed here is a conceptual model which can be offered to parents and parent educators. It is based on strategic and systemic models but attempts to go beyond a narrow re-working of the strategic-systemic literature. Instead, the writers 1) present a three-dimensional model of the ways in which individuals within systems "connect" with each other; 2) combine this three-dimensional model with basic developmental concepts to produce a systemic-developmental model of a child's changing position in a family; 3) describe strategic-systemic methods available to parents that will allow positive interactions and growth that are consistent with this systemic-developmental model.

The authors wish to thank the following people for their ideas and examples: Jeff Bogdan, Hendon Chubb, Joanne Johnston, Midge Lane, H. Merl, and Ericka Mirc.

Background: Review of Existing Parenting Literature

Popularization of theories of psychology into advice for parents is drawn
directly from developmental psychology and promotes the authors' philosophical stance on the ways we need to shape the next generation. Dr. Spock, from
1947 to the 1970s, was the main advisor to parents. More recent works such
as *Parent Effectiveness Training* (Gordon, 1970) and *Systematic Training for
Effective Parenting* (Dinkmeyer & McKay, 1976) are noted for their emphasis
on parent-child communication on both affective and instrumental levels.
Dobson's *Dare to Discipline* (1975) suggests a return to autocratic parental
leadership in a hierarchical vision of family. Dreikurs' *Children: The Challenge* (1964) prescribes scenarios which illustrate ways for parents to avoid
power struggles. He promotes the use of logical consequences, consistency,
and encouragement.

These works all have value, but they do not fit with systemic models of
explaining behavior change. They remain cause-effect, "linear," and deterministic in their orientation.

GOALS AND ASSUMPTIONS ABOUT A STRATEGIC-SYSTEMIC PARENTING MODEL

A strategic-systemic parenting model must offer to parents a way for them
to "handle" their children's problems in a new manner — one which escapes
the traditional cause and effect focus of the standard parenting manuals. They
must be "educated" to understand their children's actions as being more than
simply the result of their intrapsychic workings. The use of strategic techniques by parents must be presented as a way for them to live more happily
with their children and engage in less unnecessary conflict, while allowing
them to become productive members of society. In other words, the "payoff"
for using these ideas and styles must be that both child and parent benefit
when strategic-systemic ideas are incorporated into parenting styles.

It should not be too difficult to "sell" parents on the idea that the techniques of strategic-systemic therapies can be used in a positive parenting
model. Recently, readers of the *Journal of Strategic and Systemic Therapies*
were asked to send in examples of the use of strategic-systemic therapy ideas
in non-therapy situations, preferably with their own children. These examples
show that therapy ideas can be shifted into parenting.

Example One

A father of a 16-year-old son is asked by the boy to transport him daily
to an early morning religious class. They agree to get up at 4:45 A.M. so that
the father has time to drop the boy off and then make profitable use of the

morning. A second, somewhat older boy, also is transported. For almost a year, Mr. M. finds himself trying to force the boys to wake up, yelling at them, and trying to convince them he is doing them a favor. Matters only get worse. Eventually, Mr. M. realizes that "it was me who was keeping the problem going." He announces to them that he is giving up trying to force them to get up, has decided it is their responsibility, and is willing to leave without them. Following through on this, he is about to leave the house the next day when he hears his boy rushing to him saying that he wants to go with him to class. He congratulates the boy and they leave behind the still sleeping older boy. The father follows up by buying his son a louder alarm clock, which he does over the protests of the son that he has gotten used to his Dad waking him up. After this, Mr. M's son not only has no difficulties in waking up but also manages to awaken his friend too.

Example Two

A nursery school teacher says that her nursery children (usually around age 3) often balk at leaving the school when parents arrive. Sometimes they would run up the slide and hold to the railing. She notes that parents usually attempt to "overcome" the defiance directly by yelling and physical force or by "sweet talking" and offering promises of future favors. She has had far more success by giving the child alternatives such as "Would you like to run down the slide or slide down?" Giving a choice in this apparent no-choice situation invariably prompted the child to make his choice and then leave quite willingly.

She goes on to say that, "This principle of 'extending freedom while preserving (appropriate) hierarchy' can be applied to homework, chores, and bedtime. Parents are often ambivalent about how much control they wish to have or think they should have over their children. As a result, they can vacillate wildly between 'laying down the law' and 'letting the child decide.' I have seen many parents respond well to this 'middle ground' where the child exercises a measure of freedom within a hierarchical structure where the parents identify the requisite outcome."

Example Three

Hendon Chubb of San Francisco says that he used the following technique with parents to get children to clean up their rooms. He developed it after thinking about his own mother's unsuccessful attempts to get him and his five siblings to clean up their rooms when they were children. She tried to "make" him clean up the room — *now*! Eventually, she had to give up in the face of continued resistance. Hendon believes that to get out of this cycle, parents need to give up on the "now." Instead . . .

1) Schedule a Saturday morning, just after breakfast.
2) Tell the child, "You can do whatever you wish when you are finished, but until then stay in your room. Come tell me when it is done."
3) When the child says he or she is done, go in and say, "Great progress, and as soon as it is done you can come out." *Don't* tell the child what to do. Don't remind him of all the fun he can have when he finishes.
4) Always speak positively. Say, "You can go when you are done," not "You can't go until you are done." Say, "You've made great progress," not, "Look at all the things you have to do still."
5) Don't push the child to finish. Leave her alone for enough time and she will push herself.

Example Four

A father is eating breakfast with his 12-year-old son when his toddler son stomps into the room blowing loudly on a whistle. The older boy demands that the parent make the child stop so he can eat his breakfast in peace. The situation is set up so that the father seems to be heading for a confrontation with either the older or younger son. Instead, the father turns to the younger child and says, "I'll bet I can't hear that whistle if you blow it in the bedroom." The child runs off to the bedroom to blow the whistle as loudly as he can, to see if indeed it is loud enough for his dad to hear. He returns every few minutes to see if he has been heard. The older child is able to finish his breakfast in peace while father is able to avoid an argument.

Example Five

A father has taken his two daughters, ages 9 and 7, to the circus. Midway through the circus, the younger girl begins to whine and say she is tired. Attempts to cheer her up, cajole her, or distract her are all tried but the behavior escalates, becoming quite annoying to both the father and other daughter. After realizing that his attempts to help have only worsened the situation, the father hits upon the idea of pretending that he is even more tired than she. He begins to yawn and soon puts his head on her shoulder. Both of the children respond playfully to this by joking with their father, pretending to sleep, etc. Within a few minutes, the younger child has stopped complaining and is once again enjoying the circus.

Example Six

A father reports that a time of great stress and frustration with his four-year-old son often occurred immediately upon his return home after a day's work. The young child often demanded some play time or attention. The parent, having struggled through a day's work, was more in need of relaxation and letting go than immediately taking on the job of recreational director for his child. Given the differing needs of himself and his child, the scene often ended up with a demanding child, a harassed parent, and a no-win situation. In the following example, the strategic father chose to utilize fantasy and role play in order to bring about a situation where both individuals got what they needed.

The father, upon being confronted with this situation, quickly set up a small table and prepared a jug of lemonade. He armed himself with a pocket full of pennies and sat his son behind the table. The bewildered four-year-old sat in awe, wondering what was going to happen next. The father reached into his pocket and pulled out a penny and slapped it on the table. He exclaimed, "Give me a drink, waiter, and let me tell you all about my day." The four-year-old immediately responded by pouring his father a drink in a small container and pocketing the penny. This waiter game continued for the next hour. Both the four-year-old's need for contact with his father and the father's need for rest and a break from the day's work were met.

Example Seven

"I've lived for the last five years with a woman who has two kids from when she was married. The boy is 15 and the girl 12. They bicker a lot and sometimes they get very loud. I used to handle this by unplugging TV sets, sending them to their rooms — the usual stuff. One day I figured out a way to exploit my special, ambiguous relationship to the kids and I've used it to interrupt fighting between them ever since.

"Because I'm not the 'real' father, or any sort of father as far as they are concerned, there are certain rules no matter how close we might feel to one another. The main one is no hugging, kissing, or other open shows of affection (except, maybe a brief hug before they go off to visit their father for six weeks each summer). One day it occurred to me, when the kids were screaming at each other, that all I had to do to break it up was to say, 'If you don't stop this, I'm going to give both of you a big, wet kiss on the face.' As I had thought, they immediately separated and ran screaming and giggling 'No, no, anything but that,' to their respective rooms."

Example Eight

This is not really a parenting example, but it isn't therapy either. A psychometrist reports that recently she saw a child of about six years who refused to respond to her request to say the alphabet from a written sheet in front of him. He constantly said that he would not tell her the letters. She attempted numerous times to elicit his cooperation without success. Each time he ended by repeating that he would not tell her the alphabet. Eventually, the psychometrist said, "OK, I know you won't TELL me the alphabet, so could you please READ it to me." The boy immediately complied. The psychometrist reports that it wasn't until he had completed the task and she thanked him that he seemed to realize that he had somehow cooperated.

If anything, the danger of this approach may be that it might be too easy to present techniques. In other words, a "cookbook" style of presentation could give parents new techniques without any inherent understanding of the thinking underlying the techniques. This is the same problem faced in training any student. To counter the threat of cookbook learning, parents must be given a conceptual understanding which will allow them to place the techniques within a framework. This framework, the strategic-systemic parenting model, will be developed here. Before presenting the model in detail, certain aspects of attempting to apply strategic and systemic concepts to parenting must be considered.

First, it is preferable that the model be basically positive in focus and not contain ideas which are too connected with therapy. Parenting is generally a very satisfying experience and the difficulties which arise in parenting do not usually lead to any permanent damage to either parent or child. This is especially true when the difficulties are met with understanding and restraint. Thus the strategic parenting model is closer to the MRI brief therapy position than to many other systemic models. Because of this, it would not be appropriate to present to parents any material regarding the "function" of a child's behavior in maintaining a system. Such an approach is all too likely to become quite negative; whatever clinical value it may have, it certainly is out of place in a parenting model.

Secondly, whatever the value of the model it would be ill advised to suggest that it "replace" current parenting views. To do so would force the authors to "reinvent the wheel." A lot of very good thinking has gone into previous parenting models. It seems unwise and arrogant to suggest to parents that they drop all these ideas and replace them with nothing except strategic-systemic techniques.

Again, it is important to consider the difference between therapy and parenting. In therapy, it is often necessary to adapt as if it were truth that only the systemic ideas are effective in producing change. But systemic models say little about cuddling — children need cuddling. Systemic models say little about providing basic care — children need basic care. The strategic parenting model has much to add to parenting — but it should remain an addition, not a replacement. Thus, this model proposes to parents that they add strategic-systemic ideas on top of the basic parenting skills they have learned elsewhere. Parents are, therefore, given suggestions about when to use strategic and systemic parenting tools instead of being asked to use them continually and exclusively.

Hopefully, this will result in a relatively simple and flexible model which parents can use without resorting to any major changes in their lifestyle or basic assumptions. However, to use these models at all does require a certain amount of mental dexterity. It may very well be that not many parents will, in fact, feel comfortable with these ideas and techniques. Certainly, parents completely committed to the idea of not manipulating children will have discomfort. As with all use of strategic methods, there is an assumption that what is being done is being done in the best interests of all and is, therefore, worth the price of manipulation. As these models are presented as additions of basic parenting, there is less danger of parents losing sight of the negative aspects of manipulation. Parents, after all, will have to live with their decisions. If they go overboard to try to solve one problem, they might find themselves in trouble later.

A final consideration is that the strategic-systemic parenting model must incorporate certain basic ideas that have been derived from developmental psychology. One pragmatic reason for doing this is it allows the model to address the child as he/she grows and changes within a normal context and hence allows the parent to decide more effectively on when and how to use the tools presented to them. Also, philosophically, the addition of the developmental models is needed because of the blindness of most systemic models to the manner in which current behaviors are often limited by the potential of the systemic members. Developmental approaches seem much better at being able to describe upper and lower limits of expected and possible behaviors for members of a system at a current point in time than do pure systems approaches which often seem to assume that each family member is inherently equal and all actions inherently possible (Haley, 1980).

BASIC SYSTEMIC CONCEPTS

Strategic and systemic therapies are far from a unified, self-consistent body of work. Major questions arise as to whether the various models can, in fact, be integrated into an effective meta-model.* However, it does seem possible to offer parents a fairly simple model of systems which can suit the needs for a parenting model. It is suggested that the following concepts can provide an effective base for using strategic and systemic ideas in parenting:

---

*For a detailed study of this, readers are referred to two guest edited issues of the *Journal of Strategic and Systemic Therapies*. These are Vol. 3 (1984), issue 3, Guest Edited by J. Scott Fraser and Vol. 3 (1984), issue 4, Guest Edited by Janine Roberts.

1) Systemic thinking is distinguished from "linear" thinking by the insistence that the behavior of the members of a human group is somehow more than the sum of the individual components of the system (Watzlawick, Beavin & Jackson, 1967). The parts do not determine the behavior of the total group, nor even the behavior of any one member. The actual behavior displayed is the result of the systemic interconnections between the members.

Thus, a child's behavior in a family must be seen as making sense within his interactional context. It is not determined by his unique set of individual experiences. The same child, with exactly the same background, can and will behave quite differently when placed in different contexts, in the face of differing expectations, etc. Similarly, the behavior of parents is not predetermined by their heritage, for they too might show drastically differing behaviors depending on the context in which they find themselves.

2) A second key concept of human systems is that all behavior is thought of as mutually interactive. Behavior does not "originate" in one member. Rather, behaviors are always continuing between members of the system and always influencing other behaviors so that the vast numbers of interactions really never "start" anywhere. "Punctuation," the determining that a behavior started at time "X" by person "Y," is arbitrary and misleading. It is better to think of actions as always continuing in a sea of connections, never being confined to any one person or any one time (Watzlawick et al., 1967).

3) A third concept of human systems thinking is that this mutually interconnective aspect of human behavior does not occur randomly (Watzlawick et al., 1967). Without this assumption, it would be possible to conceive a system in which, though all actions were interconnected, essentially nothing could ever be predicted. Instead, human systems appear to have regularities so that behaviors recur with somewhat predictable regularity in somewhat predictable sequences. The sequences might be quite complicated, all elements of the sequences might not be readily visible, and there might be enormous variability, but essentially people respond to each other, in their systems, in *patterns*.

4) A fourth concept for human systems is that behaviors are not only interconnected in patterns but are also self-reflexive and subject to positive and negative feedback. By this, we mean that a behavior is not simply emitted, but is also observed and responded to by all members of the system. This act of observing in itself becomes part of the interactive pattern. Because of this, patterns of behavior can be monitored by the members of the system and can be changed. Human systems are hence much more complicated than mechanical systems, which do not have the ability to "know" what they are doing. The self-reflexive aspect allows systems to change even when they are not being imposed upon from the environment.

5) Finally, human systems are seen as "*open*" systems (Watzlawick et al., 1967). They are not "closed" to new information from the outside world.

Rather, they exist in the midst of many other systems, some larger, some smaller, some intimately connected, some quite peripheral. Each of these other systems affects and is affected by any human system. Still, to be defined as a system at all, there is at least some boundary between the human system (say an individual family) and all other systems. The boundary is "open," but still serves to differentiate this particular family from all other people.

Multiple Connections Between System Members:
The Three-Dimensional Model of Interconnections

The assumptions discussed until now suggest that human systems are made up of interconnected units which interact in some fashion with each other so as to produce a result which is not directly dependent upon the individual units themselves. The interactions produced by these interconnections are non-random and often complex. The people making up a family system can interact as a system in more than one fashion. In fact, there are at least three distinctively different means by which system members can interact with other system members and yet still retain all the characteristics of systemic interaction. It is important to realize that each type of interactive systemic pattern has its own characteristics and can be changed systemically in different ways for the other types. Thus, when therapists talk about producing systemic change, they might be talking about change of any or all of these types of interactive patterns.

Confusion between systemic therapists arises when the types of interactive patterns are not separated. Similarly, in a parenting model, confusion would arise if each type of interactive sequence were treated identically. Distinctions between systemic interactive patterns must be added to the model to avoid such confusion.

In the strategic parenting model this is done by presenting *HABIT* patterns, *ROLE* interaction patterns, and *UNDERSTANDING* patterns as three distinctive forms of systemic interactions. Each form of interaction differs in the manner in which individuals within the family "connect" with each other. The first pattern is in the form of *HABITUAL* and semi-automatic behaviors that occur regularly whenever an individual finds himself in repeating situations. For example, a mother might find herself mechanically putting a diaper on her infant each and every time the baby cries in a particular manner. Habitual activity could also take the form of "becoming anxious" whenever certain circumstances arise, for example, frowning whenever a child raises his/her voice to a high pitch. These everyday reactions seem to occur so often that they probably compose the bulk of human activity (Wilk, 1982).

At first glance, they appear to be idiosyncratic but as they occur in the context of human systems they are not actually the "possession" of the individual member of the system. Obviously, they can be altered by the reaction of the system to them or by the proactions of the system before they can occur. Thus, they still conform to actions within a system. They connect with other actions in that they form part (perhaps the greatest part) of the vast amount of interactions between the members of the system. They often form complex circular patterns with other habitual or non-habitual behavior.

A second manner in which people can interconnect is through *ROLES* (Bateson, 1979). A role is a complementary relationship and so, by definition, a role MUST connect with other roles, for there is no such thing as a role in a vacuum. One cannot be a mother without a child, a husband without a wife, etc. Thus, when one member of a system acts out a role, then other system members playing their role must necessarily interconnect. This role behavior certainly is not simply a collection of habits. For example, a mother diapering a baby THIS way has different habits than a mother diapering her baby THAT way yet both fulfill the role of mother equally.

The third manner of interconnecting in a system is through shared *UNDER-STANDINGS*. This term includes such things as religious values, conceptions of the way in which the world operates, beliefs about how children should be raised, and indeed all the myriad ways in which actions are evaluated and judged, both within the system and between the system and outside systems. A member's expression of belief, or his action on the basis of his beliefs and understandings of the situation also connects with others in the system as they necessarily respond to it. As with habits, it cannot be said that the individual "possesses" these understandings completely apart from the system. Clearly, activities by others of the system will have a great effect on how and when these beliefs are expressed, changed, or maintained.

The three types of systemic interactions can be seen as forming distinct and separate categories. For simplicity, it is possible to refer to a behavior sequence as being a habit, role, or understanding "level" sequence. In this fashion, the three types can be separated into three levels, with habits forming the base, roles in the middle, and understandings on top. To do this, though, immediately produces a need to have airtight definitions as means of deciding which level is "really" operative. Though this might be productive in some cases, it is more productive to view the three systemic interactive types as forming three "dimensions," as illustrated in Figure 1.

The Roles-Understandings dimension suggests that family behaviors can be considered from the point of whether they are primarily concerned with understanding, with roles, or with both. For example, when a child sacrifices himself for the good of the family, this behavior can be described as both a Role (the good child) and an Understanding (my family needs to be saved and I can do it). Behavior noted by the Milan group (Selvini-Palazzoli, Boscolo, Cecchin & Prata, 1978) such as living according to generations-old instructions can be more clearly placed further "up" the R-U dimension towards Understandings and less toward Roles per se. On the other hand,

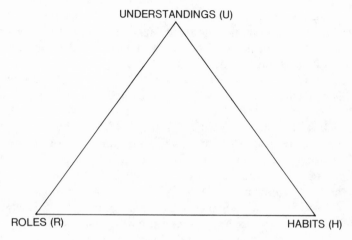

Figure 1.

a child usurping parental authority because he "understands" he can get away with it, even though all family members would not think that right, is toward the Roles end of the R-U dimension.

Similarly, family behaviors could be considered from the point of view of the Roles-Habits dimension. A father who could correct his wife's fruitless efforts to reassure a baby by comforting the baby every few minutes (thus ensuring a growing need for comforting) but who doesn't because the family wants him to be peripheral can be placed on the Role end of this dimension. The wife's behavior, though, can be placed on the Habit end. If, on the other hand, when the father's role was changed and he was given the right to be involved, he then formed the same habit pattern as did the wife — of "comforting" the baby every few minutes — then that behavior would also fall in the Habit end.

The third dimension is the Understanding-Habit dimension. Habitual behavior slowly fades into Understanding behavior and vice-versa. For example, the habitual "anxiety" behavior of a family member can be triggered off by the entire family's definition of situations as dangerous. A habitual pattern of withdrawal and refusal to attend school might very well merge into a family's understanding that no one outside the family can be trusted.

The Systemic Assumptions and the Parent's Role

From the assumptions about systems and the three dimensions of systemic interconnectiveness, we present a picture of the parent of a child as more of an active partner in the family system than is usually presented in parenting models.

The child is an active shaper of his environment, engaged in complex interactive patterns with parents and other family and nonfamily members of the systems in which she moves. The parent's job is to use his/her knowledge of habits, roles and understandings to influence the child so that the child can become what she might be in this world. In this view, the parent must necessarily *guide* the child into accepting certain habits, roles and understandings. To paraphrase the familiar saying, one cannot not influence the child (Watzlawick et al., 1967). Knowing this, the systemically aware parent will often use his relationship to ensure that certain things become part of the child's repertoire and others do not. It is inherent in strategic parenting that the parent must do more than simply let the child choose her own way. There must be an active interactional effort on the part of the parent.

This seems to be challenging one possible tenet of the systemic therapies — that it is not possible to change a system from within. It is certainly true that systemic connections are usually unnoticed. They form the background in which the content is displayed. But there seems to be no inherent reason to suggest that people within a system cannot learn to recognize at least some of the interactional patterns of the background. They can then bring them into the foreground, at least temporarily, and effect changes in the patterns. It isn't easy and, to a certain extent, it isn't "normal" to concentrate in this way on the background, but there is no reason to assume it is impossible.

The Inclusion of Developmental Concepts

A strategic-systemic model of parenting benefits by incorporation of basic developmental concepts. Inclusion of these concepts provides greater flexibility and an ability to address the reality that all "parts" of a family system are not equal in cognitive capacity, moral reasoning ability, and social interactive ability. While it is not possible to use this chapter to present developmental concepts in any detail, it is necessary to present the basic ideas underlying the developmental approaches.

Developmentalists view the human child as constantly growing and developing new capacities both physically and cognitively. This growth proceeds gradually, but the overall result is more than quantitative. Qualitative changes occur which allow the older child to perform, think, and interact differently than a younger child (Wolff, 1973). The child develops from an instinctive creature to a social one soon after infancy, gradually realizing that in fact he/she is a separate individual. The child's thinking is "animistic," egocentric, and preoperational at age two and remains so until it becomes "realistic" around age seven. Gradually, children move from concrete operational thinking to abstract thinking (Wolff, 1973). Many substages can be observed before the final stage where humans are capable of "true formal thought where construction of all possible combinations of relations, systematic isolation of variables, and deductive hypothesis testing" is possible (Kohlberg & Gilligan, 1980).

An important point is that stages do not occur automatically. Kohlberg points out that North American interpretations of Piaget have sometimes failed to realize that the stages are not "wired in" to children. Though they depend on inborn organizing tendencies, they also depend upon social experience for their formation. "Stages are, rather, the products of interactional experience between the child and the world, experience which leads to a restructuring of the child's own organization rather than to the direct imposition of the culture's pattern upon the child" (Kohlberg & Gilligan, 1980).

Kohlberg also suggests that children develop, in addition to cognitive and logical abilities, their ability to conceive of truth and reality—their epistemology. Their view of "reality" changes so that by their teens many children question the "validity of society's truths and its rightness." This particular "revolution" in thinking, unlike the earlier change in thinking which occurs almost universally around age 5–7, occurs over a wide range of time (in fact, often not until into the thirties) and for many people never occurs at all (Kohlberg & Gilligan, 1980). "Moral development" occurs in stages, moving from obeying rules strictly to avoid punishment to conforming to avoid self-condemnation, but because of the wide variance in development it is quite difficult to know where a child, or even an adult, is in his or her moral development level. However, moral development, as with cognitive development, proceeds in stages and is longitudinal. Stages can't be "skipped," but have to be gone through sequentially. Cognitive development is a necessary but not sufficient precondition of moral development (Kohlberg & Gilligan, 1980).

Many developmentalists believe that regression at both emotional and moral levels can occur either under stress or because of a combination of social factors and difficulties in "freeing" from earlier moral stages (Wolff, 1973; Kohlberg & Gilligan, 1980). The regression does not eliminate the learning that has preceded it, but does put it temporarily out of the picture. Usually, after the situation which produced the regression is removed, the child or adult will once again exhibit the thinking and behavior associated with the stage reached before the regression.

From a parental viewpoint, the constantly growing child presents ongoing challenges. The parent can do much to further the child's growth, but lack of knowledge or lack of patience may mean that a parent cannot respond properly to the child. He or she either demands too much or too little. Ideally, parents should have a working knowledge of psychosocial development, a good capacity for nurturing and caregiving at all stages of the child's development, and flexibility to respond differently to the child as the child makes both quantitative and qualitative changes.

It would be unwise to assume that parents come to Strategic Parenting with a well-developed knowledge of developmental ideas. Thus, in this approach some time is spent in introducing developmental ideas. Materials included are basic development concepts, realistic development expectations at various stages, major developmental milestones, developmental-systemic organization, and major child/parent themes. A chart is provided at the end of this chapter (see Appendix), which includes this material and also includes the Strategic Parenting techniques associated with habits, roles, and understandings at each stage of the child's development.

Combining Systemic and Developmental Concepts

The developmental concepts can be joined with the strategic-systemic assumptions to produce a model of the child's interactive world which speaks to both areas simultaneously. The key to this joining is the realization that the different forms of systemic interaction—Habits, Roles, and Understanding—can be placed within a developmental framework. The increasing capabilities of the child allow a change of interaction from Habits to Roles and, finally, to Understandings. Thus, the increasing complexity of the child as an individual is matched by increasingly complex systemic interaction patterns. Instead of contradicting a systemic view of the child in the family, the developmental concept of individual growth complements that idea and shows how complex systems can incorporate individual members that are themselves changing in their relationship to other system members.

Combining developmental and systemic ideas in this fashion facilitates using the rich material of the developmental approach without losing the emphasis of change associated with strategic and systemic concepts. This is particularly useful in a parenting model where parents must continually deal with the reality of the ever-changing quality of family life. Each child in the family constantly grows, both quantitatively and qualitatively. This development forces systemic responses by other family members. Strategic and systemic tools can help the parent deal with these changes.

Figure 2 is presented to parents to help them understand the manner in which the child becomes increasingly complex over time and hence changes his interactional patterns with the rest of the family.

Model of the Child's World—Three Areas of Growth

Figure 2 is meant to represent the growth of a child from being a creature entirely of instinct (with a few early habits) to an adult who behaves primarily according to a code of behavior which has particular meaning and value to him or her. The child, at the start, is not developmentally able to act accord-

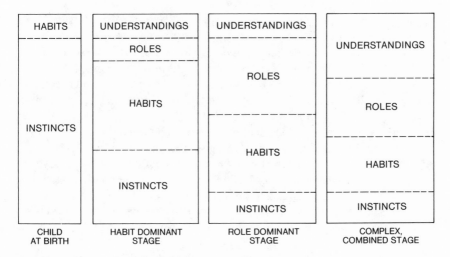

Figure 2.

ing to any set roles or values. At first, he must act according to instinct until able to learn habits. He is primarily a creature of habit until he can learn socially appropriate roles for himself. Finally, he learns to guide his life by understandings going beyond simply following a role or carrying out habit patterns.

As the child matures, he is biologically able to think in a more complicated manner which will eventually allow him to develop a set of values to guide his life. Nevertheless, it would be simplistic to think that, once developed, this set of interpretations will control all areas of his life. Rather, it is better to see each child as a collection of the habits, roles, and understandings which make up his total interactive pattern.

Figure 2 suggests that the child's interaction with others around him will gradually change from being entirely reactive to being a mixture of reactions and proactions. When he only knows habits, then he will react in a habitual way to certain situations. Parents will be able to predict his behavior to a high degree. As he learns roles, the interaction will become far more equal. He will expect others to play their role if he is to play his. A role contains far more behavioral possibilities than does a habit and so he will be far less easy to predict. Finally, when he moves on to the stage of being guided by internally important understandings, he may very well move out of his roles entirely from time to time. For example, a teenager might insist that even though he is still technically a child, nevertheless his values are so strong that he simply cannot follow the rules of the house in this or that area. In this way, the child grows from being merely fulfilling the role of son or daughter to suggesting a new value for the entire household.

It is important to stress that though the growth of the individual child is a key element in changing the interactional patterns of the family system, the system is still not determined by the nature of the individual members, including the child. It is limited. Not all actions or interactions are possible at all times. The family system with a child of six months has far more limited interactive patterns than does the family with a child of six years. The family with a child of 16 might interact using shared understandings as the basis of connectiveness much of the time. This is not possible with the family with the six-year-old when they are dealing directly with the child, just as it is unlikely that mutually agreed upon and shared roles can make up the majority of the actions of the family members with a six-month-old. The child's developmental level necessarily imposes an "upper limit" on possible interactive patterns.

From a parenting view, this normal, predictable developmental aspect of the child needs to be responded to by changes in the family system. Direct interactive patterns with the child must change and, usually, interactive patterns around the child must also change. From an original focus almost entirely on habits, parents must move to greater role interaction with the child. Eventually, the two further dimensions of Habit-Understandings and Role-Understandings must be built into the system.

In this model, parents need to be instructed about making changes along all dimensions and at all three endpoints. This is not an easy task because a large amount of flexibility, awareness, and patience is necessary. The goal remains to help parents make the necessary systemic interactional changes with the least amount of fuss and conflict. The methods of strategic and systemic therapies can be applied successfully by parents as an aid in this task. In the following section, the techniques proposed to "teach" parents to help them in interacting with their children along the dimensions of habits, roles, and understanding are examined.

STRATEGIC-SYSTEMIC TACTICS AND THE SYSTEMIC-DEVELOPMENTAL MODEL

Overview

The strategic parenting model described so far suggests that a growing child in a family will gradually become increasingly complex, both individually and in relation to others in the family. As he develops, the family will need to interact with him along all three dimensions of systemic interconnectiveness. Normally, parents are unlikely to have been given adequate means to know when and how to "intervene" in the child's interactive pattern so that the goals of greater happiness, elimination of unnecessary conflict, and growth of the child can be obtained. Should they attempt to get guidance from existing parental books or resources, they will not usually be given advice which incorporates the systemic awareness that has occurred in the last decades. Parents will thus find themselves locked into behavioral and attitudinal positions which are counterproductive. Needless or exaggerated conflicts over the fact of change, the rate of change, and the direction of change will occur.

Within the strategic parenting model, parents are offered techniques to avoid or lessen such traps. The techniques per se should be familiar to readers of strategic, systemic and Ericksonian literature. They have been modified and simplified so that parents could more easily use them. As is consistent with the previous assumptions, the model does not offer techniques to parents which are designed to help them understand or change the "function" of a child's behavior for the family. The techniques offered here are "safe" for use by parents. Most importantly, these techniques are presented in such a way that they are seen as complementary to nonstrategic methods.

The presentation of techniques to parents is preceded by discussion of the criteria that will help parents decide if and when to use these methods and by a general discussion of how parents can "set the stage" for success with the techniques. "Setting the stage" itself uses general strategic-systemic concepts.

Criteria for Using Strategic-Systemic Techniques

In parenting, strategic-systemic methods work best when used sparingly. It would be unwise to suggest that parents use these methods frequently. A trend to using only strategic techniques would endanger the basic care-giving aspects of family life which, after all, are quite different in nature from treatment situations. Consequently, parents are offered criteria which enable them to make intelligent decisions. They can choose the time to shift from their usual methods of parenting to strategic methods. The goal is to encourage parents to use these methods when necessary and while they still have a good chance of success.

The first criterion is that a parent might decide to use strategic methods if the child's Habit, Role, or Understanding interactive pattern is such that the child's behavior is dangerous to herself or others, extensively damaging to the positive relationship between the child and others, greatly limiting the child's potential for future growth, or is very obnoxious to the parent. Parents are asked not to use these techniques for those behaviors or thoughts of the child which are simply unusual or not what they would prefer. If the child is merely expressing her own particular way of going through the world — her own style or character — then the parents are advised to let it be.

A second criterion is that parents should not use strategic methods without at least some plan of what they are attempting to do, how they are going to do it, and the likely consequences. A parent who jumps into activity and attempts to influence a child in a certain direction MUST have some kind of plan in mind that actually does have a chance of doing the job. Otherwise, he is going to simply get over his head, do something ineffective, and set himself up to be seen as merely interfering instead of parenting. A parent who does this too often will, by and large, find himself losing control of the situation. There is no better way to LOSE effective involvement potential than by always jumping in to try to direct a child's life. The child, after a while, becomes immunized from the constant overinvolvement and the parent simply becomes part of the background, never emerging as an effective influence on the child.

Of course, having a plan does not mean that the parent must always have a crystal-clear outline of what he is going to do each and every time he decides to get involved. He can always indicate to the child that he will soon do something about a certain situation and buy time if he knows that something can and should be done but doesn't know exactly what yet. Nevertheless, there is no sense in buying time if the parent is going to be stuck anyway.

The use of strategic parenting is recommended only when the criteria of dangerousness, limitation, or obnoxiousness are met; when the child is not merely expressing his own style or character without meeting the criteria for involvement; and when the parent has a good chance of effectively involving himself. Each parent then faces the task of deciding if the criteria are met and if he or she has a real chance of effective involvement.

If parents decide that they must become involved, then the next step is to decide whether they will use strategic parenting or other methods. Strategic parenting methods are best used when either of two conditions prevails: 1) the events which the parent are concerned about are positive or negative CHANCES; 2) the events are ongoing and have proven resistant to other parenting methods, including straightforward rewards, punishments, consistency, and open communication.

An event is a CHANCE when the child's behavior in a situation is notably at odds with the expected, predictable behavior of the child in previous, similar situations. The child's sudden and often dramatically different behavior alerts everyone to the possibility of using strategic parenting methods to either increase the odds that the positive behavior will occur again or decrease the odds that the negative behavior will re-occur.

An event may also be a chance when the child's environment suddenly changes greatly or when he is placed in markedly different roles than he played in the past due to events such as moving into a new neighborhood, reaching a particular birthday, etc. While changes in environment do not ensure that chances will occur, such shake-ups in a child's life can increase his receptivity to strategic methods of parenting.

Non-chance events, such as the regular appearance of a particularly irritating habit, can be addressed through strategic parenting methods when it becomes clear that other methods are not helping. Also, a parent might wish to attempt to bring out a never displayed aspect of a child's personality through strategic methods when all ordinary methods have not brought it out. Such non-chance use of strategic methods should be carried out only when other methods have had more than a fair attempt at working. Further, the appearance of a chance event itself does not mean that ordinary methods have failed. In other words, a parent should not give up on ordinary methods for an area of a child's life just because the child exhibits the odd chance behavior. The Chance can be addressed with strategic methods while the vast remaining events can be handled nonstrategically. Strategic methods should be applied only if other methods have been given a fair trial in situations where there is enough stability in the child's environment to ensure that they have had every opportunity to succeed.

Setting the Stage

If parents are to use strategic techniques successfully, they need to be instructed in methods to make it more likely that their ideas will be met with as little resistance as possible by children. In therapy training, this would probably be called "joining." Although some parenting books have addressed some aspects of this issue, there has not been a "translation" to parents of material commonly taught to strategic-systemic therapists. Yet, without such knowledge, the task of using strategic techniques is made doubly difficult. Three areas of setting the stage are presented to parents: Speaking the Language of the Child; Maintaining Maximum Flexibility; and Setting Attainable Goals.

Speaking the language of the child. Parents are introduced to the concept of differing types of language styles. It is suggested that they observe their children to find out which style the child most frequently uses—the Visual, Auditory, Kinesthetic Modalities of Bandler and Grinder (1979) are briefly presented, though without any major effort to introduce sophisticated nuances. At a more basic level, parents are asked to study the language and gestures of their children to be able to use some of their verbal and nonverbal material when talking to them (Gindhart, 1983). They are warned not to get carried away and make themselves look as if they are trying to imitate the children.

It is also suggested that they develop different styles of communicating with the children depending on the mood of the child. After all, the same message given to a happy child will often produce a different effect when given to a sad or angry child. It is recognized that some parents may not be able to change their style to match the child's mood. In this case, it is suggested that the parent find the child's mood that is most receptive to the parent's style of talking and wait until the child is in that mood before trying to talk to him. Basically, the parent's awareness of his child's communicative styles is increased, as is his flexibility to better match those moods.

Maintaining maximum flexibility. One of the most overworked phrases in all of parenting is that parents should be "consistent." Consistency is needed, but if it gets to the point that strategic parenting must be used, then flexibility becomes more important. In this model, parents are advised that when using these methods they must be able to make a U-turn (Fisch, Weakland & Segal, 1982) when needed and always be willing to modify what they are doing by observation of the results of their efforts.

Under the heading of flexibility, "avoiding inescapable commitment" is discussed. Parents are used to being told that they *must* follow through with promises to their children. The strategic parenting model suggests that there can be exceptions to this rule—for example, when a child has decided to use a promised gift as a weapon over the parent's head—and that the parent can and should be willing to escape from the commitment. This is similar to a therapist realizing that he doesn't really have a "contract" with a client after all, only some vague feeling that he is trapped and the client is free. Maintaining maximum flexibility and avoiding inescapable commitment allow the parent to retain greater requisite variety than the child.

Finally, it is suggested to parents that they avoid "diagnosing" their children with such common terms as "immature," "always cranky in the morning," or "emotionally disturbed" (Imber Coppersmith, 1981). The effect that such labels have on reducing parental flexibility—namely by binding them to what fits with that definition of reality—is discussed. As an alternative, parents are requested to concentrate on specific behaviors and to develop a plan to influence the activities not only of the child but of the people involved with the child about these specific behaviors.

Setting attainable goals. As in therapy, unreasonably high goals or goals which could only be obtained with sudden, almost magical change can stop parents from effectively using strategic methods. Although the parent may, in fact, find major changes being obtained, we believe that success is most likely if a "Small Steps" approach is used. Long-range goals are separated into a number of smaller steps. Parents are asked if they can do something to produce a minimal change in the right direction (Fisch et al., 1982). They are told, for example, that a parent trying to influence her child to become interested in classical music should begin her attempt at influencing the child by showing interest in the child's present musical interests — such as rock and roll. The first step to change would then be to have the child inform the parent about the child's musical interests rather than the parent attempting to first convince the child to be interested in "her" music. Analogies are also presented showing how politicians, salesmen, etc. use small steps to eventually obtain their goals. Parents are told that each small step, once taken, is itself a sign that change can occur without painful and needless confrontation. Each step becomes a context marker (Wilk, 1982) for future steps. At the same time, the parent retains flexibility as each small step allows him to evaluate the outcome and decide on future moves.

The Strategic-Systemic-Ericksonian Methods Given to Parents

Habit-level methods. There is always the danger that a child will develop habit patterns which are unacceptable to parents. The parents may elect to use strategic parenting to attempt to influence the child's habits. To do so they will need to add to their repertoire — to go beyond the typical reward-punishment ideas available to them. Thus, it is suggested to them that the child's behavior is always part of a larger sequence of actions in which the parents' own actions play a major part (Storm, 1982). They are encouraged to change their actions, changing the sequence of behaviors, and hopefully influencing the habit in a positive direction. Parents retain their authority as adults, so their basic role vis à vis the child is not changed. The difference is entirely in the way they use the authority to interrupt ongoing sequences.

Although sequence interrupting can be done by almost any random change of parental behavior (O'Hanlon, 1982), it seems best to offer a positive view of sequence stopping. It seems unwise to suggest to parents that they simply do randomly different behavior. Parents would be justified in complaining that they were not being offered constructive guidelines. In addition, it is possible that some parents might do things which they would later regret or which might make matters worse. Again, the difference between parenting and therapy must be recognized. With disturbed families it might be wise to suggest that almost any change would be for the best. With normal families, this is clearly not the case. Parents should be given positive alternatives whenever possible.

Parents are instructed that to change habit-level sequences they should perfect the art of "Adding Alternatives" to the child's sequences. Adding alternatives is basically the strategic idea of providing new options for a client while retaining the basic framework of the situation. Thus, it does not depend on reeducating the client (or child) or on traditional rewards and punishments. The possibility of adding alternatives exists at all age levels, whenever basic habit-level interactions are involved. The main thrust in the model is to have the parents develop their own habit of using these strategic alternatives while the child is young. Examples such as the following one are suggested so that parents can recognize similar situations in their own children:

> One reader had a one-year-old daughter who had developed the unfortunate habit of crying and carrying on when it was time to end her bath. Apparently, she so enjoyed the bath and bath toys that she wanted to stay. The usual efforts to coax her out had failed and the mother was getting frustrated. This type of situation could easily lead to an escalating conflict. Instead, she went to the closet and got out her daughter's favorite towel. It was a towel with a picture of the "Pokeroo," a children's TV show character. She placed the towel on the floor beside the tub and began to dance on it as if she were the Pokeroo. After watching her carefully for a while, the daughter wanted to come out of the tub so that she, too, could dance on the towel. A new habit was quickly formed whereby at the end of her bath she and her mother danced on the towel.

Through examples such as these, parents are "trained" to seek new alternatives to problematic habit sequences within the child's developmental and systemic framework. Parents are told that providing such new possibilities does not automatically insure that the child will, in fact, choose the new alternative over the old all the time or even most of the time. But they are encouraged to try on the grounds that positive and playful alternatives will often be chosen, thus eliminating or diminishing less desirable habit sequences. Parents are asked to see if they can decrease undesired habits or increase desired ones through providing such new possibilities for the children.

It is assumed, and parents are told, that it is most likely that they, rather than the child, will come up with new behaviors. If they wait for the child to change his/her behaviors, they may eventually succeed as the child keeps growing and often leaves the troublesome habit behind. But if they do not wish to passively wait and hope, then the strategic move is to add alternatives. There is also the possibility that eventually the entire family, including the child, will develop the routine of seeking alternative solutions to situations.

Within the framework of adding alternatives, it is possible to address a related point — namely, that parents and children often find themselves oscillating between two positions, neither of which effectively deals with the difficulty at hand (Fisch et al., 1982). For example, a child might alternate between trying harder and giving up entirely, or a stepparent might oscillate between trying to be a "real father" to a child or back off altogether. This is identified to parents as a "Cycle of Limited Alternatives." They are given suggestions on how to recognize that they or their children are in such a cycle. For example, it is suggested that feelings of frustration, anger, and even boredom can be used as clues that such a cycle exists. Parents are urged to utilize these feelings as guides to finding the cycles. Once they discover these, they are urged to develop new choices for themselves and others.

Again, it is stressed that it is best if they can stay within the general systemic and developmental framework of the child and family, changing things as little as possible while at the same time introducing a really different alternative. For the most sophisticated parents, some discussion about planned failures and rituals can be presented as examples of some of the more exotic new alternatives that parents can add to the system (Penn, 1981). Some parents can successfully utilize these ideas, though perhaps most will be content to use simpler strategic ideas.

Role-level methods. While habit-level strategic actions may greatly lessen conflict in families, they need to be supplemented by role-level methods. This is especially true as the child advances to the age where cognitively he is capable of knowing what his role is in relation to others. When his actions are not just a series of learned habits but clearly reflect that he is in an interactive role, then pure habit-level actions may not suffice. In effect, at this point in the child's life, a parent will need to be able to utilize his/her role as parent by sometimes "stepping out" of this role to achieve the goal of changing the sequences of systemic interaction (Ferrier, 1981).

Role difficulties tend to develop when the child is not only capable of knowing he or she is playing a role but can also challenge the role. In normal parenting, struggles for power occur at early ages (the well-known "terrible twos") and generally continue thereafter. Though undoubtedly "normal" for our culture, they can still be bothersome. Parents can diminish the negative aspects of the role conflicts by using "role stretching," "positioning," and "pretending."

Role stretching is a term used to suggest that a parent not use his role just to try to influence his child, but actually modifies the role, "stretching" it so that it can better be used. This can mean anything from complete role reversal to minor changes. The common theme is that the parent shifts from one way to "Play" his role to another and, in so doing, succeeds in changing enough interactional patterns so that the targeted behaviors change.

An example of role stretching occurs when teenagers come into conflict with parents over the rules of the home. Assuming that the rules are in fact fair and that the conflict is a developmentally appropriate one, the parent may very well choose to step out of his normal role for some time to see what will happen. He might, for example, alleviate the conflict by putting the child "in charge" of the house for a week or so, knowing that the responsibilities of actually running a household will most likely reduce the child's need to assert himself so unilaterally in the future. Or he might begin to let his own responsibilities slip until the child begins to get concerned and so becomes more willing to bargain in good faith.

With younger children, interlocking roles might develop into a concern when, say, a child doesn't seem happy but won't tell the parents about it. The parents, trying to be good parents, might then begin to try to find out what is behind this behavior and unwittingly make things worse. To rectify this, they could stretch their role by dropping their attempts to find out what is bothering the child and simply announcing that because the child is obviously unhappy, they as parents have the *duty* to TRY to talk to him about it. They could make it clear that they do not really expect this to do any good, but because they are parents, this is their job. If the child doesn't respond (and often he or she will under these changed circumstances), the parents can then say that they are happy themselves because at least they have fulfilled their own job, thank the child for the talk, and offer to play ball or a game. The effect of this type of role stretching is to change the parent's position from being concerned and pressuring the child to being concerned but only doing his duty. The child might then talk, if he in fact has something to say, or might simply cheer up because he has been so helpful to his parents and they no longer seem so very concerned about how happy he is.

Role stretching is perhaps done best when parents can stretch the role so that something which was bringing them into conflict with the child now serves as a new bond between them. The above example does this by using the fact that the parent as parent is supposed to worry about a child if the child looks unhappy. This worry becomes the stepping-stone for the parent to declare that something OK has occurred. Very often the end result is some type of game, but it doesn't have to be. The result might be a pause in the constant battling or even some down-to-earth talk. Role stretching differs from pure habit-level actions in that the added alternatives are being added for both child and adult. The adult is freed to slip out of roles which have become too rigid. The child is responded to but is shown that there can be a new way for both parties and not just a fight to the finish.

"Positioning" and "Pretending" are other ways in which interlocking roles can be maneuvered to influence a child. In positioning, the parent escapes the role expectations which are not effective by a type of "relationship Judo" move in which he surprises the child by not only agreeing with her over some previously or potentially contentious issues, but actually goes even further in that direction than the child (Fisch et al., 1982). For example, a father might stop trying to make his child get interested in attending the YWCA each Saturday morning and instead begin to agree with the child that cartoons are really more important. This could then lead him to get so interested in cartoons that he would suggest she watch them all Saturday afternoon too. There would be a strong likelihood that the child would within a reasonable time period decide on her own that there might be more to life than cartoons. Even if this preferred solution doesn't occur, at least the father would be out of the position of being "forced" to bother her about it and perhaps some other area might open up for him to influence her positively.

"Pretending" is another use of role playing which can be valuable for a strategic parent (Imber Coppersmith, 1981). Here, the parent suggests to the child that they pretend they are doing something good or "pretend" they are doing something bad together (such as fighting). This would usually be followed by a "role play" of the event in question. At this time, both parent and child can "practice" being different and playing different roles. The father could pretend to be a child for an hour and vice versa. Highly charged negative areas can be played at in a calm or even humorous fashion and so greatly change the usual perception of both the event and of each other. Sometimes the parent will just begin to play or pretend without actually suggesting it to the child. Usually, the child will voluntarily pick up and join the adult. In any event, pretending tends to open the door for increasing options for parents and children.

Whatever the parent chooses, the key concept in this area is that she can influence her child by "connecting" with the child at the role level. The methods of sequence change are different from those used at the habit level, but the results would hopefully be the same — an undesired sequence diminished or eliminated, a new sequence put in its place.

At this time, it is also possible to introduce again the concept that habits and roles form a "dimension" and are not, in fact, opposites. An example, again given by the mother of the one-year-old daughter, illustrates this quite well. She and her husband had become concerned because her daughter had developed a tendency to "whine" at various times. The child was gaining real control over her parents by this behavior as it obviously upset them. Thus the behavior, although undoubtedly a habit, also had role level aspects. To change this pattern, Joanne and Jim began to play a "whiner game" in which they both would whine together whenever the child started to whine. Sometimes they would also choose to initiate the whining before she had a chance to whine. Within a short time, the whining had greatly diminished. Joanne and Jim's game clearly is a good strategic move. It utilizes their role as parents very creatively while serving to interrupt the usual angry response to the whining. Habit and role level changes occur simultaneously.

Understanding-level methods. Focus on understandings as a distinctive area of concern for systemic therapists came relatively recently (Selvini-Palazzoli et al., 1978). Interactive patterns within the family and between family and outside systems are greatly affected by their shared understandings of the situation and of each other. Children in families gradually gain the cognitive capacity to go beyond their habits and roles. They begin to interact with other family members at a new level where the shared understandings are at first unquestionably accepted, then reviewed, and possibly rejected. Conflicts at this level can easily be confused with conflicts as habit or role levels, but such confusion dampens effective action both in therapy and in parenting.

Understanding-level strategic methods which we share with parents include "Framing" (or reframing), use of "Context Markers" and use of analogies and metaphors.

Understanding-level methods are basically concerned with defining the meaning of actions in ways that lead to happier results than other possible meanings. Because this is not an obvious way of thinking about actions, especially the actions of children, it is necessary to spend some time discussing with parents the "reality" that reality is defined and not given (Lewis, 1983). It is to be expected that not all parents will be able to follow these arguments. If so, then these methods will be of little use to them.

For those who are able to accept this position we present "framing" or "reframing" (Watzlawick et al., 1974). Parents are told that how they define a situation will often greatly influence what will occur in the future. Suggestions are made about when the parent might be wise to deliberately not notice something a child does or about when it might be best to define the action as negative but just the exception that proves the rule, etc. The possibility that the parent might "slow down" the child when the child seems to be carried away with momentary success and is in fact setting himself up for failure is explored (Fisch et al., 1982). Examples of alternative ways to frame the same situation are given to help parents learn to think and act in these terms.

Context marking is similar to framing in that once again the influencing attempt is directed at the child's understanding of his own actions and the actions of others (Wilk, 1982). In context marking, some aspect of the context in which the desired or undesired action occurs is "marked" by the parent quite deliberately as a signal for some particular meaning to be given to the action. This, in turn, allows the child to change his responses to the behavior in some particular way. For example, if a parent noted that his child got upset because the child thought the father wasn't spending enough time with him, and if in fact the father thought that he was spending enough time or that no more time was available anyway, then he might attempt to mark certain activities as "deeper" or "more intense" activities which could be defined as being "worth" more than other ones. In this way the child's belief that the father wasn't spending enough TIME with him could be replaced by a belief that the father was spending enough "intense" TIME with him. The father might indicate that certain activities such as going fishing together, or building a model were more important than just watching TV together. These would be the ones defined as more intensive.

This framing could then be "marked" by the father each time the intensive event occurred by putting his arm around the child and/or talking to him in a "deeper" way. In other words, the father would develop special phrases or gestures which would mark these times as special. The special actions by the parent then serve as markers because each time they are done, the child is reminded of the meaning of the activity.

Finally, parents are advised that a child's understandings can be influenced by parents' use of analogy and metaphor (Young, 1981). The two terms are defined and examples given. Useful metaphors and analogies are based on knowing the child and his language; therefore, material addressed before in "setting the stage" (pp. 293–295) is reexamined. It is suggested that skillful strategic parents can make use of the gentle power of metaphor and analogy as a way to influence a child's understanding.

CONCLUSION: EXAMPLES REVISITED

At the beginning of this paper several examples were presented. It is time now to reexamine the examples in relation to the developmental-systemic model which has been outlined.

The enactments reflect an appreciation for the child's developmental stage and appreciation for the interactive dimensions that best reflect the child's functioning. The strategies used by the parent or adult all interrupt undesirable sequences so that different sequences can occur. In each example, the adult perceived a problem with the interactive sequence. The adult avoids a confrontational power struggle and introduces new alternatives which free both child and adult. The sophistication and complexity of the alternatives introduced are dependent upon the adult's perception of the dimensions of the child's interconnectiveness.

Consider the first example. It deals with two adolescent boys' difficulty in waking early and their father's frustration with unsuccessful attempts to rouse them. This example covers all three dimensions of habit, role, and understanding. Their habit of depending on father to wake them is the behavior targeted for change. This father's intervention of role stretching and positioning alters the targeted behavior. Also it allows the sons to assume more autonomy and independent behavior in their roles. And it bears an understanding-level message that they are capable of more responsible behavior.

The second example presents preschool age children whose parents are attempting to resume their parenting role at the end of the day at nursery school. As parents and children reconnect, all three dimensions of interconnectedness are addressed. There is a meaning-level message being conveyed about redefining the family unit, roles of parents and children are reenacted, and habits of defiance which challenge the parental position of influence are focused on as the behaviors needing to change. The introduction of choice into the sequence of interaction enhances the child's emerging sense of identity while clearly defining the context as one in which parents are in charge. Developmentally, children at this age need this structured context for their primarily egocentric behavior.

In the third example, the often difficult problem of cleaning up one's room is addressed. Although no child age is specified, this example targets behavior which can be a source of parent-child conflict from school age through to adolescence. The rules of the family system — that parents expect their children to assume responsibility for the maintenance of their private space — are kept clear. The role-understanding dimension is addressed through the use of the strategic intervention of positive framing and punctuation of the sequence on the "when the job is done" rather than on the child's immediate compliance to a parental demand. This example illustrates the usefulness of the strategic tactic of planned change in small steps. Here the parent alters his or her posture over the course of the process of room clean up.

The fourth example involving a parent with children at very different stages illustrates the importance of appreciation of developmental themes. Whereas the 12-year-old needs some young "adult to adult" time, the toddler needs to mark his presence by egocentric actions. When the father chooses to intervene in the sequence between himself and the toddler only, he introduces an acceptable alternative for the child's behavior, and marks the context for the older child as separate from the younger child.

The fifth example of the two daughters at the circus deals with a context that is meant to be pleasurable but is threatened by the seven-year-old's attention-seeking behavior. The role-understanding dimension of the parent-child interactive sequence is the focus of this example. Here the parent uses the strategic intervention of role stretching and pretending. The parent speaks the child's language of actions rather than words and the child quickly responds to the change in the parent.

In the sixth example, with the father and four-year-old in conflict over time spent together, the role-understanding dimension of the parent-child interaction is addressed. By reframing the interactions into a novel context, the parent stretches his role. The important understanding of the need for quality parent-child time is preserved and conflict is bypassed by the use of context marking, pretending and role reversal within a clearly defined time span.

The seventh example depicting a reconstituted family highlights the often difficult and impotent position of a stepparent in influencing child behavior. This adult is able to acknowledge and address the background meaning of the family's interactions and his more ambiguous position, as well as the latency- and adolescent-age children's need for control and struggle for identity in their roles. This intervention plays with the distance-closeness theme with children who can appreciate the subtleties of altered role behavior.

The eighth example, while not a parenting one, again demonstrates the importance of understanding the child's developmental theme and the systemic context in planning an intervention to alter an undesirable sequence of adult-child interaction. This child is struggling at the role end of the habit-role dimension — his habit of playing the role of noncompliance with an authority figure. The new sequence between the psychometrist and six-year-old preserves the structure of their relationship, yet allows some choice for the child to continue to feel "in charge" of his behavior.

In summary, these examples have been revisited to illustrate the potential of this model with parents, parent-educators, or counsellors. Armed with this simplified outline of developmental and systemic concepts, adults will be able to take meta positions to their potentially conflictual interactions with children. With a repertoire of a handful of simple strategic interventions, dramatic shifts in interactional sequences are possible. Added alternatives, role stretching, positioning and pretending, framing, context marking and the use of metaphors are strategic interventions which can safely be taught to parents who have first been taught to perceive systemic connections. As parents learn to read the background to the scenes of conflict or undesirable behaviors, they will be able to supplement their traditional parenting with strategic parenting.

REFERENCES

Bandler, R., & Grinder, J. (1979). (Edited by John O. Stevens). *Frogs into Princes*. Moab, UT: Real People Press.
Bateson, G. (1979). *Mind and Nature: A Necessary Unity*. New York: Dutton.
Dinkmeyer, D., & McKay, G. D. (1976). *Systematic Training for Effective Parenting, Parent's Handbook*. Circle Pines, MN.
Dobson, J. (1975). *Dare to Discipline*. Wheaton, IL: Tyndale House.
Dreikurs, R., with Stoltz, V. (1964). *Children: The Challenge*. New York: Hawthorn Books.
Ferrier, M. (1981). Lying: A family perspective. *Journal of Strategic and Systemic Therapies, 1* (2).
Fisch, R., Weakland, J., & Segal, L. (1982). *The Tactics of Change*. San Francisco: Jossey-Bass.
Ginott, H. (1965). *Between Parent and Child*. New York: MacMillan.
Gindhart, L. R. (1983). The use of serial metaphor in therapy: A case report. *Journal of Strategic and Systemic Therapies, 2*(1), 15-23.
Gordon, T. (1970). *P.E.T. Parent Effectiveness Training*. New York: Peter H. Wyden.
Haley, J. (1980). *Leaving Home*. New York: McGraw-Hill.
Imber Coppersmith, E. (1981). Developmental reframing. *Journal of Strategic and Systemic Therapies, 1*(1), 1-8.
Kohlberg, L., & Gilligan, C. (1980). The adolescent as philosopher: The discovery of the self in a post-conventional world. In S. Harrison and J. F. McDermott, Jr. (Eds.), *New Directions in Childhood Psychopathology*. New York: International Universities Press.
Lewis, H. C. (1983). Teaching therapists to use their right brain. *Journal of Strategic and Systemic Therapies, 2*(1), 44-57.
O'Hanlon, B. (1982). Splitting and linking: Two generic patterns in Ericksonian therapy and strategic pattern intervention. *Journal of Strategic and Systemic Therapies, 1*(4), 21-34.
Papp, P. (1983). *The Process of Change*. New York: Guilford Press.
Penn, P. (1981). Multigenerational Issues in Strategic Therapy of Sexual Problems. *Journal of*

Strategic and Systemic Therapies, 1(3), 1–13.

Protinsky, H. (1983). The strategic use of hypnosis in family therapy. *Journal of Strategic and Systemic Therapies, 2*(1), 23–30.

Rohrbaugh, M. (1984). The strategic systems therapies: Misgivings about mixing the models. *Journal of Strategic and Systemic Therapies, 3*(3), 28–33.

Selvini-Palazzoli, M., Boscolo, L., Cecchin, G., & Prata, G. (1978). *Paradox and Counterparadox.* New York: Jason Aronson.

Spock, B. (1974). *Raising Children in a Difficult Time.* New York: W. W. Norton.

Storm, C. (1982). Sexual problems: An opportunity to work strategically. *Journal of Strategic and Systemic Therapies, 1*(3), 14–23.

Watzlawick, P., Beavin, J., & Jackson, D. (1967). *Pragmatics of Human Communication.* New York: W. W. Norton.

Watzlawick, P., Weakland, J., & Fisch, R. (1974). *Change.* New York: W. W. Norton.

Wilk, J. (1982). Context and know-how: A model for Ericksonian psychotherapy. *Journal of Strategic and Systemic Therapies, 1*(4).

Wolff, S. (1973). *Children Under Stress.* Baltimore: Penguin.

Young, F. (1981). Front-door, side-door, and back-door approaches. *Journal of Strategic and Systemic Therapies, 1*(1), 16–27.

APPENDIX

PHASE I
(0–24 months)

MAJOR DEVELOPMENTAL MILESTONES	*Bio* —initially, simple nurturance needs are paramount —later, the sensory/motor skills must be stimulated —optimal frustration in a secure, enriched environment allows for maximum growth potential *Psycho* —psychological hatching occurs via separation/individuation —parents must provide a consistent, reliable frame of reference in which the foundations of personality are established *Social* —social interactions have more meaning and significance to parents and others in the infant's social context
DEVELOPMENTAL-SYSTEMIC ORGANIZATION	*Habits* —early in this phase the infant is attempting to maintain homeostasis on a comfort/discomfort continuum —later, habits are formed and broken easily, but reliability is important —parents need to view habit-forming as a positive process to be reinforced —surprise and confusion are distressing at this age *Roles* —roles are essentially ascribed by others, i.e., peace-maker, peace-breaker —roles that are ascribed can greatly influence parental response and therefore must be recognized and understood *Understanding* —understanding is also ascribed by others, although the search for meaning can be a delightful pastime for parents
MAJOR PARENT/ CHILD THEMES	—parenting the parents is important —nurturing time for each other —increasing parent empathy for child's developmental phase —finding new ways to experience developmental milestones
STRATEGIC PARENTING TECHNIQUES	—habit-level techniques are useful with the infant. Changing sequences of behavior can be employed in the later stages of this phase. Slowing as applied to the infant's progressions and regressions is effective —role-level techniques are only useful with the parents themselves, but are not that necessary since understanding-level techniques can be employed —understanding-level techniques are highly useful with the parents. Reframing, metaphors and storytelling can all be effective ways of sensitizing and providing positive alternatives for the parents

PHASE II
(24–48 months)

MAJOR DEVELOPMENTAL MILESTONES	*Bio* —large muscle skills improve, i.e., kicking, throwing, running —fine muscle skills develop, i.e, dressing, page-turning, filling/emptying of containers —increased capacity for language (500–700 words near end of phase) —names become important *Psycho* —beginning of identity formation and object constancy —focus on self in relation to others —imitation of adult roles *Social* —play is solitary, but parallel —sustained affection for significant adults
DEVELOPMENTAL-SYSTEMIC ORGANIZATION	*Habits* —behavior is more sophisticated —gratification can be delayed —capacity for anticipation —stimulus-response patterns can be internalized *Roles* —still essentially ascribed —some roles are sought by toddler in play *Understanding* —still adult-based —helpful for parents to observe and note patterns in child's behavior
MAJOR PARENT/ CHILD THEMES	—parents need relief occasionally so they can respond with maximum flexibility —child moves toward autonomous actions —reasonable chance for success in environment reinforces autonomous behavior
STRATEGIC PARENTING TECHNIQUES	—habit-level techniques are still effective, especially adding alternatives —role-level techniques become more useful, such as role-stretching and pretending —understanding-level techniques, especially storytelling, become useful

PHASE III
(4–6 years)

MAJOR DEVELOPMENTAL MILESTONES	*Bio* — capacity for gross and fine motor movement increases significantly, i.e., dancing, jumping — capacity to both recognize and produce words and phrases increases *Psycho* — still primarily egocentric, but relationship world expands — sexual differences are noted and become important *Social* — friends become important — social interactions become more reciprocal, although still primarily one-to-one
DEVELOPMENTAL-SYSTEMIC ORGANIZATION	*Habits* — provision of basic needs must remain consistent, but doesn't have to be constant — habits tend to govern behavior — rules become important and at times are cherished *Roles* — roles that carry even minimal responsibility are valued — parents can set artificial boundaries which may be more acceptable *Understanding* — primitive understanding of good/bad actions — memory of these becomes foundation for later values — not yet capable of moral thought
MAJOR PARENT/ CHILD THEMES	— parents welcome relief from constant care and can err by only stepping in to discipline — one-to-one time can help child learn the skills to build relationships — group and sibling involvement is needed, but is still troublesome
STRATEGIC PARENTING TECHNIQUES	— habit-level techniques can become more sophisticated in scope and range — role-level techniques become highly useful, such as role play, positioning, pretending — understanding-level techniques become more useful such as context marking, reframing

PHASE IV
(6–9 years)

MAJOR DEVELOPMENTAL MILESTONES	*Bio* —few external changes —eye/hand coordination improves skills and proficiency in physical activities *Psycho* —egocentricity decreases —ordered and systematic thought increases —gender specific activities are engaged in *Social* —functioning in groups becomes important in school and other activities —readiness for cooperative activities
DEVELOPMENTAL-SYSTEMIC ORGANIZATION	*Habits* —increased frustration tolerance and capacity for delayed gratification —symbolic rather than concrete satisfaction is possible —habits are well formed and more subtle —habits can be challenged and questioned *Roles* —have value in and of themselves —less fantasy, more reality-oriented —take functional roles which offer little concrete return *Understanding* —good/bad measured by obedience/disobedience —behaviors have meaning —language and words become much more important and impactful
MAJOR PARENT/ CHILD THEMES	—mastery and competence —development of problem-solving abilities as both a means and an end —competitiveness can become a positive outlet for aggression
STRATEGIC PARENTING TECHNIQUES	—habit-level techniques must be used more sparingly or they lose their effectiveness —role-level techniques are highly effective and can be blended with understanding-level techniques —understanding-level techniques become more sophisticated —use of analogy increases, reframing extremely helpful

PHASE V
(9–13 years)

MAJOR DEVELOPMENTAL MILESTONES	*Bio* —body image becomes all important —secondary sex characteristics greatly affect sense of self *Psycho* —independence and initiative become important —achievements versus feelings of inferiority —idealism and heroism are common *Social* —much greater emphasis on peer groups —playing on teams or joining clubs
DEVELOPMENTAL-SYSTEMIC ORGANIZATION	*Habits* —habits and instincts are devalued—viewed as unchangeable and debilitating —parent can help child discover value in these areas *Roles* —highly significant in terms of position on hierarchy —help to dispel feelings of inferiority —offer tangible means to measure success/failure *Understanding* —children see meaning in their own behavior —purposeful not just reactive —interactions become more complex
MAJOR PARENT/ CHILD THEMES	—acceptance by group is critical —independent functioning —parents must develop more sophisticated methods of communication (not just admonishment or consequences) —also more subtle communication techniques
STRATEGIC PARENTING TECHNIQUES	—habit-level techniques are less helpful except in combination with role- and understanding-level techniques —role-level techniques are still useful, but must be employed more in the context of the child than before; positioning and role reversal can be useful —understanding-level techniques become highly useful in this phase; child becomes more logical and literal; paradox and reason can be employed; metaphors and analogies become more effective

Index